The Economics of Beer

Edited by
Johan F. M. Swinnen

OXFORD
UNIVERSITY PRESS

OXFORD
UNIVERSITY PRESS

Great Clarendon Street, Oxford ox2 6DP

Oxford University Press is a department of the University of Oxford.
It furthers the University's objective of excellence in research, scholarship,
and education by publishing worldwide in

Oxford New York

Auckland Cape Town Dar es Salaam Hong Kong Karachi
Kuala Lumpur Madrid Melbourne Mexico City Nairobi
New Delhi Shanghai Taipei Toronto

With offices in

Argentina Austria Brazil Chile Czech Republic France Greece
Guatemala Hungary Italy Japan Poland Portugal Singapore
South Korea Switzerland Thailand Turkey Ukraine Vietnam

Oxford is a registered trade mark of Oxford University Press
in the UK and in certain other countries

Published in the United States
by Oxford University Press Inc., New York

© Oxford University Press, 2011

British Library Cataloguing in Publication Data
Data available

Library of Congress Cataloging in Publication Data
Library of Congress Control Number 2011934714

Typeset by SPI Publisher Services, Pondicherry, India
Printed in Great Britain
on acid-free paper by
Clays Ltd, St Ives plc

ISBN 978–0–19–969380–1

2

This book is dedicated to my friends and colleagues from all over the world with whom, over the past decades, I have had the immeasurable pleasure of discussing the economics of everything—'how the world works'—while enjoying wonderful beers.

Preface

The inspiration for this book came from colleagues who study the economics of wine. The economics of wine has now become a serious sub-discipline within economics, with annual conferences, a professional association, academic papers and publications, and a *Journal of Wine Economics*. Living in Belgium, with its large diversity of beers, and working in the city (Leuven) which hosts the headquarters of the world's largest brewery, the thought occurred naturally that, if there was such a wide interest in wine economics, there should be room for a modest contribution on 'the economics of beer'.

The beer market and brewery industry are and were economically (and politically) important. Beer was the drink of choice in many ancient societies and throughout much of the Middle Ages in large parts of the world. Right now, it is globally by far the most important alcoholic drink, in volume and value terms. There has been a strong interaction between governments (politics) and markets (economics) in the beer industry. For centuries, taxes on beer or its raw materials have been a major source of tax revenue for governments. Public authorities have also regulated the beer industry for reasons related to quality, health, and competition.

The beer market is a dynamic market. It is characterized by strong growth in emerging economies but also a substantial decline of beer consumption in traditional markets, and by a shift to new products. The largest brewing companies have developed into global multinationals, but in recent years there has been a strong re-emergence of small and local breweries.

The chapters in this book demonstrate that 'beeronomics' covers a vast set of issues. The contributions cover history and development, demand and supply, trade and investment, geography and scale economies, technology and innovation, health and nutrition, quantity and quality, industrial organization and competition, taxation and regulation, etc. This not only makes the beer market an interesting sector to study in itself, but it also yields important general insights on how an economy (and the world) works.

When I raised the idea among fellow economists of organizing the first conference on the economics of beer and brewing, I received enthusiastic responses. My Ph.D. students were immediately excited. Inspired by this, I decided to go ahead, with the help of many. In late May 2009, around sixty economists from all over the world gathered in Leuven for the first

Beeronomics Conference. It was a memorable conference—for more than one reason. The conference inspired enthusiasm for continued activities in this field. Since then workshops on Beeronomics have been organized in Davis, California, and Bolzano, Italy. The second Beeronomics Conference will be organized in Munich in 2011. More will follow. In fact, we have just launched The Beeronomics Society: the International Association for the Study of the Economics of Beer and Brewing.

The Leuven conference also provided the inputs and the raw material for this book. Several of the chapters in this book are based on presentations at the conference. These chapters are complemented by contributions from experienced researchers in this field, drawing upon their earlier work on the economics and history of beer, and new research inspired by the conference.

I need to thank many people for their contributions. First and foremost, the members of the local organization committee of the Beeronomics Conference (Liesbeth Colen, Tim Goesaert, Giulia Meloni, Damiaan Persyn, Piet Sercu, Thijs Vandemoortele, Kristine Van Herck, Bert Van Landeghem, Stijn Vanormelingen) were a source of inspiration, enthusiasm, and encouragement throughout this project. They did a wonderful job in planning and organizing the conference. Without them, there simply would have been no conference, and no book.

Also the members of the international scientific committee were enthusiastic supporters of the conference and the follow-up work. I thank, in particular, Julian Alston, Kym Anderson, Jill McCluskey, Tim Josling, and Scott Rozelle. Adriano Profeta and Klaus Salhofer have taken the lead in organizing a new beeronomics conference. I also need to thank colleagues at the Katholieke Universiteit Leuven for their support of the conference and the follow-up activities. In particular, vice-rector Filip Abraham, dean Luc Sels, vice-dean Patrick Van Cayseele, my colleagues global development experts and trappist lovers (Jan Wouters, Hans Bruyninckx, and Patrick Develtere), as well as my critical local VIbPs (Cis Van Peer, Bert Wouters, Wif Mostinckx) for their support throughout this less-than-traditional project and their presence and support at crucial times. The city of Leuven generously hosted the conference participants in its wonderful sixteenth-century city hall; Freddy Delvaux and his brewing students brewed a special beer for the participants; and my fellow bikers in the Tour du Provence generously joined in celebrating the book contract.

Oxford University Press responded enthusiastically to the proposal to publish this book and it has been a pleasure working with them. Anna Sabadesh provided much appreciated help in the editing process. The Research Council of the Katholieke Universiteit Leuven (Methusalem Project) and the Flemish Scientific Research Foundation (FWO) provided financial support for the research for several of the book chapters.

Thijs Vandemoortele has been an extremely efficient and reliable organizer, a great editorial assistant, and wonderful research collaborator throughout this entire process—and the past years in general.

My final thanks go to my wife and daughters who had to suffer from the—even greater than usual—absence of mind due to the combination of economics and beers.

Contents

Part I: History

Part II: Consumption

List of Figures

List of Tables

List of Contributors

William James Adams is the Arthur F. Thurnau Professor of Economics at the University of Michigan. He specializes in public policy toward business and the European economy. Educated at Harvard University (AB, AM, and Ph.D.), he has been a visiting professor at Aix-Marseille, Basel, LUISS, the Academy of International Law (Florence), Paris-Dauphine, and Paris Panthéon-Sorbonne.

Abhimanyu Arora is a Ph.D. student in economics at the LICOS Centre for Institutions and Economic Performance at the University of Leuven (KUL). He holds a Master's in Quantitative Economics from the Indian Statistical Institute, New Delhi, India.

Junfei Bai is a senior research fellow at the Centre for Chinese Agricultural Policy (CCAP) and Institute of Geographical Sciences and Natural Resources Research, Chinese Academy of Sciences. He received his Ph.D. in economics from Washington State University (WSU).

Anjor Bhaskar is an independent researcher working on development issues in India. He obtained his M.Sc. in Economics at the University of Warwick, UK. Since then he has worked extensively on child nutrition and has a special interest in environmental issues. Formerly, he was a research analyst at the International Food Policy Research Institute (IFPRI).

Matt Boswell is the General Project Manager of the Rural Education Action Project (REAP), a joint research program of Stanford University and the Chinese Academy of Sciences. REAP is primarily engaged with rigorous impact evaluation in China's poor rural areas and migrant communities.

Liesbeth Colen is a Ph.D. student in economics at the LICOS Centre for Institutions and Economic Performance at the University of Leuven (KUL). She obtained a Master's in Agricultural and Food Economics. Her research focuses mainly on agricultural supply chains, gender, and food companies' foreign investments.

Koen Deconinck is a Ph.D. student in economics at the LICOS Centre for Institutions and Economic Performance and holds a Master's in Economics from the University of Leuven (KUL).

Kenneth G. Elzinga is the Robert C. Taylor Professor of Economics at the University of Virginia. He has a BA and honorary doctorate from Kalamazoo College, a Ph.D. from Michigan State University, and has received numerous teaching awards. An expert in antitrust economics, he has testified in several precedent-setting antitrust cases, including three Supreme Court decisions. Mr Elzinga is also known for his mystery novels, co-authored with William Breit (under the pen name Marshall Jevons).

Donald G. Freeman is Professor of Economics, Sam Houston State University. He holds a Ph.D. from Southern Methodist University. His recent publications include studies of alcohol demand, the effects of alcohol legislation on traffic fatalities, and the relationship between poverty and the macroeconomy.

Lisa M. George is Associate Professor of Economics at Hunter College and the Graduate Center, City University of New York. Professor George completed her Ph.D. at the University of Pennsylvania in 2001. She is an empirical applied economist specializing in the fields of industrial organization and political economy, with a particular interest in the economics of media markets. She is editor-in-chief of the journal *Information Economics and Policy*.

Jikun Huang is the Director of the Centre for Chinese Agricultural Policy (CCAP)and Professor at the Chinese Academy of Sciences. He received a Ph.D. in Economics from the University of the Philippines at Los Banos. His research covers a wide range of issues on China's agricultural and rural economy, including work on agricultural R&D policy, water resource economics, price and marketing, trade policy, and rural development.

Jill J. McCluskey is a Professor in the School of Economics Sciences at Washington State University. She received her Ph.D. from the University of California, Berkeley. Her research interests centre on the economics of product quality, consumer behaviour, and consumer preferences. She teaches Ph.D. courses in industrial organization and microeconomic theory.

Bart Minten is a Senior Research Fellow at the International Food Policy Research Institute (IFPRI), New Delhi (India). Previously he worked at the World Bank. He holds a Ph.D. from Cornell University. He has published on issues such as agricultural marketing, technology adoption, environmental degradation, poverty, crime, and social service delivery in developing countries.

John V. C. Nye holds the Frederic Bastiat Chair in Political Economy and is Professor of Economics at George Mason University in Fairfax, VA. He obtained his Ph.D. from Northwestern University. He is a specialist in European economic history and the new institutional economics. He is the author of *War, Wine, and Taxes* (Princeton University Press, 2007). With John Drobak, he co-edited the volume, *Frontiers in the New Institutional Economics* (Academic Press, 1997).

Damiaan Persyn is a postdoctoral researcher at VIVES at the University of Leuven (KUL). He studied Economics at the Humboldt Universität in Berlin and obtained a Master's degree in Statistics and a Ph.D. in Economics from the University of Leuven (KUL). His research interests are imperfect regional labour markets, institutional organization, and the economics of regional growth.

Eline Poelmans is a lecturer at the Faculty of Economics and Management of the Hogeschool Universiteit Brussel (HU Brussel). She has degrees in History, International Relations, and a Ph.D. in Economic History from the University of Leuven (KUL). She specializes in economic history and international economics.

Scott Rozelle holds the Helen Farnsworth Endowed Professorship at Stanford University and is Senior Fellow and Professor in the Food Security and Environment Program and the Shorenstein Asia-Pacific Research Center, Freeman Spogli Institute (FSI) for International Studies. He holds a Ph.D. from Cornell University. Dr Rozelle's research focuses on agricultural policy, rural resources, and poverty, education and health in China. Dr Rozelle is the co-director of the Rural Education Action Project (REAP).

Sanatan Shreay is a global health economist at Amgen Corporation in Los Angeles. He received his Ph.D. in Economics and Master's in Statistics from Washington State University. His research interests are in applying discrete choice/limited dependent modelling to industrial organization issues and health and labour markets.

Margaret E. Slade is a Professor of Economics Emeritus at the Universities of British Columbia and Warwick, where she taught Industrial Organization. She was awarded an Honorary Doctorate from the Helsinki School of Economics and was President of the European Association for Research in Industrial Economics (EARIE). She held visiting positions in France, Germany, the UK, Belgium, Finland, and the US. Margaret also worked for the US Federal Trade Commission and has consulted for competition authorities in Canada, the US, the UK, and the EU, as well as for private firms.

Johan F. M. Swinnen is Professor of Economics and Director of the LICOS Centre for Institutions and Economic Performance at the University of Leuven (KUL). He holds a Ph.D. from Cornell University. He is a Senior Research Fellow at the Centre for European Policy Studies (CEPS), Brussels. He was Lead Economist at the World Bank and Economic Advisor at the European Commission, and Visiting Professor in Cornell University, Stanford University, SciencesPo, Wageningen University, European College Bruges. He is President (elect) of the International Association of Agricultural Economists (IAAE).

Anthony W. Swisher is a Partner in the Antitrust Practice Group at Akin Gump Strauss Hauer & Feld LLP, where he focuses on defending companies in government antitrust merger investigations. He serves as Co-Chair of the Unilateral Conduct Committee of the American Bar Association Section of Antitrust Law, and teaches antitrust policy in the Department of Economics at the University of Virginia. He holds degrees from the University of Virginia and The George Washington University Law School.

Carol Horton Tremblay is Associate Professor of Economics at Oregon State University. She obtained her Ph.D. from Washington State University. Her interests are in applied microeconometrics. She has co-authored *The U.S. Brewing Industry: Data and Economic Analysis* (MIT Press, 2005) and edited *Industry and Firm Studies* (M.E. Sharpe Inc., 2007).

Victor J. Tremblay is Professor of Economics at Oregon State University and editor of the Industry Issues section of the *Review of Industrial Organization*. He obtained his Ph.D. from Washington State University. His interests are in industrial organization and applied game theory. He has co-authored *The U.S. Brewing Industry: Data and Economic Analysis* (MIT Press, 2005) and edited *Industry and Firm Studies* (M.E. Sharpe Inc., 2007).

Richard W. Unger (Ph.D., Yale 1971) taught Medieval and Early Modern History at the University of British Columbia until retirement in 2010. His work on the history of technology has included studies of shipbuilding and shipping, beer brewing, cartography, and energy use in pre-industrial societies. His most recent books include *Ships on Maps: Pictures of Power in Renaissance Europe* (Palgrave Macmillan, 2010) and an edited volume, *Shipping Efficiency and Economic Growth 1350–1850* (Brill, 2011).

Kristine Van Herck is a Ph.D. student in economics at the LICOS Centre for Institutions and Economic Performance at the University of Leuven (KUL). She holds a Master's in Bio-engineering from the University of Leuven (KUL). Her main research interests focus on supply chains, agricultural policy, and transition countries.

Frank van Tongeren heads the Policies in Trade and Agriculture division at the OECD Trade and Agriculture Directorate. He has previously worked at the Agricultural Economics Institute (LEI-WUR) in The Hague and at Erasmus University Rotterdam. He has taught at the Chinese Academy of Sciences; Wageningen University; Monash University; ESSEC Business School; and Purdue University. He holds a Ph.D. in economics from Erasmus University Rotterdam and has published widely on trade policy issues.

Thijs Vandemoortele is a postdoctoral researcher at the LICOS Centre for Institutions and Economic Performance at the University of Leuven (KUL). He obtained a Ph.D. and M.Sc. in Economics from the University of Leuven (KUL). He has published several articles in international journals related to the political economy of standards, and has consulted for the OECD on these issues. He holds a scholarship from the Research Foundation—Flanders (FWO).

Anneleen Vandeplas is a postdoctoral researcher at the LICOS Centre for Institutions and Economic Performance at the University of Leuven (KUL). She obtained a Ph.D. in Economics from the University of Leuven (KUL). She has worked on projects of the FAO, IFPRI, the European Commission, and World Bank.

Stijn Vanormelingen is a postdoctoral researcher at the IESE Business School in Barcelona. Previously he was a lecturer at HU Brussels. He obtained his Ph.D. in Economics with 'Essays on Empirical Industrial Organization' at the University of Leuven (KUL). His research interests include empirical international trade, strategic firm behaviour, on-the-job training and the economics of media markets.

Units of Measurement

Contributors use different units of beer consumption, production, and trade—reflecting differences in geographic coverage, history, and traditions. The table below lists these units of measurement and the conversion factors that can be used to convert one unit into another.

Units of beer consumption and production, and conversion factors

	Litre	Hectolitre	Imperial (UK) gallon	US gallon	Barrel	Old ton	Can (12 ounces)
Litre	1	100	4.546	3.785	117.348	954.679	0.355
Hectolitre	0.01	1	0.0455	0.0379	1.173	9.547	0.00355
Imperial (UK) gallon	0.220	21.997	1	0.833	25.813	210	0.0781
US gallon	0.264	26.417	1.201	1	31	252.199	0.0938
Barrel	0.00852	0.852	0.0387	0.0323	1	8.135	0.00303
Old ton	0.00105	0.105	0.00476	0.00397	0.123	1	0.000372
Can (12 ounces)	2.816	281.633	12.803	10.661	330.49	2688.694	1

Part I
History

1

A Brief Economic History of Beer

Eline Poelmans and Johan F. M. Swinnen

Introduction

Throughout history, different types of alcoholic beverages made from a whole range of products (fruits, sugar cane, honey, and cereals such as barley, wheat, oats, millets, rye, and maize), have been labelled 'beer'. If we look at all these historical 'beers' through contemporary glasses, some of them would now be classified as 'wine' or some kind of 'distilled alcoholic beverage'.[1] Predecessors of our modern beer were found several thousands of years ago in places all over the world, including Asia and Europe. It is not clear whether the technique to produce 'beer' was discovered in one place and then spread among people and continents, or whether it was discovered in various places independently (Nelson 2005).

In this brief historic overview, we discuss the evolution of beer production and consumption and the industrial organization of breweries throughout history. Our overview draws significantly on some excellent and more detailed studies of beer and brewing in different historical periods, such as those by Aerts et al. (1990); Baron (1962); Clark (1983); Eßlinger (2009); Hornsey (2003); Nelson (2005); Rabin and Forget (1998); Tremblay and Tremblay (2005); and Unger (2001, 2004).

The chapter is organized as follows. We first discuss the discovery and use of beer in ancient history, and the monasteries as centres of the beer economy in the early Middle Ages. Subsequently, we analyse innovation and taxation in brewing in the Middle Ages, after which we move on to the growth of commercial breweries and the decline of the monasteries in early modern

---

[1] Nelson (2005: 1–2) defines beer as: 'any sort of maltose-based alcoholic beverage, whether or not the ingredients include other products (fermented or not)' and 'a fermented drink made essentially from malted cereal, water and yeast'.

times. Furthermore, we discuss the globalization and new competition for beer in early modern times, as well as scientific discoveries and the development of modern brewing in the eighteenth and nineteenth centuries. Then, we look at the growth and decline of different types of beer and the consolidation and globalization of breweries in the last two centuries.

The Discovery and Use of Beer in Ancient History

The Neolithic Revolution—i.e. the gradual transition from the nomadic life of hunters (the 'extractive economy') to a more settled life as farmers (the 'agrarian economy')—which happened in several parts of the world between 9000 and 7000 BC, is often seen as the major turning point in early human history (Dineley and Dineley 2000). It is possible, and even probable, that even before this revolution, 'beer' was already brewed to some extent, because some of the fermentation materials necessary for the brewing of beer (e.g. sugar in tree saps or certain kinds of fruits) were already available in sufficient quantities to the nomadic humans living before the Neolithic Revolution (Hornsey 2003). However, some of the earliest evidence that 'beer' was produced and consumed comes from China more than 7000 years ago (Bai et al., Chapter 15, this volume). Outside China, it is known that by the beginning of the fifth millennium BC, people in southern Mesopotamia—in a region known as Sumeria, which included the fertile region between the Tigris and Euphrates Rivers—were making 'beer'. During archeological excavations, a clay tablet dated 6000 BC, containing one of the oldest known beer recipes, was found in Mesopotamia (Patroons 1979). Moreover, the Sumerians already understood that beer could be used as a form of 'currency'. Around 3500 BC in the Sumerian city of Uruk—one of the first modern cities in which grain production gradually increased thanks to the rich soil and the introduction of improved farming methods—people traded grain and beer for other, more scarce natural sources, such as timber, metals, or even precious stones (Rabin and Forget 1998). During the second millennium BC, after the Sumerian Empire had collapsed, the Babylonians ruled the fertile Mesopotamia. Beer brewing was important and they issued laws to protect and preserve their beer-brewing methods (Röllig 1971).

Around 3000 BC, beer production started to spread to ancient Egypt. All ranks of society, male and female alike, drank beer (Brewer and Teeter 2007). It is said that Ramses III, one of Egypt's greatest pharaohs, found beer to be such a noble drink that he and his guests drank it in golden cups. At the height of the Egyptian Empire, beer was the drink of choice for both festive and ordinary dining occasions (Geller 1992). It was only (much) later, i.e. after Egypt had been conquered by the Roman Empire, that wine became widespread and the Egyptian elite started to prefer wine over beer. However, even then, beer remained the drink of choice for the Egyptian 'masses' (Meussdoerffer 2009).

In these ancient civilizations, it was customary to drink unfiltered beer—beer that had not gone through any sieving or settlement phase—directly from large jars through straws in order to avoid gross sediment (Hornsey 2003). The straw was used to get through the layer of yeast and hulls that was floating on the surface of the beer (Katz and Voigt 1986).

The earliest indications of beer production in Europe date from 3000 BC. It is uncertain whether European people discovered the fermentation process themselves or whether the beer-producing technology used in Europe was based on knowledge from the Near East.

At the beginning of the Greek Empire (around 500 BC), the Greeks brewed beer as some of their ancestors had done before them, until the growing of grapes for wine became both more common and more popular. Subsequently, the Greeks increasingly started to drink wine instead of beer, which coincided with the increasing notion of wine as a more 'civilized' drink that was 'suitable for gods' (Nelson 2003). This shift in preferences is reflected in their writings. While many Greek writers saw beer as a barbarian drink, inferior to wine, some of the works of the early Greek writers and philosophers adopted a more neutral position towards the qualities of beer versus wine and even attributed positive qualities to beer.[2]

According to the historian Pliny (AD 23–79), the Romans learned brewing techniques from the Egyptians. However, the Romans generally drank only wine, and they generally despised beer and its drinkers, whom they referred to as 'barbarians' and 'uncivilized' people.[3] The expansion of the Roman Empire coincided with the spread of wine consumption and viticulture in Europe.

In many other European regions which are now associated with wine, people drank not wine but beer for thousands of years. For example, in what

---

[2] Sophocles (496–406 BC) considered beer to be 'healthy' and was in favour of a 'diet of moderation', which consisted not only of bread, meat, and vegetables, but of beer as well (Rabin and Forget 1998). Xenophon (430–354 BC) wrote that beer could be 'very good' once people got used to it (Nelson 2005). Diodorus of Sicily (first century BC) saw both wine and beer as 'gifts from the gods' and according to him, it was just a matter of climatological conditions which of the two beverages was produced. This meant that in places where grapevines could not grow, beer would be produced instead (Nelson 2005).

[3] For example Cornelius Tacitus (AD 56–120) referred to the drink of the German Teutons as: 'a horrible brew fermented from barley or wheat, a brew which has only a very far removed similarity to wine' (Rabin and Forget 1998). Later on, the Roman Emperor Julian (who ruled from AD 361 to 363) wrote a poem about what he called the 'two Dionysi', i.e. two gods, one for wine and one for beer. His poem goes as follows: 'Who and from where are you Dionysus? Since, by the true Bacchus, I do not recognize you; I know only the son of Zeus. While he smells like nectar, you smell like a billy-goat [or spelt]. Can it be that the Celts because of lack of grapes made you from cereals? Therefore one should call you Demetrius [that is born from Demeter or born of two mothers], not Dionysus, rather wheat-born [than fire-born] and Bromus [that is, oats], not Bromius [that is, roarer of the thunder].' (Nelson 2005: 30–1).

is now France, Spain, Portugal, and northern Italy, people drank beer, not wine, in the millennia before the advent of the Roman Empire. Nelson (2005: 66) states that 'there is no doubt that Celtic peoples in Europe from what is now France, Spain, Belgium, Germany, and Britain were all avid beer drinkers, probably from very early times'.

Together with the Roman conquest of Europe, the Roman wine culture and (later) production spread to northern Italy (above the Po River) and southern Gaul (France), followed by the Iberian peninsula (Spain and Portugal), and later still by northern Gaul (northern France and Belgium). Although the introduction of wine consumption and production was usually to the detriment of the local beer-drinking cultures in the regions that were conquered by the Romans—especially for the upper classes—some Celtic tribes continued to drink beer. Especially in the outer, northern areas of the Roman Empire where the influence of Germanic tribes was strong and where wine was difficult to obtain, i.e. in what is now called Britain, Belgium, and Germany, beer was still consumed in large quantities during the Roman rule (Patroons 1979).

In the fifth century AD, the Germans took control of large parts of the West Roman Empire, which heralded a 'great beer revival'. The early German tribes drank beer in considerable quantities (Meussdoerffer 2009). After half a millennium of wine-drinking rulers, beer-drinking rulers took over again, and the negative perception of beer and beer-drinking people as uncivilized—which had been commonplace under Roman rule—became rare (Nelson 2005).

Monasteries as the Centres of the Beer Economy in the Early Middle Ages

> The church and the monasteries were . . . the birthplaces of brewing science
> (Jackson 1996: 1)

In early history, women brewed beer. The Egyptians saw brewing as a domestic—and thus female—chore (i.e. the preparation of food), and to them, the goddess Hathor was the 'inventress of brewing'. The production of wine was seen as a more complicated process, and thus an activity assigned to men (Hornsey 2003). Only by the eighth century AD and with the spread of Christianity and large monasteries, did men take over the task of brewing beer from women (Rabin and Forget 1998), although women continued to have an important role in small home breweries throughout the Middle Ages (Unger 2001).

When Charlemagne started ruling his Holy Roman Empire around AD 800, he drew up rules regarding how a town should be organized. He also gave a place to the brewers in his 'ruling hierarchy' (Unger 2004). Charlemagne's empire, which had started as a loose confederation of Germanic tribes living in Gaul (modern Belgium and France), expanded to other regions in what is now Germany, Italy, and Spain. Across his empire, Charlemagne built many monasteries, many of which became centres of brewing. Initially, most of the monasteries were located in southern Europe, where the climate permitted the monks to grow grapes and make wine for themselves and their guests. However, when later monasteries were established in northern regions of Europe, where the cooler climate made it easier to grow barley instead of grapes, the monks started to brew beer instead of wine (Jackson 1996). In this respect and throughout the early Middle Ages, the principle of 'monastic brewing' spread widely in the British Isles, and to many parts of Germany and Scandinavia (Unger 2004).[4] In fact, the growth in brewing in the Low Countries in the ninth and tenth centuries was mainly due to this extension of the Carolingian authority northwards. Only in the twelfth and thirteenth centuries would brewing emerge as a commercial venture. Before that, the monastery was probably the only institution where beers were manufactured on anything like a commercial scale (Hornsey 2003). The beer brewed by the monks was used for their own consumption, as well as to be given to pilgrims and the poor (Bickerdyke 1889).[5] The oldest known drawings of a modern brewery were found in the monastery of Saint Gall, in present-day Switzerland and were dated AD 820. The plans of the Saint Gall monastery show three breweries, all producing beer, but for different groups of consumers: one brewery for the guests, one brewery for the pilgrims and the poor, and one brewery for the monks in the monastery. The beer that was produced for the guests was of a better quality than that brewed for the pilgrims, poor, and the monks (Horn and Born 1979).

However, the monks soon started to brew beer for other people as well, such as noblemen. In addition, monks were allowed to sell their brew in so-called 'monastery pubs'. There were also so-called 'church ales', celebrations and feasts of the church where peasants were allowed to drink large quantities of beer for free, reducing the demand for commercial brewing (Rabin and Forget 1998).

Studies indicate that monks often drank large quantities of beer. Statistical sources even mention beer consumption of up to five litres a day for each

---

[4] 'The English abbot Aelfric in a tenth-century work has a novice answer the question of what he would drink with the following response: beer if I have it and otherwise water... In the early days of the Cistercian reform movement around 1100 the monks, aware that wine was allowed by the rule of St Benedict, were too poor to drink much of it and so had to settle for beer or just water... Early medieval churchmen both inside and outside of monasteries may have preferred wine but it seems certain that they commonly drank beer' (Unger 2004: 29–30).

[5] According to the rule of Saint Benedict (AD 480–547), the founder of 'modern monasticism', the Benedictine monks not only had to live in their own community and be self-sufficient, but they also had to offer hospitality to travellers and people in need (Nelson 2005).

monk in some monasteries. Several factors seem to have played a role (Rabin and Forget 1998). First, monks preferred beer over water, as the water in the Middle Ages was often polluted. Second, apart from nutritional reasons, beer was often used in monasteries for spiritual and medicinal purposes. Third, an average meal in the monasteries of the early Middle Ages was rather frugal, and beer provided a welcome nutritious addition for the monks and their guests. Fourth, although beer contained alcohol, it was seen as a liquid like water, and was, as such, not forbidden during a fasting period. Beer was the 'ubiquitous social lubricant' and this not only because it was an essential part of the—often dire—medieval diet, but also because during the Middle Ages every occasion that was even remotely 'social' called for a drink (Unger 2004).

Innovation and Taxation in Brewing in the Middle Ages

An important innovation was the use of hops in brewing. There is evidence that as early as around AD 800, German monasteries were adding extracts of the hop plant to preserve their beer longer. Moreover, the bitterness of the hops also balanced the rather sweet flavour of the malt, the other main ingredient of Germanic beer (Behre 1983 and 1999).

This innovation would ultimately transform the entire global beer economy. However, despite its benefits, the use of hops did not spread rapidly through the beer-producing regions of Europe. In fact, it would be several centuries before its use would be widely accepted. The main reason for the slow diffusion of this innovation was its impact on the local tax base in many regions.

Before hops were used, breweries were subjected to a so-called 'Grutrecht' or 'flavouring licence' in many regions. This Grutrecht was named after the 'grut', a combination of herbs that were used to flavour beer (or to 'disguise faults' in the brew) and to preserve the beer. Grut was an important factor in distinguishing between different beer brews (Doorman 1955). The 'Grutrecht' was determined by the local authorities and was used to tax breweries. It stated explicitly which particular flavouring additive could be added to the beer. All brewers were obliged to buy grut for their brews from the local rulers and brewing beer without grut was forbidden. To avoid tax evasion, the exact composition of grut was kept a secret (Mosher 2009).

While the addition of hops improved the taste and preservation of the beer and allowed for transportation over longer distances, hops threatened the Grutrecht. By using hops, brewers no longer needed grut (or needed less of it). Hence, the introduction of hops threatened local rulers' revenue from the Grutrecht tax on beer. Therefore, in many regions, including Britain and Holland, the use of hops was prohibited for a long time. The official reason was that the taste of hopped beer could be very different from the well-known taste of the 'older style' Germanic beers and that adding hops was seen as a 'contamination of good ale'. The real reason was that, if the use of hops was allowed, the local authorities would lose tax revenues (Unger 2004).

For this reason, it took several centuries before the use of hops became commonplace in some European regions. For instance, using hops was initially forbidden in the British Isles. Only after the Hundred Years' War between France and England (1337–1453), were hops allowed to be used in brewing English ales (Meussdoerffer 2009). In Holland too, rulers did not allow the domestic brewers to use hops until the early fourteenth century (Hornsey 2003). An interesting illustration of how the (compulsory) addition of grut to beer still has repercussions to the present day comes from Belgium, where breweries on opposite sides of the Schelde River continue to use different brewing processes (Degrande 2010).[6]

It is important to mention that, after the addition of hops as a brewing technique had become generally accepted, the beer terminology changed as well. 'Old' beer, made without the addition of hops, was now called 'ale', whilst 'new' beer, made with the addition of hops, was just called 'beer'. However, somewhat confusingly, the terms 'ale' and 'beer' would take on different meanings again several centuries later. With the introduction of the bottom (cold) fermentation processes, in the twentieth century, the 'new' beer was called the (cold lagering) 'beer' and the 'old' beer the (warm fermentation) 'ale' (see further).

The Growth of Commercial Breweries and Decline of the Monasteries in Early Modern Times

In the fourteenth century, the central position of the monasteries in the beer-brewing industry changed dramatically. Commercial breweries emerged and grew in importance. These changes coincided with the overall growth of the brewing industry. Unger (2004: 107) sums up the brewing industry in early modern times as follows:

> The years from around 1450 to the early seventeenth century were a golden age for brewing... From Flanders to the Celtic Sea to northern Scandinavia to Estonia and Poland to Austria to the upper reaches of the Rhine River—

---

[6] Breweries that were located on the left bank of the Schelde River were subject to German rule and obliged to use grut. Several of them currently still brew sour beers (which is due to grut not being protected against acidification by bacteria). Breweries located on the right bank of the Schelde were under German rule and allowed/obliged to use hops. Today these breweries still produce less sour beer.

brewing expanded...It enjoyed unprecedented economic success. Beer invaded new parts of Europe, claiming or reclaiming territory where wine was the preferred drink. The higher quality of hopped beer compared to its predecessors, the greater efficiency of producers..., and improved distribution all combined to make beer an increasingly popular drink.

Several factors, affecting both the demand and the supply, played a role in this process (Rabin and Forget 1998 and Unger 2004). In the Early Middle Ages, many people only drank beer at religious festivities, because it was free. Incomes were too low to sustain a large demand for beer. Demand for beer only increased in the late fourteenth and fifteenth centuries, after the Black Death (1347–52), during which many Europeans—rich and poor alike—died. Income growth in the fifteenth century increased demand for beer. In addition, after the Black Death, the re-expansion of existing towns and the creation of new towns also provided opportunities for developing and expanding the brewing industries and related techniques.

Demand also increased as more people started to drink beer instead of water with increasing awareness of the problems of water pollution. Drinking fouled and polluted water lowered people's general resistance to illnesses and epidemics could be transmitted by water. As a result, a growing number of people started to prefer beer, which was made from boiled water (in which bacteria had been eliminated), over water.

Another reason for the growth in beer demand was that an increasing number of merchants were travelling between town markets and regional fairs. These travelling merchants needed a place to sleep, as well as food and drink. The increasing demand for lodging facilities, food, and drink led to the emergence of 'inns' and 'taverns' (Clark 1983). With it, the demand for beer grew in these places. As merchants became used to spending the night in these facilities, the taverns became true meeting places, where people would come not only to sleep and eat but also to do business. A prime example are the famous Hanseatic cities that maintained a trade monopoly between the Middle Ages and early modern times (thirteenth to seventeenth centuries) along the coast of northern Europe.[7] Around 1376, the city of Hamburg was called 'the Hanseatic League's Brewhouse'. Afterwards, other important centres of brewing were associated with the League, such as Wismar, Rostock, Lübeck, and Danzig (Von Blanckenburg 2001).

Together with the emergence of commercial breweries and a real 'brewing industry', many government regulations were implemented. Regulations imposed a variety of taxes and rules that described how beer had to be produced, the duration of the brewing process, the required composition of

---

[7] These Hansa brewers were the first brewers to develop a beer that could be transported great distances over land and sea (Meussdoerffer 2009).

beer, rules that fixed beer prices, etc. (see Chapter 2 by Unger in this book for more details on these regulations). The first brewing regulations of this kind had already been introduced in Nuremberg (Bavaria) in the early fourteenth century. In 1487, a famous brewing 'law' was actually enacted in Munich in Bavaria: the so-called 'Reinheitsgebot' (or 'Purity Law'), which survived until 20 years ago. The 'Reinheitsgebot' stipulated that only barley, hops, and pure water could be used to produce beer (Hackel-Stehr 1987).[8]

As more beer was brewed and commercially traded, its quality, as well as its distribution and export, increased. Increasing competition between breweries contributed to the fact that beer had become more tasty because of increased experimenting with the flavour of the finished brews. In addition, real 'brewing centres' developed (e.g. Leuven, Bruges, Ghent, and Antwerp in Flanders; Haarlem and Gouda in Holland; Hamburg, Lübeck, and Munich in Germany; and London in England (Unger 2004)).

While the commercial breweries arrived, the role of monasteries as centres of brewing declined. This was heavily influenced by political considerations and actions. First, to compensate for the lost tax income from the 'Grutrecht', local rulers wanted to impose taxes on beer itself. However, beer-brewing monasteries were linked to local parishes which did not have to pay this tax. As a result of the privileged position enjoyed by the monasteries, local rulers favoured private brewers, which would have to pay the taxes on beer (Meussdoerffer 2009).

Later on, during the Reformation, which took place in Europe in the early sixteenth century, the monasteries' breweries lost further market share as the Catholic Church lost a lot of its power (Holt 2006). In the northern European regions which turned to Protestantism, the Reformation eliminated Catholic monasteries and, along with them, their beer production. Commercial breweries would emerge to take their place. In those countries that continued to be Catholic, monasteries carried on brewing, with the advantage of being exempt from some taxes (Wrightson 1981).

The final element that completed the shift from monasteries to commercial breweries as centres of brewing came at the end of the eighteenth century. During the French Revolution in 1789, many European monasteries—along with their breweries—were destroyed. As many monasteries were destroyed

---

[8] The purity laws had been issued by cities as part of urban legislation and they never attained more than local significance. In 1516, however, Wilhem IV, the Duke of Bavaria, extended this law to the whole state of Bavaria (Meussdoerffer 2009). However, in some rural regions of Bavaria that escaped state surveillance, beer was still brewed by adding 'grut'. In this respect, the Reinheitsgebot was seen by some as an early Protestant measure to break the dominance of the Grutrecht through which the often Catholic local rulers earned a lot of money (Unger 2004). The Reinheitsgebot was ultimately extended to the whole of Germany, became federal German law in 1919, and was only repealed in 1988. For a more detailed account of the issues surrounding the Reinheitsgebot, we refer to Chapter 3 by Van Tongeren in this book.

and/or the monks had been chased away in the preceding years, beer brewing was no longer a priority for the monks that remained. Instead, commercial breweries took their place (Patroons 1979). Hence, from the Napoleonic era onwards, on the whole, the role of monasteries in brewing became (much) less important. That said, the role of monasteries and abbeys in brewing has seen a remarkable revival in recent decades, and particularly so in Belgium (see Chapter 5 by Persyn et al. in this book).

Globalization and New Competition for Beer in the Early Modern Times

During early modern times, the European superpowers of the time (initially Spain and Portugal, followed by England, France, and the Netherlands) made voyages to the 'New World', which gave another indication of the importance that Europeans attached to their beer (Mathias 1959 and Stubbs 2003). Convinced that water in newly discovered territories was polluted and carried diseases, the European discoverers took beer as a very important cargo on their ships. The Europeans also introduced beer-brewing methods into the territories they conquered (Schmölders 1932). In some conquered regions, however, such as in the southwestern region of North America, they found that native Americans were already brewing some form of 'beer', made from fermented maize (Rabin and Forget 1998). Another example could be found in Latin America, where the Aztecs—who lived in what is now Mexico—already produced some sort of beer made from the sprouted kernels of maize (Dickenson and Unwin 1992).

However, the globalization process also had very different effects on the European beer industry. Apart from finding new markets in which to sell their beer, the European beers faced stiff new competition from other, non-alcoholic, beverages coming from the new territories, such as tea, cocoa, and coffee. Other important competition for beer in the seventeenth century was found closer to home. As incomes in Europe increased, more people could afford wine, which had also become more widely available because of improved transport infrastructure. In addition, distilled alcoholic beverages, such as gin, rum, vodka, and whisky, were increasingly produced and traded (Aerts and Unger 1990).

Not surprisingly, such competition induced lobbying for protectionist measures. A well-illustrated case is the introduction of high taxes in the UK on the import of French wine and alcoholic spirits in the early eighteenth century, causing a dramatic decline in cheap wine consumption. The British masses collectively turned to beer as their most important and widely consumed alcoholic beverage, and hence, with a largely protected beer industry, the UK became a 'beer-drinking nation' (see Chapter 4 by Nye in this volume).

Apart from increasing competition from 'New World' non-alcoholic beverages, from the end of the nineteenth century onwards, 'soda water', another non-alcoholic drink, became a strong competitor for beer. In 1767, after experiments in his Leeds brewery, the Englishman Joseph Priestley (1733–1804) invented artificially 'carbonated water'. After this invention, several other scientists experimented with ways of producing carbonated water and, in Hungary, Ánios Jedlik (1800–95) produced consumable 'soda water'. In 1886, the American John S. Pemberton (1831–88) invented the soda water that would become known as 'Coca-cola'. In the decades that followed, consumption of coca-cola and similar sodas grew very rapidly.

Scientific Discoveries and the Development of Modern Brewing in the Eighteenth and Nineteenth Centuries

During the eighteenth and nineteenth centuries, several scientific discoveries had a dramatic impact on beer production. Increasing knowledge about the function and composition of yeast made it possible to produce new types of beer and better control the production process. Other important discoveries were the improvement of the steam engine, the invention of the refrigerator and of glass beer bottles, the introduction of new methods to seal beer bottles and—in the twentieth century—the invention of metal cans. A final important invention was the ability to control the 'stability' of beer once it had been bottled.

First, an important innovation constituted the discovery of a new beer production process called 'lagering'. Although a 'lager' kind of beer was already being brewed in southern Germany in the late Middle Ages, lager as we know it today is the pale and almost gold-coloured drink first brewed in the mid-nineteenth century by Josef Groll (1813–87) (Michel 1899).[9] To produce lager beer, a 'bottom-fermentation process'—in which the (slow-fermenting) yeast sinks to the bottom of the brewing vessel—was used. Before this method was invented, the yeast rose to the top of the fermenting brew, i.e. the top-fermentation process (Hornsey 2003).

By 1818, scientists had discovered that the beer fermentation process could be divided into a first phase, in which saccharine was transformed into alcohol and carbon dioxide, and a second phase, in which the beer 'ripened' and remaining impurities were removed. This knowledge led to experiments to

---

[9] This new beer is associated with the brewery of Pilsen (Plzen) in West Bohemia (now part of the Czech Republic) from which the name 'Pils beer' derives.

produce new beers by manipulating the yeast's environment. Experiments by two brewers, Gabriel Sedlmayr (1811–91) in Munich and Anton Dreher (1810–63) in Vienna, led to the discovery of the 'process of lagering' (Sedlmayr 1934).[10] To control the activity and suspension of the yeast, they used slow-acting yeast and storage at a low temperature over a period of several weeks (Meussdoerffer 2009). In this way, the German 'lager'—literally 'storage'— beer was produced. The 'lager' beer was clearer and brighter than the then existing beers.

This scientific approach led to the creation of 'brewing schools' and to more new beers.[11] By 1840, in the Munich 'brewing school', Dreher was producing large quantities of so-called 'pale lager beer', which represented a mix of the 'crispness' of lager beer and the paler colour associated with English ale beer (Hornsey 2003).

Around the same time that the lager brewing process was developed, the exact composition of yeast was discovered. Although yeast had been used to produce beer for several centuries, it was only in the nineteenth century that yeast was identified as the actual cause of fermentation in malted barley water: one of the most important steps in the beer-making process. While the first principles of the operation of yeast were discovered during the seventeenth and eighteenth centuries (Barnett 2003),[12] it was not until the mid-nineteenth century that the French scientist Louis Pasteur (1822–95) was able to demonstrate that yeast consists of living cells that are responsible for the fermentation process (Barnett 2000). Whilst doing research into the causes of 'diseases' associated with wine in the 1860s, Pasteur developed the so-called 'Pasteurization' method, in which he found that wine could be preserved much longer if he heated the wine to a specific temperature and cooled it immediately to destroy pathogens in the wine.[13] Later on, he conducted

---

[10] At first and in order to gather as much knowledge as possible, both Sedlmayr and Dreher visited the breweries of England, where newer and more 'scientific' brewing methods had already been introduced. Subsequently, they tried to implement the beer-brewing methods they had learned about in England in their own breweries at home. In this respect, Sedlmayr started to apply the English 'pale ale' brewing techniques in his 'Spaten' Brewery in Germany. In addition and after taking over his father's brewery in Vienna in 1836, Dreher started experimenting with the English malting process.

[11] In 1836, the German Professor Cajetan Kaiser started teaching on brewing. A real 'brewing school' was established in Munich to conduct further research into the brewing of 'lager beer'. In 1876, following the 'Munich example', new brewing schools were established in Paris and Berlin. Belgium followed in 1887, with new brewing schools in Ghent and Leuven (Patroons 1979). In the USA, a zymotechnic institute was established in 1872 (Baron 1962).

[12] Three scientists, namely, the Dutch Antoni Van Leeuwenhoek (1632–1723), the German George Ernst Stahl (1660–1734) and the Dutch Hermann Boerhaave (1668–1738), all contributed to the understanding of how yeast causes fermentation. Building further on the theories of these three scientists, the French scientist Antoine Laurent Lavoisier (1743–94) demonstrated for the first time that, through the process of fermentation, sugar molecules were broken down into alcohol and carbon dioxide (CO_2) (Hornsey 2003).

[13] Pasteur (1866).

similar research with regard to beer in his *Etudes sur la Bière* (1876).[14] Around the same time, the Danish scientist Emil Christian Hansen (1842–1909) studied the 'diseases' that affected beer production (Michel 1899). In the Carlsberg laboratories in Copenhagen, Hansen succeeded in isolating the strain of yeast that produced the German lager beer. Other breweries could now also produce lager beer, which became very popular (Hornsey 2003). The 1880s heralded the transition from top to bottom fermentation. With the success of this new fermentation process, the brewery industries in continental Europe embarked on the road to industrialization (Teich 1990).

Two other technological innovations in the late eighteenth and nineteenth centuries were important for the growth of lager beer and the beer industry, namely, the improvement of the steam engine[15] and the invention of refrigeration. First, the refined Watts steam engine not only made it possible to use more complicated, steam-operated machinery during the brewing process, but it also reduced transportation costs. With trains and steamboats, it became much cheaper to export beer throughout Europe and to the USA, Canada, and even Australia. Second, the invention of the refrigerator in 1876 made it possible to brew lager beer—which required cooling—all year round and not just during the winter months, when natural ice was available to cool the beer (Meussdoerffer 2009).

Other important innovations affected storage of beer (Hornsey 2003). Using glass bottles was important for the transportation of the beer, as it enabled beer to be preserved much better than cask beer, especially on long journeys. In the seventeenth century, glass beer bottles were hand blown and therefore expensive.[16] After the invention of the 'chilled iron mould' in the 1860s, glass bottles could be produced relatively cheaply in mass quantities, as of the 1890s (Teich 1998). Equally important was the invention of new methods to seal beer bottles. Glass beer bottles were initially sealed with a cork held in place with wire (Meussdoerffer 2009). Later on, beer bottles were closed with a 'screw stopper', invented by Henry Barrett in 1872. Another 20 years later, in 1892, William Painter patented the 'crown cork', which enabled automatic bottling machines to be developed. In the first half of the twentieth century, metal beer cans were invented and introduced in the USA. They soon became popular in the USA, but not in the UK and the rest of Europe, where their widespread use did not occur until (much) later.[17]

---

[14] Pasteur (1876).

[15] In 1769, James Watts (1736–1819) considerably improved and reduced the operating costs of the steam engine that had been invented by Newcomen in 1712.

[16] In some regions, there was a kind of 'excise duty' on glass. For instance, in England and Wales, there was such an excise duty from 1745 to 1845. This stalled the further development of glass bottle technology in those regions for many years.

[17] Data from the USA show also a clear historical change in the way beer was sold. In the early twentieth century, 85 per cent of beer was kegged and sold in bars or saloons and only 15 per cent

In summary, scientific progress in the eighteenth and nineteenth centuries had a major impact on the brewing industry. The mechanization and use of steam engines was followed by the introduction of refrigeration, making control of the environment in breweries possible. Moreover, these developments came at the same time as detailed research on yeast which made it possible to produce a consistent and reliable pilsner beer of high quality throughout the entire year and at lower costs. With an improved product which brewers could distribute using cheaper and faster transportation networks, beer production and consumption grew and spread throughout the entire world (Unger 2004). In addition, throughout beer history, one of the main goals of brewers had always been to achieve consistency in their brew. Lack of technology and knowledge had made this very difficult for centuries. However, with increasing knowledge of how the actual brewing process took place and, thanks to the introduction of beer bottles, beer cans, and crown corks, it became increasingly possible to control the 'stability' of beer once it had been bottled (Gourvish 1998).

Growth and Decline, Consolidation and Globalization in the Nineteenth to the Twenty-First Centuries

Growth and Decline

The nineteenth century was characterized by strong and continuous growth in beer production (see Table 1.1 and Figure 1.1). Beer production and consumption increased particularly sharply in the last quarter of the nineteenth century and up to the eve of World War I, a period characterized by a strong decline in global grain prices (Swinnen 2009). By the early twentieth century, the beer markets of Germany, the UK, and the USA were the largest in the world and of similar size: between 5 to 7 billion litres each.

However, evolution in the twentieth century is characterized by both growth and decline. In most countries, beer production declined dramatically in the 1915–50 period, but for different reasons. To illustrate the changes better, Figure 1.2 presents beer production in indices, with 1900 = 100. In Europe, production fell by around 70 per cent during World War I. The brewing industry suffered greatly, particularly in the occupied parts of Europe

---

of the beer was canned or bottled. By 1935, 30 per cent of the sold beer was canned or bottled, partly caused by the spread of home refrigerators, which could preserve beer, and the decrease in the price of canned and bottled beer. After World War II, more and more beer was sold in bottles. By 1980, 80 per cent of total beer sales was packaged in bottles or cans and only 20 per cent of beer sales consisted of draught beer (Stack 2003). By 2000, beer packaged in cans and bottles represented 91 per cent of total beer sales in the USA, whilst draught beer only represented 9 per cent of these sales (Tremblay and Tremblay 2005).

Table 1.1. The largest beer producers by continent (1820–2000), in billion litres

	1820	1840	1860	1880	1900	1920	1940	1960	1980	2000
Europe										
Belgium		0.531	0.656	0.924	1.462	1.041	1.023	1.011	1.429	1.551
France		0.424	0.657	0.823	1.071	1.155	1.815	1.726	2.129	1.599
Germany		1.310	1.700	3.850	7.086	2.344	4.872	6.075	11.320	10.988
UK	1.110			4.496	6.001	4.485	4.173	4.337	6.483	5.891
Czechoslovakia	0.116				0.587	0.589	0.599	1.409	2.339	1.780
Netherlands							0.176	0.355	1.568	2.496
Poland							0.150	0.673	1.116	2.523
Russia							1.213	2.498	6.133	5.156
America										
USA				1.561	4.635	1.080	6.441	11.094	22.777	
Canada					0.124	0.161	0.359	1.149	2.266	2.452
Mexico							0.179	0.853	2.688	5.985
Argentina							0.148	0.243	0.228	1.269
Brazil						0.082	0.206	0.643	2.782	6.695
Colombia							0.078		1.287	
Africa										
South Africa						0.032	0.066	0.097	1.144	
Nigeria								0.022	0.399	
Asia										
China									0.688	
Japan					0.015	0.122	0.311	0.929	4.559	5.464
South Korea								0.018	0.579	1.654
Thailand								0.008	0.124	1.165
Oceania										
Australia					0.200	0.325	0.427	1.053	2.023	1.768
New Zealand					0.031	0.071	0.083	0.245	0.378	0.298

Note: For the period until 1830, the data for the UK refer to Great Britain only. From 1880 onwards, the data refer to the United Kingdom of Great Britain and Northern Ireland (UK). Alsace-Lorraine is included in Germany rather than France from 1871 to 1917, though it is not included in the French statistics until 1922. For the period 1945–89, the figures of West Germany and East Germany were added together. With regard to Russia, figures until 1913 apply to the Russian Empire. For the period 1913–39, they apply to the USSR territory of 1923. In 1940, they include territories incorporated in 1939–40. After 1990, they apply to the present territory of Russia. For Czechoslovakia (which came into existence from 1918), the figures for the period 1938–44 are for the Czech lands only. From 1993 onwards, they refer to the Czech Republic.

Source: Mitchell (2007a), table D23, 506–12; Mitchell (2007b), table D26, 602–10; Mitchell (2007c), table D21, 415–21.

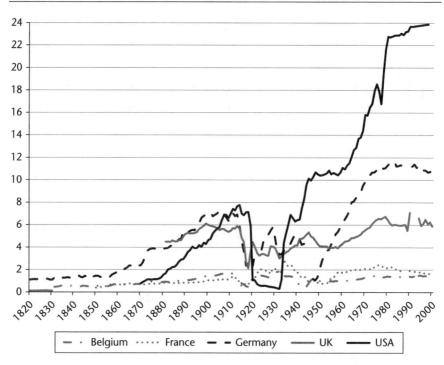

Figure 1.1. Beer production in the nineteenth and twentieth centuries in Europe (Belgium, France, Germany, and the United Kingdom) and the USA (1820–2000), in billion litres

Note: For the period until 1830, the data for the UK refer to Great Britain only. From 1880 onwards, the data refer to the United Kingdom of Great Britain and Northern Ireland (UK). For the period 1945–89, the figures for West Germany and East Germany were added together.

Source: Mitchell (2007b), table D26, 602–10; Mitchell (2007c), table D21, 415–21.

(e.g. Belgium and France). The mobilization caused many workers in the brewing industry to be scattered, which led to a shortage of employees in the breweries. Moreover, metal materials (such as copper), vehicles, and draught animals were requisitioned by the occupying forces. As a consequence, a lot of breweries had to close their businesses (Patroons 1979). In Germany too, the beer industry suffered, as other industries (especially the war industries) had priority in the allocation of resources. Moreover, grains were scarce and expensive, with food and feed shortages throughout Europe.

After the war, the scarcity of raw materials persisted for several years. Breweries that wanted to start up again, or to increase production, had to manage with what they could find. For several years after the war, all kinds of grains, peas, beets, and beans were used to produce beer. Yet beer production recovered strongly in some European countries after the war. For example, in France, beer production increased four-fold between 1918 and the late 1930s. Recovery was less marked in Germany and the UK (see Figure 1.2).

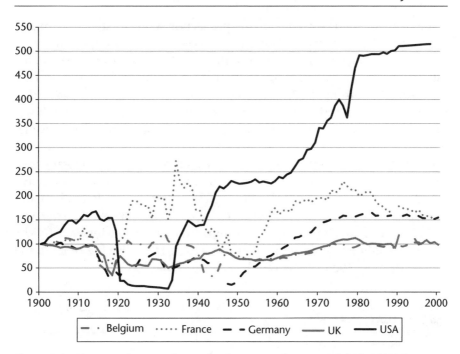

Figure 1.2. Change in beer production in the twentieth century (1900–2000), base year 1900 = 100

Note: For the period 1945–89, the figures of West Germany and East Germany were added together.
Source: Mitchell (2007b), table D26, 602–10; Mitchell (2007c), table D21, 415–21.

Production declined again dramatically in the 1940s. During World War II, food was rationed and raw materials for the European breweries were scarce and expensive. As during the previous shortages, breweries tried to cope by using substitutes for normal brewing ingredients. Examples of substitutes included several types of malt that had been flavoured/aromatized, beets (rich in sugar content), and several flavouring substances, such as coriander seed, camomile blossom, and the skins of lemons and oranges (Patroons 1979). As the war continued, metal and cork—needed to seal beer bottles—became scarce as well. Cork was increasingly substituted by cardboard with an added layer of paper, by recycling used crown caps, or by using 'swing-top bottles', with rubber rings made from used car or plane tyres to close the bottle.

The impact of the world wars was smaller in the USA. During World War I, there was an approximately 10 per cent decrease in American beer production. Grain rationing, which was imposed by the American government because of 'war-time emergencies', induced the American brewers to brew beer with a lower alcohol content (i.e. only 2.75 per cent) (Stack 2003).

A much more radical decline in beer production was caused by government regulation. The 'temperance movement' succeeded in securing a nationwide prohibition on alcohol in the USA from 1919 to 1933. During this period, the sale, manufacture, and transportation of alcohol of more than 0.5 per cent were banned (Hartung 1932). As a result, the USA had no legal beer production for 14 years. There was some illegal beer production in this period, but it was minimal. Total beer output collapsed (Figure 1.2). Many American breweries were closed down. Some sold their plant and equipment as soon as possible, at substantial losses. Others, who expected the Prohibition to be temporary, tried to use their equipment to produce related products: such as beer containing less than 0.5 per cent alcohol (Stack 2003). In 1933, the Prohibition was repealed. The manufacture and sale of certain kinds of alcoholic beverages, including beer, was allowed again. The impact on the US brewing industry was severe. According to official figures, there were 1,345 active breweries in the USA in 1915. By 1934, 50 per cent had closed (Table 1.2).

Table 1.2. The number of breweries and the average brewery size in Belgium, in the UK, and in the USA (1900–1980)

	Belgium		UK		USA	
	No. of breweries	Average brewery size (x million litres)	No. of breweries	Average brewery size (x million litres)	No. of breweries	Average brewery size (x million litres)
1900	3223	0.454	6447	0.901	1816	2.556
1910	3349	0.478	4398	1.310	1568	4.466
1914	—	—	3746	1.540	—	—
1915	—	—	—	—	1345	5.224
1920	2013	0.517	2914	1.966	Prohibition	Prohibition
1930	1546	1.078	1418	2.850	prohibition	Prohibition
1934	1362	1.081	—	—	756	5.859
1940	1120	0.914	840	4.898	684	9.430
1946	755	1.431	—	—	468	21.741
1950	663	1.529	567	7.437	407	25.634
1960	414	2.442	358	11.613	229	48.488
1965	305	3.637	—	—	197	64.408
1968	256	4.646	220	22.424	—	—
1970	232	5.610	—	—	154	102.769
1973	190	7.732	162	35.119	—	—
1975	174	7.929	—	—	117	158.565
1977	159	8.691	144	44.488	—	—
1980	123	11.619	142	48.108	101	219.154

Note: The average brewery size was measured in million litres for Belgium, in UK barrels for the UK, and in US barrels for the USA. We calculated all figures in million litres, taking 1 UK barrel = 36 imperial gallons (43 US gallons) and 1 US barrel = 31 US gallons (26 imperial gallons). 1 UK gallon = 4.55 litres and 1 US gallon = 3.79 litres. (The Finnish Foundation for Alcohol Studies 1977: 33).

Source: Calculated from Hornsey (2003: 618); Patroons (1979: 18); 'History of Beer', The Belgian tourist office, Wallonia and Brussels; Union of Belgian Brewers; Stack (2000: 49); Stack (2003).

Some authors (e.g. Rabin and Forget 1998) also claim that the Great Depression (reducing demand) and the dust bowl[18] (increasing grain prices) reduced production in the 1930s. However, as Figure 1.2 illustrates, within a few years of the repeal of prohibition, beer production increased to the level of the pre-prohibition years. The dust bowl seems to have affected the nature of the brewing process rather than the amount of beer produced, just as, during World War I, US breweries reacted to increased grain prices by switching ingredients. Instead of barley, cheaper grains such as corn and rice were used, and, with these 'substitutes', 'lager' style beer was brewed.[19]

Strong growth was temporarily interrupted by World War II, but resumed soon afterwards. The 1950–80 period was characterized by strong growth in beer production and consumption, both in Europe and in the USA. Technological innovations and increasing incomes lowered real prices and increased demand, causing growth in beer consumption.

The 1980s were the start of a major structural change in beer consumption in Europe and the USA. In Chapter 7 of this volume, Colen and Swinnen show that there is a non-linear relationship between income and beer consumption. Beyond a certain level of income, per capita beer consumption falls instead of rises. In addition, alternative alcoholic drinks, in particular wine, became more readily available in traditional beer-drinking countries. Hence, since 1980, per capita consumption declined in all major beer-producing countries, with consumers switching to other beverages because of increased choice and higher incomes (Colen and Swinnen, Chapter 7, this volume). Total production continued to increase in some countries. It increased in the USA because of population growth as a result of migration, leading to an increase in total demand. In some European countries, such as Belgium, production grew because increasing exports more than offset declining local demand (Persyn et al., Chapter 5, this volume).

Growth in global beer markets has shifted elsewhere. Beer consumption in emerging countries has grown rapidly over the past 20 years. The strongest growth in beer consumption is in Russia (Deconinck and Swinnen, Chapter 16, this volume), while Brazil, India, and China have also shown strong growth in beer consumption. While per capita consumption in India is still very low, China has, since 2003, become the largest beer market in the world (Arora et al., Chapter 17 in this volume; Bai et al., Chapter 15, this volume).

---

[18] An enormous drought during the 1930s transformed many grain fields into a massive 'dust bowl'. As a result, grain became very expensive and many breweries started to look for alternatives.

[19] These adjustments to using cheaper substitute grains had important lasting effects. To this day Budweiser and Bud Light—the main US beer—are brewed based on a portion of rice.

Consolidation in the Twentieth Century

The twentieth century was also characterized by a strong consolidation in the brewery industry (Table 1.2). For example, the number of breweries in the UK decreased from 6,447 in 1900 to 2,914 in 1920. In the next 30 years, the number of UK breweries decreased further to 567 in 1950. The average size of UK breweries grew from 0.9 million litres in 1900 to 2.0 million litres in 1920, and to 7.4 million litres in 1950. In Belgium, the number of breweries decreased from 3,223 in 1900 to 2,013 in 1920, to 663 in 1950. In the same period, the average Belgian brewery size increased from 0.45 million litres in 1900, to 0.51 million litres in 1920 and 1.5 million litres in 1950 (Persyn et al., Chapter 5, this volume).

The world wars played an important role in this consolidation process, in particular in continental Europe. Many breweries that had to start again from scratch after World War I decided to mechanize their brewery or merge with larger breweries. Similarly, many European breweries in the occupied countries suffered damage during World War II. These breweries needed to invest substantially in new brewing equipment. As a result, in the immediate post-war period, many breweries merged or concentrated because of the investments that were necessary to re-equip and modernize the breweries. Other breweries expanded their activities by producing mineral water and several types of lemonade. The production of these types of non-alcoholic drinks did not pose high technical demands and there were substantial cost savings through scale economies in the distribution of the drinks, which could happen through the same channels (Patroons 1979).[20]

In the USA, the number of breweries decreased from 1,816 breweries in 1900 to 1,345 in 1915. The average size of the American breweries grew from 2.6 million litres in 1900 to 5.2 million litres in 1915 (Table 1.2). Prohibition disrupted this process.[21] After the end of prohibition, 756 breweries started brewing again. By 1940, 684 breweries were still active on the American market, and their average size increased enormously after prohibition: from 5.9 million litres in 1934 to 9.4 million litres in 1940, to 25.6 million litres in 1950, reflecting a huge increase in the USA's total beer production: from 4.4 billion litres in 1934 to 10.4 billion litres in 1950 (Table 1.1 and Stack 2003).

---

[20] In the USA, in the same period, all large mergers were vertical, as horizontal types of merger were forbidden by the country's antitrust laws. For a more detailed discussion of postwar developments in America, see Chapter 13 by Adams in this book.

[21] Some American breweries—e.g. Anheuser-Busch—were granted special licences by the American government to produce beer for medical purposes. This made it possible for those breweries to keep their staff active and still to use their equipment and plant to make beer, which gave them a competitive advantage over the breweries that were not granted such a government licence (Stack 2003).

The consolidation process continued after World War II. Between 1950 and 1980, the number of UK breweries decreased from 567 breweries in 1950 to 142 in 1980. The average size increased accordingly, from 7.4 million litres in 1950 to 48.1 million litres in 1980. Similarly, in Belgium, the number of breweries decreased from 663 in 1950 to 123 in 1980. As in the UK, the average Belgian brewery size increased strongly, from 1.5 million litres in 1950 to 11.6 million litres in 1980.

As in Europe, consolidation in the US beer industry continued in the second half of the twentieth century. The number of US breweries decreased sharply, from 407 in 1950 to only 101 in 1980. The average size of US breweries grew from 25.6 million litres in 1950 to 219.2 million litres in 1980 (Table 1.2). Large national breweries, such as Anheuser-Busch and Pabst, grew in importance, to the detriment of small local breweries. An important cause was scale economies in advertising, in particular with the arrival of TV (see Chapter 12 by George in this book). The five largest American breweries' share in total USA beer production rose from 19 per cent in 1947 to 75 per cent in 1981 (Stack 2003).

Globalization in the Late Twentieth Century

During the 1980s and 1990s, an increasing number of breweries started looking abroad for additional sales. To this end, European and American breweries started to export more beer overseas, establish new firms abroad, and engage in 'licensing deals' in some countries where the already existing breweries started brewing their products. For example, in 1995, Anheuser-Busch entered into licensing accords to brew Budweiser in two breweries outside the USA, namely, one brewery in the UK to serve the European market and one in China to serve the East Asian market (Stack 2003).

Also non-US breweries went 'global' in the last decades of the twentieth century. In particular, companies such as Heineken (Holland), SABMiller (South Africa), and Interbrew (Belgium) made a large number of acquisitions across the globe. In the 1990s, they bought a whole series of breweries in Eastern Europe (Swinnen and Van Herck, Chapter 14 in this volume) and extended their operations in North and South America (e.g. Canada, Mexico, Brazil, and the USA) and China. These days, the holdings that resulted from these brewing companies dominate the global beer market. For example, in 2002, SABMiller plc—with its head office in London, UK—was created through the merger between South African Breweries (SAB) (the dominant brewery of South Africa, with many operations in Europe), and the second largest US brewery, Miller (Stack 2003). Another example is Anheuser-Busch Inbev NV—with headquarters in Leuven, Belgium—that resulted from the

2004 merger between the Belgian Interbrew and the Brazilian AmBev and the 2008 merger with Anheuser-Busch (<http://www.ab-inbev.com>).

From Ales to Lager to Light to Specialty Beers

As already explained, the introduction of the lagering technology revolutionized brewing and dramatically changed the global beer markets in the nineteenth and twentieth centuries. All over the world, traditional ales produced with top fermentation lost market share to lager beer brewed with bottom fermentation. Lager came to dominate the beer market globally. However, some breweries continued to produce other types of beer, particularly in some European regions, such as Belgium, Ireland, England, and Bavaria.

During the first half of the twentieth century, several grain shortages caused a further shift in beer brewing and ultimately in consumer preferences in the USA. First, during World War I, grain rationing was imposed by the US government, causing US brewers to brew beer of a lower alcohol content (i.e. only 2.75 per cent) (Stack 2003). Second, the 'dust bowl' drought during the 1930s made grain very expensive. In response, breweries looked for alternatives. Instead of barley, other and cheaper grains such as corn and rice were used. With these substitutes, the resulting lager beers were lighter in colour. They were called 'light lager' or 'American lager' beer. A few years later, during World War II, grain was again in short supply and, as a result, American brewers kept producing 'light lager'. Consequently, by the end of the war, the 'light lager' had gained a major share of the North American beer market and US consumers had become used to drinking 'light lager' (Rabin and Forget 1996).

Later in the twentieth century, new types of beer were developed in response to a growing demand for low calorie foods and drinks (Tremblay and Tremblay 2005). Many beer producers discontinued the production of dark beer and started producing 'diet' or 'light' beers. These beers, brewed with more water relative to hops and grains and with an enzyme called amylogucosidase—added during fermentation—contained less alcohol, fewer calories, and fewer carbohydrates than the 'regular' beers (Robertson 1984). In 1975, Miller introduced Miller Lite, successfully marketed as 'America's fine light beer'. The new drink became an enormous success and similar brews were introduced in the following years. Light beer has been a great success ever since and, in 2005, it was the most popular beer category in the United States (Tremblay and Tremblay 2005).

However, the growing domination of increasingly standardized lager and light beers produced by increasingly fewer brewing companies has led to a counter-movement in the past 25 years. This reaction against consolidation and lack of variety started in the USA. During the 1980s, people started to show a renewed interest in 'older' beer styles, such as porter, pale ales and brown cask ales, stout, and bitters. At the beginning of the 1990s, this trend of (re-)appreciating and brewing 'special beers' and 'older' style beer was labelled the 'microbrewery movement' because of the small scale of the new breweries that started to brew different types of beer (see Chapter 8 by Tremblay and Tremblay in this volume).[22] The size of these new breweries was much smaller than that of the existing breweries. However, because of their success, some of these microbreweries have since outgrown the 'micro' term, but are still labelled 'microbreweries' because of the style of beer they are producing. Some are now referred to as 'regional specialty brewers' (Tremblay and Tremblay 2005). At the beginning of the twenty-first century, the microbreweries accounted for approximately 5 to 7 per cent of the total US beer market (Stack 2003 and Duffy 2010).

Although this process first started in the USA, similar developments can now be observed in many traditional beer-consuming countries. While the share of the 'microbreweries' in total global beer production is still relatively small, these breweries have influenced the beer markets significantly and in various ways. In countries like Belgium, beer brewing in (collaboration with) monasteries and abbeys has known a remarkable revival. Abbey beers are the fastest growing segment of the Belgian beer market (Persyn et al., Chapter 5, this volume), but only a few of these abbey beers—mainly the very popular 'Trappist' beers—are still produced in monasteries nowadays. The other abbey beers are either based on old recipes from monasteries or they represent an attempt to brew 'abbey-style' beers in commercial breweries. The latter reflects an important strategy of the larger brewing companies. In recent years, many large beer brewers have tried to 'copy' the taste of the 'microbrews' or have bought (shares in) microbreweries or abbey-type beers (Stack 2003).

As a concluding comment in this review of the changes from the nineteenth to the twenty-first centuries, it is interesting to point to Tremblay and Tremblay's (Chapter 8, this volume) observation that today the largest US-owned brewery is the Boston Brewing Company, which started only a few years ago as a 'microbrewery'. This is a consequence of the simultaneous process of consolidation and global mergers and acquisitions of traditional (lager and light

---

[22] The term 'microbrewery' can have different meanings. Originally, the term—which was already in use in the UK in the late 1970s—was used to describe the *size* of the breweries producing these older types of beer, i.e. breweries with a beer production of between 5,000 to 100,000 barrels a year. Very quickly, however, the term was used to denote a new and 'fresh' approach to brewing, one that, instead of competing on the basis of low prices and advertising, tried to compete on the basis of the inherent *product characteristics*, leading to a greater quality and diversity of the 'end beer product', i.e. in terms of taste, added flavours, the freshness of the ingredients, etc. When this kind of 'microbrewing' became more popular in the USA as well, the term was used for American breweries that adopted the 'brewing philosophy' described above and that produced fewer than 15,000 barrels of beer a year (Stack 2003).

beer) brewers (which has caused all the large US breweries to be acquired or to be majority owned by foreign brewing companies) and the growth of microbreweries. This is a powerful illustration of the dramatic changes that have taken place in global beer markets during the twentieth century and which are ongoing in the twenty-first century.

References

Aerts, E., L. M. Cullen, and R.G. Wilson (eds.) (1990). *Production, Marketing and Consumption of Alcoholic Beverages*. Leuven: Leuven University Press.

—— and Unger, R. W. (1990). 'Brewing in the Low Countries', in Aerts et al. (1990), 92–101.

Barnett, J. (2000). 'A History of Research on Yeasts 2: Louis Pasteur and his Contemporaries, 1850 +/– 1880'. *Yeast*, 16/14: 755–71.

—— (2003). 'Beginnings of Microbiology and Biochemistry: The Contribution of Yeast Research'. *Microbiology*, 149: 557–67.

Baron, S. (1962). *Brewed in America: The History of Beer and Ale in the United States*. Boston, MA: Little, Brown.

Behre, K.-E. (1983). *Ernährung und Umwelt der wikingerzeitlichen Siedlung Haithabu: die Ergebnisse der Untersuchungen der Pflanzenreste*. Neumünster: Karl Wachholtz.

—— (1999). 'The History of Beer Additives in Europe—A Review'. *Vegetation History and Archaeobotany*, 8: 35–48.

Bickerdyke, J. (1889). *The Curiosities of Ale & Beer: An Entertaining History*. London: The Leadenhall Press.

Brewer, D. J., and E. Teeter (2007). *Egypt and the Egyptians*. Cambridge: Cambridge University Press.

Clark, P. (1983). *The English Alehouse: A Social History, 1200–1830*. Harlow: Longman.

Degrande, G. (2010). *Tournée générale: De geheimen van het Belgische bier*. Leuven: Uitgeverij Van Halewyck.

Dickenson, J., and T. Unwin (1992). 'Viticulture in Colonial Latin America: Essays on Alcohol, the Vine and Wine in Spanish America and Brazil', in Institute of Latin American Studies, Working Paper 13.

Dineley, M., and G. Dineley (2000). 'Neolithic Ale: Barley as a Source of Malt Sugars for Fermentation', in A. S. Fairbairn (ed.), *Plants in Neolithic Britain and Beyond*, Oxford: Oxbow, 137–54.

Doorman, G. (1955). *De middeleeuwse Brouwerij en de Gruit*, 's-Gravenhage: Nijhoff.

Duffy, J. (2010). 'The Plight of the Micro-Brewers'. *BBC News Online*, 28 November.

Eßlinger, H. M. (2009). *Handbook of Brewing: Processes, Technology, Markets*. Weinheim: Wiley-VCH Verlag GmbH & Co. KGaA.

Geller, J. (1992). 'From Prehistory to History: Beer in Egypt', in R. Friedman and B. Adams (eds.), *The Followers of Horus (Egyptian Studies Association Publication 2)*. Oxford: Oxbow, 19–26.

Gourvish, T. R. (1998). 'Concentration, Diversity and Firm Strategy in European Brewing, 1945–90', in R. G. Wilson and T. R. Gourvish (eds.), *The Dynamics of the International Brewing Industry since 1800*. London: Routledge, 80–92.

Hackel-Stehr, K. (1987). *Das Brauwesen in Bayern vom 14. bis 16. Jahrhundert, insbesondere die Entstehung und Entwicklung des Reinheitsgebotes (1516)*. Dissertation, Berlin 1987, herausgegeben von den Gesellschaft für Öffentlichkeitsarbeit der Deutschen Brauwirtschaft zum Jubiläum der Gesellschaft für die Geschichte und Bibliographie des Brauwesens e.V. 1913–1988, Bonn–Bad Godesberg: den Gesellschaft für Öffentlichkeitsarbeit der Deutschen Brauwirtschaft, 1989.

Hartung, J. (1932). 'Die Brautechnik in den Vereinigten Staaten vor und nach der Einführung der Prohibition', in G. Schmölders, *Die Brauindustrie in den Vereinigten Staaten in ihrer technischen und wirtschaftlichen Entwicklung*. Berlin: Institut für Gärungsgewerbe, 101–90.

Holt, M. P. (2006). 'Europe Divided: Wine, Beer, and the Reformation in Sixteenth-Century Europe', in M. P. Holt (ed.), *Alcohol: A Social and Cultural History*. Oxford: Berg, 25–40.

Horn, W., and E. Born (1979). *The Plan of St Gall: A Study of the Architecture and Economy of, and Life in a Paradigmatic Carolingian Monastery*. Berkeley, CA: University of California Press, 3 vols.

Hornsey, I. (2003). *A History of Beer and Brewing*. Cambridge: The Royal Society of Chemistry.

Jackson, M. (1996). *All About Beer Magazine*, 1 March.

Katz, S., and M. Voigt (1986). 'Bread and Beer: The Early Use of Cereals in the Human Diet'. *Expeditions*, 28/2: 23–34.

Mathias, P. (1959). *The Brewing Industry in England 1700–1830*. Cambridge: Cambridge University Press.

Meussdoerffer, F. G. (2009). 'A Comprehensive History of Beer Brewing', in Eßlinger (2009).

Michel, C. (1899). *Geschichte des Bieres von der ältesten Zeit bis zum Jahre 1899*, Augsburg: Verlagsbuchhandlung Gebrüder Reichel.

Mitchell, B. R. (2007a). *International Historical Statistics: Africa, Asia and Oceania, 1750–2005* (6th edn.). Basingstoke, UK: Palgrave Macmillan.

—— (2007b). *International Historical Statistics: Europe 1750–2005* (6th edn.). Basingstoke, UK: Palgrave Macmillan.

—— (2007c). *International Historical Statistics: The Americas, 1750–2005* (6th edn.). Basingstoke, UK: Palgrave Macmillan.

Mosher, R. (2009). *Tasting Beer: An Insider's Guide to the World's Greatest Drink*. North Adams, MA: Storey Publishing, LLC.

Nelson, M. (2003). 'The Cultural Construction of Beer among Greeks and Romans'. *Syllecta Classica*, 14: 101–20.

—— (2005). *The Barbarian's Beverage: A History of Beer in Ancient Europe*. London and New York: Routledge.

Pasteur, L. (1866). *Études sur le vin, ses maladies, causes qui les provoquent, procédés nouveaux pour le conserver et le vieillir*. Paris: Imprimerie Impériale V. Masson.

Pasteur, L. (1876). *Études sur la bière, ses maladies, causes qui les provoquent, procédés pour la rendre inaltérable avec une théorie nouvelle de la fermentation*. Paris: Gauthier-Villars.

Patroons, W. (1979). *Bier*. Antwerp: Standaard Uitgeverij.

Rabin, D., and C. Forget (eds.), (1998). *The Dictionary of Beer and Brewing* (2nd edn.). Chicago: Fitzroy Dearborn Publishers.

Robertson, J. D. (1984). *The Connoisseur's Guide to Beer*. Ottawa, IL: Jameson Books.

Röllig, W. (1971). 'Das Bier im Alten Mesopotamien', in Gesellschaft Für Geschichte Und Bibliographie Des Brauwesens, *Jahrbuch*. Berlin: Institut für Gärungsgewerbe, 9–104.

Schmölders, G. (1932). 'Die Brauindustrie in den Vereinigten Staaten von der Kolonialzeit bis zur Gegenwart', in G. Schmölders, *Die Brauindustrie in den Vereinigten Staaten in ihrer technischen und wirtschaftlichen Entwicklung*. Berlin: Institut für Gärungsgewerbe, 3–100.

Sedlmayr, F. (1934). *Die Geschichte der Spatenbrauerei unter Gabriel Sedlmayr dem älteren und dem Jüngeren 1807–1874 sowie Beiträge zur bayerischen Brauereigeschichte dieser Zeit*. Munich: Kommissionsverlag von Piloty & Loehle.

Stack, M. (2000). 'Local and Regional Breweries in America's Brewing Industry, 1865 to 1920'. *Business History Review*, 74, autumn: 435–63.

—— (2003). 'A Concise History of America's Brewing Industry', in Robert Whaples (ed.), *Economic History Net Encyclopedia of Economic and Business History*, available at <http://eh.net/encyclopedia/article/stack.brewing.industry.history.us>.

Stubbs, B. (2003). 'Captain Cook's Beer: The Antiscorbutic Use of Malt and Beer in Late 18th Century Sea Voyages'. *Asia Pacific Journal of Clinical Nutrition*, 12: 129–37.

Swinnen, J. (2009). 'The Growth of Agricultural Protection in Europe in the 19th and 20th Centuries'. *The World Economy*, 32/11: 1499–537.

Teich, M. (1990). 'The Industrialisation of Brewing in Germany (1800–1914)', in Aerts et al. (1990), 102–13.

—— (1998). 'The Mass Production of Draught and Bottled Beer in Germany, 1880–1914: A note', in R. G. Wilson and T. R. Gourvish (eds.), *The Dynamics of the International Brewing Industry since 1800*. London: Routledge, 75–9.

The Finnish Foundation For Alcohol Studies And The World Health Organization Regional Office For Europe (1977). *International Statistics on Alcoholic Beverages: Production, Trade and Consumption*, 27. Helsinki: Finnish Foundation for Alcohol Studies.

Tremblay, V., and C. Tremblay (2005). *The U.S. Brewing Industry: Data and Economic Analysis*. Cambridge, MA: MIT Press.

Unger, R. (1995). 'The Scale of Dutch Brewing, 1350–1600'. *Research in Economic History*, 15: 261–92.

—— (2001). *A History of Brewing in Holland, 900-1900, Economy, Technology, and the State*. Leiden and Boston: Brill Academic Publishers.

—— (2004). *Beer in the Middle Ages and the Renaissance*. Philadelphia: University of Pennsylvania Press.

Von Blanckenburg, C. (2001). *Die Hanse und ihr Bier: Brauwesen und Bierhandel im hansischen Verkehrsgebiet*. Dissertation. Cologne: Böhlau Verlag.

Wrightson, K. (1981). 'Alehouses, Order and Reformation in Rural England 1590–1660', in E. Yeo and S. Yeo (eds.), *Popular Culture and Class Conflict 1590–1914*. Brighton: Harvester, 1–27.

2

Beer Production, Profits, and Public Authorities in the Renaissance

Richard W. Unger

Introduction

Brewers in northern and western Europe enjoyed a significant advantage for much of the period from the fifteenth through the seventeenth centuries. The market for their product was booming. Average levels of consumption reached their highest ever. Urban populations were drinking on average about 0.75 litres per person per day. The market was a broad one, including everyone from monks and nuns to small children to building labourers. It was not just the traditional beer drinkers known in later centuries but everyone in every walk of life who understood beer on the table at meal time to be a normal part of life.

Despite the positive circumstances, the producers of beer had to face a range of emerging problems which made it increasingly difficult for them to maintain profitable businesses. Technology, though in general well established, was subject to process innovation, to changes in the ways beer was made. Capital requirements were on the rise because of, among other things, those process innovations. The success of the industry drew the interest of governments and so brewers faced increased regulation and taxation. Location presented difficulties not only because of rising land costs but also because of environmental degradation. The cost structure of the industry made brewers heavily dependent on the prices of some raw materials where they were competing against other buyers who could heavily influence prices brewers paid. Eventually the hurdles brewers had to clear proved too high and profits, along with brewing, stagnated or declined in the second half of the seventeenth century. Trends were all but universal in the beer-drinking regions of

Europe. Examples from the Low Countries and especially the Dutch Republic offer useful illustrations of the general pressures created by supply, demand, and technical change.

Data on brewers' profits, like data on the Renaissance economy in general, are notoriously sparse. Production figures and government regulations are often well documented. Records of individual brewing enterprises, either technical or financial, are extremely rare. The character of the sources limits the scope of any discussion of the industry and also limits the reliability of any conclusions drawn. For example, efforts to calculate profits based on what is known about costs and prices of beer are suspect not only because of the scarcity of figures from firms in the trade, but also because short-term changes in input prices and in taxes could generate significant fluctuations. There was some consistency in the breakdown of expenditures for sixteenth-century breweries, though, and there are indications of a profit rate in the range of 20–30% in some German Hanse towns in the early seventeenth century. Both brewers and governments had an interest in the success of the industry, a joint interest which was regularly tested when matters of profit came to be considered. Direct taxation on beer and indirect taxation on inputs and on land was undoubtedly a heavy burden for the brewing industry. That burden increased through the sixteenth century and to the point at least, in some German towns, where profits may by 1600 have fallen to zero (Huntemann 1971: 41–2, 71–2; Langer 1979: 72; Unger 2004: 161–5). Still there must have been enough gain possible for so many people, from investors to workers to retailers, to remain in the business of making and selling beer. The survival and continued success of sales through to the middle of the seventeenth century, and in southern England and Bavaria into the nineteenth century, strongly suggest that at least in some places there was money to be made in brewing. Even so profits were always under threat from rising capital costs, increasing government regulation and taxation, pollution of water supplies, and rising raw material costs.

Technology and Changing Capital Requirements

Renaissance brewing became prosperous because of the adoption of hops as an additive in making beer. That technological breakthrough in the thirteenth century took some time to work its way through the industry. By 1400 the equipment and processes for making beer were more or less fixed. A century later, with the new practice all but standard, brewers turned to process innovation to reduce costs and enhance profits. The principal change over time was to increase the scale of production, which led to rising capital costs. Small operators with limited access to capital were forced out of business and production came to be concentrated in fewer hands.

Brewers had probably used hops from the early Middle Ages, but it was from around 1200 onwards that people learned the most effective combinations of hops, grains, and water to make beer of higher quality. One sign of the superiority of hopped beer was that it lasted longer and could tolerate shipment over some distance. Starting in north Germany in the thirteenth century, making hopped beer spread across northern Europe, reaching as far south as Austria by the sixteenth century.

By the standards of the early sixteenth century, a brewery and associated maltery involved a sizeable investment in fixed capital. Brewing was different from most contemporary economic activities in that it had a relatively high ratio of capital to labour (Soly 1975: 345), a fact dictated by the technology and continuing efforts to exploit existing technology more effectively. By the early sixteenth century, the biggest lump of capital, the brewing kettle or copper, sat on top of an iron grate with walls or platforms around it (Doorman 1940: 272; Langer 1979: 70). Kettles had to be in a fixed place, so breweries took on the appearance of something more permanent, more massive, and more expensive (Langer 1979: 71; Nef 1954: 99). Copper remained the best and most common material for the brew kettle. The unit was indivisible and, for the sizeable investment to be worthwhile, brewers needed to increase production so that they could reap the potential economies of scale.

Examples from a number of towns indicate how big kettles were and how big they became. At Leuven in the southern Low Countries, the size of a single brew doubled in the fifteenth century, going from about 850 to 1,700 litres (Uytven 1978:154–5; Uytven 1961: 325–7). Around 1400, Gouda brewers made from 1,000 to 2,000 litres at a time (Pinkse 1972: 100, 108). A fifteenth-century Lübeck kettle was considerably larger at 4,630 litres. In 1568 Munich kettles probably had a capacity of around 4,700–4,800 litres and a Wismar kettle from 1602 may have been just short of 4,000 litres. The last-named was said to weigh 406 kilograms, so it is no surprise that for a long time kettles were treated for tax purposes as immovable goods (Langer 1979: 70–1; Techen 1915: 333). At Einbeck, a small town which enjoyed a reputation for producing better beer among consumers in the late sixteenth century, the communal beer kettle could hold 2,200 litres (Frontzek 2005: 23). The kettles in the towns of northern Poland in the seventeenth century were in the range of 1,200–1,700 litres—small perhaps by Dutch or German standards, but still significantly larger than those used in the Polish countryside which ranged between 60 to 900 litres (Klonder 1983: 158).

The Regulatory Context

Governments from the fourth millennium before the start of the Common Era took an interest in beer. That meant brewing was subject to official oversight, always having to function within a body of rules set by authorities. Regulations fixed the parameters within which brewers worked, regulations which fixed much more than just levels of output. Throughout the Renaissance authorities in beer-producing regions were typically more interested in improving their tax income than in protecting small brewers. The larger brewers, expanding the scale of operations and exploiting new technology, became something of a political force. That had an effect on what civic governments required of brewers and also on the ways in which those governments dealt with what was in very many towns the principal source of tax income. The decline in the number of brewers in the sixteenth century can largely be attributed to the increasing size of brew kettles and the increasing scale of brewing operations (Pinkse 1972: 121). The rising capacity of breweries meant a decrease in their numbers and that translated into easier surveillance for tax purposes, as well as a decrease in the risk of fire in the towns, two things much desired by governments throughout northern Europe (Glamann 1962: 133).

Often governments restricted the size of the kettle and even the number of times per week, or per month or per year, that a brewer could turn out the maximum amount allowed under the rules. The result was to dictate the scale of the brewing operation and the upper limit of what any brewer could produce and so limit potential scale economies. The first regulations on maximum production date from early in the fifteenth century. In general, under pressure from some powerful brewers, governments relaxed restrictions and the number of barrels allowed per brew did go up through the fifteenth and sixteenth centuries. The tendency was not only for kettles to get larger, but also for the frequency of brewing and so the total output of those brewers with larger kettles to increase dramatically. Rising levels of investment forced smaller commercial brewers out of business. Brewers with great fixed costs agitated for relaxation of production limits to enhance their profits. A number of examples of such agitation exist, but one from the province of Holland in the sixteenth century graphically illustrates the trend.

In 1548 the ruler of the province of Holland set up a commission to investigate the status of the brewing industry, and to explain why exports had fallen off, and so why his tax income was lagging behind (Bleyswijck 1667: 709–10). A petition from a prominent citizen of the town of Delft inspired the setting up of that commission. The petition claimed that big brewers in the town had control of capital and that this made it impossible for small brewers to compete. Bigger kettles made it possible, so the petitioner said, for brewers who used to brew 4,300 litres at a time to make 8,600 litres. The integration of cooperage and the grinding of grain into brewing enterprises all hurt smaller firms, the petitioner claimed (Woltjer 1987: 265–6, 274–5). The debate in Delft and court cases at Haarlem, as well as petitions from Gouda, contributed to the government decision to carry out a full-scale investigation. Commissioners went to the towns of Delft, Leiden, Haarlem, Gouda, Rotterdam, and Schiedam and asked how many times each week each brewer brewed, how many barrels each brewer made each time, and how much of which types of grain each used. Those members of town governments who were brewers themselves were excluded from any discussions. The governments of Delft and Leiden produced a report for the commission in 1550, showing conclusively that there were scale economies to be reaped and that the savings were greater the more expensive the beer. The biggest gains came from lower average capital costs, since the investment in buildings and equipment was spread across a larger number of litres produced (Yntema: 1992: 163–7).

The commission's report led to a spate of legislation affecting the province of Holland, but reflecting general trends across northern Europe. Not all brewers were pleased with the results. The general decision was that a brewer could brew up to twice a week, that is, a maximum of 104 times each year, and produce about 5,000 litres each time. With permission, though, a brewer could produce 10,000 litres at a time, but then could brew only once a week or 52 times a year. Town bailiffs had to give permission for such double brewing. In addition, the price of beer was to be fixed in relation to the price of grains used in making it. Any decision on price change was to be made by knowledgeable town officials who were not brewers. Officials were put in place to oversee the enforcement of the rules and the maintenance of the quality of the beer in terms of grain used and in terms of taste. Beer is easily infected by various bacteria which can make it overly acidic and, at the extreme, turn it into vinegar. The inspectors made sure that brewers used the required amounts of grain, did not contaminate their beer, and only sold drinkable beer (Cau et al. 1658–1770: II, 2059–66; original document, 1549). A provincial government investigation of the effects of the legislation was undertaken immediately. The results of that enquiry led to a change in 1551 which dropped the limits on the frequency of brewing altogether, another victory for the bigger brewers in the major brewing towns. The price-fixing system was dropped too. It proved impractical (Bijlsma 1910: 78; Clement 1959: 70–1; Timmer 1920: 366–8; Woltjer 1987: 267–8).

The threat to small commercial brewers led them in 1552 to ask for a tax on beer made by a brewer outside his own house and for a prohibition on a brewer holding an interest in more than one brewery. Earlier legislation in the sixteenth century had prohibited brewing in a house unless the brewer owned it or had leased it for a minimum of one year. Their request was granted, the new rules reaffirming earlier practice. The 1552 legislation was renewed in 1562. The problem was that there were brewers with the capacity to go well beyond the traditional limit of 4,900 litres per brew and they continued to press for increases (Timmer 1920: 360–1). Maximum annual production was raised 6% in 1564 and inexpensive small or ship's beer was no longer included in the basic limit, but given a new quota which potentially added another 30% to a brewer's total output. The smaller brewers tried to get the 1564 increases overturned, but in 1566 the courts reaffirmed the raised limits. It seems doubtful that the town of Delft enforced the rules with any vigour, so even the maxima set in the legislation may understate what actually came out of the breweries (Bleyswijck 1667: 714–20; Timmer 1920: 368–72; Woltjer 1987: 268). By 1572 the anticipated average size of a brew was 5,400 litres (General State Archive, The Hague, Het Archief der Rekenkamer te Auditie: 332).

Brewing on a larger scale won out in a number of other towns, invariably in the face of resistance from producers fearful of bankruptcy. In Gouda in Holland, for example, larger brewers complained that they could not compete without increases in the limits placed on them, while smaller brewers said it was only those limits that made it possible for them to stay in business (Clement 1959: 63–4, 67–70; Pinkse 1972: 102–3). In sixteenth-century Liège, smaller brewers, as elsewhere, tried to impede the growth of the larger brewers. An effort to raise production limits from 3,800 to 4,300 litres was successfully overturned and in 1586 the number was forced back to 4,800 from 6,600 litres, a limit in force for only two years (Santbergen 1949: 66–9, 236–7). By the end of the fifteenth century, brewers at Utrecht had had the limit raised from one brewing per week to two. Over time they also got the maximum size of the brew increased from 2,400 or 2,520 litres to 2,900 litres and even to 3,400 litres, the last limit probably before 1530. In that year the town changed the rule from being a maximum to being a minimum, and insisted that brewers fill no fewer than a fixed number of barrels with a fixed quantity of grain in each brew. Their goal was to guarantee the number of taxable units for each quantity of grain (Muller Fz. 1900: 63–6). Wismar, on the other hand, remained highly restrictive and continued to limit the maximum number of times a brewer could make beer in a year through the sixteenth and into the seventeenth century, but exceptions could be and were granted (Techen 1915: 186–289, 294–6).

Restrictions may have slowed the pace of consolidation of production, but the general trend was clear. Enforcement of regulations on maximum output was also a contentious issue, with larger brewers opposing oversight of what they did. At Haarlem there was a long and drawn-out struggle over how much beer could be brewed at one time. The maximum, set early in the sixteenth century, was widely ignored (Houwen 1932: 16). It was so common for brewers simply to overbrew that the town government in 1501 appointed seven beer tasters. They measured the fermenting vessel in each brewery and sealed and marked each one, trying to control the maximum that could be produced at any one time. Brewers had to send to those men a quarter of a barrel of about 30 litres from each brew so the officials could determine the strength of the beer.

Haarlem was not alone. Many towns appointed inspectors to check on brewers to be sure they did not get too much beer out of a fixed amount of grain. The system of limitation and brewers' transgressions forced the establishment of such overseers. An inspector with similar responsibility in fifteenth-century Utrecht asked those who worked in breweries to state under oath whether brewers conformed to production regulations (Muller Fz. 1900: 64). Gouda had five officials responsible for overseeing the maximum brew by 1518 and probably before that date (Couquerque and van Embden 1917: 278). By 1549 at the latest, Delft had inspectors to check, under oath, that brewers conformed to the rules (Bleyswijck 1667: 711–13).

Haarlem brewers tried to get rid of the limits and of the officials who enforced them. That led to a suit in 1519 which the town won before both the high court of Holland and the supreme court of appeal in the Low Countries. In 1520 the town reaffirmed the system of surveillance, but the maximum brew was raised to 4,000 litres (van Loenen 1950: 36–41, 64–67, 103). In 1546 Haarlem brewers renewed their attack on the officials. A petition from 30 brewers and brewsters to the high court of Holland claimed that existing legislation was causing decline in the industry. A supporting letter from the small town of Monnikendam helped the case. It said that forcing Haarlem brewers to prove the quality of their beer caused an unnecessary increase in costs. In 1548 the brewers finally won. The high court ruled that the system of oversight was not needed and it was abolished (van Loenen 1950: 41–3; Woltjer 1987: 266–7). It was yet another victory for bigger brewers with access to greater capital. The fight at Haarlem and elsewhere was ultimately between brewers interested in export, producing more for a wider market, and smaller-scale brewers interested in supplying the home market. At Hamburg, as at Haarlem, there had been separate legislation on the scale of operation for those brewing for export and those producing for the domestic market, but as the fifteenth century progressed, the distinction faded (Bing 1909: 248) as it did in the Low Countries in the sixteenth century.

Fewer bigger brewers was the long-term trend, fed by improving technology. Resistance from small operators and from governments typically failed. Not every town in northern Europe succumbed to the tendency towards consolidation, but it was the norm. The tendencies in technology, investment, production, and legislation all clearly favoured larger brewers. Bigger brewers expanded the scope of their operations and integrated those operations horizontally as well as vertically. They acquired smaller breweries, usually to increase capacity but also in a number of cases to acquire a larger production quota in towns where quotas prevailed. They sold beer at retail in their breweries, built and operated their own malteries, and became grain merchants. Despite lobbying by lesser producers and town regulations, there is every indication that it was bigger brewers who prospered in the second half of the sixteenth century (Timmer 1920: 372). Many towns in the sixteenth century were battlegrounds between a small number of expansion-minded large brewers and conservative smaller ones. The efforts of the latter did not prevent the continued growth and success of the larger brewers nor did they prevent their own decline and disappearance.

Political circumstances could dramatically change the regulatory environment. The more lax regimen in the northern provinces of the Netherlands after the Dutch Revolt of the 1560s worked to the advantage of larger brewers. In the Dutch Republic any efforts to limit the size of the brew came to an end (Woltjer 1987: 269–77; Yntema 1994: 74–5). The new government dropped any attempt at careful regulation of brewing. It took a revolt against the established authorities to give big brewers a better regulatory environment. While political change was an important factor in the consolidation trend in the Netherlands, other jurisdictions throughout northern Europe followed the same pattern, even without such dramatic political transformation.

Smaller brewers were always at a disadvantage because successful businessmen were the source of personnel for town governments and the big brewers were therefore likely candidates. Brewers sat in town governments in Germany, the Low Countries, and Scandinavia from the fifteenth through the eighteenth century. Already in 1370 there was a brewer on the town council of Nuremberg (Schultheiss 1978: 69). In 1465 at Wismar, 21 of the 24 members of the town council came from among the 182 brewers in the town (Techen 1915: 269). By the mid-fifteenth century, a brewer of Leiden became mayor. The collection of excise taxes was typically auctioned in towns, and brewers often found it highly profitable to buy the right to collect the beer excise (Prevenier and Blockmans 1986: 178). There was no perceived problem in combining politics with the brewing trade, and there were real advantages to the brewer. Collecting taxes enhanced his income as well as his political status. Brewers' critical role in supplying tax income to civic and regional governments made them popular with the public authorities, but also made them part of the public authority. Cooperation between government and brewers to increase public income had already in the fifteenth century led to the merging of the profession and public power. In Munich in 1610, 17% of brewers belonged to the highest level of taxpayer, most being in the middle range of wealth, and only one brewer was classed as poor

(Huntemann 1971: 77–8). In many places, the larger brewers gained the political upper hand and so gained tolerance or even government support for the expansion of their activities and eventual dominance of the industry.

Brewers' Guilds

Labour organization in brewing varied, though guilds of brewers were the traditional institutions to protect as well as control hiring practices in the industry. Some guilds were of long standing by 1600 (Dirks 1878: 171, 214; Yntema 1992: 224). The march towards greater restriction through guilds was prevalent from the late sixteenth century, limiting brewers' flexibility in deploying labour. Regulations of brewers' guilds covered much the same ground as from the earliest days, but became more extensive, more detailed, and more repetitive over time. The towns approved, and sometimes even dictated, legislation. The underlying principles of regulation were stable and so, therefore, was the language of rules.

In Holland even porters, men organized separately in guilds who made deliveries from breweries to pubs and homes, received more complex and elaborate rules. Their role as agents of the excise tax collectors increased, especially in smaller towns. Brewers took an active interest in the rules of porters' guilds and that helped promote an increase in regulation. In England no such groups existed. Brewers had to organize deliveries themselves. They had to hire porters, which meant more employees, always men, and with a very different range of skills from the rest of the brewery workers. At least the English system offered greater potential for controlling costs, even if controlling what was at times an unruly group created a new set of problems for brewers.

Guilds needed a monopoly and the town had to grant this to the guild. Only members of the guild could brew beer and that had to be stated clearly in any set of by-laws (Hoekstra 1935: 36; Timmer 1916: 741). Otherwise the guild had no purpose. Guild members had to pay annual dues, which constituted both a licence fee and a way of sustaining the finances of the organization. Granting membership in the guild meant granting a licence to operate a brewery. Failure to enter the guild and pay the annual dues led to a prohibition on working in the trade. Membership applied to all those building, buying, or inheriting a brewery. Brewers' guilds became more exclusive. First, small-scale producers who sold from pubs in their own houses were driven out, and then fees for master status were driven up, so limiting membership. Though guilds raised entry fines, these were still small in comparison to the capital needed to start up a brewery. Customers who fell into debt with guild members were a common topic of regulation, as were hours and days of work. At Haarlem, for example, brewers had to work by sunlight and not on Sundays or on days of commemoration without the explicit consent of the town government (Hoekstra 1935: 35–6). Guilds also had rules about the hiring of brewery workers. To avoid conflict between brewers over the pirating of talented employees and, even more important, to prevent workers from bidding up wages, a worker had to get a statement of release from his old employer. Without that piece of paper, acknowledging that he had left with the agreement of both parties, the worker could not be hired by any other brewer. In Leiden, from 1638 no worker could be hired until he had been separated from the former employer for at least six weeks. Rules covered both employers and employees who might want to move before the end of their contracts (Unger 2001: 290–1). The guild may well have been a creature of the town, but it also acted as the brewers'representative in relation to the town, petitioning the government and striking agreements with the government and with third parties (Yntema 1992: 228).

Guild regulations included social provisions which might generate benefits to producers, but which also created costs that could erode profits. There were festive meetings, requirements for members to attend the funerals of their brothers, provisions for payment for funerals, and, in a few cases, for retirement. In general, the more elaborate the guild institution, the more limits there were on brewers' flexibility in deploying personnel. Invasive and sustained government oversight, the ability of town governments to veto virtually any action by the guilds, made it extremely difficult for members to use the organization to enhance their financial position. Governments made every effort to scoop up any monopoly gains in the form of taxes. Increases in restrictions over time, as with production limits, could present problems for the profitability of brewing enterprises. Despite the presence of brewers in government, regulatory limitations on them were a general trend through the sixteenth and seventeenth centuries.

Pollution and Environmental Problems

Rising population and increasing urbanization in the fifteenth and sixteenth centuries benefited brewers by creating a concentrated market for beer. But bigger towns created problems too. The greater numbers forced up land values which further raised the capital requirements of urban brewers. More people and more industrial activity also meant threats to the environment, especially to the purity of water supplies. Brewers developed different strategies to deal with the problems generated by growth in towns, not all of them successful.

One option to combat rising land values was to move to the countryside. Any savings might be wiped out, however, by the added cost of shipping beer into population centres. Being in town, with many consumers nearby, created potential scale economies. Shipping bulky beer, which was mostly water, added significantly to prices, so setting up operations outside towns could be counterproductive. Towns also offered concentrated supplies of other raw materials, such as grain. All towns, because of the population concentration, had well-organized grain markets which drew on a number of regions both near and far, so brewers could count on access to a variety of grains on a regular basis, without having to invest either capital or effort in guaranteeing supplies. Staying in town had clear advantages.

A compromise solution to the problem of urban land costs was to operate on the outskirts of urban centres. The short distance to market meant shipping did not translate into large price increases. There was also the chance that some drinkers might be willing to come to the brewery and its associated pub, thus transporting the beer back into town themselves in their own stomachs. In the sixteenth century, the province of Holland outlawed manufacturing on the edges of towns. The ability of the province to borrow depended on the stream of tax income from the towns and forcing the concentration of production in towns made it possible to limit evasion of levies on beer. For the same reason, there were also restrictions on locating ale houses close to town limits (Brünner 1918: 126–134, passim; Tracy 1984: 87; Unger 2001: 182–90). There were similar cases of such legislation elsewhere and for the same reason, that is, to secure for governments what was due from taxes (Unger 2004: 200–3). The presence of a large market kept most brewers in towns and cities. But being in town created a different set of problems for brewers.

By the sixteenth century, pollution in most towns was a threat to brewers. Their need for large quantities of good water led them to focus more on ecology. As a result, their guilds often took on different responsibilities from those common among guilds in other trades. Finding good, clean water was a constant problem for brewers. About 85% of their product was water and in addition they needed large quantities for cooling and cleaning. It took about 2.5 litres of water for each litre of beer produced (Frontzek 2005: 34; Soly 1972: 105). As the industry grew, especially in towns with sizeable export markets and high levels of production, the problem became more acute. Troubles with pollution forced the creation of joint capital-intensive schemes to give access to much-needed sweet water. Such schemes increased the pressure for concentration in the industry, though such projects were infrequent and had only limited success.

One solution tried was to transport good water to town by boat. The whole profession of water carriers or transporters was a product of the Middle Ages. In England, when water supplies in London, Bristol, Coventry, and elsewhere became less reliable because of the multiple uses of streams, tradesmen emerged to supply brewers with the water they needed (Corran 1975: 31; Schultheiss 1978: 56). As early as 1497, Amsterdam brewers had to bring water from outside the town and, by 1514, town legislation restricted suppliers to one waterway as a source. The water was to be landed at a specific site and only sound vessels could be used. Brewers could use no water other than that shipped in. Those hauling water for brewers had to swear that they had got the water from the designated place and from no other. Fines were to be levied for violation of the by-laws (Breen 1902: 569–70, paras 6–9; van Dillen 1929: No. 18, paras 1, 2). The rules laid down by the town were, as in many other cases, designed to assure the standard of quality of beer, so that consumers in the town would not be unhappy with the local product and so that the beer would enjoy a positive reputation elsewhere which might translate into exports. In Amsterdam, by 1530 all canal water proved too foul for use. That was despite by-laws, repeated in 1547, that levied fines on polluters. As the sixteenth century went on, the distances covered to bring in good quality water increased.

At nearby Haarlem, brewers were in intermittent conflict through their guild with other manufacturers over pollution of streams, but the organization was also the agent responsible for lobbying the town government to make changes in streams and water sources (Hoekstra 1935: 19–21, 36–7). In 1478 the brewers and the town agreed to share equally the costs of deepening a canal to bring sweet water to brewery sites in the centre. They also agreed to share the costs of repairs, so that foul water could not enter the canal. Other industries, and in Haarlem that meant bleaching, created demands on supplies and made water unusable for brewing. The rivers and canals that passed through towns in Holland and in many other parts of northern Europe did not move swiftly, so the location of various industrial activities in relation to where brewers drew their water became critical to the quality of the beer. The chemical composition of the water affected taste, while the presence of contamination could make the beer 'go off' and be undrinkable. Haarlem brewers resorted to a law suit in 1577 to try to get rid of bleachers who dumped their waste in the canals. The brewers petitioned the town government to take action against the bleachers in 1581 and 1583 and in the latter year they got the judgement they wanted from the courts. Next, they went after the preparers of flax, who used water in the town and polluted the canals. Then in 1591 it was the turn of the paint makers. In 1599 the brewers again complained about the bleachers, so any victory over polluters was hard to enforce.

The constant problems with foul water forced brewers to try to improve existing water sources or even to find new ones. All the efforts to deal with problems of water pollution involved joint action by brewers, negotiation with public authorities, and a threat to profits. In early sixteenth-century Haarlem, there were complaints about water being brackish and those difficulties led, as early as 1549, to the organization of a system for bringing in water by ship (Hoekstra 1935: 19–21, 36–7; Houwen 1932: 44–6, 49–58;

van Loenen 1950: 102–3; Unger 2001: 166–7). In seventeenth-century Amsterdam, brewers united to get water from the Vecht, a stream in North Holland. It was one of the few things on which Amsterdam brewers cooperated, though with difficulty (Unger 2001: 167–9). The brewers' college, a group that acted much like a guild, took over the task of organizing the shipping of water to the town (Hallema and Emmens 1968: 91–2; Wagenaar 1760–8: IX, 233–4). As the largest city in Holland and one which grew extremely rapidly during the sixteenth and seventeenth centuries, Amsterdam faced the greatest problems of access to good water. Its brewers had to make joint capital investment in boats and, later, even in an icebreaker to guarantee supplies in winter, another cost of doing business and a threat to profits.

Other Dutch towns faced problems similar to those of Amsterdam and did so much earlier. Gouda brewers, like their Haarlem counterparts, could only operate in certain streets and along certain canals. They took water from those canals and also used canals to bring in water by boat (Clement 1959: 199). In Delft, as early as 1450, there were rules about the use of canal water for brewing. The water literally stank. One mill had to be moved because it was creating stinking pools of stagnant water. Delft town regulations of 1473 prohibited brewers from using canal water in the summer and, in the same year, the ruler of the province noted that the canals of the town had become dirty and that the resulting pollution was hurting the brewing trade. He authorized the construction of a sluice to carry water into the town (Bleyswijck 1667: 700–6; Doorman 1955: 57; Hallema and Emmens 1968: 66). Incidentally, it was not just water pollution that troubled Delft brewers. In 1547 the provincial government prohibited the construction and operation of limestone ovens within half a mile of the town and even insisted on shutting one down because the smoke and stench were bad for the brewing industry (Bleyswijck 1667: 707–9; Unger 2001: 167).

The alternative to using water from streams running through towns or bringing in water by boat was to build dedicated water supply systems, with conduits bringing water directly to brewers. Fixed systems implied brewers' cooperation with governments and considerable investment. Lübeck had perhaps the earliest system for supplying water to brewers, dating from 1294. Over the following three centuries, the town developed an elaborate system of pipes for the distribution of water from nearby unpolluted streams to breweries. The system in Hamburg also included piping, but the water source was wells (Frontzek 2005: 33–9). Brewers in early seventeenth-century Edinburgh, Scotland, built a special reservoir to guarantee their supplies of water (Donnachie 1979: 2) and Wismar in northern Germany had a system of piped water that connected houses, including breweries, to a reservoir. In such cases, users paid for the systems. In mid-sixteenth-century Antwerp, a public/ private partnership between the town and a property speculator tried to revive and expand the brewing industry through the construction of a system to convey good quality water to one place. The new source of water centralized the industry and had a deep and lasting effect on its operation. The entrepreneur did not completely fulfil his part of the bargain, however, and the project had its financial, legal, and political problems. The investment in water supplies paid off though. Between 1565–6 and the early 1580s, total production rose by more than 50%. The goal of promoting exports was also achieved. Early in the sixteenth century only some 5–7% of Antwerp output was sold outside the town, but by the 1570s the average was some 25% (Soly 1968: 352–7, 360–3, 367–74, 1166–76, 1182–3, 1194–5, 1203; Soly 1977: 288–307, 310–19). Capital investment in water supplies added to brewers' costs and so contributed to the trend towards consolidation both geographically and in terms of firm size. While increased cost might threaten profitability, without reliable supplies of large quantities of good water brewing could not survive at all.

The Costs of Inputs

Rising population in both towns and the countryside led to sustained and long-term increases in grain prices. While those prices fluctuated widely throughout the year and from year to year, depending on various factors, the trend throughout Europe in the sixteenth and early years of the seventeenth centuries was unquestionably toward higher costs for the users of grain. Since buying grain typically constituted around two-thirds of the direct costs to the brewer, the price of barley and other food grains was always critical to the success of any firm. Brewers faced a long-term price trend which worked against them and short-term fluctuations which could spell disaster.

In Ghent, for example, between 1527 and 1585, grain prices rose fourteen-fold and the cheapest beers did not even double in price. The increase over those 58 years was a result of local circumstances, but it did reflect the kind of dramatic change beer producers could face. Brewers' range of options to deal with higher grain prices was small. Since prices of beer were often controlled and taxes were included in those prices, lowering quality through using less grain per litre produced was one of the few ways brewers had to protect profitability. Brewers thinned their beer and so made it a less appealing drink. The tendency in a large number of German towns from about 1500 to about 1600 was clearly towards making more beer from the same quantity of malt. To do that effectively, the work was typically done in larger batches, with the quantity of malt increasing and the quantity of beer increasing even faster (Huntemann 1971: 10, 75). As the sixteenth century wore on and grain prices rose, it became more likely that brewers had to adjust the amount of grain used in their beer to maintain sales. In Wismar, from the second half of the fourteenth century to 1640, the amount of beer produced from the same quantity of malt increased threefold. In Nuremberg, it increased twofold in the short period from 1521 to 1564 (Aerts 1996: 173–7, 195–8; De Commer 1981: 91; Schultheiss 1978: 23). Innovation in beer making and rising capital investment might explain part, but typically a small part, of the long-term improvements in output per unit of grain.

It was government regulation that set the quantities of grain to be used, so such sharp falls in the quality of beer, especially over short periods of time, must have had the approval of the civic authorities. In periods of high grain prices, such as the 1530s, brewers in both Gouda and Delft approached town governments for an increase in how much they could make from a fixed quantity of grain. In 1526 Gouda brewers had already asked for an increase in the price at which they sold beer on account of the adverse state of the Baltic grain market, which was driving up their costs (Brünner 1918: 108, 159). In general, the calorific content of beer deteriorated, consumers were dissatisfied, and brewers were forced to seek ways of improving productivity to protect their threatened profit margins.

Another solution over the long term was to make high-quality beers with more grain or with malt that had been heated longer in the drying process to enhance flavour, or with more expensive additives, including various spices. Such better beers commanded considerably higher prices and offered a valuable complement to weaker beer sold at a price that could be kept, more or less, constant. Using less grain for each barrel of weak beer lowered costs and also lowered the alcohol content. The small or *klein* beer brewed in Lier in 1434 was 6% alcohol, but by 1505–8 it was down to 3.355. Less alcohol meant beer was less durable and so less likely to be a traded good. Brewers brought new types of beer to market, changing their names and so opening the door to changing prices. That way they could mask, or potentially mask, quality deterioration (De Commer 1981, 1983: 84–9, 115–23; Unger 2004: 185–8). The gains, whatever they were, proved temporary, since drinkers spotted the strategy with little difficulty. Another way to degrade beer was to use substitutes like buckwheat, beans, or peas instead of the traditional brewing grains: barley, wheat, oats, and rye. In Wismar, town rules set the amount of beer that could be made at one time with an implied, and sometimes explicit, regulation of the amount of grain used in each brew. Where the amount of grain was controlled, in some cases the government might allow the quantity of grain per brew to decrease. This yielded thinner beer, without allowing the scale of operations to increase. Such regulations might keep a larger number of brewers in place, but offered no opportunity to defend profits (Techen 1915: 337, 339–40).

In the eighteenth century, when grain prices rose again, brewers repeated the strategies. Brussels brewers used one-third less grain for the same quantity of the inexpensive low grade of beer in the eighteenth century than in the fifteenth. In Holland the drop was even more dramatic. The amount of grain used to make a litre of beer by the 1770s may have been as much as a quarter of the amount used two centuries before. Along with the grain input, the alcohol content fell for lesser beer from 3–4% down to 2–3% and for better beers from about 9% to between 5% and 7% (Vandenbroeke 1975: 536). The fall in alcohol content and the reaction of governments are clear indicators that it was not that brewers could get more out of each unit of grain, but that brewers were lowering the ratio of vegetable matter to water in their brew kettles. The pattern was repeated in northern Germany and throughout the Low Countries despite efforts, such as those in Haarlem in 1749, to keep brewers from lowering the quality of their beer by using less grain per litre produced (Magré 1936: 2; Techen 1915: 339–41). The decrease in the quantities of grain meant less potent and less nutritious beer, with fewer calories and lower quantities of various vitamins per litre. Such a decline threatened sales volumes. In the eighteenth century, brewers in Dutch towns offered a litany of explanations for the decline in brewing. High taxes and fees figured prominently in their accounts, as did competition from other drinks, but so too did the high cost of land, the high cost of maintaining a stock of barrels, and the high cost of raw materials. Brewers did not mention that the beer they were making had less taste, strength, and fewer calories, but such deterioration in quality was a significant source of their troubles (Unger 2001: 263–6).

Supplies of grain were always uncertain, but at least there were some circumstances that worked to brewers' advantage. When grain prices went down, a 1636 English report said, brewers increased their profits, but when grain prices went up they used less grain to keep profits at the former level (London, Public Records Office: SP 16/341/124). While grain prices in Germany went up faster than beer prices through the second half of the sixteenth and the first years of the seventeenth centuries, from around 1620 grain prices fell, while beer prices held firm into the eighteenth century (Huntemann 1971: 93–4, 104–6). At least in the seventeenth century, brewers were able to benefit from the stickiness of beer prices.

In addition to rising grain costs, sixteenth-century brewers faced increases in outlays for virtually all other items in their budgets. There was no relief from fuel costs. On average, firewood prices rose much faster than even grain prices through the sixteenth and first half of the seventeenth centuries in England, and there are indications of problems with firewood supplies in other parts of Europe as well. The limitations of relying on trees for thermal energy was a problem only circumvented in the eighteenth and nineteenth centuries (Nef 1932: 161–2, 165–89; Sieferle 2001: 157–78 and *passim*). Dutch brewers were insulated to some degree from problems with wood supplies because they used peat as their principal source of heat, but even they faced threats to profitability from rising fuel prices. The cost of peat in seventeenth-century Holland was said to be 2.5 times that in other parts of the Low Countries. One reason for this was the taxes levied on it. Another had to do with the exhaustion of peat bogs. Holland towns relied on suppliers of peat throughout the Dutch Republic. Not just any peat would do. Brewers needed heavier, darker, more dense types, with less moisture content, to derive adequate heat intensity for their tasks (Grönloh 1936: 14; Hoekstra 1935: 19, 32–3). As regions in the western part of Holland were dredged for all their peat and the land converted to agriculture, suppliers turned to sources in Friesland. Access to those deposits required greater capital investment in canals and digging equipment. Frisian peat was said to give off less heat than the darker peat dug in Holland. All this affected prices directly.

A trend to substitute for increasingly expensive peat started around 1600 and was all but complete in the early eighteenth century. By 1715 only 10% of total fuel supplies for Holland brewers came from peat (Gerding 1995: 320–1; Wijsenbeek-Olthuis 1982: 67). The rest came from coal. English brewers had gone over to coal in the sixteenth and early seventeenth centuries, but old prejudices against using coal did not disappear easily. Fears of polluting the beer through the noxious gases given off by some fuels, especially coal, made brewers willing to stay with more traditional heat sources. In areas of abundant wood supplies, in Austria, Bavaria, and Bohemia for example, fuel costs may not have presented problems (Allen 2003: 479). In regions where price structures led to a shift to coal, brewers needed to improve their furnaces to get the most out of the fuel and to prevent contamination of the beer. Savings on fuel costs had to compensate for the greater capital investment. Towns might sometimes, as happened in Amsterdam in 1638, restrict the shift to coal, preventing brewers from taking advantage of potential savings (Unger 2001: 274). Such ordinances against the use of coal at the very least limited the flexibility of those making beer in the face of changes in costs.

From the late fifteenth through the first half of the sixteenth centuries, the long-term rise in average grain prices posed a threat to the profitability of brewing. While some years or months might see lower prices, the tendency was towards increasing input prices, with resistance to any increase in what consumers paid for beer. Converting barley or oats or wheat into beer implied, for consumers, significant losses in nutrition per measure of grain. If beer prices rose too much, buyers would, even if reluctantly, take their grain in solid rather than in liquid form.

Even if brewers had wanted to raise the price of their product, often government regulation limited their ability to do so. Government regulation of the quantities of which grains brewers used to make the types of beer they produced restricted their ability to lower costs. The scissors of rising raw material costs and more or less stable prices for beer created a long-term problem for much of the European brewing industry.

The End of the Golden Age of Brewing

The overall success and probable profitability of the industry obscure significant changes in the brewing industry from the fifteenth through the seventeenth centuries. Rising grain prices, rising land costs, problems with water supplies, and increased taxation posed serious threats. To combat the danger to profits, brewers took advantage of existing technology and increased capital investment. The defence of profits led to consolidation in the industry. Some brewers—those with access to funds and political influence—were able to prosper, while others, operating on a small scale, were driven out of business. The tightening of regulation on labour, enforced through the guilds, decreased the flexibility of brewers in deploying their workforces. Since labour costs were a small share of total costs, that did not present great problems. The guilds proved to be valuable vehicles for joint action by brewers dealing with governments or in handling problems with raw material supplies and pollution. Only the very largest of the brewers, though, proved able to thrive in the face of the next threats to profits in the eighteenth century, a combination of rising grain prices and the appearance of substitutes for beer. Gin and later tropical drinks, that is tea, coffee, and cocoa, forced contraction, even more consolidation, and, with very few obvious exceptions, the end of profits in brewing.

Brewers in regions of rising incomes and greater urbanization fared better through the eighteenth and early nineteenth centuries. Efforts to advance technology through experiment, through the exchange of information, and, in some cases, through the theft of knowledge using industrial espionage made it possible for a few brewers to survive and even prosper (Glamann 1984: 186–94). This was in the face of a sharp decline in beer consumption compared to the sixteenth century. Renaissance brewers could expect average consumption of more than 250 litres per person per year, while their nineteenth-century counterparts were lucky to see figures one-third of that. Though brewers in London and Bavaria, Austria and Bohemia may have fared well, they were the exceptions. The success of modern brewing and the restoration of profitability came with falling transport costs thanks to railways, technical advances in refrigeration, and scientific breakthroughs in understanding the properties and behaviour of yeast. By the 1880s varied forces had come together to transform the industry. The combination of technical changes made possible the marketing of a different kind of beer, lager, to a much larger population with a growing taste for beer. From the closing years of the nineteenth century, a new industry emerged that was not constrained by the forces which had led to the long-term contraction of brewing in late Renaissance Europe.

References

Aerts, E. (1996). *Het bier van Lier: De economische ontwikkeling van de bierindustrie in een middelgrote Brabantse stad (eind 14de-begin 19de eeuw)*. Brussels: Paleis der Academiën.

Allen, R. C. (2003). 'Was there a Timber Crisis in Early Modern Europe', in Simonetta Cavaciocchi (ed.), *Economia e Energia Secc. XIII-XVIII: Atti della 'Trentaquattresima Settimana di Studi', 15–19 aprile 2002*. Prato: Le Monnier, 469–82.

Bijlsma, R. (1910). 'Rotterdams Welvaren in den Spaanschen Tijd'. *Rotterdamsch Jaarboekje*, 8: 75–100.

Bing, W. (1909). *Hamburgs Bierbrauerei vom 14. bis zum 18. Jahrhundert*. Hamburg: Von Lütcke und Wulff.

Bleyswijck, D. Van (1667). *Beschryvinge der Stadt Delft*. Delft: Arnold Bon.

Breen, J. C. (1902). *Rechtsbronnen der Stad Amsterdam*. The Hague: Martinus Nijhoff.

Brünner, E. C. G. (1918). *De order op de buitennering van 1531: Bijdrage tot de Kennis van de economische Geschiedenis van het Graafschap Holland in den Tijd van Karel V*. Utrecht: A. Oosthoek.

Cau, C., S. Van Leeuwen, J. Schultus, P. Schultus, and I. Schultus (eds.). (1658–1770). *Groot Placaatboek vervattende de Placaaten, Ordonnantien en Edicten van den Hoog Mog: Heeren Staaten Generaal der Vereenigde Nederlanden . . .*, 7 vols. The Hague: Hilldbrandt Jacobus van Wouw, Jacobus, Paulus and Isaac Schultus.

Clement, A. Van Der P. (1959). 'De Bierbrouwerijen van Gouda in middeleeuwen en 16e eeuw.'. Incomplete and unpublished doctoral dissertation, Town Archive of Gouda.

Corran, H. S. (1975). *A History of Brewing*. Newton Abbot: David and Charles.

Couquerque, L. M. R., and A. Meerkamp Van Embden (1917). *Rechtsbronnen der Stad Gouda*. The Hague: Martinus Nijhoff.

De Commer, P. (1981 and 1983). 'De Brouwindustrie te Ghent, 1505–1622'. *Handelingen der Maatschappij voor Geschiedenis en Oudheidkunde te Gent*, Nieuwe Reeks, 35: 81–114 and 113–71.

Dillen, J. G. Van (1929). *Bronnen tot de Geschiedenis van het Bedrijfsleven en het Gildewezen van Amsterdam*. The Hague: Martinus Nijhoff.

Dirks, J. (1878). *De Noord-Nederlandsche Gildepenningen*. Haarlem: De Erven F. Bohn.

Donnachie, I. (1979). *A History of the Brewing Industry in Scotland*. Edinburgh: John Donald Publishers Ltd.

Doorman, G. (1940). *Octrooien voor Uitvindingen in de Nederlanden uit de 16e–18e Eeuw*. The Hague: Martinus Nijhoff.

—— (1955). *De Middeleeuwse Brouwerij en de gruit*. The Hague: Martinus Nijhoff.

Frontzek, W. (2005). *Das städtische Braugewerbe und seine Bauten vom Mittelalter bis zur frühen Neuzeit Untersuchungen zur Entwicklung, Ausstattung und Topographie der Brauhäuser in der Hansestadt Lübeck, Häuser und Hofe in Lübeck.* Neumünster: Wachholtz Verlag.

Gerding, M. A. W. (1995). *Vier Eeuwen Turfwinning De verveningen in Groningen, Friesland, Drenthe en Overijssel tussen 1550 en 1950.* Wageningen: Afdeling Agrarische Geschiedenis, Landbouwuniversiteit.

Glamann, K. (1962). *Bryggeriets Historie i Danmark indtil slutningen af det 19. århundrede.* Copenhagen: Gyldendal.

—— (1984). 'The Scientific Brewer: Founders and Successors during the Rise of the Modern Brewing Industry', in D. C. Coleman and P. Mathias (eds.), *Enterprise and History: Essays in Honour of Charles Wilson.* Cambridge: Cambridge University Press, 186–98.

Grönloh, C. C. J. (1936). 'De Brouwerij in Amsterdam van 1700 tot 1800'. University of Amsterdam, Unpublished doctoral dissertation, Economisch-Historisch Seminarium, No. 117.

Hallema, A., and J. A. Emmens (1968). *Het bier en zijn brouwers: De geschiedenis van onze oudste volksdrank* Amsterdam: J. H. De Bussy.

Hoekstra, P. (1935). 'Het Haarlems Brouwersbedrijf in de 17e eeuw'. University of Amsterdam, Unpublished doctoral dissertation, Economisch-Historisch Seminarium.

Houwen, A. (1932). 'De Haarlemsche Brouwerij 1575–1600'. University of Amsterdam, Unpublished doctoral dissertation, Economisch-Historisch Seminarium.

Huntemann, H. (1971). *Das deutsche Braugewerbe vom Ausgang des Mittelalters bis zum Beginn der Industriealisierung. Biererzeugung—Bierhandel—Bierverbrauch.* Nuremberg: Verlag Hans Carl.

Klonder, A. (1983). *Browarnictwo w Prusach Krolewskich [2 Polowa XVI-XVII W.].* Warsaw: Zaklad Narodowy Imienia Ossolinskich Wydawnictwo Polskiej Akademii Nauk.

Langer, H. (1979). 'Das Braugewerbe in den deutschen Hansestädten der frühen Neuzeit', in Konrad Fritze, Eckard Müller-Mertens, and Johannes Schildhauer (eds.), *Hansische Studiën IV Gewerbliche Produktion und Stadt-Land-Beziehungen.* Weimar: Hermann Böhlaus Nachfolger, 65–81.

Loenen, J. Van. (1950). *De Haarlemse Brouwindustrie voor 1600.* Amsterdam: Universiteitspers.

Magré, T. (1936). 'De Brouwnering in Haarlem van 1700–1800'. University of Amsterdam, Unpublished doctoral dissertation, Economisch-Historisch Seminarium.

Muller Fz., S. (1900). *Schetsen uit de Middeleeuwen.* Amsterdam: S. L. van Looy.

Nef, J. U. (1932), *The Rise of the British Coal Industry*, London: Routledge (reprinted London, 1966).

—— (1954). 'The Progress of Technology and the Growth of Large-Scale Industry in Great Britain, 1540–1640', in E. M. Carus-Wilson (ed.), *Essays in Economic History*, I. London: Edward Arnold, 88–107.

Van Noordkerk, H. (1748). *Handvesten; ofte Privilegien ende Octroyen; mitsgaders Willekeuren, Costumen, Ordonnantien en Handelingen der Stad Amstelredam . . .* Amsterdam: Hendrik van Waesberge, Saloman en Petrus Schouten.

Pinkse, V. C. C. J. (1972). 'Het Goudse Kuitbier, Gouda's Welveren in de Late Midde-leeuwen 1400–1568', in Arie Scheygrond (ed.), *Gouda Zeven Eeuwen Stad*. Gouda: *Oudheidkundige Kring* 'Die Goude', 19 July: 91–128.

Prevenier, W., and W. Blockmans (1986). *The Burgundian Netherlands*. Cambridge: Cambridge University Press.

Santbergen, R. Van (1949). *Les Bons Métiers des Meuniers, des Boulangers et des Brasseurs de la Cité de Liège*. Liège: Faculté de Philosophie et Lettres.

Schultheiss, W. (1978). *Brauwesen und Braurechte in Nürnberg bis zum Beginn des 19. Jahrhunderts*. Nuremberg: Schriftenreihe des Stadtarchivs Nürnberg Band 23.

Sieferle, R. P. (2001), *The Subterranean Forest Energy Systems and the Industrial Revolution*, Michael Osmann, trans. Cambridge: The White Horse Press (Original German edition published as *Der unterirdische Wald*, Munich: C. H. Beck, 1982).

Soly, H. (1968). 'De Brouwerijenonderneming van Gilbert van Schoonbeke (1552–1562)'. *Revue Belge de Philologie et d'Histoire*, 46: 337–92, 1166–204.

—— (1972). 'De economische betekenis van de zuidnederlandse brouwindustrie in de 16e eeuw. Problematiek'. *Handelingen van het Colloquium over de economische geschiedenis van België. Behandelingen van de Bronnen en Problematiek*. Ghent: Rijksuniversiteit. Afdeling Geschiedenis van de Faculteit der Letteren en Wijsbegeerte, 97–117.

—— (1975). 'Nijverheid en kapitalisme te Antwerpen in de 16e eeuw'. *Studia Historica Gandensia*, 193: 331–52.

—— (1977). *Urbanisme en Kapitalisme te Antwerpen in de 16de Eeuw: De stedebouwkundige en industriële ondernemingen van Gilbert van Schoonbeke*. Antwerp: Gemeentekrediet van Belgie.

Techen, F. (1915 and 1916). 'Das Brauwerk in Wismar'. *Hansisches Geschichtsblätter*, 21: 263–352 and 22: 145–224.

Timmer, E. M. A. (1916). 'Uit de nadagen der Delftsche brouwnering'. *De Economist*, 65: 740–73.

—— (1920). 'Grepen uit de geschiedenis der Delftsche brouwnering'. *De Economist*, 69: 358–372, 415–29.

Tracy, J. D. (1984). 'The Taxation System of the County of Holland during the Reigns of Charles V and Philip II, 1519–1566,' *Economisch- en Sociaal-Historisch Jaarboek*, 48: 71–117.

Unger, R. W. (2001). *A History of Brewing in Holland 900–1900: Economy, Technology and the State*, Leiden: E. J. Brill.

—— (2004). *Beer in the Middle Ages and the Renaissance*. Philadelphia: University of Pennsylvania Press.

Uytven, R. Van (1961). *Stadsfinanciën en Stadsekonomie te Leuven van de XIIe tot het einde der XVIe Eeuw*. Brussels: Paleis der Academieën.

—— (1978). 'Bestaansmiddelen'. *Arca Louvaniesis Jaarboek*, 7: 129–94.

Vandenbroeke, C. (1975). *Agriculture et alimentation*. Ghent and Leuven: Centre belge d'histoire rurale.

Wagenaar, J. (1760–8). *Amsterdam in zyne opkomst, aanwas, Geschiedenissen, voorregten, koophandel, Gebouwen, kerkenstaat, schoolen, schutterye, Gilden en Regeeringe*. 18 vols. Amsterdam: Isaak Tirion.

Wijsenbeek-Olthuis, T. F. (1982). 'Ondernemen in Moeilijke Tijden: Delftse Bier-brouwers en Plateelbakkers in de Achttiende Eeuw'. *Economisch- en Sociaal-Historisch Jaarboek*, 44: 65–78.

Woltjer, J. J. (1987). 'Een Hollands stadsbestuur in het midden van de 16e eeuw: brouwers en bestuurders te Delft', in *De Nederlanden in de late middeleeuwen*. Utrecht: Aula, 261–79.

Yntema, R. J. (1992). 'The Brewing Industry in Holland, 1300–1800: A Study in Industrial Development'. Unpublished doctoral dissertation, The University of Chicago.

—— (1994). 'Een kapitale nering: De brouwindustrie in Holland tussen 1500 en 1800', in R. E. Kistemaker and V. T. Van Vilsteren (eds.), *Bier! Geschiedenis van een volksdrank*. Amsterdam: De Bataafsche Leeuw, 72–80.

3

Standards and International Trade Integration: A Historical Review of the German 'Reinheitsgebot'

Frank van Tongeren

Introduction

The Bavarian beer law of 1516, which later morphed into the German 'Reinheitsgebot' (purity law), is often seen as one of the oldest known food laws, and German brewers take great pride in referring to it as a guarantee of traditional quality. The law is also an example of a unilateral production standard that became a non-tariff barrier to trade as the economic integration of Europe proceeded. Some 470 years after it was decreed, the European Court of Justice decided in 1987 that the German standard hampered the free movement of goods in the European Community and forced a national repeal of the law. Today, German beer producers are still subject to legal production standards that have their origins in the original Reinheitsgebot, but imported beers need not adhere to the strict requirements concerning the ingredients to be used in brewing.

This chapter provides a brief historical overview of the evolution and adoption of the Reinheitsgebot. It proceeds by presenting a simple analytical framework to analyse its economic effects on consumers, domestic producers, and foreign suppliers. Finally, there is a discussion, using statistical data, of developments in the German beer market after it opened up to imports.

Historical Overview: From the Bavarian Beer Law in 1516 to the German Biersteuergesetz 1993

The 1516 beer law that was decreed by the Bavarian ruler Herzog Wilhelm IV was an extremely concise way to formulate a food production standard: it stipulated that only barley, hops, and water could be used to brew beer. The existence of yeast, and its essential role in fermentation, had not yet been discovered and it was therefore not mentioned in the law. The text of the law is provided in Box 3.1.[1] But the Bavarian law regulated more than just the ingredients of beer making. It also set maximum prices depending on the season of the year. It had wider impacts on the beer market, as well as on the grains market, which may be summarized as follows:

- Consumer protection: it kept beer free from additives and often unhealthy ingredients, such as rushes, roots, mushrooms, and animal products.

- Price regulation: it set maximum prices depending on the season (a low price between 23 April and 29 September, and twice that price during the rest of the year).

- Guild protection: it created an entry barrier into the sector by setting a potentially cost-increasing standard.

- Agricultural policy: it had direct as well as indirect market effects on grain prices by diverting wheat into bread making, in combination with setting maximum prices in the downstream beer industry. This kept overall demand for the relatively expensive wheat lower and reduced wheat prices.

Over the centuries, acceptance of the law spread gradually from Bavaria northwards to other German states. By the time of the Second German Empire in 1871, it was in force in many of the kingdoms and principalities that formed the new union. By 1906, it became the official law of the entire realm of the German Kaiser, with the additional mention of yeast as a basic ingredient and malted wheat as an allowable component in top-fermented beers, such as Alt and Kölsch, which originate in the north-western parts of Germany in North Rhine-Westphalia, and Weissbier (Hefeweizen), which is a Bavarian specialty.

---

[1] The German Reinheitsgebot has documented predecessors ranging back to the times of Emperor Barbarossa. The town law of Augsburg (also in Bavaria), 'Justitia Civitatis Augustensis', mentions beer as early as 1156: 'Wenn ein Bierschenker schlechtes Bier macht oder ungerechtes Maß gibt, soll er gestraft werden...' ('If an innkeeper pours bad beer or uses unfair measure he shall be punished', own translation by the author). The punishment was heavy and amounted to 5 guilders; on the third infringement the beer licence was revoked.

Box 3.1 THE TEXT OF THE BAVARIAN BEER LAW, 1516

The law was decreed by the Bavarian ruler Herzog Wilhelm IV in April 1516 in Ingolstadt.

How the beer must be served and brewed in summer and winter

We decree, together with the Council of our Principality, that henceforth everywhere in the Principality of Bavaria, in the countryside and in the towns and markets that do not have a special rule for this, from Michaeli (29 September) to Georgi (23 April) one Maß (a Bavarian Maß = 1,069 Litre) or one Kopf (a half-spherical container for liquids, not quite one Maß) of beer shall be sold for no more than one Munich Pfennig, and from Georgi to Michaeli the Maß shall cost no more than two Pfennig of the same currency, the Kopf no more than three Heller (equals usually half a Pfennig), by threat of punishment specified hereunder. If someone does not brew or sell March beer but some other beer, the price shall be no higher than one Pfennig per Maß. In particular do we wish that henceforth, everywhere in our towns, markets and in the countryside, no beer must be made from other ingredients than barley, hop and water. Anyone who knowingly infringes this decree shall be punished each time by law by the taking from him those barrels of beer. If, however, an innkeeper obtains from a brewer in our towns, markets and in the countryside one, two or three Eimer (= 60 Maß) of beer and serves it to the common folks, he alone shall be entitled to, and shall not be forbidden to charge, one Heller per Maß or Kopf more than specified above. (Author's own translation)

WIE DAS BIER IM SOMMER UND WINTER AUF DEM LAND AUSGESCHENKT UND GEBRAUT WERDEN SOLL

Wir verordnen, setzen und wollen mit dem Rat unserer Landschaft, daß forthin überall im Fürstentum Bayern sowohl auf dem Lande wie auch in unseren Städten und Märkten, die kein besondere Ordnung dafür haben, von Michaeli (29 September) bis Georgi (23 April) ein Maß (bayerische = 1,069 Litre) oder ein Kopf (halbkugelförmiges Geschirr für Flüssigkeiten = nicht ganz eine Maß) Bier für nicht mehr als einen Pfennig Münchener Währung und von Georgi bis Michaeli die Maß für nicht mehr als zwei Pfennig derselben Währung, der Kopf für nicht mehr als drei Heller (Heller = gewöhnlich ein halber Pfennig) bei Androhung unten angeführter Strafe gegeben und ausgeschenkt werden soll. Wo aber einer nicht Märzen-, sondern anderes Bier brauen oder sonstwie haben würde, soll er es keineswegs höher als um einen Pfennig die Maß ausschenken und verkaufen. Ganz besonders wollen wir, daß forthin allenthalben in unseren Städten, Märkten und auf dem Lande zu keinem Bier mehr Stücke als allein Gersten, Hopfen und Wasser verwendet und gebraucht werden sollen. Wer diese unsere Anordnung wissentlich übertritt und nicht einhält, dem soll von seiner Gerichtsobrigkeit zur Strafe dieses Faß Bier, so oft es vorkommt, unnachsichtlich weggenommen werden. Wo jedoch ein Gauwirt von einem Bierbräu in unseren Städten, Märkten oder auf dem Lande einen, zwei oder drei Eimer (= enthält 60 Maß) Bier kauft und wieder ausschenkt an das gemeine Bauernvolk, soll ihm allein und sonst niemandem erlaubt und unverboten sein, die Maß oder den Kopf Bier um einen Heller teurer als oben vorgeschrieben ist, zu geben und auszuschenken.

With the formation of the Weimar Republic in 1919, the old Bavarian beer ingredients law, now renamed the Reinheitsgebot (purity law), became firmly anchored in German beer tax law. An important driving force in this development was the Free State of Bavaria, which made its nationwide application a condition for joining the new Republic. Making the production standard compulsory in the entire Republic had an impact on competition between varieties, and hence on competition between brewers from different regions of Germany. The exclusion of additives, especially sugar and spices, put at a disadvantage those brewers, mainly from northern Germany, who traditionally used such ingredients in beer making.

Intra-German beer trade disputes have been observed since the early twentieth century. For example, Adams (2006) reports the case of Süssbier, which complied with the German purity requirements, but failed to comply with the even stricter rules applied by the Free State of Bavaria, and hence which could not be sold in that part of Germany, leading to legal disputes between 1949 and 1965.[2] But European economic integration meant the first serious threat to the unilateral German production standard. In 1987 the German Reinheitsgebot had to give way in the interests of free trade within the European Community.

Foreign competitors had long complained about the trade restrictions that were created by the German law (and an almost identical one in Greece (EEC case 176/84)). The European Court of Justice ruled in March 1987 that the German purity law created intra-European trade barriers, in direct violation of the Rome Treaty (Article 30, banning protectionism). The Court ruled that the beer's alcohol content threatened public health more than any otherwise legal additive, and that Germany itself violated the law on occasion at public festivals, without any apparent damage to health. The Court forced a national repeal of the law to balance requirements within the European Community, although it noted that domestic production requirements could remain in effect.

Since the ruling, it has been legal to import beers into Germany that are brewed with adjuncts such as corn, rice, non-malted grains, spices, and sugar, and treated with chemical additives to produce an artificial head and a longer shelf life.

However, beer that is produced and sold in Germany has to follow production standards akin to the Reinheitsgebot. Today, the purity law is part of the German tax code (Bundesministerium der Justiz 1992, 2000, 2009). It states that, in bottom-fermented beers (lagers), brewers may use only barley malt, hops, yeast, and water. Specifically, this rule forbids the sale of lagers *brewed in*

---

[2] Such divergence of state laws from federal German law is still possible today, and is enacted in German beer tax law (§9 (7), VorlBierG 1993; see Bundesministerium der Justiz 1992).

Germany that contain spices (as do many Belgian beers), corn, or rice (as do virtually all mass-produced industrial beers in the rest of the world), sugar (to be found in many Belgian and British beers), unmalted grains (required for many Belgian and British style beers), as well as chemical additives and stabilizers.

For top-fermented beers (ales), the Reinheitsgebot is somewhat more generous in terms of allowable ingredients, in part to accommodate an ancient and varied, mostly barley-based ale-brewing tradition in northern Germany, in part to accommodate the wheat-based Weissbier from Bavaria in the south. German ales may contain—in addition to barley malt, hops, yeast, and water—'other' malted grains, including, of course, malted wheat for Weissbier, as well as various forms of sugar and sugar-derived colouring agents—but still no chemicals or other processed compounds.[3]

The German production standard for beer has created new frictions in the context of German reunification after the fall of the Berlin Wall in 1989. A brewery in east German Brandenburg that has a brewing tradition dating back to 1410 was not allowed to sell its traditional bottom-fermented black beer under the name 'beer', since sugar syrup had been added to give it a dark colouring and distinct taste. The Klosterbrauerei Neuzelle had to call its brew 'Schwarzer Abt' instead of beer. It took a lengthy legal battle, as far as the German administration court, to allow the production and distribution of the product under the name 'beer'. In February 2005 the court ruled that adding sugar syrup in this case was not a substitute for barley malt, since it was added after brewing and filtration (Bundesverwaltungsgericht 2005).

Analysis: An Economist's View on the German Production Standard

The Reinheitsgebot erected a non-tariff barrier to trade, as prior to the 1987 decision of the European Court of Justice all produce had to adhere to this unilateral production standard. The effects of the domestic production standard can be analysed in a simple partial equilibrium setting of supply and demand for beer in Germany.[4]

Assume that two types of consumers of beer can be distinguished: 'traditionalists', who care about drinking only beer produced according the Reinheitsgebot, and 'experimentalists', who venture into consuming imported varieties

[3] Once again, the exception is Bavaria, where no sugar and chemical additives are allowed in beers, including in beers for the export market.
[4] This is a variation of a model for the analysis of non-tariff measures developed in van Tongeren, Beghin, and Marette (2009).

that may contain additives not allowed under the German standard. The traditionalists' demand is denoted D_2 in Figure 3.1, while the experimentalists' demand is denoted D_1. With imports allowed, there are two supply functions: S_0 denotes the domestic German supply, S^F the foreign supply. Note that Figure 3.1 assumes that German brewers face higher costs than foreign producers due to the production standard that prohibits using cheaper substitute ingredients, and hence their supply function lies above the foreign one. It is further assumed that consumers are able to distinguish perfectly between beers made according to the Reinheitsgebot and imported varieties, so that they choose to buy either domestic or foreign beer. Two cases can now be distinguished.

In case 1, imports of non-compliant beers are allowed. As a result, two equilibrium prices are observed: p_2^L where the traditionalists' demand clears the market for domestic beers, and p_1^L where the experimentalists' demand intersects with foreign supply. The outcomes in this segregated market can be compared to the equilibrium under autarchy.

In case 2, imports that do not comply with the German Reinheitsgebot are prohibited. With the Reinheitsgebot in place, there were (virtually) no imports, and hence the standard acted as an import ban. Figure 3.1 illustrates this

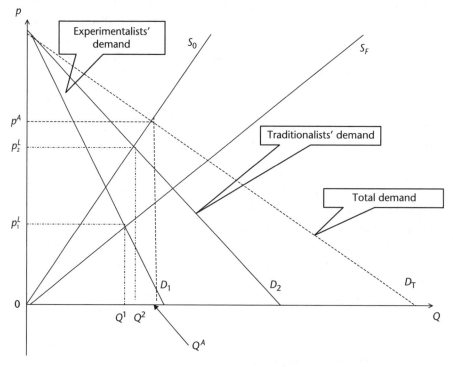

Figure 3.1. Segmented market for beer

situation, where domestic supply S_0 intersects with total domestic demand D^T at the autarchy equilibrium price p^A and a quantity Q^A is sold and consumed.

Hence, this simple model suggests that by allowing imports of beer that do not comply with the Reinheitsgebot:

- The price for German brews will decline, due to competition from abroad $(p_2^L < p^A)$.
- Total consumption increases: $Q^1 + Q^2 > Q^A$.
- Consumer welfare increases due to greater variety and lower prices: traditionalist consumers are still able to buy the Reinheitsgebot beer, and experimentalists can enjoy alternative varieties, and prices are lower for both varieties.
- Producer surplus for German brewers declines due to lower prices and substitution towards imported products, while producer surplus of foreign suppliers increases.

Evidently, the strength of these effects depends critically on (1) consumer preferences, as reflected in the shape of the demand functions and (2) the size of the two consumer groups distinguished, as well as on (3) cost factors, encapsulated in the supply functions.

The Facts: What has Happened to the German Beer Market since 1987?

The previous analysis would suggest an increase in total beer consumption since 1987, holding everything constant but the change in import regime. Per capita beer consumption in Germany reached its peak in the late 1970s and early 1980s, with more than 148 litres of beer consumed per inhabitant. Since then, there has been a steady decline in beer consumption, reaching 111 litres per capita in 2008. Population growth has not counteracted the declining consumption per capita, so that aggregate beer consumption is also declining slowly, but it still represents a sizable 9.2 billion litres (see Figure 3.2).[5] The decline in per capita beer consumption is not unique to Germany. It is observed in most European countries and is explained by substitution towards wine and other alcoholic beverages, in combination with a general decline in consumption of alcohol.

---

[5] Note that the steep increase in total beer consumption between 1990 and 1992 is explained by German reunification and the consequent broadening of the population base over which beer consumption is counted.

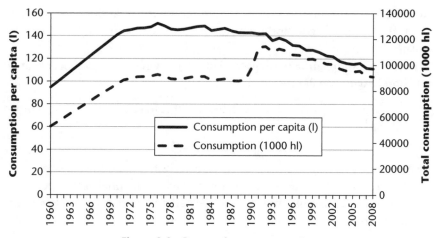

Figure 3.2. German beer consumption
Source: Deutscher Brauer-Bund (2007, 2008).

The number of breweries in Germany has been quite stable at around 1,300 since 1995. Adams (2006) notes that market concentration in the German beer market is relatively low, although it has increased slightly between the late 1950s and 2005.

The decline in consumption is not what might be expected from the analysis above and is probably unrelated to the repeal of the Reinheitsgebot in 1987. In terms of Figure 3.1, either overall demand for beer has shifted downward, or beer prices have increased, leading to less consumption. What has happened to imports and domestic prices?

Recall that the simple model predicts an increase in imports (as would any common-sense reasoning). Indeed, as Figure 3.3 shows, imports have increased steadily since 1987. This increased openness of the German beer market is surely related to the decision of the European Court of Justice in 1987. In 1987 the import share of domestic consumption amounted to 1.5%, and in 2003 imports represented only 3% of German beer consumption. Indeed, a sharp rise in imports is observed only after 2003, and by 2008 the import share had climbed to 7%. This degree of import penetration is relatively low within Europe. In comparison, Italy (34%), France (32%), and the United Kingdom (18%) have much higher import penetration of their beer markets, with the European average amounting to 13% (Ernst and Young

2009). The exporting countries most in evidence on the German beer market are, in decreasing order of market shares in 2008: Denmark (2.4%), the Czech Republic (1.6%), and Belgium (1.5%). Beer exporters from the Czech Republic in particular have increased their presence in the German market after accession to the EU in 2004.

The data thus show that imports have been increasing since 1987, the year when import beers that did not comply with the German Reinheitsgebot started to get access to the German market. In that sense, the German beer market is no longer an exception to the internalization of the beer market. However, import penetration remains relatively low in comparison with other large countries in Europe. What can explain this low level of imports?

Consumer preferences may partly explain the low import penetration. The reference to the Reinheitsgebot of 1516 on German beer bottles signals a certain quality that German beer drinkers seem to value highly. The German beer market is also quite particular regarding the dominance of local beers. The presence of many (1,300), often small, producers serving a regional or local market is testimony that many German beer consumers have a taste for their preferred local varieties. However, the local preference argument is contested by Adams (2006), who argues that German beer preferences evolve towards a more homogeneous taste for Pilsener-style beers, hence indicating a decline in local preferences.

Preference for local brews is not the only factor that determines ease of market access on the German beer market. Another important factor is the bottling and distribution of beer, which is dominated by a return-bottle system in Germany. The German packaging rules favour more costly reusable bottles rather than the use of cans, hence making access to the distribution system an important factor in market access.

Consumer preferences, brand loyalty, and access to the distribution system may favour foreign direct investment, including through acquisitions and takeovers, rather than trade. The presence of foreign firms in the German beer market is greater than the import figures suggest. However, foreign firms have to brew beers that comply with the Reinheitsgebot, and consequently that route to penetrating the German market with alternative, non-compliant, beer varieties is closed.

The rise in imports has coincided with a fall in real consumer prices for beer. Beer consumer prices relative to the overall consumer price index have fallen by 6% during the period 1996 to 2008.[6] While this is consistent with the conclusions of the simple model, it is unclear which portion of the price fall can be attributed to import competition, since other factors such as efficiency

---

[6] Note however that nominal consumer beer prices rose in the same period by about 15%.

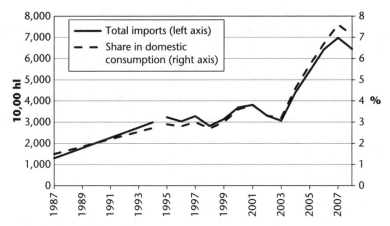

Figure 3.3. German beer imports

Note: The data points between 1987 and 1995 are estimated by linear interpolation between observations for 1987 from Karrenbrock (1990) and the start of the time series 1995–2008 from Deutscher Brauer-Bund (2007, 2008, 2009).

Source: Karrenbrock (1990); Deutscher Brauer-Bund (2007, 2008).

gains, and falling input prices, may also play a role. However, available statistics indicate that nominal German producer prices rose faster than nominal consumer prices, which lends support to the conclusion that import competition has played a role in lowering the average price of beer on the German market, even though the import share is relatively low.

Conclusions

The German Reinheitsgebot, which dates back to a Bavarian law of 1516, is sometimes said to be the oldest known food law. While this is probably an exaggerated claim, it is perhaps true that it is one of the oldest food laws that is still in existence in more or less unchanged form. Almost 500 years of influence is a considerable achievement for any regulation or law, anywhere in the world.

Five hundred years ago, beer was not very much traded across the European continent. But with greater economic integration, the unilateral German production standard became a non-tariff barrier to trade, which was challenged in the context of the European single market. Today imported beer can use a wider set of methods and ingredients than is allowed for beer produced and sold in Germany. In some sense, this could be seen as discrimination against domestic producers.

The opening of the German beer market means that consumers have a wider choice of varieties, thereby improving their welfare. However, import penetration remains relatively low and many German beer drinkers prefer domestic and often local varieties that are still produced according to the comparatively strict requirements that originate in the original Bavarian law of 1516. Deregulation has meant a wider choice for consumers, but one cannot deregulate against consumer preferences. Other important factors in import penetration are access to the German distribution system, which disfavours the use of non-reusable containers, and the fact that foreign beers brewed in German plants still have to satisfy the Reinheitsgebot.

References

Adams, W. J. (2006). 'Markets: Beer in Germany and the United States'. *The Journal of Economic Perspectives*, 20/1: 189–205.

Bundesministerium der Justiz (1992). *Biersteuergesetz 1993*. Berlin: Bundesministerium der Justiz.

—— (2000). *Verordnung zur Durchführung des Vorläufigen Biergesetzes*. Berlin: Bundesministerium der Justiz.

—— (2009). *Biersteuergesetz (BierStG)*. Berlin: Bundesministerium der Justiz. <http://bundesrecht.juris.de/aktuell.html>.

Bundesverwaltungsgericht (2005). Leipzig, BVerwG 3 C 5.04—Ruling 24 February 2005. <http://www.bverwg.de>.

Deutscher Brauer-Bund (2007). *Die deutsche Brauwirtschaft in Zahlen 2006*. Berlin, Deutscher Brauer-Bund e.V. <http://www.deutsches-bier.net>.

—— (2008). *Die deutsche Brauwirtschaft in Zahlen 2007*. Berlin: Deutscher Brauer-Bund e.V. <http://www.deutsches-bier.net>.

—— (2009). *Die deutsche Brauwirtschaft in Zahlen 2008*. Berlin: Deutscher Brauer-Bund e.V. <http://www.deutsches-bier.net>.

Ernst and Young (2009). *The Contribution Made by Beer to the European Economy*. Report commissioned by The Brewers of Europe. <http://www.brewersofeurope.org/docs/flipping_books/ey_full_2009/index.html>.

European Court of Justice (1987). Judgment of the Court of 12 March 1987. *Commission of the European Communities v Federal Republic of Germany*. Failure of a State to fulfil its obligations—Purity requirement for beer. Case 178/84. European Court Reports 1987: 1227. <http://eur-lex.europa.eu/LexUriServ/LexUriServ.do?uri=CELEX:61984J0178:EN:HTML#SM>.

Karrenbrock, J. D. (1990). 'The Internationalization of the Beer Brewing Industry'. *Federal Reserve Bank of St Louis Review*, 72/6: 3–19.

van Tongeren, F., J. Beghin, and S. Marette (2009). 'A Cost-Benefit Framework for the Assessment of Non-Tariff Measures in Agro-Food Trade'. OECD Food, Agriculture and Fisheries Working Papers, 21. OECD Publishing, <http://dx.doi.org/10.1787/220613725148>.

4

Brewing Nation: War, Taxes, and the Growth of the British Beer Industry in the Eighteenth and Nineteenth Centuries

John V. C. Nye

Introduction

Why do some nations drink beer, not wine? Most especially, why did Britain evolve into a beer-drinking nation despite a growing taste among the upper classes for French wine in the seventeenth century?

An English state eager to reduce its trade deficit with France in the late seventeenth century found that opportunity as a result of the wars that ran from 1689–1713. War with Louis XIV's France provided the excuse that protectionists had long sought to cut off virtually all commerce with the French. This was especially important for the trade in wine and spirits, one of the largest components of the seventeenth-century English trade deficit. Prohibition and protection led to the creation of powerful interests at home and abroad (notably the brewing industry in London and the English-dominated wine industry in Portugal) that benefited from the absence of competing French imports. These groups successfully lobbied to impose new and nearly prohibitive tariffs on French goods—notably on wine and spirits—when trade with France resumed after the war. Protection of domestic interests in turn allowed the state to raise domestic excises in a credible fashion, therefore leading to a dramatic increase in government revenues without a need to increase taxes on landed property. The state ensured compliance not simply through the threat of lower tariffs on foreign substitutes, but also through the encouragement of oligopoly in the production and sale of beer. Thus, the rise of the eighteenth-century British brewing industry is not just the story of tariff protection and import substitution, but is a direct window into the process by which the state Leviathan extended its scope and acquired the revenue essential to sustain the government during a period of expansion, war, and nascent imperialism.

Beer had emerged as the most important, mass-produced beverage during the years of the Anglo-French wars at the end of the seventeenth century. Technical improvements leading to economies of scale in brewing, coupled with the growth of London as the major British urban centre, promoted beer as the common beverage and also encouraged the transformation of the industry from small-scale home production to concentrated large-scale industry. This tendency was further enhanced by laws designed to limit entry into the brewing industry and to lessen concentration in the retail trade as well (Mathias 1959; Nye 2007). Thus, the brewing industry was well-placed to benefit from protection afforded by wine tariffs, but also to bargain directly with the government as a powerful special interest which could (and did) argue for continued protection throughout the eighteenth century. Attempts to invade the oligopoly tended to fail as late as the early nineteenth century (Nye 2007).

The net result was an expansive British state, with revenues collected through the newly created central tax administration and a cooperative brewing industry that found it easy to shift much of the burden of this taxation onto consumers, who had little say in the matter. The growth of British revenues in the eighteenth century was so dramatic that it made possible Britain's rise to prominence as a world power (Brewer 1988).

In addition, the protective tariffs had long-term consequences for the pattern of British domestic consumption, perhaps even altering, or at least shaping, the fundamentals of British 'taste'. Deforming the centuries' old wine trade with France meant that wine was kept out of the British Isles during the century and a half which included the Industrial Revolution and the rise of mass consumption. It ensured that beer would be the dominant component of the ordinary Briton's drinking habits, and it restricted the consumption of fine Bordeaux and Port to the upper classes.

War and Wine Tariffs

The tariffs on wine and spirits had their origins in the period 1689–1713 when England ceased trading with France as a result of the Nine Years' War and the War of Spanish Succession. This cessation of trade was especially significant because France was England's largest trading partner in the seventeenth century and the largest source of her imports. Stopping trade with France turned

England's large merchandise trade deficit into a surplus for several years. And a very large portion of Anglo-French trade—at least 20%—was wine.

The cessation of imports from France led to a surge in imports from Spain and, more significantly, Portugal. As Portugal was not noted for its capacity to produce wine and spirits prior to this period, the heavy shift in production directed almost exclusively towards the English market was quite significant (Nye 2007). Portugal was an ally, even something of a dependency of England, and Englishmen dominated the Portuguese wine and spirits trade as growers, producers, merchants, and shippers. When the fabled Methuen Treaty of 1704 was signed, England was granted the right to sell textiles freely to the Portuguese in exchange for a promise that Portuguese wine would enter England (and later Britain) at a duty level never to exceed two-thirds of duties imposed on other nations (Nye 2007). Since Portugal was not particularly successful at selling wine to other nations, this arrangement was a clear distortion aimed at creating a supplier of alcoholic beverages that would be favourable to England. Indeed, as Portugal had enjoyed only the most minimal success in exporting wine and spirits prior to the quarter century of war with the French, the Methuen Treaty virtually created the overseas wine market for Portugal. Table 4.1 illustrates the decrease in French imports from 13,401 tuns to 1,261 tuns, and the increase of Portuguese imports from 434 tuns to 10,334 tuns during the period 1686–1715.

The end of war with France did not restore trade with France to anything like the former levels. Rather, a highly limited trade arose that was based on elevated volume tariffs specifically designed to exclude the bulk of French products, including wine, from the British market. Supplementary tariffs on items that passed through French ports, or were delivered by French ships, or duty reductions on colonial products increased the favouritism against France and in favour of British domestics and allies.

The significance of the wine tariffs can be seen by comparing the ex post ad valorem rates of protection on wine (using total wine import duties divided by wine import value) with the excise on beer. Using average tariff rates on wines and comparing them to the ad valorem rates on domestic beer shows that the wine rates were several times higher than the rates on beer until the 1860 Treaty of Commerce. For the rest of the century, the average wine tariffs were approximately two to three times the rate charged on beer (Figure 4.1). However, even these differences understate the differences between the wine tariffs and the beer excises, because the wine and spirits duties were set by volume, rather than ad valorem. This meant that cheaper products were entirely excluded from Britain, while small quantities of higher end alcohol, such as

Table 4.1. Evolution of British wine imports, 1686–1786

	France	Portugal	Spain	Other	Total
Averages for the Years					
1686–9	13,401 (2,814,210)	434 (91,140)	9,914 (821,940)	955 (200,550)	18,704 (3,927,840)
Averages for the Years					
1690–6	0	5,491 (1,153,110)	6,253 (1,313,130)	900 (189,000)	12,954 (2,720,340)
Year					
1713	2,458 (516,180)	5,861 (1,230,810)	4,116 (864,360)	3,472 (729,120)	15,907 (3,340,470)
1714	1,196 (251,160)	8,652 (1,816,920)	5,605 (1,177,050)	3,180 (667,800)	18,633 (3,912,930)
1715	1,261 (264,810)	10,334 (2,170,140)	6,768 (1,421,280)	3,354 (704,340)	21,717 (4,560,570)
1716	1,568 (329,280)	8,923 (1,873,830)	4,718 (990,780)	3,596 (755,160)	18,805 (3,949,050)
Ten-year averages:					
1717–26	1,297 (272,370)	12,066 (2,533,860)	7,458 (1,566,180)	1,675 (351,750)	22,496 (4,724,160)
1727–36	845 (117,450)	12,211 (2,564,310)	8,467 (1,778,070)	1,409 (295,890)	22,932 (4,815,720)
1737–46	374 (78,540)	12,330 (2,589,300)	3,305 (694,050)	1,023 (214,830)	17,032 (3,576,720)
1747–56	490 (102,900)	10,321 (2,167,410)	3,867 (812,070)	991 (208,110)	15,669 (3,290,490)
1757–66	541 (113,610)	11,221 (2,356,410)	3,555 (746,550)	1,247 (261,870)	16,564 (3,478,440)
1767–76	491 (103,110)	11,849 (2,488,290)	3,554 (746,340)	1,271 (266,910)	17,165 (3,604,650)
1777–86	436 (91,560)	11,300 (2,373,000)	2,434 (511,140)	744 (156,240)	14,914 (3,131,940)

Note: Wine imports are expressed in old tuns. The values in parentheses are expressed in imperial gallons.

Source: Francis, A. D. (1972) and Nye, J. V. C. (2007: 39). *War, Wine, and Taxes: The Political Economy of Anglo-French Trade 1689–1900.* Princeton: Princeton University Press.

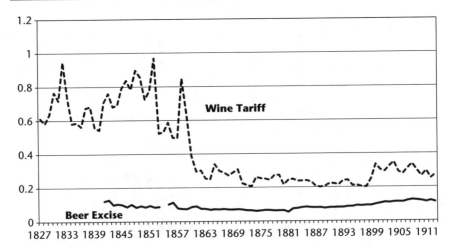

Figure 4.1. Beer excise ratio and wine tariff protection, Britain, 1827–1913

Source: Figure 6.4 in Tena, A. (2006). 'Assessing the Protectionist Intensity of Tariffs in Nineteenth-Century European Trade Policy', in J. P. Dormois and P. Lains (eds.), *Classical Trade Protectionism 1815–1914*. London and New York: Routledge.

the best claret from Bordeaux, would continue to make their way to Albion (Nye 2007).[1]

The tendency to levy them first by volume, and then (after 1860) by alcoholic content, would mean that the cheapest and lowest alcoholic beverages would be most highly discriminated against. Those drinks of course would have been the ones most likely to be competitive with beer, even though the 1860 reform partially redressed the discrimination between French wine and Portuguese products. But domestic beer remained somewhat protected from foreign competition throughout the nineteenth century. In addition, high tariffs on weak substitute beverages such as coffee or tea also added a layer of protection.

Most important of all, the mere fact of high taxes on the entire class of beverages, both non-alcoholic and alcoholic, would have distorted British production and consumption to favour those industries (manufactures) in which Britain enjoyed a strong comparative advantage.

[1] Detailed records of what types of wines were being imported and in what quantities are not available but, as Nye (2007) has demonstrated, one can infer the extent of the quality shift simply by examining the ratio of wines imported in the barrel versus those in the bottle. Given high transportation costs and the possibilities of breakage, only the best wines tended to be shipped directly in bottles. Hence, it was typical for the ratio (by volume) of barrel to bottled wines from France to reside in the range of 15 to 1 up to 25 to 1. In contrast, the ratio for Britain tended to be of the order of 3 gallons of barrel wine for every gallon imported in bottles (Nye 2007).

British Wine Tariffs and Increased Government Revenues

The history of tariffs on imported alcohol was deeply protective by design, and this protection was tied into the state's capacity to extract revenue from the protected beer industry. The growth in eighteenth-century British revenue essentially reflects the growth of the excise.

A simple examination of the British budgets indicates that an overwhelming part of the excises derived from taxes on alcoholic beverages. Table 4.2 is reprinted from O'Brien's (1988) work on British revenue sources in the eighteenth century. The table gives the principal sources of British revenue for the late eighteenth century and covers perhaps 90% of the central government's budget. Customs revenues from wine and spirits and domestic excises on beer and spirits and intermediate products in beverage production total nearly 40%.[2]

Thus, the growth in eighteenth-century British revenue essentially reflects the growth of the excise, which in turn was politically sustainable because of British tariff policy. Figure 4.2 shows the steep rise in income earned by the British state throughout the eighteenth century, of which the largest share was due to earnings from customs and excises. The striking feature is the stability of the share of revenues from property and land; it remained fairly constant throughout the eighteenth century. Taxes on land, customs, and the excise each accounted for roughly a million pounds each in the first decade of the eighteenth century (varying in a range from about 500,000 to 1,500,000 pounds sterling). By the 1780s land brought in some 2 to 3 million pounds at the most and customs another 3 million or so, while the excise accounted for upwards of 7 to 8 million pounds sterling. Since roughly 5 millions pounds came from beer, malt, and domestic spirits and another 2 million of the customs revenues derived from wine and spirits, it is safe to say that the story of British tax success in the eighteenth century is predominantly the story of the successful imposition of tariffs on alcoholic beverages.

The Peculiar Position of the Brewing Industry

Although Brewer (1988) has argued that it is the professionalization of the tax administration that explains the rise in British receipts, the nearly exclusive focus on alcoholic beverages and their substitutes cuts against that technocratic argument.

---

[2] Note that this figure also leaves out the revenues from excises and tariffs on sugar used in the production of alcoholic beverages; their inclusion would bring the total closer to one-half of all government revenues.

Table 4.2. Major taxes, Britain, 1788–1792

	Average annual yield 1788–92 (thousands of pounds £)	Type of tax	Percentage distribution of taxes	
1 Direct taxes				
Land, windows, etc.	3388	Direct		21.2%
2 Food				
Tea	583	Customs	3.6%	
Salt	999	Customs	6.3%	
Sugar	425	Excise	2.7%	
			subtotal	12.6%
3 Heat, light, fuel	969	Cust & Exc		6.1%
4 Construction materials	648	Cust & Exc		4.1%
5 Clothing, footwear	1010	Cust & Exc		6.3%
6 Soap and starch	501	Excise		3.1%
7 Alcohol and tobacco				
Beer	1968	Excise	12.3%	
Malt	1838	Excise	11.5%	
Hops	121	Excise	0.8%	
Wine	739	Customs	4.6%	
Foreign Spirits	990	Customs	6.2%	
Domestic Spirits	654	Excise	4.1%	
Tobacco	607	Customs	3.8%	
			subtotal	43.3%
8 Commercial services				
Newspapers, etc.	533	Stamp		3.3%
Overall total	£15,973			100.0%

Source: O'Brien , P. K. (1988: 11). 'The Political Economy of British Taxation, 1660–1815'. *Economic History Review*, 41/1: 1–32. John Wiley and Sons.

The increase in London's population and its development as the centre for a new urban proletariat with less opportunity for home-brewing seems to have been an important development for the success of the excise. Furthermore, technological developments resulting in the easy production of beer—primarily porter—in mass quantities led to the increasing concentration of the brewing industry. The coincidence of the war from 1689 to 1713, the rise of London, the concentration of the brewing industry, the stoppage in trade with France, and the rise of a mostly English beverage trade from Portugal allowed a situation in which the government now had a limited number of players to bargain with.

It was both easier to see who benefited from different policies and who would be responsible for payment of excises.[3] In exchange for protection

---

[3] This is merely the legal incidence of course. As we know, it is likely that much of the tax was eventually passed on to the consumer, who was a passive player in this whole process. A

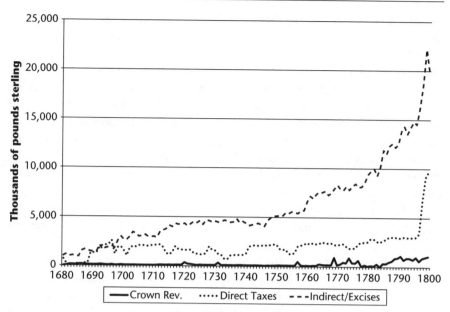

Figure 4.2. Net public revenue, Britain, 1680–1800
Source: O'Brien and Hunt (1993).

from tariffs, the brewing industry would comply with tax payments. It was in the interests of government and the leading brewers to promote oligopoly in beer production through the encouragement of concentration and continued restrictions on entry both at the wholesale and the retail level. The government fixed prices and inspected production of these large brewers on a regular basis.

The ease of collection seems key to understanding the success of the excise. The more scattered were the sources of production, the more troublesome it was to collect the excise. Just as the land tax fell most heavily on the largest holdings because the state could obtain more income for the least effort, excises that had to be collected from a variety of small producers would quickly run up against diminishing returns as the high costs of dealing with multiple producers would not be offset by the small income from the

comparison of the lobbying power of the brewers and English consumers demonstrates how this passing was most possible. At this time, English consumers were not in any position to successfully protest the taxes imposed on them. The problem with most excises—as is evidenced by the problems the British had with the beer excise in the seventeenth century—is that resistance to their imposition is likely to be more successfully prosecuted by the producers than by the consumers of the good in question. It is usually only this group that has the organization and the political influence to evade the tax.

multitude of sources. Smuggling, fraud, and other forms of evasion would place a heavy burden on authorities seeking to correctly assess as well as collect the tax.

The claim that alcoholic beverages were a 'natural' revenue source runs up against the problem that attempts to raise excises brought only limited success in the late 1600s and the early 1700s. Charles Davenant (1695) and other contemporaries were of the opinion that excises were becoming counterproductive as they seemed to be lowering demand to the point where only limited gains were possible at best. This was indeed the situation facing the Crown in the seventeenth century, when continued attempts to raise revenue by raising tax rates could only go so far.

By the standards of the seventeenth century, Britain was moderately successful in raising taxes and revenues in the late 1600s. In the late seventeenth century, tariffs and excises were jointly implemented on imported wines and domestic beer. At this time, the high tariffs were not yet very discriminatory; so revenues collected were actually quite similar from both excise and customs sources. From May 1643, beer paid a duty of 2s. a barrel on beer valued at 6s. or over, while beer valued under 6s. a barrel paid 6d. Furthermore, these impositions were begun at a time when beer still had to face competition not just from substitutes like wine, but also from imported beers which were not yet prohibited. Eventually, differential tariffs and, later, outright prohibitions were imposed on beer imports. By this time, though, these protections had already come at a price.

Although the British wine tariffs were not directly revenue maximizing, they did serve to promote the development of an effective fiscal system to extract tax revenues from the consumption of alcoholic beverages. By protecting domestic producers of beer and spirits, tariffs on imported wine and brandies made it possible for the state to impose high excises on local beverage production, while minimizing resistance to the imposition of high taxes.

A belief had formed in the industry that the end of the Cromwell government would mean the elimination of the beer duty. Unfortunately for these brewers, this would not be the case. A Royal proclamation in 1660 further extended the excise (Monckton 1966: 118). The gradual acceptance of the beer excises would lead to its use to finance a variety of government ventures, notably the wars with France. With the regularization of the domestic levies on beer came the joint problem of evasion, as well as increased agitation by domestic producers against imports of all sorts. Initial attempts to raise greater amounts of revenue simply through an increase in the rate of excise taxation did not produce the desired results. In 1689 and 1690, the duty on beer was raised so that it was virtually double the initial level of 2s. 6d. a barrel for strong beer and 6d. for small beer. This led to a decrease in the number of common brewers and stagnation in the revenue levels after the initial increase. Eventually, income began to fall. Protecting the industry from foreign competition would be necessary if the taxes were to become viable. The government took advantage of this consolidation in the industry to encourage the oligopoly dominance of brewing in London by a dozen or so firms.

Yet none of this compares to the astonishing rise in income following the Glorious Revolution of 1688 that initially took place with only modest increases in the number of taxes and tax rates. It is therefore collection, not the taxes themselves, that needs to be the focus of the explanation. To speak of collection is really to speak of compliance of taxpayers to pay their taxes, without which the government would have been in the position of squeezing blood from a stone.

Changes in Technology and Protectionism

The story I have presented here permits us to derive fresh insights into the evolution of the eighteenth-century brewing industry, especially in combination with the story told by Peter Mathias (1959). Mathias's great work on the rise of the London beer industry makes three important points relevant to our discussion.

The beer industry, notably the porter breweries, saw an 'industrial revolution' in brewing in the early to mid-eighteenth century, which led to a rise in the minimum efficient scale of operations. The changes in technology and organization led to very high levels of concentration in the brewing industry, with only a dozen or fewer firms dominating the market by the end of the eighteenth century. The change in concentration at the wholesale level was associated with the rise of tied houses in the retail market, which led to enhanced regulation by the state of the entire industry, with the cooperation of the brewers themselves.

These changes will be examined in more detail because an understanding of the industrial organization of brewing will illustrate how the policy of restricting wine imports came to be sustained by institutional developments at the level of domestic industry.

The revolution in brewing was primarily a revolution in the production of porter rather than ale. Porter 'seems to have been the first beer technically suited for mass-production at contemporary standards of control, unlike ale which needed "attemperated fermentation" for stability in large-scale brewing' (Mathias 1959: 13). Porter was the brew of choice because porter was capable of being mashed in large quantities while surviving operations in which the release of tannins would cloud and, therefore, make the mash unacceptable for fine ale. No grain brew other than porter could survive the many mashings of industrial strength brewing at the time, which made it the natural choice of growing industry. Perhaps porter would not have displaced ale at the time had there not been such concentration in population in London, which worked to promote both demand and supply. Not only could large-scale production flourish, but home-brewing was both more difficult and, hence, less economical than in the countryside. Furthermore, the greater opportunities for employment and distraction in the City undoubtedly raised the opportunity cost of attempting to avoid the market product, and, of course, war with France destroyed the only other drink with a realistic chance of making inroads into the drinking habits of the small but growing middle class.

Changes in regulation and taxation since 1660 'had been having an effect in concentrating the industry into fewer and larger plants: in particular, Common Brewers had favourable excise allowances' (Mathias 1959: 21). Porter was a relatively undifferentiated product as produced by the most efficient firms, making it much easier to market and sell. The combination of increasing urbanization, the central importance of London, and the successful adoption of porter as a basis for large-scale wholesale production contributed to a situation that moved large numbers of people away from home-brewing towards just consuming market products.

Such production and the attendant problems of distribution apparently had enough scale economies to make for a concentrated industry dominated by a few powerful brewers (cf. Mathias 1959: 63, 'this first generation of industrialists exploited the commercial success of a new product in the main by organizing their establishments deliberately for its large-scale production and distribution'). The number of brewers registered by the authorities steadily declined from the late 1600s to the early 1800s, hovering in the range of 160–190 in 1684 to 1708 and falling below 100 in the period up till 1830 (Mathias 1959: 22). As Mathias notes, 'The fall in absolute numbers did not coincide with any great increase in absolute quantities . . . It is this important relative change in relation to the modest aggregate expansion of production which distinguished the industrial revolution of the brewing industry from that of others, such as cotton or iron, which represent the Industrial Revolution' (1959: 22).

The third point is of great importance because it underlines the extent to which fiscal and tariff policy did in fact suppress the growth in demand for all alcoholic beverages. Demand for wine and beer as a category usually has a high income elasticity. Despite the growth in income that accompanied the British Industrial Revolution, the increases in total demand for both products were minor till the mid-nineteenth century because taxes and tariffs were so high.

If the industry did not see any substantial growth in demand or output, though, why then did they support policies which limited the industry's growth? The answer lies in distinguishing the gains to the industry as a whole from the gains to a restricted industry with monopolistic elements.[4] In a nutshell, control and regulation made possible an oligopoly which derived substantial monopoly profits from the increased concentration in the beer industry. These profits were more easily taxed by the government, and the maintenance of such profits were held hostage to government policy towards international trade in wine and spirits.

The brewing industry became larger and more concentrated in both structure and organization in eighteenth-century London. The concentration of power in the hands of the largest brewers is confirmed by the value of these establishments over time. For example, Anchor Brewery was purchased in 1729 for £30,000. It was later valued at £78,800 in 1749. This value later rose to £149,200 by 1780, when it was apparently sold cheaply for £135,000. The firm of Benjamin Truman showed similar rises in valuation from £23,340 in 1741 to £225,090 in 1790 (Mathias 1959: 24). In Mathias's words, 'Before the mid-eighteenth century, a large porter brewery was as different from the inn brewhouse as the later cotton mill was from a large cottage workshop. As the process continued so the pyramid of production developed ever more steeply sloping sides' (1959: 24).

The rise in the control of brewing can be seen from Table 4.3, which analyses beer output throughout the mid-eighteenth to early nineteenth

Table 4.3. Production of strong beer in London, 1748–1830 (figures in 1,000 barrels)

Year	Total brewed	First twelve houses	Percentage of total
1748	915.5	383	41.9
1750	979.5	437	43.6
1760	1114.5	525.5	47.1
1776	1289	707	54.8
1780	1319.5	680	52.8
1787	1251	965	77.1
1795		978.2	
1800		994.5	
1810		1320.5	
1815	1768.5	1401.5	77.7
1817	1532.5	1226.5	80
1830	1441.5	1200	85

Note: Collected originally from excise returns, where available. First 12 houses, MSS. And printed lists at the breweries.

Source: Mathias, P. (1959). *The Brewing Industry in England: 1700–1830*. Cambridge: Cambridge University Press.

---

[4] Mathias (1959: 24) notes: 'Great knowledge, enterprise and skill, both in the actual brewing and in management, were needed for success. For those with such qualities, and sufficient capital, ... the "Profits returned are proportionately considerable".'

centuries. Notice that the total amount of beer brewed was at most 50% greater in 1830 than in 1748, despite the rise in income and population that had been experienced by London. At the same time, the share of total output accounted for by the top 12 houses rose from 42% to some 85%.

Further evidence of the role of the relationship between protection for the dominant brewers and the ease with which the government could collect excise taxes can be seen in the evolution in the central government's attitudes towards restrictions on retailing, especially state support for the notion of the tied house. In the late seventeenth century, the government favoured unrestricted licensing as the best means to facilitate revenue generation. Yet by the eighteenth century both the government and the leading brewers supported regulation restricting licensing of new pubs and beer houses. Policy that had heretofore been designed to promote revenue through unrestricted retail trade became focused on cautious regulation and protection of the public health. When 16 licences were eliminated in Bedfordshire in 1689, the complaint arose from the government that 'suppression of Ale Houses is a growing mischief to the Revenue', and encouragement had been given earlier to the Treasury to license on the grounds that 'The more Ale Houses there are the better it is for the Excise' (Mathias 1959: 125–6).

In contrast, this theme is not taken up at all in the eighteenth century, and there was little concerted complaint from those whose interests lay in the sale of beer against those anxious to control it. Increasingly, arguments emerged as to the need to restrict licensing for the purposes of preserving the public health or to protect the public from fraudulent practices. Whereas before the government's attitude was clearly 'the more, the merrier', the 1700s saw the state involved in fastidious attempts to restrain the uncontrolled expansion of retail establishments. From the 1730s on, 'surplus' houses were routinely restricted. As the vast majority of retail establishments came to be related to the leading brewers through tie-in sales and franchise arrangements deriving from ownership of the retail sellers by the large producers, the industry was eager to encourage efforts on the part of the Treasury or any other branch of the state to restrain competition in the sale of all alcoholic beverages. In effect, the government worked to limit entry into the retail market.

Government support for monopoly practices and the self-evident increase in the profitability of the large London brewers actually made for an interesting concordance between the temperance and the free trade movements at the beginning of the nineteenth century. For the first few decades of the 1800s, the temperance movement was actually allied with the free traders. For instance, Cobden believed that beer monopolies with their tied houses and the economically inefficient restrictions on the wine trade drove the working classes to hard liquor in unhealthy conditions. While they were not in favour of broader consumption of spirits, those in the movement did feel that wider consumption of wine and lighter beverages would more effectively substitute for rum and whisky (an argument equally made by lobbyists for the vignerons of Bordeaux).

In describing the logic that united the temperance movement with the free traders, Brian Harrison writes:

> The free licensing argument went something like this: government attempts to regulate the drink trade foster four related evils: high prices, adulteration, smuggling and drunkenness. High taxation and monopoly enable drink manufacturers to make large profits and to adulterate their product at the expense of the poor. Inefficient and corrupt government inspectors do nothing to improve its quality and fail to curb smuggling. Therefore, sweep away medieval sumptuary laws and monopolies, reduce taxes, and institute free competition! This will reduce prices, eliminate adulteration and smuggling, and curb drunkenness—which flourishes only when governments bestow artificial attractions on drink. If drink is made as accessible as bread and cheese, and as cheap as wine in France, it will be taken for granted, drunkenness will fall to the French level and supply will settle down to meet demand. (Harrison 1971: 64–5)

By the time of the 1860 Anglo-French treaty, however, a large group of temperance activists, though socially emerging from the same circles as the free traders and other libertarians, came to view prohibition as the only solution to the problem of drunkenness and vice. This they recognized to be a difficult proposition to pass by their colleagues inasmuch as the prohibitionist United Kingdom Alliance was headquartered in Manchester, the spiritual and political centre of libertarian free trade.

The passage of the 1860 Anglo-French Treaty of Commerce led to the removal of French prohibitions on British goods in exchange for a lowered tariff on French wine.

Consequences of the Tariffs

The imposition of high tariffs on French imports led to an increase in government revenues which brought major socio-political consequences in Britain.

First, at a time when Britain managed a dramatic increase in the size of the state and built up its military to become the dominant power in world affairs, the shift in the relative source of the tax burden was quite remarkable. Moreover, there has been no rigorous analysis of why only Britain and none of the other major powers were able to accomplish this. North and Weingast (1989) famously point to the role of the Glorious Revolution in making state borrowing and taxation more credible, but give no reasons why the government was able to collect more revenue. A focus on the struggle over wine tariffs and brewing excises makes clear that this shift in interest group politics led to a configuration of interests in which taxes could be imposed and credibly collected from the parties most likely to attempt evasion (Nye 2007).

Second, this meant that when the time came to reform the British tariff system in the nineteenth century, the importance of the tariffs for revenue—not primarily for the direct revenue they generated but for their ability to collect revenue from producers of domestic substitutes—served as a drag on legislators' capacity to implement reforms that substantially altered duties on these new luxuries. Indeed, even the repeal of the Corn Laws, which were a much later set of agricultural tariffs than the various duties on alcohol and luxuries, proved so politically difficult that the proponents of the legislation were forced out of power as a result in the 1840s (Schonhardt-Bailey 2006).

Third, the way in which the tariffs were imposed drastically reshaped the consumption patterns of the British citizenry. As previously analysed, fixed volume duties had the effect of excluding all trade in the lowest quality wines and of tilting the import mix of the remaining products towards wine that was high in alcoholic content or to very high quality products. The Portuguese wines benefited from the double effect of their higher alcoholic content and of course from the lower level of the duty itself. Spanish products did not have quite the same preference as that of wines from Portugal, but they still benefited from the shift towards more alcoholic products. For the most part, an overwhelming share of the market left to the French was at the very highest end.

Hence, the perception of wine as primarily being a luxury product in Britain had less to do with any essential qualities of the wine itself or any peculiarities of British culture. Rather, a policy designed to exclude cheap wine and promote beer shaped what we think of as the canonical British penchant for beer, whisky, gin, and rum for the masses, and claret, sherry, and port for the elites.

Conclusions

Breweries' domestic protection derived from high import tariffs on French wine led to the creation of powerful interests which allowed an increase in excises. This provided a stable increase in government revenues maintained by the threat of the protectionist measures and by the encouragement of an oligopoly beer production.

Both entry into wholesale brewing and retail distribution were more tightly regulated and restricted throughout the eighteenth century, making for a concentrated domestic interest that could work in concert with Parliament. The steep rise in income earned by the British state was in largest part due to earnings from customs and excises. This entailed that the group that benefited tremendously from protection were local brewers and distillers.

It is hard to see how the small-scale, often home-brewed world of seventeenth-century English beer could have provided the level of revenues and easy collection that the eighteenth century witnessed. The advantage of the political system that emerged from the wartime restrictions on trade with France was that the beer excise was easily imposed on a group whose continued profitability was highly dependent on cooperation from the government and coordination on matters of trade policy. Tariffs on imported alcohol provided the state with a reliable means of imposing a credible tax on domestic consumption of beer and spirits. Whereas previous attempts (in the seventeenth century) to raise the excise on beer only raised revenues by a modest amount (due to the varieties of evasion that were practised), the eighteenth century saw the successful imposition of a variety of excises that were effectively enforced and paid to the government. The great successes of the eighteenth-century excises were twofold: first, the narrowing of the range of commodities bearing the primary burdens of the excise to alcoholic beverages; second, making the producers of domestic beverages so dependent on protection that cooperation would be enhanced or opposition weakened to increased excises.

Furthermore, technical changes in production contributed to a dramatic rise in the size of the most efficient brewers. From the government's perspective, the change in the industrial organization of the brewing industry, especially the trend towards increased concentration in production begun around 1700, and the rise in the scale of production made it substantially easier to monitor and implement the tax than would otherwise have been the case.

The stable and consistent increase in government revenues allowed Britain to build up its military to become the dominant power in world, allowing legislators to implement reforms that substantially altered duties on alcohol and luxuries. Moreover, this allowed the growth of the British beer industry and led to Britain becoming a beer-drinking nation. Perhaps ironically, more liberal treatment of both imported wine and domestic beer would have led to substantially greater amounts of all beverages being consumed in the eighteenth century, without perhaps biasing British consumption to favour not-so-cheap beer for the masses and only the finest claret and port for the elites. And of course, we do not yet know whether the dramatic rise in tax levels throughout the eighteenth century restrained growth during the critical early decades of the Industrial Revolution.

References

Brewer, J. (1988). *The Sinews of Power*. Harvard, MA: Harvard University Press.

Davenant, C. (1695). *An Essay upon the Ways and Means of Supplying the War*. London: Jacob Tonson.

Francis, A. D. (1972). *The Wine Trade*. London: A & C Black.

Harrison, B. (1971). *Drink and the Victorians: The Temperance Question in England 1815–72*. Pittsburgh: University of Pittsburgh Press.

Mathias, P. (1959). *The Brewing Industry in England: 1700–1830*. Cambridge: Cambridge University Press.

Monckton, H. A. (1966). *A History of English Ale and Beer*. London: Bodley Head.

North, D. C., and B. R. Weingast (1989). 'Consitutions and Commitment: The Evolution of Institutions Governing Public Choice in Seventeenth-Century England'. *Journal of Economic History*, 49/4: 803–32.

Nye, J. V. C. (2007). *War, Wine, and Taxes: The Political Economy of Anglo-French Trade 1689–1900*. Princeton: Princeton University Press.

O'Brien, P. K. (1988). 'The Political Economy of British Taxation, 1660–1815'. *Economic History Review*, 41/1: 1–32.

—— and P. A. Hunt (1993). 'Data Prepared on English Revenues, 1485–1815'. *European State Finance Database*. Accessed at <http://www.le.ac.uk/hi/bon/ESFDB/frameset.html>. Files used: <http://\obrien\engd002.ssd>.

Schonhardt-Bailey, C. (2006). *From the Corn Laws to Free Trade: Interests, Ideas, and Institutions in Historical Perspective*. Cambridge, MA: MIT Press.

Tena, A. (2006). 'Assessing the Protectionist Intensity of Tariffs in Nineteenth-Century European Trade Policy', in J. P. Dormois and P. Lains (eds.), *Classical Trade Protectionism 1815–1914*. London and New York: Routledge.

5

Belgian Beers: Where History Meets Globalization

Damiaan Persyn, Johan F. M. Swinnen, and Stijn Vanormelingen[1]

> The great beers of Belgium are not its lagers. Its native brews are in other styles, and they offer an extraordinary variety, some so different from more conventional brews that at the initial encounter they are scarcely recognisable as beers. Yet they represent some of the oldest traditions of brewing in the Western world.
>
> (Michael Jackson, <http://www.beerhunter.com>)

Introduction

When you ask people around the world what they associate 'Belgium' with, some of them say 'Belgium?' Those who have heard of the country typically associate it with chocolates, Brussels or Bruges, the older ones with Eddy Merckx, the young ones with Kim Clijsters or Justine Henin and with . . . 'Belgian beers'. Beers have become one of the country's prime points of recognition and fame. In this age of globalization, Belgian beers, with their ancient histories, have become the true ambassadors of the country, increasingly to be found across the globe. The uniqueness of Belgian beers relates to some marked characteristics of the Belgian brewery sector and beer market which will be the focus of this chapter.

First, Belgium has a huge variety of wonderful beers, on a per capita basis higher than any other country. Many breweries have a history going back many centuries and continue to operate in traditional ways, but at the same

[1] We would like to thank Nele Vanbeneden and Leander Price for their useful comments on an earlier version of this chapter.

time are very much alive in this age of globalization. For example, brewery Roman, located near Oudenaarde, has been run by the same family since 1545 and has since grown into a mid-sized brewery with a yearly production of 9 million litres and 85 employees. Another example is the increasingly popular trappist beers which are still brewed by trappist monks, a tradition that dates back to the Middle Ages.

Second, at the same time, Belgium is also the home country of the largest brewing multinational in the world, Anheuser-Busch (AB) InBev. The company is not just the largest brewing company in the world, it is also the largest player in many countries in the world, including the United States, the UK, Canada, Belgium itself, and many others. Interestingly though, its roots can be traced back to a small Belgian brewery that started producing beer in the fourteenth century, and for six centuries it remained a relatively small local brewery. Its international expansion did not start until a mere 20 years ago, when it merged with another Belgian brewery. The brewery went on a global acquisition and merger spree which, in only two decades, led to the creation of the largest global beer company.

Third, despite this global image of Belgium as the country of beer, beer consumption in Belgium has actually been declining for decades. For over 30 years now, Belgians have been drinking less beer each year.

Fourth, Belgian breweries have developed export-oriented strategies to compensate for the declining consumption in their home markets. These strategies have included both the takeover of breweries in other countries and the actual export of Belgian beers. Around 1990 export accounted for around 10% of beer production and 90% was domestically consumed. This has changed drastically: in recent years, around half of all beer production is exported.

Fifth, as in many other countries, the number of breweries has fallen rapidly over the past century, with strong consolidation taking place. Interestingly, however, over the past decade the number of breweries has stabilized, and for the first time in more than a hundred years, the number has been increasing again in recent years—reflecting the growth of craft and microbrewery type innovations in the brewery sector. Despite, or as some would argue, because of, the globalization of the beer market with the domination of standard quality beers, alternative breweries catering to niche markets with special tastes are re-emerging.

In this chapter we will review, document, and explain each of these developments and, in doing so, analyse the most important economic dynamics and characteristics of Belgian beers. The chapter is organized as follows. The next section gives some background on the various beer types which are brewed and consumed today in Belgium, several of which are unique to the country. The following section gives an overview of the history and current structure of the consumer market for beer in Belgium. The international performance of Belgian beers is then analysed and the industrial organization of the Belgian brewery sector and its increasing concentration is discussed. Next, the recent history of the trappist beers and of the AB InBev brewery are considered in two case studies which illustrate the main trends in the Belgian brewery sector. A final section concludes.

Belgian Beers

The Belgian beer market was and, especially in terms of international comparison, still is, characterized by the production and consumption of an exceptionally large variety of different styles of beer. This section will provide a concise overview of the main types of beer. A basic classification of beer styles can be made according to the fermentation process, namely bottom, top, or spontaneous.

Bottom-fermented lager beers represent around 70% of total beer consumption in Belgium.[2] Some Belgian lagers are well known and appreciated internationally (such as Stella Artois, for example). Despite its current market domination, bottom fermentation is a relatively recent technology, at least from a historical perspective. Lager beers were introduced in the late nineteenth century, but experienced rapid growth afterwards. The yeast typically ferments at low temperatures (6–15 °C) and is collected at the bottom of the fermentation vessel, hence the term bottom fermentation. After fermentation, the resulting beer needs to be stored for up to 30 days before it is fit for consumption. The result of this process is lager beer.[3] Bottom fermentation tends to better convert sugars into alcohol and produces less esoteric side-products in the process, leading to beers which are characterized by a cleaner, less sweet, and crisp taste compared with top-fermented beers.

Typically Belgian is so-called 'table beer'—beer with a low-alcohol content of about 2%. Nowadays such beer tends to be bottom fermented, but it was traditionally consumed as a meal-time drink—even by children—dating from the days when water was still contaminated by bacteria which could be killed off during the brewing process.[4] Table beer remained popular for much of the nineteenth century, but it has lost market share to soft drinks in recent decades.

---

[2] The dominance of lager beers is even more pronounced in other countries, since lager beers accounted for 90% of worldwide beer consumption.

[3] The name stems from the German noun 'lager', which means 'storehouse', because of the longer storage time for this type of beer.

[4] Recently, a Belgian beer lovers' movement has launched the idea of providing pupils at school with table beer instead of soft drinks. They claim that table beer is a healthy alternative to soft drinks because it contains less sugar. The alcohol content is at such a low level that even 6-year-olds can drink it.

Top-fermenting yeasts have been used since ancient times for brewing. Yeasts are added to the fermentation vessels, which are kept at a higher temperature (18–28° C). During fermentation the yeast settles as foam on the top of the wort, where it was traditionally skimmed off by the brewer; hence the term top-fermented beers. The smaller market for top-fermented beers is highly geographically concentrated: Belgium, Germany, the USA, and the UK account for 55% of worldwide consumption (Euromonitor 2009b, 2010). In contrast to lager beers, bottom-fermented beers constitute a family of rather heterogeneous beers, and the wide variety in taste reflects significant differences in ingredients, yeasts, and brewing processes used.

An example of a typical Belgian top-fermented style is the 'Spéciale Belge' beer, which is somewhat similar in style to British Pale Ale, a spin-off of a competition set up in 1904 to help the industry cope with the strong new competition from imported lager beers. The winning recipe 'Belge du Faleau' was appreciated so much that it was copied with variations by many brewers. Some of the results survive today (Palm, De Coninck, Op-Ale). The characteristic haze and taste of top-fermented white beers (Hoegaarden, Blanche de Bruges, . . .) is due to the use of unmalted wheat and spices such as coriander and orange peel.

Unique to Belgium are spontaneously fermented beers. This fermentation technique is typical of the region around Brussels and is the survival of what is probably the oldest fermentation technique, which operates without cultivated yeast. Fermentation of Lambic beer relies on contamination of the wort in open vessels by a variety of wild yeasts, lactic acid bacteria, acetic acid bacteria, and enterobacteria, which are carried by the air and are specific to the region and the brewery dwellings. The lactic acid gives spontaneously fermented beers a rather distinctive, refreshing sour taste. Typical for spontaneously fermented beers is the use of unmalted wheat, the addition of fruits such as sour cherries in some varieties (Kriek), and the use of the 'méthode champenoise', where Lambic beers of different ages are mixed before bottling (Geuze). Mixed fermentation approaches are also used, where a mixture of top-fermenting yeasts strains and lactic acid bacteria is mostly used (Rodenbach, Liefmans).

Some Belgian beers stand out not so much because of a specific brewing technique, but rather due to their brewing tradition. Prime examples are the 'abbey beers' which originated in the Middle Ages when abbeys started to brew and sell beer to finance their needs. Nowadays, several of these ales are brewed in commercial breweries. Mostly production still happens in collaboration with the abbey, which has a say in the commercialization of the abbey beer. Moreover, royalties, which can be used for charity, are paid to the abbey.[5]

---

[5] For example, probably the most famous Belgian abbey beer internationally is Leffe. The Notre Dame de Leffe Abbey was founded in the twelfth century. The abbey and brewery were destroyed

The increasing popularity of abbey beers and their image as authentic and high quality products have recently led several brewers to introduce their own abbey beers. Often these new beers were named after a former abbey that no longer exists and without any involvement or approval by the abbey. The Union of Belgian Brewers reacted by introducing a certificate setting out specific requirements which have to be met in order for a beer to be labelled as an abbey beer.

Trappist beers are a special kind of abbey beers. These are top-fermented (often bottle-conditioned) ales which are still brewed in a monastery by trappist monks themselves or under their supervision. They account for 2.3% of the total beer market, lagers included. In the last section of this chapter, we document their strategy in the age of globalization.

Table 5.1 lists some well-known examples of beers from the largest Belgian breweries according to their style and whether they belong to the top, bottom, spontaneous, or mixed fermentation group. Together these breweries and brands represent a large share of the total Belgian market, but they do not reflect the large variety of beers that exist on the market: Hilde Deweer (2007) counted 756 different beers which are brewed and sold commercially in Belgium in 2007, excluding special-occasion brews and varieties which differ only in packaging or name (so-called 'label beers').

Beer Consumption in Belgium

By world standards, Belgium is a major beer producer with a long history and an extensive culture of beer drinking. Around 1900, Belgium was character-ized by an exceptionally high beer consumption level of more than 200 litres per capita, more than double the per capita consumption in the UK and Germany at that time (Van der Hallen 2009). As noted by Van der Hallen, among the reasons for this historically high level of beer consumption in Belgium were the comparatively low taxes on beer, the absence or high price of alternatives beverages such as imported wine, and government policy aimed at discouraging the consumption of distilled beverages. Figure 5.1 shows the evolution of total beer consumption in Belgium and consumption per capita.

Since 1900 there has been a downward trend in total consumption, with the exception of a revival in beer consumption after World War II. Beer consump-tion started to fall again in the mid-1970s, namely from over 1.3 billion litres

during the French Revolution. In the twentieth century, the abbey was reopened. Beer production continued after World War II in collaboration with Lootvoet brewery, which was acquired by Interbrew, later to become AB InBev. Nowadays, Leffe is brewed at the AB InBev brewery in Leuven, but AB InBev still pays royalties to the Leffe Abbey.

Table 5.1. Belgian beer brands of the major Belgian breweries, by style

Fermentation	Type	AB InBev	Alken-Maes (Heineken)	Haacht	Duvel Moortgat	Palm
Bottom	Lager	Jupiler Stella	Maes Cristal	Primus Adler	Bel pils Vedett	Bock pils Estaminet
	Table beer	Piedboeuf	Maes Nature	Blonde		
	Non-alcoholic	Jupiler N.A.	Tourtel	Star		
Top	Abbey	Leffe	Grimbergen Ciney	Tongerlo	Maredsous	Steenbrugge
	White beer	Hoegaarden	Brugs Witbier	Witbier Haacht	Vedett Extra White	Steenbrugge Wit
	Amber ale	Vieux Temps		Spéciale 1900		Palm
	Blonde ale	Julius	Judas Hapkin	Keizer Karel	Duvel La Chouffe	Brugge Tripel
	Non-alcoholic					Palm Green
Spontaneous	Lambic-based	Belle-Vue[1]	Mort Subite[2]			Boon
Mixed	Brown ale				Liefmans	
	Red ale					Rodenbach

Notes: [1] Only one of the varieties of beers sold under the name 'Belle-Vue' can be categorized as a spontaneously fermented beer, namely the rare 'Belle-Vue Sélection Lambic'.
[2] Only a subset of the varieties of beers sold under the name Mort Subite are of spontaneous fermentation, such as, for example, the Mort Subite Oude Geuze, Oude Kriek, Faro, and Witte Lambik beers.

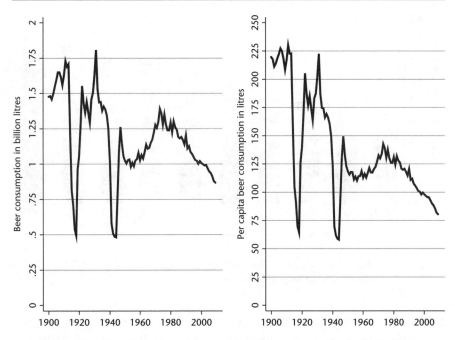

Figure 5.1. Total and per capita beer consumption in Belgium, 1900–2007
Source: Union of Belgian Brewers and Mitchell (2007).

to only 870 million litres in 2009, a decrease of over 30% over three decades. The fall in beer consumption has been even more pronounced on a per capita basis, since beer's decreasing popularity was initially compensated by population growth. By 2004, Belgium ranked seventh in the list of countries by per capita beer consumption, with an average consumption of 93 litres per capita (Kirin Holdings Company 2005). Frequently cited explanations for falling beer sales include a lower tolerance for alcohol (ab)use and a shift in consumer preferences to sweeter drinks. Sales of soft drinks have more than doubled over the same period and beer has lost its number one position in the ranking of most sold beverage to soft drinks and bottled water since the 1980s, as can be seen from Figure 5.2. The shift towards soft drinks has coincided with the fading tradition of drinking beer with a low alcohol content during meals, and has been linked with an increase in the susceptibility to breast cancer of youngsters (Janssens et al. 1999). The change in consumer preferences has even led breweries to reduce the bitterness of their beers. For example, InBev admitted in 2004 to having changed the composition of the hops added to their lagers to sweeten the taste (Hinderyckx and Kamoen 2008). Also contributing to the decline is a change in consumer habits and preferences regarding the location of consumption: over the years, on-trade sales, i.e. sales through

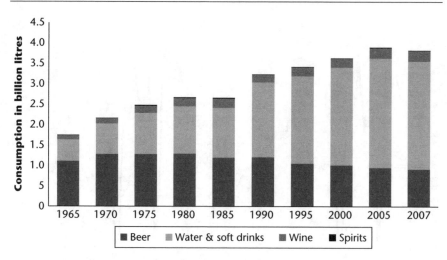

Figure 5.2. Consumption of beverages in Belgium, 1965–2007
Source: Union of Belgian Brewers.

bars and restaurants, have decreased substantially, while the rise in off-trade sales, i.e. sales through supermarkets and shops, has not compensated for these sales losses. In 2008, on-trade sales accounted for 53% of total volume sold, down from 73% at the beginning of the 1990s.

Standard lagers make up the bulk of the Belgian beer market. In 2006, lagers held a market share of around 70%. However, total sales of lager beers in Belgium have been declining over the years. The rest of the beer market is dominated by top-fermented beers. The most important types and their respective market shares are displayed in Figure 5.3.[6] The evolution of consumption is displayed in Figure 5.4. For expositional reasons, the left axis measures non-lager beer consumption, while the right axis measures consumption of lager beers.

Abbey beers are the most popular next to standard lagers. As Figure 5.4 shows, despite their traditional approach, trappist beers, together with abbey beers, have seen the strongest growth among Belgian beers in terms of domestic consumption. Total volume sales of abbey and trappist beers have more than doubled over the period to almost 100 million litres, in spite of a shrinking beer market.

Wheat-based white beers rank third, with approximately 5% of the market. The 'amber ales' category mainly contains top-fermented beers of the 'Spéciale Belge' variety. Turning to the evolution of sales, the underperformance of wheat beers and amber ales stands out. Over a period of 15 years, sales of

---

[6] For expositional reasons, we excluded standard lagers from the bar chart.

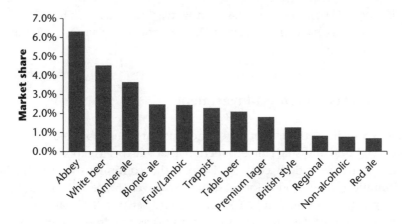

Figure 5.3. Market share of non-lager Belgian beers, 2003
Source: Union of Belgian Brewers.

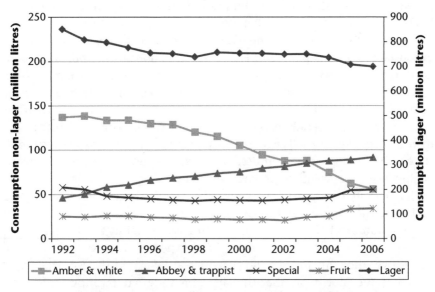

Figure 5.4. Evolution of consumption of different types of beers
Source: Union of Belgian Brewers.

white beers and amber ales dropped by more than 50% due to an ageing consumer base, combined with increasing competition from abbey-style beers (both abbey beers and trappist beers). Spontaneous fermentation beers, such as fruit beers and other lambic-based beers, make up around 2.4% of the total beer market. The once very popular low-alcohol table beers hold a market share of only 2%. Special beers[7] have on aggregate seen a rise in their sales over recent years, as have fruit beers, reflecting consumer tastes switching to sweeter products.

Trade and Foreign Direct Investment

Figure 5.5 displays the evolution of the amount of beer brewed in Belgium since 1900 and the share of production that has been exported since the middle of the twentieth century. Despite the continuous decline in beer consumption, total production has increased over the period thanks to the growing export performance of Belgian beers. Between 1975 and 1995, exports rose by approximately the same amount as the drop in consumption, leaving total production fairly stable. Over the past 15 years, exports have soared, compensating for more of the decline in domestic consumption. Consequently, the Belgian brewery sector has changed from a sector focused on production for domestic consumption towards an export-oriented sector. In 2009, almost 60% of production was exported, compared to less than 20% at the beginning of the 1990s.[8] The recent evolution of exports to the six largest export destinations is plotted in Figure 5.6. Traditionally, the bulk of exports went to neighbouring countries—France, the Netherlands, and Germany—but in recent years exports to the USA have risen exponentially, reflecting increased demand by American consumers for specialty beers (Tremblay and Tremblay 2005). Over the last decade, exports to the USA have risen tremendously from a mere 2 million litres in 2005 to over 130 million litres in 2009. As a result, the US is now the third largest export destination for Belgian beer, leaving Germany behind. A similar evolution can be observed for exports to Canada.

The majority of exports are accounted for by the largest breweries such as AB InBev. The top five exporting Belgian breweries accounted for 78.5% of the export volume in 1995, and this number increased slightly to 79% in 2009. In terms of the value of exports, the top five export share rose from 62.5% to 68.7% over the same time period. The increasing export share of the largest breweries does not imply that the larger breweries are pushing the smaller ones out of the export market. Figure 5.7 compares the export growth of the top five exporters, the sixth up to twentieth ranked exporters, and the remaining smaller exporters. The figure clearly shows that the largest breweries were

---

[7] This category is a collection of other beer types such as British-style beers and blonde or brown ales.

[8] Imported beers have always been a small minority of the market, since foreign brands have difficulty entering the Belgian market, although their volume has been increasing over the last decade. In 2009 imported brands made up only 10% of total consumption (90 million litres) in Belgium.

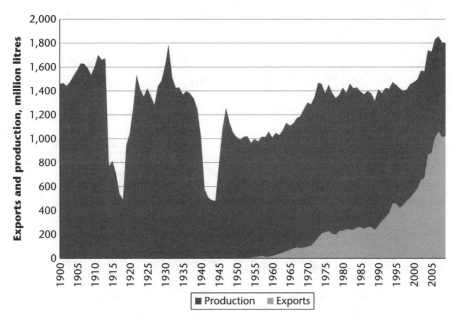

Figure 5.5. Belgian beer production, 1900–2009
Source: Union of Belgian Brewers.

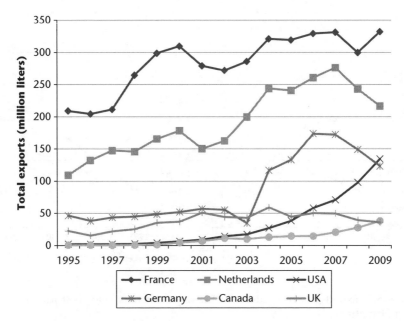

Figure 5.6. Exports of Belgian beers by main destination countries, 1995–2009
Source: COMEXT, Eurostat.

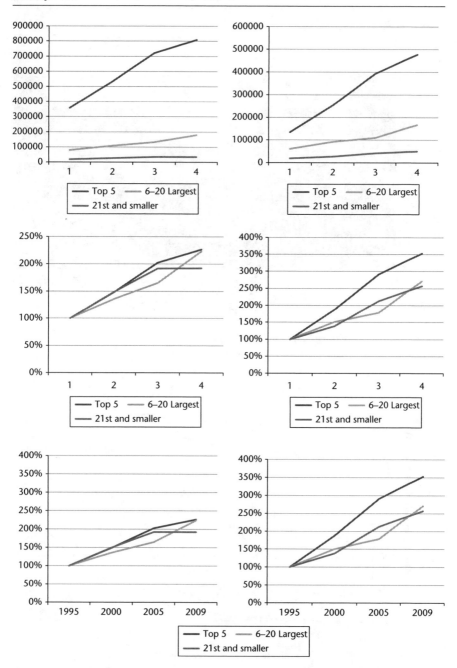

Figure 5.7. Export growth for different brewery sizes, by volume (left panel) and by revenue (right panel)

Source: Nationale Bank België, COMEXT.

able to significantly increase their export volume between 1995 and 2009 (+125% for the top five exporters); but the medium-sized and smaller exporters followed suit, recording increases of 92% and 123% respectively. The fact that the increase in the market share of the largest exporters is more marked in revenue terms indicates that larger breweries are increasingly successful at charging higher prices for their products. But the difference in pricing between the larger and smaller exporters remains large: in 2009 the average price per litre of exported beer was 1.48 euros for the small exporters (twenty-first ranked and smaller), 0.93 euros for medium-sized exporters (sixth to twenty-first ranked exporters), and 0.59 euros for the top five exporters. Smaller breweries sell products which are on average more differentiated (allowing breweries to charge higher markups) and of a higher quality. Taken together, these figures clearly show that large and small Belgian breweries alike are benefiting from the increased worldwide demand for Belgian beers.

An illustrative example of the increasing popularity of Belgian beers throughout the world in general and in the United States in particular, is the export performance of the Duvel Moortgat brewery. This mid-sized brewery, founded in 1871, produces around 60 million litres of specialty beers annually. Its main brand is the luxury strong blond ale called Duvel,[9] with an alcohol percentage of 8.5%. The brewery has witnessed a remarkable increase in its international sales over the last decade, with double-digit yearly growth rates, leading to a turnover in international markets which is 600% higher compared with ten years ago. The brewer received an award as the best-performing Flemish exporter in 2006 for its international expansion. The largest increase has been realized in the United States, where the brewer benefited from American consumers' switch to degustation beers. Nowadays the company realizes a turnover of 12.5 million euros on the US market, representing 11% of total turnover, compared with a mere 500,000 euros ten years ago.[10]

Several smaller breweries have also developed specific export strategies. The family-owned brewery 'De Troch' from Wambeek near Brussels, for example, has been brewing lambic-based beers since the eighteenth century. The brewery, with a production capacity of only 600,000 litres, has survived the large consolidation movement in this subsector by diversifying into distinctively sweet lambic-derived fruit beers, specifically targeting export markets. Exports represented 85% of this brewery's revenue in 2010. A different example is the 'Dolle Brouwers' brewery located near Diksmuide in West Flanders. This brewer of specialty beers realizes 45% of its turnover through exports, but voluntarily restricts its sales to a selection of foreign distributors in order to

---

[9] 'Duvel' is Flemish for 'Devil'.
[10] Some of the US sales are accounted for by the 100% subsidiary Brewery Ommegang, located in Cooperstown, New York. The beers brewed in Cooperstown are marketed as Belgian beers.

Table 5.2. Market shares of local and foreign producers on the Belgian beer market

Company	Market share 2004	Market share 2007
AB–InBev (mainly through Inbev)	55.3%	55.0%
Alken-Maes (owned by Heineken)	13.6%	13.9%
Brouwerij Haacht nv	3.1%	3.2%
Duvel Moortgat nv	2.1%	2.2%
Brouwerij Palm nv	2.4%	2.0%
Others	10.8%	11.1%
Private label	12.7%	12.6%
Total	100.0%	100.0%

Source: Adapted from Euromonitor (2009a).

guarantee brand reputation and adequate sales service. The company recently turned down an offer to export its products to Japan for this very reason.

The Industrial Organization of the Belgian Brewery Sector

The Belgian beer market is dominated by AB InBev. In 2007, the brewer held a market share of 55%, as shown in Table 5.2. This dominance is mainly a result of the popularity of its lager brand Jupiler,[11] which on its own accounts for about one-third of total beer sales in Belgium. In the submarket of Belgian ales (including trappist and abbey beers), the dominance of AB InBev is less pronounced. The second largest brewer active in the Belgian market is Heineken, which recently acquired the Alken-Maes brewery (previously owned by Scottish and Newcastle). Alken-Maes was the result of a merger between two old Belgian breweries and holds 13.9% of the Belgian beer market. The third largest brewery is Haacht, which is now the largest fully Belgian owned beer producer. Its market share is only 3.2%, however. The other beer producers each have a market share of below 3% in the total beer market.

Given these market shares, it is safe to state that the Belgian beer market is characterized by heavy concentration. The three largest breweries hold 72% of the market and one company, AB InBev, clearly dominates. The Herfindahl-Hirschman index is around 3,300, well above the cut-off value of 1,800 which distinguishes moderately from heavily concentrated markets according to US merger guidelines.

Although the market is highly concentrated, the number of available varieties remains high. One reason for this might be that large brewers attempt to brew a portfolio of beers in the most important styles. In Table 5.1 the largest

[11] While Jupiler is AB InBev's top brand in Belgium, the most exported lager beer is Stella Artois. A standard lager in Belgium, with a market share of 7%, Stella Artois is branded as a premium lager abroad. For example, Stella Artois has been promoted for years in the UK with the slogan 'Reassuringly Expensive'.

Belgian brewers and a non-exhaustive list of their different brands is displayed, classified by the different types of beers (submarkets). Clearly, the largest brewers are active in multiple submarkets, except for the submarket for regional and trappist beers, for obvious reasons. While trying to cover the most interesting submarkets, the larger breweries go to great lengths to preserve the image of a regional quality product. This is obvious in the case of those abbey beers which are brewed not in abbeys but in commercial breweries, and for which the breweries attempt to create an image of authenticity. Examples of large breweries producing a wide array of varieties are the Palm and Duvel Moortgat breweries, which recently purchased the Rodenbach and Liefmans breweries that produce red and brown ales with a very specific traditional production process involving mixed fermentation, blending, and year-long maturation in oak casks. Because of the specificity of the production process of these beers and their regional characteristics, it would have been undesirable (and probably even technically impossible) for Palm or Duvel Moortgat to centralize the production of these beers in their main breweries. It can therefore be said that, at least in these cases, the acquisitions actually saved the various brands of Liefmans and Rodenbach from disappearing altogether. Similarly, AB InBev recently had to cancel plans to move production of the Hoegaarden white beer from the village of Hoegaarden because it turned out to be difficult to reproduce the Hoegaarden beer in Jupille, and also because consumers, employees, and the Hoegaarden community strongly objected.

A second reason for the existence of a large variety of Belgian beers, despite the heavy concentration of the market, is the large number of small-scale craft breweries. As can be seen from Table 5.3, almost 95% of all Belgian breweries produce less than 10 million litres per year. Together, they make up only 7% of total production. The number of varieties of beers is larger still, since most craft breweries produce multiple varieties. The finding of a dual market structure, where a large number of small breweries coexist next to a small number of large breweries that account for the vast majority of production, mimics the

Table 5.3. Size distribution of Belgian breweries

Size Class (million litres)	No. firms		Production (million litres)	
	Percentage	Cumulative Percentage	Percentage	Cumulative Percentage
< 1	72.1%	72.1%	0.7%	0.7%
1 –< 10	22.5%	94.6%	6.3%	7.0%
10 –< 100	1.8%	96.4%	6.1%	13.1%
100+	3.6%	100%	86.9%	100%

Source: Zythos; Caldéron (2009); own calculations and enquiries.

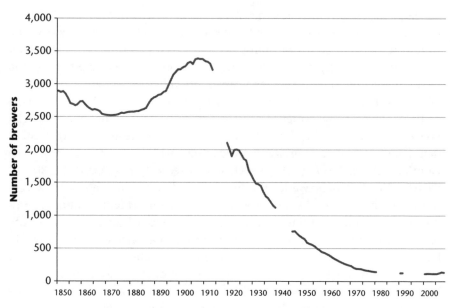

Figure 5.8. Number of Belgian brewers, 1850–2006
Source: Union of Belgian Brewers.

market structure found in other countries. For example in 2000, Anheuser-Busch, Miller, and Coors together held a market share of 95% of the US beer market, while the rest of the market was served by around 1,400 small-scale beer producers (Adams 2006).

Figure 5.8 illustrates how the number of breweries increased during the latter part of the nineteenth century, but then declined dramatically throughout the twentieth century. Around 1900, there existed over 3,300 breweries in Belgium, producing 1.6 billion litres of beer. Since then, the number of breweries has declined rapidly, while the survivors have increased the scale of their operations considerably. There were 1,120 breweries remaining in 1940, but their number dwindled to about 100 in 1980. Since the 1990s, the number has stabilized. Recently, the number of breweries has been increasing again, as can be seen in Figure 5.9, which shows the evolution of the number of active breweries since 1988, together with the yearly number of exits and entries.

Several hypotheses have been proposed to explain the large consolidation in the beer market, not only in Belgium but also in other countries (Tremblay and Tremblay 2005). One important factor is technological progress which leads to greater economies of scale, mainly due to automation of the beer production process and the acceleration of packaging (Adams 2006). A second factor is that more effective advertising can explain (at least part of) the increased concentration in a consumer product industry such as the beer

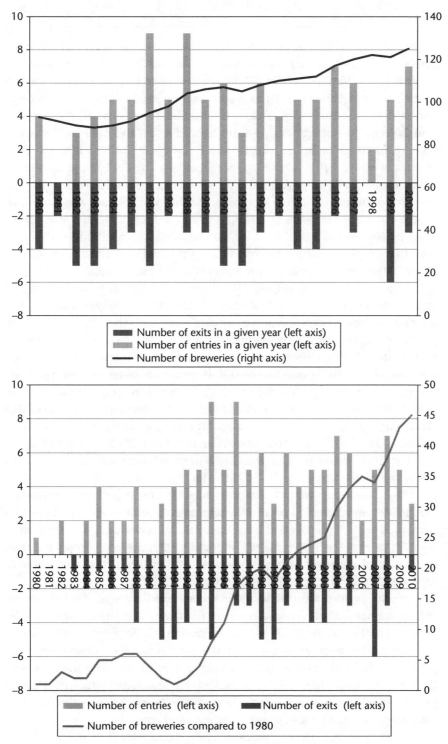

Figure 5.9. Number of Belgian brewers, 1988–2008

Source: Zythos.

sector (Sutton 1991; George 2009). The following paragraphs provide more detail about the causes of the consolidation wave in the Belgian beer industry.

According to Van der Hallen (2009), the decline in the number of breweries in the first part of the twentieth century was triggered by the introduction of bottom-fermented beers in Belgium. Wielemans-Ceuppens was the first Belgian brewery to start producing lager beer in 1884, followed by the Artois brewery and the Haacht brewery. However, it was not until the interwar years that there was a real breakthrough for lager beers in Belgium, an evolution which may have been triggered by the German occupation, which exposed Belgian consumers to lager. Moreover, World War I forced the closure of a large number of breweries, as copper from the brewing kettles was confiscated by the Germans and used for ammunition. The retribution payments after the armistice enabled brewers to recover some of their setup costs and invest in bottom-fermentation breweries (Van der Hallen 2009).

During the interwar period, lager beers were considered to be at the high end of the consumption market. Not only did they have a longer shelf life, but their production process was also more controlled such that the quality of the product could be guaranteed. In contrast, due to older machinery and a higher fermentation temperature, the quality and taste of top-fermented beers varied considerably. A final reason for the shift in consumer tastes to lagers was their different appearance. While top-fermented beers were quite turbid in those days, bottom-fermented beers had a bright, shiny, and clean appearance. This was an important selling point for lager breweries, as transparent glasses were introduced in the nineteenth century (Van der Hallen 2009). For example, the brewery Alken named its lager beer Cristal to stress its (crystal-) clear look. Also the name Stella Artois—stella is Latin for 'star'—was chosen to stress its sparkling appearance when it was introduced in the 1920s. All these factors led the bottom-fermented beers to be seen as a superior product and the top-fermented beers to be seen as a product for the lower-class worker. Consequently, sales of lager beers soared, especially when its price dropped due to technological improvements. The market share of lagers rose from a low of 15% after World War I to a high of 70% after World War II.

Typically, brewers needed to incur higher fixed costs in the brewing of bottom-fermented beers compared to top-fermented beers, since lagers require artificial cooling during the fermentation and throughout the longer maturation time. Moreover, in reaction to the introduction of lager beers, top-fermentation breweries invested in new equipment to increase the quality of their brews. Both these factors increased the minimum efficient scale of production in the beer sector and caused smaller breweries to exit the market, since they were not be able to recover their fixed costs.

The concentration trend continued after World War II as the minimum efficient scale of breweries continued to increase. For example, Kerkvliet et al.

(1998) find that technological change considerably increased the minimum efficient scale of operation in the US brewing industry between 1960 and 1990. More effective and automated control of the brewing, fermenting, and conditioning process, automated canning and bottling techniques, and more effective distribution through high capacity trucks and improved road networks all contributed to larger economies of scale (Gourvish 1994).

Next to increases in minimum efficient scale, higher advertising effectiveness has been proposed as an explanation for the rising concentration since World War II (Tremblay and Tremblay 2005). Over time, advertising possibilities increased substantially, thereby ameliorating the effectiveness of promotional activities, which led to an escalation of sunk advertising costs. Consequently, only a few breweries were sufficiently large to earn back the costs of advertising, resulting in a more and more concentrated market structure. For example, George (2009) finds that increases in television penetration are associated with the decline of local breweries in the USA. Together with the observation that the introduction of national television increased returns to advertising, this may explain the observed market concentration. Note that commercial television started only at the end of the 1980s in Belgium. Before that, there were no opportunities to advertise on national television networks. However, advertising possibilities in other media such as newspapers, billboards, as well as in movie theatres increased considerably. Note that this theory can serve as an explanation for the observed 'dual' structure in the Belgian beer market, namely very high concentration in the lager submarket and a less concentrated market structure in the market for top-fermented beers. Top-fermented beers are highly differentiated due to the possible addition of different kinds of ingredients and, as a result, each brewery's beer definitely has a taste of its own (Van der Hallen 2009). Lager beers, on the other hand, are much more homogeneous products. The likelihood of an escalation in endogenous sunk costs depends crucially on how much rival market share a firm can capture by advertising (Sutton 1991) and as such on the homogeneity of the market. Consequently, an escalation of advertising spending was more likely to take place in the lager segment than in the top-fermentation segment, where each brand can serve a niche market.

The consolidation wave did not only materialize through the exit of small inefficient breweries. Mergers and acquisitions between larger players also played an important role. An example of this is the story of the Wielemans-Ceuppens brewery. In 1930 this Brussels-based brewery constructed the single largest brewing site in Europe, and retained market leadership for many years. In 1978 the Artois brewery started to accumulate shares in the company and took over the administration. In 1980 the Wielemans-Ceuppens brewery was liquidated and by 1988 all its brands had disappeared completely from the market.

Another example is the history of the spontaneously fermented lambic-based beers brewed in the Brussels area. At the beginning of the twentieth century, these beers were the standard beverage in the wider Brussels area, with hundreds of active breweries. The combined shifts in consumer taste and market structure during the twentieth century caused the lambic-style beers to disappear almost completely, with only a handful of breweries surviving today. The remaining varieties now enjoy a 'Traditional Speciality Guaranteed' status in the EU and are increasingly enjoyed by beer lovers worldwide, in spite of (or maybe because of) the fact that the most authentic of these beers are an acquired taste.

Recently, the number of active breweries in Belgium has stabilized and has even started to increase. Figure 5.9 shows the evolution of the number of active brewers since 1988, and firm creation and destruction in each year. At first sight, a tentative conclusion would be that a revival of small-scale breweries is taking place, comparable to the enormous increase in craft breweries in the USA since the end of the 1980s. For example, the number of small-scale brewers in the USA soared from 461 in 1993 to over 1,500 in 2001 (Tremblay and Tremblay 2005). However, note that the number of breweries in Belgium is currently around 130 for a total population of 10.5 million people, roughly 12 breweries per million inhabitants. This compares with 1,500 breweries in the USA for a population of 300 million—around five breweries per million inhabitants—and a slightly lower beer consumption per capita, leading to the conclusion that, even without a substantial revival of small-scale brewers, the number of breweries in Belgium is already at a substantially higher level. Consequently, it is unclear whether one should expect the same kind of growth in the number of Belgian brewers as has been observed in the USA in recent decades.

Where History Meets Globalization: Two Cases

In this section, we present two very different cases of Belgian beers with a long, even ancient, history and how they have dealt with, and benefited from, the process of globalization.

AB InBev

Leuven, a small city near Brussels, hosts the headquarters of the world's largest brewer, AB InBev.[12] The roots of AB InBev date back to Brewery Den Hoorn for which tax records exist since the year 1366 and which later became the

---

[12] Some of its activities were moved to a new office in New York after the acquisition of Anheuser-Busch in 2008.

brewery Artois. It was here that the famous lager Stella Artois was launched in the 1920 and its logo still refers to the ancient brewery.[13] Shortly after the launch of Stella Artois, the Artois breweries became the largest beer producer in Belgium and remained so for the next 50 years.[14]

In 1987, the two largest Belgian breweries (breweries Artois and Piedboeuf) merged and the new company was called Interbrew. This was the start of a rapid external expansion, first through acquisitions in Belgium, such as of breweries De Kluis and Belle-Vue, afterwards through international acquisitions of a series of East European breweries in the 1990s, the Canadian brewer Labatt in 1995, and Bass Breweries in the UK in 2000. As a result of the 2004 merger with the Brazilian brewer AmBev, a new company, InBev, was created, at the time the largest brewer in the world. A provisional final step in the expansion process was taken in 2008 with the acquisition of the market leader in the United States and the fourth largest brewer in the world, Anheuser-Busch. With a price tag of over 50 billion dollars, the takeover was the largest acquisition ever by a consumer product producer (Riepl 2009). The acquisition resulted in a company that produced around 36.5 billion litres of beer worldwide, about one-quarter of the total beer consumption in the world.

In a time span of only twenty years, the company has grown from two local Belgian breweries, Artois and Piedboef, to become to AB InBev, by far the largest brewer in the world. The expansion occurred through a continuous process of foreign acquisitions. As a result, the portfolio of AB InBev consists nowadays of more than 200 brands, of which only a small number are 'Belgian beers'. The most popular Belgian brand internationally, Stella Artois, accounted in 2007 for only 3.6% of InBev's total beer volume (Riepl 2009). Consequently, the success of AB InBev has had little to do with the superior quality of Belgian beers, as many Belgians like to think, but more with the strategic decisions and choices of the shareholders and management.

The company strategy of AB InBev is to keep local beers in each country. In addition to these local brands, AB InBev holds a number of so-called global

---

[13] The Stella Artois logo shows a horn ('Den Hoorn' is Dutch for 'The Horn') together with the year 1366.

[14] The merger foundations were preceded many years earlier by a secret agreement in 1971 between Artois breweries and Piedboeuf breweries, one of its main Belgian rivals and producer of the lager beer 'Jupiler'. Officially they founded a new company to acquire an almost bankrupt brewery. However, they also secretly swapped company shares. Since, at the time, Stella Artois had a production volume of 350 million litres compared to 70 million litres for Jupiler, the ratio at which the swap was executed was 1/8 for the Piedboeuf Breweries and 7/8 for Artois Breweries. (Riepl 2009: 24) After the agreement, Stella Artois saw its market share decline every year, while sales of Jupiler boomed and by the end of the 1970s, Jupiler had taken the lead in the Belgian beer market. To fulfil demand, Piedboeuf was looking for extra production capacity and Piedboeuf and Artois started to secretly brew Jupiler at the Artois breweries in Leuven. Jupiler was brewed under the codename 'Lager', after which it was transported to Piedboeuf breweries to be bottled. Only in 1987 did the merger between Piedboeuf and Artois become official and it was only then that employees of each brewer discovered that they had been working for years for the same company.

brands which are promoted worldwide as premium brands and use the distribution networks of the local brands to gain market share. The global brands are Becks, Budweiser, and Stella Artois,[15] of which only the latter is a Belgian beer. Besides these global brands, there exist two so-called multi-country brands, Hoegaarden and Leffe, both Belgian beers, which are also sold internationally, but mainly in Europe and North America. Nowadays AB InBev concentrates the production of Belgian beers[16] in two large production facilities in Leuven and Jupille, the locations of the founding breweries Artois and Piedboeuf, and two smaller breweries.[17] Since one of the AB InBev global brands and some multi-country brands (even foreign brands) are brewed in Belgium, a large share of total exports of Belgian beers is accounted for by AB InBev, although their market share in the total AB InBev portfolio remains limited.

Trappist Beers

A totally different case of Belgian beers with a long history that have been successful in a globalizing world are the trappist beers. Trappist beers are probably the most famous type of Belgian beer and regularly obtain top scores in international competitions. While there are many beers associated with abbeys, there are only seven real 'trappist beers', six of which are Belgian. The brewing and commercialization of these beers is still controlled by trappist monks. The Trappist order is a branch of the Cistercians and originated in the seventeenth century in the Abbey of La Trappe, located in Normandy. The order began as a reform movement in reaction to a relaxation of practices in many Cistercian monasteries.[18] Trappist monks live by the strict rule of St Benedictus, which states:

> for then are they truly monastics when they live by the labor of their hands, as did our Fathers and the Apostles (Chapter 48, Rule of St. Benedict)

Consequently, Trappist monks produced different kinds of goods ranging from cheese to clothing which were sold to generate income in order that the monasteries should be self-sufficient. One of these products was beer. The French Revolution and its aftermath destroyed most of the monasteries in

---

[15] Note that although Stella Artois is internationally advertised as a premium lager, it is considered to be a standard lager in Belgium.

[16] Part of the Stella Artois production is also brewed under licence in the UK.

[17] One of these smaller facilities is the Hoegaarden brewery. In 2005, InBev wanted to close the brewery and move production of the Hoegaarden white beer to the larger plant in Jupille, which provoked a storm of protest in Belgium. However, Jupille was not able match the taste and quality of the beers brewed in Hoegaarden. Together with a sudden increase in popularity of Jupiler in the Netherlands and consequent capacity problems in the Jupille brewery, InBev revoked its decision and kept the production of Hoegaarden at its original location.

[18] The official name of the order is Order of Cistercians of the Strict Observance, but they are mostly referred to as the Trappist order after the founding Abbey of La Trappe.

Table 5.4. Trappist breweries and their production volume

Trappist Monastery	Brand	Production volume (thousand litres)
Abdij der Trappisten Westmalle	Westmalle	12,000
Abbaye Notre Dame de Scourmont	Chimay	12,300
Abbaye Notre Dame d'Orval	Orval	4,500
Abbaye Notre Dame de Saint Remy	Rochefort	1,800
Abdij van Westvleteren	Westvleteren	475
Sint-Benedictusabdij Achel	Achel	450
Abdij Onze Lieve Vrouw van Koningshoeven (The Netherlands)	La Trappe	14,500

Source: Van den Steen (2003).

Belgium and most of today's abbeys were founded or restored in the nineteenth century or even later. With the establishment of the new monasteries, the brewing of trappist beers restarted. According to the official website of the Trappist order,[19] there currently exist 169 monasteries worldwide (100 for monks, 69 for nuns) with around 2,500 monks and 1,800 nuns. However, only seven of them house active beer breweries, six of them located in Belgium and one in the Netherlands (Brewery De Koningshoeven). The seven breweries are listed in Table 5.4. The oldest trappist brewery that still operates today is Westmalle, which opened its doors in 1836. The most recent is the Achel brewery,[20] introducing the seventh trappist beer in 1998.

Over the years, trappist beers have gained a reputation of being high quality, authentic products. As a consequence, commercial breweries tried to profit from this brand image by introducing beers labelled trappist. To preserve the authenticity of the trappist beers, the International Trappist Association was founded in 1997. The association imposes strict rules on using the label 'Authentic Trappist Product', which are as follows:[21]

1. Products which carry this label are produced within the walls of the monastery or in vicinity of the monastery.

2. The monastic community determines the policies and provides the means of production. The whole process of production must clearly evidence the indisputable bond of subsidiarity, with the monastery benefiting from the production, and must be in accordance with the business practices proper to a monastic way of life.

3. The profits are primarily intended to provide for the needs of the community or for social services.

---

[19] <http://www.ocso.org>.
[20] Although today's trappist beer was only introduced in 1998, the Abbey of Saint Benedict in Achel had previously housed a brewery until the Germans dismantled it during World War I.
[21] See the International Trappist Association, <http://www.trappist.be>.

These rules were enforced in 1999 against the Koningshoeven Abbey which produces the La Trappe trappist beer, after it sold its brewery to the commercial Bavaria brewery. The brewery, in spite of being one of the founding members, was expelled from the International Trappist Association and was denied the right to use the official trappist logo. A settlement was agreed in 2005 which again allowed La Trappe to carry the official trappist logo, on condition that the monks should once again be involved in the brewing process, working several hours per day.

The production of the different trappist breweries is displayed in Table 5.4. The number of litres brewed ranges from approximately 500,000 litres in the Achel and Westvleteren breweries to more than 12 million litres in the breweries of Westmalle and Orval. The most popular trappist beer, Westmalle, has a market share of 1% of the total Belgian beer market. Among the trappist beers, Westvleteren stands out in terms of its strategy in the globalized world. The Abbey of Westvleteren restricts its sales strictly to the level required to sustain the monastery. The beer is only sold at the abbey gate. Buyers are not allowed to resell the beer and there are strict limits as to the amount which can be bought per individual in a certain span of time. When the 'Westvleteren 12' variety was rated 'the best beer in the world' by Ratebeer.com in 2005, this caused a global search for this trappist beer, much to the discontent of the monks. They refused to increase their production or prices. Since 2006 an interested buyer has to go to the lengths of obtaining an appointment with the abbey before being allowed to purchase some crates of the precious beer at the abbey gates.

Conclusion

This chapter has given an overview of the past and current trends in the Belgian beer market. As in other traditionally beer-loving European countries, Belgian domestic consumption has been steadily declining due to changing consumer preferences and slowing population growth. Changes in technology and the market structure during the last century have led to a large consolidation movement, with only about one hundred active breweries remaining today.

In spite of this, in international comparisons the Belgian brewery sector and beer market are still characterized by the production and consumption of an exceptionally large variety of beers, many of which are of styles which are unique to the country. Some prime examples of this are the Lambic-based beers of spontaneous fermentation, the renowned trappist beers, traditional beers of mixed fermentation, and the many specialty and abbey beers which are produced by both large and small breweries.

In recent years Belgian breweries have succeeded in compensating for the decline in domestic demand by increasing exports. Total production is increasing as both century-old family-owned breweries, small newly founded breweries, and the larger breweries benefit from the increasing international demand for Belgian beers.

Increasing domestic and foreign awareness of the unique position of Belgian beers may have resulted in a halt in the secular decline in the number of producers and varieties, and they may even be increasing again.

References

Adams, W. J. (2006). 'Beer in Germany and the United States'. *Journal of Economic Perspectives*, 20/1: 189–205.

Caldéron, A. (2009). *Bieren en Brouwerijen van België*. Ghent: Mens en Cultuur Uitgevers.

Cistercian Order of the Strict Observance, official website; <http://www.ocso.org> (accessed 5 February 2010).

Deweer, H. (2007). *All Belgian Beers, Les Bières Belges, Alle Belgische Bieren*. Oostkamp: Stichting Kunstboek.

Euromonitor (2009a). *Beer in Belgium*. Retrieved from <http://www.portal.euromonitor.com>.

—— (2009b). *Global Alcoholic Drinks: Beer—Opportunities in Niche Categories*. Retrieved from <http://www.portal.euromonitor.com>.

—— (2010). *Strategies for Growth in an Increasingly Consolidated Global Beer Market*. Retrieved from <http://www.portal.euromonitor.com>.

George, L. M. (2009). 'National Television and the Market for Local Products: The Case of Beer'. *The Journal of Industrial Economics*, 57/1: 85–111.

Gourvish, T. R. (1994). 'Economics of Brewing, Theory and Practice: Concentration and Technological Change in the USA, UK and West Germany since 1945'. *Business and Economic History*, 23/1: 253–61.

Hinderyckx, A., and J. Kamoen (2008). *Artikel 81 EG-verdrag: Toepassing op brouwerijcontracten*. Ghent: Story Publishers.

Jackson, M. (2010). *Beer Hunter*. <http://www.beerhunter.com/documents/19133-000213.html>. Accessed 29 August 2010.

Janssens, J. P., N. Shapira, P. Debeuf, L. Michiels, R. Putman, L. Bruckers, D. Renard, and G. Molenberghs (1999). 'Effect of Soft Drink and Table Beer Consumption on Insulin Response in Normal Teenagers and Carbohydrate Drink in Youngsters', *European Journal of Cancer Prevention*, 8/4: 289–95.

Kerkvliet, J. R., W. Nebesky, C. H. Tremblay, and V. J. Tremblay (1998). 'Efficiency and Technological Change in the U.S. Brewing Industry'. *Journal of Productivity Analysis*, 10/3: 271–88.

Kirin Holdings Company (2005). 'Beer Consumption in Major Countries in 2004'. Kirin Research Institute of Drinking and Lifestyle—Report Vol. 29.

Mitchell, B. R. (2007). *International Historical Statistics: Europe, 1750–2005*. London: Palgrave Macmillan.

Riepl, W. (2009). *De Belgische Bierbaronnen*. Roeselare: Roularta Books.

Sutton, J. (1991). *Sunk Costs and Market Structure: Price Competition, Advertising, and the Evolution of Concentration*. Cambridge, MA: MIT Press.

Tremblay, V. J., and C. H. Tremblay (2005). *The U.S. Brewing Industry: Data and Economic Analysis*. Cambridge, MA: MIT Press.

Van den Steen, J. (2003). *Trappist: Het bier en de Monniken*. Leuven: Davidsfonds.

Van der Hallen, P. (2009). 'Concentration in the Belgian Brewing Industry and the Breakthrough of Lager in the Interwar Years'. KU Leuven CES Discussion Paper 07.28.

Part II
Consumption

6

Cold Comfort in Hard Times: Do People Drink More Beer during Recessions?

Donald G. Freeman

Introduction

Do people drink more in hard times? Psychological theories suggest that alcohol consumption increases during recessions as a response to the stresses of economic downturns. In a series of papers Brenner and his colleagues (e.g. Brenner and Mooney 1983) produced evidence that a host of self- and other-destructive activities, including alcohol abuse and drunk driving, increased during periods of unemployment.

Economists on the other hand generally say no: the conventional view in the economics literature is that alcohol is a pro-cyclical normal good.[1] Ruhm (1995), Blake and Nied (1997), Ruhm and Black (2002), Freeman (1999, 2000), among many others, conclude that per capita consumption of alcoholic beverages, including beer, wine, and spirits, declines during recessions, with income elasticities varying between 0.5–0.8.[2] Tremblay and Tremblay (2005), in a comprehensive study of the beer industry, summarize eight studies of demand, with six finding beer to be a normal good and two finding beer to be inferior, with an average income elasticity of about +0.2.

Ruhm (1995) investigates the role of the macroeconomy in relation to alcohol consumption and traffic fatalities, finding that drinking and vehicle mortality decline during recessions. Freeman (1999) verifies Ruhm's finding of

---

[1] In economics, a 'normal' good is one whose consumption rises with income; the contrast is with an 'inferior' good, one whose consumption falls when incomes increase.

[2] Meaning that every 1 percentage increase in income results in a 0.5–0.8% increase in the quantity of alcohol consumed.

alcohol's pro-cyclicality using an expanded data set. Dee (2001), on the other hand, using data from the Behavioral Risk Factor Surveillance System (BRFSS), finds that binge drinking increases markedly during recessions, and argues that economic stress outweighs the income effects of recessions. Ruhm and Black (2002) counter with an expanded BRFSS sample with a larger set of explanatory variables to show that alcohol is pro-cyclical even at the micro level.

Freeman (2001) takes a somewhat different tack from previous literature to focus on beer consumption at the national level, at a monthly frequency, and over a much longer period: 1955–94. Because recessions are relatively short-lived phenomena (the average post-World War II recession has lasted only 10 months), the annual frequency used in previous research may not be adequate to pick up responses in alcohol demand to changes in cyclical economic variables. Freeman finds evidence of a long-run relationship among beer consumption, the unemployment rate, personal income, and beer excise taxes, but further tests reveal no evidence that beer consumption is responsive to short-run changes in the economic variables, indicating that beer is relatively immune to the business cycle.

Freeman's findings accord more with the prevailing view from the investment side, which is that alcohol and especially beer are recession-proof. Brewing companies (and other purveyors of 'vice' products like tobacco or gambling) are considered to be 'defensive' stocks, relatively immune to the business cycle. For instance, over the five-year period from June 1998 to June 2003, marked by the bursting of the 'dot-com' bubble, the recession of 2000–1, and the tragedy of 11 September 2001, the stocks of companies in the Alcoholic Beverages, Gambling and Casinos, and Tobacco industries rose by 46.02%, 145.18%, and 56.70% respectively, while the S&P 500 lost 14.05% (Ahrens 2004). Notably, common stocks of brewing companies typically carry 'betas' less than 1.0, meaning that their systematic risk is less than the market.[3]

In order to examine specifically the cyclicality of beer consumption, this research uses US state-level shipments data from 1970 to 2007 to estimate pooled time-series models of annual beer consumption on economic and demographic variables. Using state-level data has many advantages. Each state has its own set of consumption data, unemployment rates, etc., adding variability and allowing coefficients to be measured with greater precision. Disaggregating the data allows the researcher to control for state-and time-specific sources of variation, including the different timing and severity of

---

[3] Broadly speaking, 'beta' is the coefficient of the return of a security regressed on the return of the market. A beta of 1.0 indicates that the security has the same systematic risk as the market.

recessions across states. And the larger sample provides more potential power for tests of stationarity and cointegration.[4]

An innovation in this chapter is the incorporation of controls for changes in the age distribution of the states. Kerr et al. (2004), using the US National Alcohol Survey, show that age groups have different consumption habits regarding types and amounts consumed of alcoholic beverages. Tremblay and Tremblay (2005), using market research data, report that the prevalence of beer drinking, while declining somewhat for all groups, is highest (at around 50% in 2001) in the 25–34 year age group. As we will demonstrate below, changes in this group's proportion of the population show a close association with trends in per capita consumption of beer in the US and in the several states.

The estimation methods use recent developments by Pesaran (2006) and his co-authors to control for unobserved common factors in pooled cross-sections. The traditional way of controlling for common factors like nation-wide economic shocks has been to employ a two-way fixed effects model with 'dummy' variables for each time period in a pooled estimation. The limitation of the traditional approach is that all the cross-section units are constrained to have the same response to the (single) common time effect. In the Pesaran approach, referred to as common correlated effects (CCE) estimators, the cross-section means of the dependent variable and the regressors are used as proxies for the unobserved common effects in augmented regressions, allowing for heterogeneous responses to the proxies across the units. The CCE estimators have been shown to reduce the substantial bias and size distortions that result if cross-section dependence is ignored.

Using the CCE estimator produces the finding that beer consumption is a cyclical, normal good, varying negatively with the unemployment level and positively with income, a result that emerges only when unobserved heterogeneity is properly controlled. Hence people do drink less beer during recessions. However, we find that the estimated effect is small and that in practical terms recessions have little influence on beer consumption.

Additional results support previous research finding negative effects of excise taxes on consumption, although again the effect is small. Also, demographics have a significant and material effect on consumption; as expected, the larger the share of young adults in the population, the greater the consumption of beer per capita.

---

[4] Stationarity and cointegration tests are necessary to determine whether long-run relationships among variables are stable. If two variables are both not stationary and not cointegrated, any estimated relationship is spurious.

We proceed as follows. We first describe the data and methodology. Next, we describe the empirical approach and the regression estimates. The final section provides discussion and concludes the chapter.

Data and Methodology

Previous research on alcohol demand has typically used aggregate national time series or panels of state time series. One issue with national time series is the potential for aggregation bias from combining heterogeneous units like the US states, with their welter of different alcohol laws, demographics, and so on. Using state-level data in panels is a definite improvement: the additional degrees of freedom and the greater variety of economic circumstances allow for a greater precision in estimating the coefficients of interest. Many of the panels used thus far, however, have been relatively short. Ruhm (1995), for example, uses a panel of states for 14 years covering only two national business cycles. Given that business cycles tend to differ in magnitude, duration, causes, regional effects, and so forth, it is desirable to have more business cycles represented.

This research addresses that need by using 31 years of data for the 50 states plus the District of Columbia, a time period covering four full business cycles and parts of two others. As measures of economic activity, we use the unemployment rate, the employed/population ratio (for the working-age population), and disposable income per capita, in 2007 dollars, all at the state level, for the years 1970–2007. Each of these variables captures a different characteristic of the business cycle, and the use of multiple measures is a reflection of the fact that there is no variable that is the one best measure of the cycle. The unemployment rate and the employed/population ratio are taken from the Local Area Unemployment Survey of the Bureau of Labor Statistics; state disposable income is taken from the regional accounts database of the Bureau of Economic Analysis.

The data on beer consumption are taken from 'Beer Shipments by State', as reported in *The Brewer's Almanac*, an annual publication of the Beer Institute, formerly the United States Brewers' Association (Beer Institute, various years). The data are reported by millions of 31-gallon barrels shipped within each state annually from 1970–2007, and then converted to per capita equivalents.[5] *The Brewers' Almanac* is also the source of the state and federal excise tax rates on beer, used as a measure of inter-state price variation.

---

[5] Other methods of reporting are used in the literature, including per capita consumption above a certain age, or beer in terms of ethanol equivalents. We use per capita consumption for all ages because we incorporate the age distribution in our regressors. We acknowledge the variation in

Figure 6.1 displays annual gallons per capita beer consumption for the two largest states, California and Texas, along with the percentage of the population in each state between 20 and 35 years of age. There is much useful information in the figure. First is the general pattern of beer consumption in the two states (more or less representative of most states), wherein beer consumption peaks at about 1980 and declines thereafter. Though the earlier years are not shown in the figure, the 1980 peak marked the end of a long period of growth in consumption, beginning at least in the early 1960s in both states.

The second piece of information in Figure 6.1 is the gap in consumption between the two states, which is constant throughout and even widening in recent years. This gap is a clear indication of differences in beer consumption across states, heterogeneity that is unlikely to be fully captured by the regressors in the model. The nature of the different consumption patterns, demographics, and economic variables can be seen from the descriptive statistics in Table 6.1.

Beer consumption per capita has been highest over the sample period in Nevada (with a young population and a large tourist sector), and lowest in

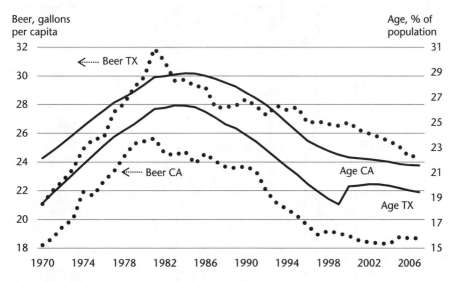

Figure 6.1. Demographics and beer consumption

Note: Dotted lines are annual gallons per-capita beer consumption in Texas (topmost) and California; solid lines are the percentages of the population aged 20 to 35 years in California (topmost) and Texas.

alcohol content in beer due to, for example, the introduction of 'light' beers, but the statistical methods employed in the estimation will likely capture much of this variation.

Table 6.1. Descriptive statistics, beer consumption, and explanatory variables, annual data, 1970–2007, 50 states and the District of Columbia

Variable		Minimum	Maximum	Average	Std. Deviation
Beer, gallons *per capita*	1970–2007	13.1 (Utah)	33.5 (Nevada)	22.9	3.7
	2007 only	12.0 (Utah)	32.4 (North Dakota)	22.8	3.9
Unemployment rate	1970–2007	3.4 (Nebraska)	8.3 (West Virginia)	5.8	1.1
	2007 only	2.6 (Hawaii)	7.2 (Michigan)	4.4	1.0
Employment/population	1970–2007	48.7 (W. Virginia)	67.5 (Minnesota)	61.5	3.7
	2007 only	53.4 (West Virginia)	71.2 (N. Dakota)	64.1	3.9
Disposable income, 2007 $('000)	1970–2007	12.6 (Mississippi)	23.1 (D.C.)	16.7	2.3
	2007 only	18.3 (Utah)	38.6 (D.C.)	23.6	4.0
Excise taxes, 2007 $/gallon	1970–2007	1.23 (Wyoming)	3.65 (S. Carolina)	1.85	0.60
	2007 only	0.97 (Wyoming)	2.90 (Alaska)	1.38	0.40
% Population ages 20–35	1970–2007	14.1 (Florida)	19.6 (D.C.)	15.7	0.95
	2007 only	11.7 (Maine)	18.2 (D.C.)	13.9	1.28

Utah, which has a large Church of Latter-Day Saints population who do not drink alcohol. The variation in consumption is quite substantial, with the 20 gallon difference between minimum and maximum consumption equivalent to about 200 12 oz cans of beer per person per year.

There is considerable variation in the independent variables as well, with maximum unemployment rates more than double minimum rates, both over the sample and in 2007. Likewise, income is not distributed equally, with the District of Columbia about twice as rich as the poorest states, both historically and recently. The employment/population ratio has less volatility and less variation than the other cyclical economic measures, and has trended upward over the sample. Excise taxes, meanwhile, differ by a factor of about three between the highest and lowest-taxed state.

Given mobility, similar cultural heritage, and so forth, the distribution of young people across states' populations is roughly similar, but there are differences. Florida and Maine are relatively old, and the District of Columbia is relatively young (as is Utah among states proper). On average, the percentage of young people in the population has risen, then fallen over the sample period as the children of the 'Baby Boomers', the large population surge in the US following World War II, have matured.

There undoubtedly remains much unobserved heterogeneity in factors influencing beer consumption across states. States have very different laws regarding the distribution and sale of alcoholic beverages, for example. Similarly, there are sources of temporal heterogeneity that affect all cross-section units in the sample, such as macroeconomic events like interest rate changes, fiscal policy, etc., or social factors like changing attitudes toward the consumption of alcohol. For example, the decline in beer consumption per capita from 1980 has likely been influenced by evolving attitudes, changing family structure, and cohort influences. The estimation techniques we employ are designed to control for these unobserved factors.

The third and final piece of information in Figure 6.1 is the relationship between the proportion of young adults in the population and the per capita consumption of beer. As noted, the highest consuming age group is the young adult category, so it is not surprising that trends in consumption would be related to the size of this group. We incorporate the states' age distributions in our analyses by including age variables in the regression model, one of the few attempts to do so in the literature on alcohol demand.

The relationship between the age distribution and beer consumption may be more subtle than the proportion of a single age group may be able to capture, however. Therefore there may be value in examining the effect of changes in the *entire* age distribution on beer consumption. This we do using a polynomial distributed lag (PDL) technique introduced by Fair and Dominguez as an alternative to the single age group, as described below.

Empirical Framework and Estimation

The least square dummy variable (LSDV) model, relying on fixed effects for the cross-sections and time periods to capture unobserved heterogeneity in the data, is the workhorse of heterogeneous panels. However, the LSDV model assumes that all heterogeneity can be captured by simple zero-one variables, and that the response of each cross-section unit to the time effects is identical.[6] Recently, Pesaran and his co-authors (Pesaran 2006; Pesaran and Tosetti 2007) have proposed a more flexible technique, the Common Correlated Effects (CCE) estimator, to control for unobserved heterogeneity in panels of moderate size in T and N. The CCE estimator, which uses cross-section averages of the dependent variable and the regressors to augment regressions of the individual units, is quite flexible and easy to use, and has been shown in Monte Carlo simulations to control for unobserved heterogeneity and cross-section dependence far more completely than the usual two-way fixed effects model. The CCE estimator is described more completely in the Appendix. Here we give a brief outline of the approach.

The basic model for estimation can be expressed as:

$$y_{it} = a_i' d_t + \beta_i' x_{it} + e_{it,} \tag{6.1}$$

where y_{it} is consumption of beer in gallons per capita, d_t is a vector of observed deterministic effects, x_{it} is a $k \times 1$ vector of regressors, and the errors, $e_{it,}$ have the multifactor structure,

$$e_{it} = \gamma_i' f_t + \epsilon_{it,} \tag{6.2}$$

with f_t a vector of unobserved common factors, and ε_{it} an idiosyncratic error term uncorrelated with f_t or x_{it}. We note that $d_t = 1$ and $f_t = 1$, $\gamma_i = \gamma$ and $\beta_i = \beta$ is the traditional two-way fixed effects model.

Our approach is to estimate (6.2) using traditional methods as well as the recently developed CCE estimator. Table 6.2 presents the results of pooled regressions utilizing various forms of controls for cross-section and intertemporal heterogeneity.

Model 1 presents the results of a pooled sample of all 51 units with only the regressors and state fixed effects as controls and using a common intercept. Beer is seen to be marginally counter-cyclical using unemployment as a cyclical control (each additional percentage point of unemployment results in about a one can increase in beer consumed per person), but pro-cyclical if the

---

[6] Another technique is to use state-specific trends. However, in the present case there is no evidence of linear trends, and the use of quadratic trends would likely overdetermine the model.

Table 6.2. Pooled estimations of per capita beer consumption, annual data, US states, 1970–2007 (p values in parentheses)

Variable	Model			
	(1)	(2)	(3)	(4)
Lagged dependent variable	—	—	—	0.245
				(.000)
Unemployment	0.050	0.016	–0.141	–0.139
	(0.092)	(0.680)	(0.000)	(0.000)
Employment/population	0.047	0.110	0.002	–0.003
	(0.079)	(0.000)	(0.955)	(0.806)
Real disposable income	–0.262	–0.100	0.083	0.075
	(0.000)	(0.002)	(0.067)	(0.094)
Excise taxes	–2.544	–2.649	–0.731	–0.467
	(0.000)	(0.000)	(0.003)	(0.052)
Age 20–35	—	—	—	—
Z_1Age PDL	12.28	15.60	42.28	34.94
	(0.000)	(0.000)	(0.000)	(0.000)
Z_2Age PDL	–0.772	–0.851	–2.661	–2.181
	(0.000)	(0.000)	(0.000)	(0.000)
Fixed state effects	Yes	Yes	Yes	Yes
Fixed time effects	No	Yes	No	No
Variable cross section means (CCE)	No	No	Yes	Yes
R—Square	0.865	0.883	0.982	0.983
Pesaran 'CD'	22.71	5.90	5.02	4.46
Heterogeneity test	(0.000)	(0.000)	(0.000)	(0.000)
Durbin—Watson	0.265	0.245	1.490	1.955
	(0.000)	(0.000)	(0.000)	(0.212)

Notes: Model 1 is a standard fixed effects estimator with controls for unobserved cross-section, but not temporal, heterogeneity. Model 2 adds controls for temporal heterogeneity in the form of time fixed effects. Model 3 is the CCE estimator using variable means as controls for heterogeneity. Model 4 adds a lagged dependent variable.

employment/population is used instead. These two results are not necessarily inconsistent—the employment/population ratio reflects, in addition to cyclical movements, longer-term trends in labour participation—but the two variables do tend to move in opposite directions during the business cycle. Beer in model 1 is an inferior good, significantly so, and taxes have a strong effect on consumption: each dollar of beer excise tax reduces beer consumption by 2.5 gallons (about equivalent to a case of 24 cans of beer) per person annually.

As noted earlier, the age distribution may affect beer consumption in more complex ways than a single age group can capture. The rationale for including the entire distribution is that the proportions of ages older or younger than normal beer-drinking age may modify the drinking of the latter. For example, the drinking habits of the 20% of the population aged 20–35 may be different if the split in the older and younger population is an even 40–40 instead of say, 50–30 or 30–50.

It is clearly not feasible to estimate 14 age-group coefficients; besides the degrees of freedom limitations, the age groups are highly collinear, leading to imprecise estimates of the true pattern of the coefficients. To proceed, we use

Fair and Dominguez's (1991) polynomial distributed lag (PDL) technique as applied to the entire age distribution. The derivation of the technique is given in the Appendix. For now we note that the coefficients of 'Z_1' and 'Z_2' describe an inverted parabola, implying higher levels of consumption for young adults, as the theory and casual observation would suggest. The shape of the responses of the age distribution are described and illustrated in connection with the discussion of model 4, below.

We note with model 1, however, that there appears to be much remaining cross-correlation in the sample. The Pesaran 'CD' test, specified as $CD = \sqrt{\frac{2T}{N(N-1)}} \left(\sum_{i=1}^{N-1} \sum_{j=l+1}^{N} \rho_{ij} \right)$, where ρ_{ij} are the contemporaneous cross-correlations of the disturbances, distributed as a standard normal variant, soundly rejects the null of zero correlation, and the pooled Durbin–Watson indicates the presence of within-unit serial correlation as well.

Model 2 introduces time fixed effects to further correct for unobserved variation in the sample due to common influences occurring in the time dimension; this is the two-way fixed effects model. Unemployment is now insignificant and the magnitude of the coefficient on income is much increased and that on the employment/population ratio is much decreased. The coefficients on the age distribution increase, as does the coefficient on taxes. Each additional dollar of excise taxes now causes a more than two and one-half gallon reduction per person in annual beer consumption. Moreover, the CD statistic, if still statistically significant, is reduced by a factor of almost four. There is no improvement in the Durbin–Watson, however, indicating that fixed time effects are insufficient to account for serial correlation in the residuals.

Model 3 introduces the main innovation in this chapter, the use of the CCE estimator. We replace the time fixed effects with a two-step procedure, first regressing each cross-section unit on an intercept and the cross-section averages of the set (y_{it}, x_{it}), then pooling and regressing the residuals e_{it}^y on the e_{it}^x. We find that the CCE estimator produces significant changes in the responses of beer consumption to the regressors. Beer consumption is now definitely pro-cyclical, with increases in unemployment producing a small yet significant reduction in beer consumption. The employment ratio now produces no response in consumption, but the sign of the income variable is also reversed and significant, indicating that beer is a normal good.

Of special note is that the coefficient of the tax variable is much reduced. We suspect that the construction of the tax variable by deflating a fixed nominal tax rate with the consumer price index, a common practice in studies of this type, is capturing some of the downward trend in beer consumption in models 1 and 2. The cross-section average of the tax variable in the first-stage regressions of model 3 is capturing more or less the same movement, thus the residuals used in the second step have been in effect de-trended and the tax variable is no longer significant.

The coefficients of the age variables are much increased in magnitude, indicating a much steeper rise and fall than in previous models in the effects on beer consumption as we move through the age distribution. The R^2 of model 3 (calculated using the variance of the original dependent variable) is somewhat improved, and the CD statistic is smaller but still large enough to reject the null of no cross-correlation. A notable difference is the size of the Durbin–Watson statistic, still indicating the presence of serial correlation, but much improved from the earlier models. We can thus be reasonably assured that much of the unobserved heterogeneity is being captured by the CCE model in a way that the traditional two-way fixed effects model could not handle.

In model 4 we add the lagged dependent variable to the CCE model. The coefficients of the regressors are little changed, except for the tax coefficient, but the pooled Durbin–Watson statistic now indicates that the null of no serial correlation cannot be rejected. The consequences of using a lagged dependent variable (LDV) in the CCE model are not well established (although it is certainly known that the use of a LDV in panel data introduces bias, especially in the coefficient of the LDV), but the lack of substantial change in the coefficients indicates that distortions are likely benign in the current circumstances. The CD statistic is also reduced, though still significant.

The estimated coefficients of the age distribution variables from model 4 are used to generate the effect of the entire age distribution on beer consumption, as displayed in Figure 6.2.

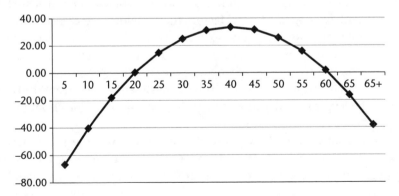

Figure 6.2. Implied age coefficient

Note: Taken from model 4, Table 6.2. Implied coefficients for five-year age intervals from a polynomial distributed lag (PDL) estimation with summation constraint zero. See Fair and Dominguez (1991).

In the figure, the markers on the line indicate implied coefficients for the five-year interval ending at that marker. The pattern shows that consumption peaks at age 40, a little later than expected, but not much at variance with the survey results reported by Tremblay and Tremblay (2005). Greater concentration of the population at very young (especially) and very old age groups subtracts from per capita beer consumption, as expected.

Model 4 yields the strongest results in terms of the economic variables; that is, the coefficients of the regressors tell a nice story of beer as a pro-cyclical, normal good that is sensitive to excise taxes and therefore price. The implied price elasticity of beer as derived from the tax coefficient is quite small, however; using the means of the variables from Table 6.1 results in price elasticity of only –0.045; the income elasticity is also small at + 0.041. These estimates are well below those of recent research, including Selvanathan and Selvanathan (2004), Clements and Johnson (1983), and Clements and Selvanathan (1987). Evidently, the results of prior research may have been overstated by the omission of controls for common effects.[7]

Conclusion

This chapter uses recent developments in the econometrics of pooled time series with unobserved common effects to re-estimate the effects of economic and demographic variables on beer consumption using US state-level data over the period 1970–2007. Previous research using pooled data relied mainly on two-way fixed effects models using 0–1 'dummy' variables to control for two quite different sources of variation in the sample that are not captured by the independent variables: (1) differences in beer consumption across states but constant over time, due to factors like religious preferences, level of tourism, alcohol control laws, and so on; and (2) differences in beer consumption over time but constant across states, such as changing national attitudes toward alcohol consumption, changes in the structure of the brewing industry, national advertising, and so on. The result is a series of intercept shifts that change the level of the dependent variable (beer consumption) from time to time and from state to state.

A major shortcoming, however, of the two-way fixed effects estimator is that the common time shock (an increase in oil prices, for example) is constrained to have the same effect on each state. The CCE estimator addresses

---

[7] Other estimations were conducted to test for regional effects, structural breaks, and the consumption of other alcoholic beverages. The CCE estimator (1) produced estimates consistent with those in Table 6.1 in a variety of different specifications; and (2) was superior to the traditional two-way fixed effects model under conditions of arbitrary breaks in the sample. For details, see the working paper version of this chapter (Freeman 2010).

that shortcoming by replacing the 0–1 dummy with the cross-section means of the dependent and independent variables, then performing a two-stage regression. In the first stage, beer consumption in each state is regressed individually on the cross-section means. In the second stage, the residuals from the first regression, which are now 'purged' of the common time shock, are then pooled and regressed on the set of independent variables. Thus the CCE estimator separates the time shock into several components (the variable means), and allows their influences to vary among the states. The overall effect is to capture more of the factors accounting for the variation in beer consumption, thus reducing the potential for omitted variable bias and increasing the efficiency of the resulting estimators.

The principal finding of the chapter is that beer is a pro-cyclical, normal good: people do drink less beer during recessions. Meanwhile, beer consumption has been quite responsive to changes in the age distribution of the states during the sample period. The results from the CCE estimator stand in contrast to those from a standard two-way fixed effects model using the same data. The latter model estimates beer consumption as being a non-cyclical, inferior good, with much smaller response to the age distribution variables.

The models also differ in the estimated effects of excise taxes on beer consumption within states across time. The two-way fixed effects models estimate the coefficient on taxes to be about four times as large as the estimate for the CCE estimator, indicating that the effect of taxes may have been overstated in previous research, a finding also reported by Dee (1999) and Young and Likens (2000) in a different context. While we have no evidence on the effect of taxes on, say, heavy versus light drinkers, we can say that taxes have only small effects on aggregate consumption.

The results of the Fair–Dominguez PDL technique of measuring the effects of the age distribution on beer consumptions estimate that peak beer consumption occurs in the 35–40 year age category, a bit later than the survey reports of beer drinking by age would indicate. It may be somewhat misleading to interpret the peak of the distribution as being the peak of consumption, however, given that the entire distribution is being modelled instead of the age group that happens to provide singly the largest coefficient. It is interesting that the two-way fixed effects model differs here too, placing the peak even later, at the 40–45 year age category.

The CCE estimator also reduces both cross-section dependence and serial correlation of the residuals compared to the traditional two-way fixed effects estimator. The use of cross-section means shows great promise in modelling unobserved common effects.

One result of practical significance is the acknowledgement that, while the estimated coefficients are statistically significant, their *economic* significance is fairly small. The estimated (or inferred) elasticities of income and price suggest that the measured effects of the economy on beer consumption will be hard to pick up in the data. Thus both the economists and the investment analysts can take 'cold comfort' in being right about their views!

APPENDIX

The CCE Estimator[8]

The so-called CCE estimator offers two advantages over the traditional two-way fixed effects estimator. First, by admitting the possibility of multiple common but unobserved factors, the CCE estimator offers the potential for consistent estimation of the coefficients of the individual regressors (i.e. the β_i in equation (6.1) in the text above). Because these coefficients, and not the factor loadings of the unobserved factors, are the items of interest in the current exercise, this method is particularly important. Second, by allowing the coefficients of the f_t to vary across units, the CCE estimator can better accommodate heterogeneous panels where some average of responses is nonetheless required.

To operationalize the CCE estimator, we proceed in two steps. First, we run regressions of each cross-section on a constant and on simple averages of the dependent variable and the regressors. Then the residuals from the cross-section regressions are pooled and regressed against the x_{it}. The effect is very similar to a pooled time-series cross-section with two-way fixed effects, except that the variable averages replace the time effects and the procedure allows a separate response for each cross-section unit. In Monte Carlo tests of the CCE estimator in generated samples with unobserved common effects that are correlated with the regressors, Pesaran (2004) and Coakley, Fuertes, and Smith (2004) demonstrate that the CCE estimator is the preferred choice on efficiency grounds when compared with the usual two-way fixed effects and demeaned mean group estimators.

In most cases, it is reasonable to assume that the observed and unobserved factors are related, and this relationship can be expressed as

$$x_{it} = A_i' d_t + \Gamma_i' f_t + v_{it,} \tag{6.3}$$

where A_i and Γi are factor loading matrices and v_{it} are error terms assumed not to be correlated with the common effects. Stacking (6.1) and (6.3), we obtain

$$z_{it} = B_i' d_t + C_i' f_t + u_{it} \tag{6.4}$$

where $z_{it} = (y_{it}, x_{it}')'$, $B_i' = (\alpha_i \quad A_i) \begin{pmatrix} 1 & 0 \\ \beta_i & I_k \end{pmatrix}$, $c_i = (\gamma_i \quad \Gamma_i) \begin{pmatrix} 1 & 0 \\ \beta_i & I_k \end{pmatrix}$. Assuming suitable rank conditions on C_i, equation (6.4) can be multiplied by $(C_i C_i')^{-1} C_i$ and solved for f_t to give

---

[8] This discussion follows closely Pesaran (2006), in which the CCE estimator is fully developed.

$$f_t = (c_i c_i')^{-1} C_i (z_{it} - B_i' d_t - u_{it}).$$ (6.5)

Thus, the unobserved common factors can be expressed as linear combinations of the dependent variable, the regressors, and the deterministic effects. Pesaran (2006) shows that asymptotically, any weighted average will be consistent, so simple averages will do.

The Fair–Dominguez PDL

In the Fair–Dominguez framework, the age distribution enters the model originally as:

$$y_{it} = \alpha_t' d_t + \beta_i' x_{it} + \delta_1 p_{1it} + \ldots + \delta_n p_{nit} + e_{it}$$ (6.6)

with p_{jit} the proportion of age group j in the population, where each j consists of five-year age groups up to age 65, and then all remaining years. Fair and Dominguez therefore propose to impose two restrictions on the coefficients: (1) that they all sum to zero; and (2) that they lie on a second-degree polynomial $\delta_j = a_0 + a_1 j + a_2 j^2$. The zero-sum constraint implies that for n groups $a_0 = -a_1 (1/n) \Sigma_{j=1}^n j - a_2 (1/n) \Sigma_1^n j^2$, and given the standard formulae for the summation of the first n numbers and first n squares, the age variables will enter (6.6) as $a_1 Z_{1it} + a_2 Z_{2it}$ where $Z_{1it} = \Sigma_{j=1}^{14} j p_{jit} - 7.5$ and $Z_{1it} = \Sigma_{j=1}^{14} j^2 p_{jit} - 72.5$.

Given estimates of the a_i's, the coefficients $\hat{\delta}_j$ can be recovered.

References

Ahrens, D. (2004). *Investing in Vice: The Recession-Proof Portfolio of Booze, Bets, Bombs, and Butts*. New York: St Martin's Press.

The Beer Institute (formerly the United States Brewers Association) (various years). *The Brewers Almanac*. Washington: The Beer Institute.

Blake, D., and A. Nied (1997). 'The Demand for Alcohol in the United Kingdom', *Applied Economics*, 29: 1655–72.

Brenner, M. H., and A. Mooney (1983). 'Unemployment and Health in the Context of Economic Change'. *Social Science & Medicine*, 17: 1125–38.

Clements, K. W., and L. W. Johnson (1983). 'The Demand for Beer, Wine and Spirits: A System-Wide Analysis'. *Journal of Business*, 56/3: 273–304.

—— and E. A. Selvanathan (1987). 'Alcohol Consumption', in H. Theil and K. W. Clements (eds.), *Applied Demand Analysis: Results from System-Wide Approaches*. Cambridge, MA: Ballinger Publishing Co.

Coakley, J., A. Fuertes, and R. Smith (2004). 'Unobserved Heterogeneity in Panel Time Series Models'. Working Paper BWPEF 0403, Birkbeck, University of London.

Dee, T. S. (1999). 'State Alcohol Policies, Teen Drinking, and Traffic Fatalities'. *Journal of Public Economics*, 72: 289–315.

—— (2001). 'Alcohol Abuse and Economics Conditions: Evidence from Repeated Cross-Sections of Individual-Level Data'. *Health Economics*, 10: 257–70.

Fair, R. C., and K. M. Dominguez (1991). 'Effects of the Changing US Age Distribution on Macroeconomic Equations'. *American Economic Review*, 81/5: 1276–94.

Freeman, D. G. (1999). 'A Note on Economic Conditions and Alcohol Problems'. *Journal of Health Economics*, 18/5: 661–70.

—— (2000). 'Alternative Panel Estimates of Alcohol Demand, Taxation, and the Business Cycle'. *Southern Economic Journal*, 67/2: 325–44.

—— (2001). 'Beer and the Business Cycle', *Applied Economics Letters*, 2001/8: 51–4.

—— (2010). 'Beer in Good Times and Bad: A U.S. State-Level Analysis of Economic Conditions and Alcohol Consumption'. Working Paper No. 09-06, Sam Houston State University.

Kerr, W. C., T. K. Greenfield, J. Bond, Y. Ye, and J. Rehm (2004). 'Age, Period, and Cohort Influences on Beer, Wine, and Spirits Consumption Trends in the US National Alcohol Surveys'. *Addiction*, 99: 1111–20.

Pesaran, M. H. (2004). 'General Diagnostic Tests for Cross Section Dependence in Panels'. CESifo Working Paper series no. 1229.

—— (2006). 'Estimation and Inference in Large Heterogeneous Panels with a Multifactor Error Structure'. *Econometrica*, 74: 967–1012.

—— and E. Tosetti (2007). 'Large Panels with Common Factors and Spatial Correlations'. CESifo Working Paper series no. 2103.

Ruhm, C. J. (1995). 'Economic Conditions and Alcohol Problems'. *Journal of Health Economics*, 14: 583–603.

—— and W. E. Black (2002). 'Does Drinking Really Decrease in Bad Times'? *Journal of Health Economics*, 21: 659–78.

Selvanathan, E. A., and S. Selvanathan (2004). 'Economic and Demographic Factors in Australian Alcohol Demand'. *Applied Economics*, 36: 2405–17.

Tremblay, V. J., and C. H. Tremblay (2005). *The US Brewing Industry: Data and Economic Analysis*. Cambridge, MA: The MIT Press.

Young, D. J., and T. W. Likens (2000). 'Alcohol Regulation and Auto Fatalities'. *International Review of Law and Economics*, 20: 107–26.

7

Beer-Drinking Nations: The Determinants of Global Beer Consumption

Liesbeth Colen and Johan F. M. Swinnen

Beer-Drinking Nations

When one thinks of the favourite alcoholic drinks of people in Italy, Spain, and France, one thinks of wine; when one thinks of Russia, one thinks of vodka; when one thinks of countries like Belgium, Germany, the Czech Republic, or Britain, one thinks of beer. The question then arises: what makes a country a 'beer (or wine) drinking nation'?

Interestingly, it appears that many regions which we now typically no longer associate with beer were initially 'beer-drinking nations'.[1] At the height of the Egyptian Empire, beer was the drink of choice for all in Egypt. It was only later that the elite in Egypt shifted to preferring wine. However, even then beer remained the drink for the masses. In more recent times, beer consumption declined in North Africa with the spread of Islam.

Also in Europe, in many regions which are now associated with wine, people drank mostly (or only) beer for thousands of years. For example, in what is now France, Spain, Portugal, and Northern Italy, people drank beer, not wine, in the millennia before the Greek and Roman empires.[2] Widespread consumption of wine and viniculture did not occur in large parts of southern Europe until the Romans conquered these parts of Europe. Both the Greeks

---

[1] See Poelmans and Swinnen (Chapter 1 in this volume) for a more elaborate discussion and for more references to the literature on the history of beer, including Nelson (2005) and Unger (2004).

[2] There is evidence that the Greeks began exporting wine to southern France, particularly via Massala (Marseille), from around 650 BC, and that there was some local production around Massala. However, even after that, for hundreds of years, in Southern Gaul (today's France) wine was a luxury item and only consumed by the upper classes. According to Diodorus of Sicily, the price of wine was high: Gauls would exchange a slave for one jar of Italian wine (Nelson 2005: 49).

and the Romans drank wine, and only wine, not beer. Moreover, they despised beer and its drinkers. They referred to them as barbarians, uncivilized, etc. With the Roman conquest of Europe, wine consumption—and later production—spread over the continent. Northern Italy (above the Po River), then Southern Gaul (France), the Iberian peninsula (Spain and Portugal), and later Northern Gaul (northern France and Belgium) were conquered one by one by the Romans, and with conquest came a dramatic geographic spread of wine consumption and production.

Celtic people in (what are now) France, Spain, Belgium, Germany, and Britain were all avid beer drinkers, probably from very early times and for the most part even after the Roman conquests (Nelson 2005). However, due to Greek and especially Roman influence, wine came to supplant beer (or honey beer or mead) as the upper-class beverage in most of these areas. The place where the old beer tradition remained most entrenched was what is now Germany, perhaps due to the Germanic influence on Celts. This is reflected in Caesar's comment about the resistance to wine by the Suevi and the Nervi, two German tribes:

> [the Germanic tribe Suevi] on no account permit wine to be imported to them, because they consider that men degenerate in their powers of enduring fatigue, and are rendered effeminate by that commodity'. (*De Bello Gallico*: Book 4, Chapter 2)
>
> That there was no access for merchants to them [the Nervii]; that they suffered no wine and other things tending to luxury to be imported; because, they thought that by their use the mind is enervated and the courage impaired. (*De Bello Gallico*: Book 2, Chapter 15)[3]

Also, in more recent times, international political and economic developments have strongly affected beer consumption across the world. For example, international conquests (e.g. the colonization of America and Australia), migration (e.g. of German settlers in the United States), and foreign investments by companies (e.g. recent investments by Western brewing companies in Russia, China, and India) have led to international transfers of technologies and knowledge of brewing and wine production.

This brief historical introduction shows that local traditions, climatic conditions, trade, technology diffusion with economic integration (through military means and conquests, or through migration and foreign investments), government regulations,[4] economic development, and religious constraints

---

[3] *De Bello Gallico*, Book 2, Chap. 15, in McDevitte and Bohn (1869). Special thanks go to Giulia Meloni for coming up with these apt quotes. See Meloni and Swinnen (2010) for more details.

[4] Governments have actively intervened in alcohol markets throughout history (Meloni and Swinnen 2010). Regulations have been religiously motivated and supported by those in favour of the prohibition of alcohol for health and social reasons (Okrent 2010). Governments have universally imposed various taxes on beer, wine, and spirits as a source of revenue or to protect

have a major impact on whether countries became 'beer-drinking nations', or not. In more recent times also each of these factors appears to have been important in explaining (changes in) beer consumption.

In this chapter we study beer consumption across countries and over time. We analyse empirically which factors have affected beer consumption. As far as we are aware, there are no earlier econometric studies analysing changes in global beer consumption across many countries and over a long period of time. There are, however, many studies analysing the determinants of alcohol consumption, including beer, in various countries.

Economic theory predicts that an individual consumer's demand for beer is a function of the price of beer, the prices of substitutes and complements, the consumer's income, the product's characteristics, and the consumer's level of consumption capital (Tremblay and Tremblay 2005). Important substitutes for beer include other alcoholic beverages, such as wine and distilled spirits, and soft drinks. The fact that beer, like other alcoholic beverages, is potentially addictive, also affects the demand for beer. Addiction influences demand directly and varies with an individual's consumption capital (Stigler and Becker 1977). For an addictive commodity, current consumption may be higher when past and expected future consumption are higher (Becker and Murphy 1988; Akerlof 1991). Finally, peer pressure and advertising that promotes the image that drinking alcohol is the social norm, may encourage alcohol consumption (Akerlof and Kranton 2000).

Studies find that the estimated price elasticities are consistent with theoretical expectations (i.e. negative own price elasticities and positive cross-price elasticities), but that the elasticities are relatively small. Fogarty (2008) and Tremblay and Tremblay (2005) summarize more than 150 studies, most of which are on OECD countries. Although there is variability in the estimates, most indicate that the demand for beer is inelastic. The mean estimate of price elasticity of demand is about –0.5 in various studies for the US, the UK, and Ireland (Fogarty 2008). That is, a 10% increase in the price reduces the quantity of beer demanded by about 5%. Regarding cross-price effects, most studies show that wine, spirits, and soft drinks are imperfect substitutes for beer, as the cross-price elasticity estimates are small—close to zero (Tremblay and Tremblay 2005).

The majority of studies conclude that beer is a normal good, but that income has a relatively small effect on demand. The mean income elasticity is between 0.35 and 0.90 for most countries (Fogarty 2008). A few studies find negative income elasticity (e.g. Niskanen 1962; Gallet and List 1998; Nelson

---

certain interests. For example, heavy import tariffs on French wines induced a massive shift from wine to beer consumption in 18th century Britain (see Nye, Chapter 4 in this volume).

2003 for the US). However, the vast majority of the studies find positive income elasticity.

Demographic and regional factors also affect the demand for beer. Typically, men are more likely to drink beer than women, and beer is more popular for consumers aged 18–44 than for those aged 45 and over. Studies that control for demographics find that demand rises with growth in the young adult population (Ornstein and Hanssens 1985; Lee and Tremblay 1992; Larivière et al. 2000; Nelson 2003). In the US, residents of the Northeast and the West are more likely to be beer drinkers than residents of other regions. Per capita beer consumption is much lower in Utah, where many Mormons live, and highest in Nevada (Tremblay and Tremblay 2005).

Before addressing the question 'what makes a country a beer-drinking nation?' more rigorously, it is obviously important to first analyse whether the images of countries in people's minds are actually true, i.e. whether our associations of a certain alcoholic drink with particular countries is consistent with actual consumption habits. In the next section we describe the evolution of beer consumption over time. We briefly discuss the role of trade in the following section. After that, we describe the empirical model used to analyse the determinants of beer, and we discuss the regression results. The last section concludes.

Beer Consumption

On a global level, beer consumption is much more important than wine or other alcoholic beverages in volume terms. Moreover, the gap has grown strongly over the past 50 years (Figure 7.1). While in the 1960s the global volume of beer was approximately double that of wine, beer consumption was more than six times larger than wine consumption by 2005. The gap with other alcoholic drinks increased substantially as well. By 2005, the total volume of beer was 153 billion litres, while the volume of wine was 24 billion litres and that of other alcoholic drinks 18.5 billion litres.

Since wine and other alcohol are typically more expensive than beer, the differences in value terms are smaller (Figure 7.1). Between 1960 and 1990 the global value of beer and 'other alcoholic beverages' was roughly equal and approximately double the value of wine. However, over the past 20 years, the value of beer has continued to increase, while that of 'other alcoholic beverages' has stagnated. The global value of beer has been double that of wine over the past 50 years, with beers accounting for about 130 billion US dollars by 2005 and wine for about 65 billion US dollars.

Figure 7.2 illustrates the evolution of beer consumption for a series of countries over the past 50 years. For most of that period the US was the largest

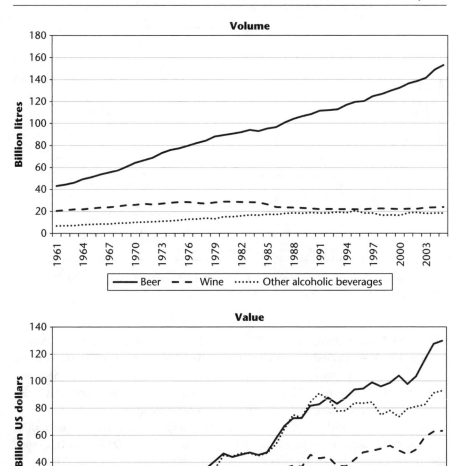

Figure 7.1. Global consumption of beer, wine, and other alcoholic beverages in volume[1] (billion litres) and value[2] (billion US dollars), 1961–2005

Notes: [1] Data on volumes in kg have been converted to litres, assuming 1 kg of liquid equals 1 litre. [2] Values are calculated using the average of global import and export prices (calculated from world trade value and volume) multiplied by volume.

Source: FAOstat (2010).

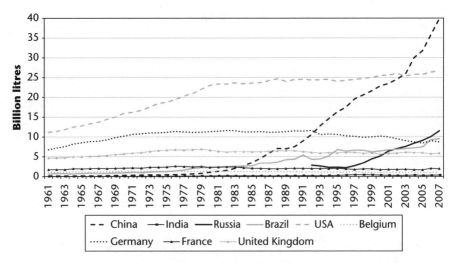

Figure 7.2. Beer consumption in the world (billion litres), 1961–2007
Source: FAOstat (2010).

beer market, consuming around 25 billion litres per year for the past 30 years. In the 1960–80 period, the other large markets were in Western Europe: Germany, the UK, and France. However, consumption of beer has declined significantly in the past 25 years in some of the traditional European beer-drinking countries such as Germany, the UK, and Belgium.

Growth in demand is concentrated in the emerging countries. In particular, the rise of consumption in China is spectacular. Since 2003 China has over-taken the US as the largest beer market and China now consumes 20% of all beer in the world. The dramatic growth of China[5] in the global beer economy is well illustrated in Figure 7.2. From close to zero beer consumption as recently as 1980, the Chinese beer market grew to 40 billion litres by 2007. Growth was strong in other emerging markets as well. In Russia and Brazil, beer consumption has increased strongly over the past two decades and today these countries are larger beer markets than Germany. In all these countries, the combination of income growth and economic liberalization has induced a dramatic growth of production and consumption. In India too there has been substantive growth in beer consumption in recent years, albeit India is far behind China. In fact, total Indian beer consumption is only slightly higher than that of Belgium (Arora et al., Chapter 17 in this volume). Table 7.1 summarizes the changes in the structure of the global beer market.

---

[5] See Bai et al. (Chapter 15 in this volume) for the fascinating story of what has been happening in the Chinese beer market.

Table 7.1. Structure of the global beer market

Country	1961		2005	
	billion litres	%	billion litres	%
US	11.2	26.01	25.81	16.86
Germany	6.79	15.77	8.45	5.52
UK	4.70	10.92	6.04	3.95
USSR/Russia[1]	2.69	6.25	9.12	5.96
France	1.71	3.97	1.67	1.09
Brazil	0.63	1.46	7.46	4.87
Belgium	0.61	1.42	1.06	0.69
China	0.15	0.35	31.76	20.74
India	0.01	0.02	0.26	0.17
Other countries	15.18	35.25	62.53	40.84
Total (World)	43.06	100.00	153.10	100.00

Note: [1] The 1961 numbers are for the former Soviet Union, the 2005 numbers are for the Russian Federation. All countries that together comprised the Soviet Union consumed 13.13 billion litres of beer in 2005, which corresponds to 5.58% of global consumption.
Source: FAOstat (2010).

Clearly the volume of total consumption is affected by the number of people living in a country. Therefore another interesting indicator is beer consumption per capita. Figure 7.3 provides details on per capita beer consumption in various countries. Per capita beer consumption is still highest in Western and Central Europe. The 'world champion beer drinkers' are the Irish and the Czech, with more than 160 litres per capita—much more than any other country. Austrians, Germans, Belgians, and British consumers also drink 100 litres per capita or more. The highest consumption in non-European countries is in Australia (89 litres per capita) and the US (86 litres per capita). Per capita consumption in other major beer markets is considerably less: 63 litres per capita in Russia, 40 litres per capita in Brazil, and 24 litres per capita in China. Per capita consumption was less than 1 litre in India in 2005.

Figure 7.4 shows the evolution of per capita consumption over the past 50 years. There are several interesting patterns. First, among the recently growing beer markets, growth in per capita consumption has been strongest in Russia,[6] almost quadrupling between 1995 and 2005, much stronger even than in China. In Brazil, growth was strongest in the 1975–95 period and has slowed since.

Second, Figure 7.4 also suggests that there is huge potential for further growth in beer consumption in the world's largest countries. In India, despite a large population that does not consume beer, there appears much room for

---

[6] Russia is a very interesting case, since beer consumption increased dramatically over the past 15 years, with consumers shifting 'from vodka to Baltika' (i.e., the most popular beer in Russia) (Deconinck and Swinnen, Chapter 16 in this volume).

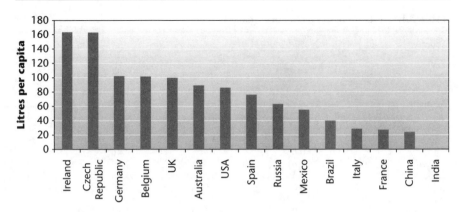

Figure 7.3. Per capita beer consumption in 2005 (litre/capita)
Source: FAOstat (2010).

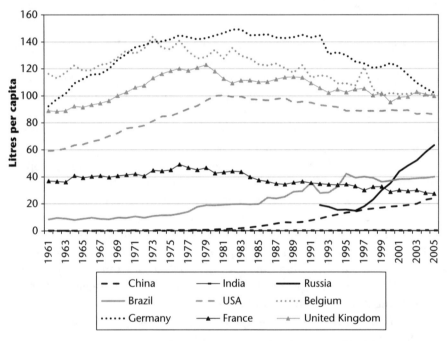

Figure 7.4. Per capita beer consumption (litre/capita), 1961–2005
Source: FAOstat (2010).

growth. Also in China, while average consumption has grown continuously since 1980, it is still far below that of the US or Western and Central Europe.

Third, a remarkable observation is that in all West European countries and in the US, per capita consumption has been declining for decades. The decline is substantial. The maximum consumption per capita was reached in 1974 in

Belgium, in 1976 in France, in 1980 in the UK, in 1981 in the US, and in 1983 in Germany. Per capita consumption has declined significantly since then: in Germany and Belgium, beer consumption declined from close to 150 litres per capita to around 100 litres per capita, a decline of around 30%.

To conclude whether a country is a 'beer-drinking nation' or not, one should not only consider total and per capita consumption, but also compare beer consumption with consumption of other drinks such as wine and spirits. Table 7.2 presents the share of beer, wine, and spirits in total alcohol consumption for several countries for 1961 and 2005. One can classify countries as 'beer-drinking', 'wine-drinking', and 'spirit-drinking nations', based on which beverage has the highest share in total alcohol consumption. With the largest proportion of alcohol intake coming from beer, the US, Germany, the Czech Republic, and Belgium have always been 'beer-drinking nations' over the past 50 years. France and Greece are 'wine-drinking nations' and Russia and China 'spirit-drinking nations'.

There are major changes in the shares for some of the countries between 1961 and 2005. For example, Spain and Poland have become beer-drinking nations in recent years, while before that they were wine (Spain) and spirit (Poland) drinkers. Interestingly, in many 'beer-drinking nations', the relative share of beer is declining and that of wine increasing. For example, in Belgium, the UK, Germany, and the Czech Republic, the consumption of beer is falling, while wine consumption has increased over the past few decades in most of these countries. In Belgium, the share of beer in total alcohol consumption has decreased from 71% in 1965 to 57% in 2005, with the share of wine consumption increasing from 15 to 37% over the same period. In the UK, the shift was even larger: the share of beer fell from 81% to 45%, while the

Table 7.2. Share of beer, wine, and spirits in total alcohol consumption

Country	1961			2005		
	Beer	Wine	Spirits	Beer	Wine	Spirits
US	**47.05**	11.15	41.79	**52.71**	16.04	31.25
Germany	**57.14**	17.32	25.54	**53.30**	26.99	19.71
UK	**80.95**	4.32	14.73	**45.35**	32.47	22.17
Czech Republic	**69.01**	19.05	11.94	**58.97**	16.15	24.88
Belgium	**71.28**	15.06	13.67	**56.83**	36.75	6.42
France	11.25	**74.41**	14.33	17.67	**62.28**	20.05
Spain	11.04	**65.39**	23.58	**47.98**	38.11	13.91
Greece	6.86	**86.14**	7.00	24.20	**49.61**	26.18
Russia	14.61	17.14	**68.26**	33.24	0.91	**62.66**
Poland	27.66	12.24	**60.10**	**55.65**	12.99	31.36
China	1.52	0.00	**98.48**	36.06	3.61	**60.34**

Note: The entries in **bold** indicate which beverage has the highest share in total alcohol consumption. Based on this criterion we classify the country as a 'beer-drinking', 'wine-drinking' or 'spirit-drinking country' in that period.
Source: WHO Global Alcohol Database (2010).

share of wine in total alcohol consumption went from 4 to 32%. Inversely, in 'wine-drinking nations' such as France, Spain, and Greece, the share of wine is declining and that of beer increasing—and substantially so. For example, in Spain, beer consumption increased from 11% in 1961 to 48% in 2005, effectively overtaking wine consumption, which was at 38% in 2005 (compared to 65% in 1961). In 'spirit-drinking nations' too, a relative increase in beer consumption is found. In 1965 the Russians, Polish, and Chinese consumed most of their alcohol in the form of spirits, while the share of beer was respectively 15, 28, and 2%. By 2005, the share of beer had increased strongly: to respectively 33, 56, and 36% of total alcohol consumption. These observations are consistent with arguments of Aizenman and Brooks (2008), Bentzen and Smith (2009), and Leifman (2001) that economic integration and globalization have led to a 'convergence' of alcohol consumption patterns.

In summary, the indicators we have reviewed in this section point to several interesting developments in the global beer market. In middle and low income countries which experience growth, such as China, Russia, Poland, and India, beer consumption grows. In rich countries, however, further growth has led to a reduction in beer consumption per capita. These observations suggest a non-linear relationship between income and beer consumption. At the same time, it seems that in many 'beer-drinking nations' beer seems to lose importance in favour of other alcoholic drinks, while the opposite is true in 'wine-drinking' and 'spirit-drinking' countries. In the regression model that we use later in the chapter, we will test whether such a non-linear, inverse-U function, relationship does indeed exist and whether there is international convergence in alcohol consumption patterns.

The Role of Trade

Before formally analysing the determinants of beer consumption, it is useful to consider the role of trade in beer markets. Convergence of alcohol consumption may occur through various mechanisms. One of them is trade.

Because beer is a voluminous product, made up mostly of water, trade is costly. That is why trade in beer has traditionally been limited and restricted to neighbouring regions. Expansion of brewing companies happens mostly through mergers and acquisitions and brewing licences for in-country production of foreign beers rather than actual trade of beer. Figure 7.5 illustrates how trade in beer has always been a small fraction of production.

In recent years, trade has grown substantially in volume and value. Trade growth was particularly strong in the past two decades, as Figure 7.6 illustrates. In the US, imports increased from around 0.5 billion litres in 1980 to 3.5 billion litres in 2007 (Tremblay and Tremblay, Chapter 8 in this volume).

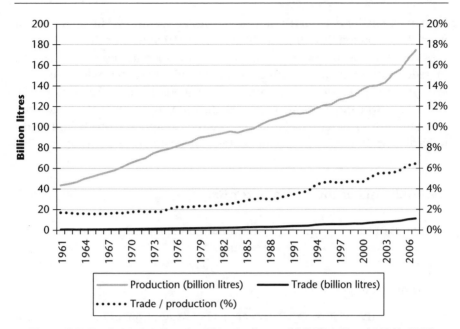

Figure 7.5. Production and trade of beer in the world (billion litres), 1961–2007
Source: FAOstat (2010).

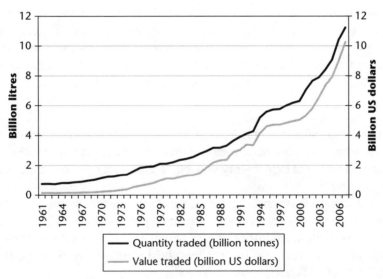

Figure 7.6. Volume and value of beer traded in the world (billion litres, US dollars), 1961–2007
Source: FAOstat (2010).

133

Belgian exports of beer increased from less than 250 million litres in 1980 to more than 1 billion litres in 2007 (Persyn et al., Chapter 5 in this volume).

However, if one looks at trade as a share of production, the relative growth in trade is rather small. In fact, the volume of traded beer increased from 2% of beer production in 1970 to around 5% over the last decade (see Figure 7.5). Still, as we will show below, increased trade openness seems to have been correlated with substantial changes in beer consumption globally and seems to have contributed to converging patterns of alcohol consumption.

Determinants of the Demand for Beer

In the rest of this chapter, we try to explain these patterns of beer consumption both across countries and over time.

Empirical Model

We estimate the relationship between beer consumption and a series of variables, such as income, climatic and religious effects, and the impact of global integration over the past decades, across a large group of countries.[7] To measure impacts and differences in beer consumption between countries and over time, we use a pooled approach, looking at both the variation *between* and *within* the countries, and an approach that focuses on the variation over time *within* countries only. First, we look at how beer consumption and the share of beer in total alcohol consumption vary between and within countries, making use of a pooled ordinary least square (OLS) regression and calculate cluster-robust standard errors. We estimate the following regression, using annual data for 104 countries for 25 years (1980 till 2005):

$$Y_{it} = a + x_{it}' \beta_1 + z_i' \beta_2 + u_{it}$$

where the dependent variable Y_{it} is an indicator of beer consumption, a is a constant term, x_{it} represents a vector of time-varying explanatory variables, z_i represents a vector of explanatory variables that do not vary over time, and u_{it} is the error term.

Second, using a fixed effects analysis, we isolate the within effect. We try to explain the evolution of beer consumption and its share in total alcohol consumption within countries over a period of 25 years (1980–2005). We include time dummies and use cluster-robust standard errors. We estimate the following fixed effects regression model:

---

[7] Due to lack of data, we cannot account for (changes in) different types of beer (e.g. between ales, lagers, light beers, premium beers, etc.).

$$Y_{it} = \alpha_i + x_{it}'\beta + \gamma_t + u_{it}$$

where the dependent variable Y_{it} is an indicator of beer consumption, α_i represents the country fixed effects, x_{it} represents a vector of time-varying explanatory variables, γ_t are the time dummies, and u_{it} is the error term.

We use two different indicators of beer consumption as dependent variables: average per capita beer consumption and the percentage of beer in total pure alcohol consumption. Average per capita consumption of beer is calculated based on production, trade, and population statistics from the Food and Agricultural Organization (FAO 2010). We compared our consumption indicators with data from the Commission For Distilled Spirits (2005) and found them to be generally consistent. FAO statistics are available for longer periods (1961–2005). Percentages of beer, wine, and spirits in total pure alcohol consumption are taken from the Global Alcohol Database (WHO 2010).

The first explanatory variable is income, measured as GDP per capita based on purchasing power parity (PPP), in constant 2005 international dollars. We include this variable also in squared terms to capture possible non-linear effects. Data on GDP per capita in PPP terms are taken from the World Development Indicators (WDI 2010).

The second explanatory variable is 'openness' as an indicator capturing potential effects of globalization. Openness is measured as the share of trade in GDP. Trade and GDP data are also from the World Development Indicators database (WDI 2010).

Third, to account for the impact of relative price effects we created a country-specific proxy for the relative price of beer to wine. There are no good price data sets available covering many countries and such long periods. The proxy variable we use is measured as the ratio of unit import prices for beer over wine. FAO data on import values and volumes for beer and wine are used (FAO 2010). We should emphasize that there may be endogeneity problems with this variable: countries with a high demand for beer are often countries where own beer production is high while wine is imported, which could be the reason for a lower relative beer-to-wine price. Hence, we should interpret the estimated coefficients of this variable with care—for several reasons.

Fourth, we use the minimum and maximum temperature and average rainfall as indicators of the environmental and climatic conditions which affect beer production. Country-level aggregated climate data are taken from the Tyndall Centre for Climate Change Research (Mitchell et al. 2004).

Fifth, we include a set of indicators to measure the impact of religion on beer consumption. Specifically, we use data on the share of different religions among the countries' population in the year 1970, taken from the Religion Adherence Database constructed by Barro and McCleary (2005). Since we expect religion to have an impact on the volume of alcohol consumption but not on the share of different types of alcohol, we include the religion shares only in the regression with 'beer consumption per capita' as the dependent variable.

Finally, to measure possible convergence effects we included a variable which indicates whether the country was initially a 'beer-drinking country'. A dummy (0–1) variable, 'beer-drinking country', equals 1 when the share of beer in total alcohol consumption was higher than that of wine and spirits in the first available data on the shares of different alcoholic drinks (WHO 2010). In the fixed effects analyses, this dummy is interacted with the openness variable.

Regression Results

We now present the key results, as summarized in Tables 7.3 and 7.4. We refer to Colen and Swinnen (2010) for more extensive statistical analyses and

Table 7.3. Beer consumption per capita

Variable	Pooled OLS regression	Fixed effects regression
GDP/cap (in 1,000 dollars)	4.485***	5.299***
	(0.831)	(1.777)
(GDP/cap)^2 (in 1,000 dollars)	−0.0708***	−0.0908***
	(0.0214)	(0.0248)
Openness	0.0774	0.0133
	(0.0509)	(0.0104)
Openness *Beer-drinking country		0.0294
		(0.101)
Relative price	−0.00555	−0.000110
	(0.0251)	(0.00452)
Minimum temperature	1.117	
	(1.426)	
Maximum temperature	−1.000	
	(1.277)	
Annual precipitation	−0.00507	
	(0.00394)	
% Catholics[1]	12.38**	
	(6.192)	
% Protestants	27.32	
	(17.89)	
% Orthodox	−0.537	
	(16.78)	
% Jews	−54.46***	
	(11.94)	
% Muslims	−8.089	
	(5.418)	
Fixed effects included	No	Yes
Year dummies included	No	Yes
Observations	2148	2148
R^2	0.733	0.173

Notes: [1] Percentage of population adhering to the Catholic religion in 1970. Similarly for other religions. Cluster-robust standard errors in parentheses. * $p < 0.10$, ** $p < 0.05$, *** $p < 0.01$.

Table 7.4. Share of beer in total alcohol consumption

	Pooled OLS regression	Fixed Effects regression
GDP/cap (in 1,000 US dollars)	0.0105**	−0.0128
	(0.00529)	(0.0109)
(GDP/cap)^2 (in 1,000 US, dollars)	−0.0000772	−0.0000258
	(0.000126)	(0.000152)
Openness	−0.000504*	−0.000112
	(0.000283)	(0.000127)
Openness *Beer-drinking country		−0.00236**
		(0.00118)
Relative price	−0.000559*	−0.0000847
	(0.000311)	(0.000120)
Minimum temperature	-0.0231*	
	(0.0125)	
Maximum temperature	0.0279**	
	(0.0108)	
Annual precipitation	0.0000406	
	(0.0000384)	
Fixed effects included	No	Yes
Year dummies included	No	Yes
Observations	2107	2107
R^2	0.096	0.156

Notes: Cluster-robust standard errors in parentheses. * $p < 0.10$, ** $p < 0.05$, *** $p < 0.01$.

robustness tests. Table 7.3 has beer consumption per capita as the dependent variable. In Table 7.4, the dependent variable is beer as a percentage of total alcohol consumption.

Our first important result is that we do indeed find an inverted-U shaped relation between income and per capita beer consumption in the pooled OLS and in the fixed effects specification (Table 7.3). The first- and second-order effects for income are strongly significant in both specifications. From the pooled OLS regression, we find that countries with higher levels of income initially consume more beer. Yet, the second-order coefficient on income is negative, indicating that from a certain income level onwards, higher incomes lead to lower per capita beer consumption. The fixed effects regression results confirm this, so the non-linear relationship for income holds not only between countries, but also *within* individual countries over time. As a country becomes richer, beer consumption rises, but when incomes continue to grow, beer consumption starts to decline at some income level. We calculated the turning point, i.e. the point where beer consumption starts declining with growing incomes, to be approximately 29,000 international dollars per capita.[8]

When looking at the percentage of beer in total alcohol as the dependent variable, the relation with income is less clear (Table 7.4). The pooled OLS

[8] This income level was reached by the US in 1985, Belgium in 1988, Germany in 1999, and the UK in 2000.

regression indicates that higher income levels correspond to a higher share of beer in the consumption of alcohol drinks, but we do not find the same results if we look only at the variation within countries over time.

The coefficients for the globalization indicator suggest that increased *openness* corresponds to higher beer consumption, but they are not significantly different from zero (Table 7.3). We do find a significant effect of openness on the share of beer in total alcohol consumption (Table 7.4). In the fixed effects regression with the share of beer as the dependent variable, we see that the interaction term of openness, with the dummy indicating whether or not the country was initially 'beer drinking', has a significantly negative coefficient. This result partially confirms earlier studies stating that countries converge in their alcohol drinking patterns. In countries where beer was the most important alcoholic drink, increased openness is correlated with a fall in the relative importance of beer in alcohol consumption. However, we do not find a significant effect of increased openness on the share of beer for those countries where beer was initially not the most important alcoholic drink.

For the other variables the results are according to expectations. For the price of beer relative to wine, the coefficients have a negative sign (Tables 7.3 and 7.4). Yet only in the regression with the share of beer in alcohol as the dependent variable is the effect significantly different from zero. This corresponds to the intuition that consumption of beer is lower when its price relative to a substitute—wine—is higher. As expected, a higher relative price of beer corresponds to a lower share of beer in total alcohol consumption.

The *climatic* variables indicate that beer consumption is higher where minimum temperatures are not too low and maximum temperatures not too high, corresponding to temperate climatic regions (see Colen and Swinnen 2010), though multicollinearity causes the effect to disappear once the variables on religion shares are inserted (Table 7.3).

The importance of different *religions* also affects beer consumption. High shares of Jews and Muslims[9] in a country correspond to lower levels of beer consumption, while countries with high percentages of Catholics and Protestants consume more beer (Table 7.3).

Conclusion

In this chapter we study the evolution of beer consumption between countries and over time. An overview of the historic evolution of beer consumption in the world indicates that consumption of beer has changed importantly over

---

[9] The coefficient for % Muslims is significantly different from zero at the 15% level (p-value = 0.12)

time. Over the past 50 years consumption patterns in beer too have changed strongly, with decreasing consumption in the traditional 'beer-drinking nations' and strong growth in emerging economies.

We analysed the determinants of beer consumption and estimate an empirical model to explain 'what makes a country a beer-drinking nation'. Our first empirical result is that the relationship between income and beer consumption is non-linear, both if we look at the variation between countries and when variation over time within countries is considered. Beer consumption initially increases with rising incomes, but at higher levels of income beer consumption falls with further income growth. Second, we find that in countries that were originally 'beer drinking', the share of beer in total alcohol consumption falls with opening of trade and increasing globalization, while this is not the case in the 'non-beer-drinking' nations. These findings are partially consistent with the idea that there is convergence in the consumption patterns of alcoholic beverages, as suggested in the literature.

Finally, other factors that can explain the different levels of beer consumption between countries are climatic conditions, the importance of different religions in the country, and the price of beer relative to other alcoholic drinks.

References

Aizenman, J. and E. Brooks (2008). 'Globalization and Taste Convergence: The Cases of Wine and Beer'. *Review of International Economics*, 6: 217–33.

Akerlof, G. A. (1991). 'Procrastination and Obedience'. *The American Economic Review*, 81/2: 1–19.

—— and R. E. Kranton (2000). 'Economics and Identity'. *Quarterly Journal of Economics*, 115: 715–53.

Barro, R. J., and R. M. McCleary (2005). 'Which Countries Have State Religions'? *Quarterly Journal of Economics* 120/4: 1331–70.

Becker, G. S. and K. M. Murphy (1988). 'A Theory of Rational Addiction'. *Journal of Political Economy*, 96/4: 675–700.

Bentzen, J. and V. Smith (2009). 'Developments in the Structure of Alcohol Consumption in OECD Countries'. Paper for the pre-AARES conference workshop, Adelaide, February 2010.

Colen, L. and J. F. M. Swinnen (2010). 'Beer Drinking Nations: The Determinants of Global Beer Consumption'. LICOS Discussion Paper.

Commission For Distilled Spirits (2005). *World Drink Trends 2005*. World Advertising Research Center Ltd, UK.

Faostat, Statistics Of The Food And Agriculture Organization Of The United Nations. <http://faostat.fao.org>, last accessed August 2010.

Fogarty, J. (2008). 'The Demand for Beer, Wine and Spirits: Insights from a Meta-Analysis Approach'. AAWE Working Paper 31, available at <http://www.wine-economics.org>.

Gallet, C. A., and J. L. List (1998). 'Elasticity of Beer Demand Revisited'. *Economics Letters*, 61/1: 67–71.

Larivière, E., B. Larue, and J. Chalfant (2000). 'Modeling the Demand for Alcoholic Beverages and Advertising Specifications'. *Agricultural Economics*, 22: 147–62.

Lee, B., and V. J. Tremblay (1992). 'Advertising and the U.S. Market Demand for Beer'. *Applied Economics*, 24/1: 69–76.

Leifman, H. (2001). 'Trends in Population Drinking', in T. Norström (ed.), *Alcohol in Post-War Europe: Consumption, Drinking Patterns, Consequences and Policy Responses in 15 European Countries*. Stockholm: National Institute of Public Health, 49–81.

McDevitte, W. A., and W. S. Bohn (1869). *Caesar's Gallic War*, translated from Julius Caesar, *De Bello Gallico*. New York: Harper & Brothers. Provided by The Internet Classics Archive at <http://classics.mit.edu//Caesar/gallic.html>.

Meloni, G., and J. F. M. Swinnen (2010). 'The Political Economy of European Wine Regulation'. Conference of the American Association of Wine Economists, UC Davis, California, USA, 27 June 2010.

Mitchell, T., T. R. Carter, P. Jones, and M. Hulme (2004). 'A Comprehensive Set of High-Resolution Grids of Monthly Climate for Europe and the Globe: The Observed Record (1901–2000) and 16 Scenarios (2001–2100)'. Tyndall Centre Working Paper 55. Tyndall Centre for Climate Change Research, <http://www.cru.uea.ac.uk/cru/data/hrg/>.

Nelson, J. (2003). 'Advertising Bans, Monopoly, and Alcohol Demand: Testing for Substitution Effects Using State Panel Data'. *Review of Industrial Organization*, 22/1: 1–25.

—— (2005). *The Barbarian's Beverage: A History of Beer in Ancient Europe*. London: Routledge.

Niskanen, W. A. (1962). 'The Demand for Alcoholic Beverages'. Ph.D. thesis, University of Chicago, Department of Economics, Chicago, IL.

Okrent, D. (2010). *Last Call: The Rise and Fall of Prohibition*. New York: Scribner, Simon & Schuster.

Ornstein, S. I., and D. M. Hanssens (1985). 'Alcohol Control Laws and the Consumption of Distilled Spirits and Beer'. *Journal of Consumer Research*, 12/2: 200–13.

Stigler, G. J., and G. S. Becker (1977). 'De Gustibus Non Est Disputandum'. *American Economic Review*, 67/2: 76–90.

Tremblay, V. J., and C. H. Tremblay (2005). *The US Brewing Industry: Data and Economic Analysis*. Cambridge, MA: MIT Press.

Unger, R. W. (2004). *Beer in the Middle Ages and the Renaissance*. Philadelphia: University of Pennsylvania Press.

WDI (World Development Indicators), <http://databank.worldbank.org>, last accessed August 2010.

WHO (World Health Organization), Global Alcohol Database, <http://apps.who.int/globalatlas/default.asp>, last accessed August 2010.

8

Recent Economic Developments in the Import and Craft Segments of the US Brewing Industry

Carol Horton Tremblay and Victor J. Tremblay

Introduction

The emergence and ascent of microbreweries over the past three decades stands in stark contrast to the erosion of the number of traditional macro-brewers in the US. The evolution of micros has been accompanied by an expansion in the import sector as well. How do the microbrewery and import segments of the beer industry differ from the macrobrewery segment?

The macro or mass-producing brewers produce traditional light lager beer, frequently called American lager. Lightness is achieved by limiting hop content, replacing malted barley (or malt) with adjuncts such as rice or corn, and using bottom-fermenting yeast. Historically, important players in the macro segment include the Anheuser-Busch, Miller, Coors, and Pabst brewing companies with brands such as Budweiser, Miller Lite, Coors Light, and Pabst Blue Ribbon, respectively.

Since 1938, the number of macrobrewers has fallen from approximately 700 companies to only 20 today. Still, they produce most of the beer consumed in the US, accounting for over 80% of the US market in 2009. Brewing a relatively homogeneous product in large quantities enables the macrobrewers to take advantage of scale economies and produce beer at a low unit cost.

On the micro side, the number of 'craft brewers' grew from two to over 1,700 enterprises from 1977 to 2009. Craft brewers include microbrewers, brewpubs, and regional craft brewers. In contrast to the macrobrewers, they are small in size and produce beer that is more in keeping with the brewing traditions of Europe. Like the imports, domestic craft beer comes in a variety of styles, including ales, porters, stouts, and lagers.

Most craft and import brands are made with malted barley and without adjuncts.[1] The use of malted barley makes European-style lagers darker and richer in flavour than traditional American lagers. Ales, porters, and stouts use bottom-fermenting yeast and more darkly roasted malt. This produces an even darker brew that is more bitter in flavour, is higher in alcohol, and has more calories than American and import/craft lagers (*Consumer Reports* 2001). Porters and stouts are so dark that they are almost black and nearly opaque.

There is limited competition between the macro and import/craft groups: they produce very different styles of beer and sell at different price points. For example, the typical import or domestic craft beer sells for over 50% more than premium American lager. Some beer connoisseurs believe that this price premium reflects the fact that imported and craft beers have more flavour and are superior in quality. In fact, Jim Koch, president of the Boston Beer (Samuel Adams) Company, calls craft and import beers the 'better beer' category of the market (*Modern Brewery Age* 1999).

The macro and import/craft groups are not perfectly distinct, however, as the macrobrewers do compete with the import and craft brewers to a certain extent with their so called 'super-premium' brands (e.g. Michelob). Super-premium beer lies between import/craft beer and American lager in price and also in heartiness, being lighter than most import and craft brands, but darker than domestic premium beer. For these reasons, leading trade journals identify a 'high end' category of beer, which includes super-premium, craft, and imported beer.[2]

In this chapter, we focus on the high end, paying particular attention to the import and domestic craft brewers. These relatively new entrants are capturing a growing share of the market and have invigorated the industry with a new and expanding array of products. Our main goal is to describe and explain recent economic trends in the import and craft sectors of the US beer market.[3]

The High End

Figure 8.1 graphs the market share of US sales for the super-premium, import, and craft beer sectors of the industry for 1970–2009. It reveals several

---

[1] An important exception is wheat beer, which is made from malted wheat and other grains. Examples include Hefeweizen and Weizenbier.

[2] For example, see *The High End: 2007*, Beer Marketer's Insights, Suffern, NY.

[3] Much of our discussion will focus on recent trends. For a more complete discussion of the history of the macros, import suppliers, and craft brewers from 1950 through 2000, see Tremblay and Tremblay (2005) and Tremblay et al. (2005).

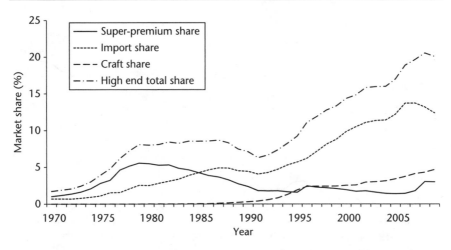

Figure 8.1. The market shares of super-premium, craft, and imported beer in the US, 1970–2009

interesting trends. For the most part, the long-term trends for imports and crafts have been positive over this period. Super-premium brands made a strong showing into the early 1980s, but have lost considerable share since that time. Imports had the greatest gains relative to craft and super-premium beers, except during the recessionary periods of the early 1990s and the late 2000s. The craft beer segment grew at a rapid rate from the mid-1980s through 1996. Growth has continued since then, albeit at a slower pace. In 2009, the high-end category accounted for 20.1% of US beer consumption, including 3.0% for super–premium, 12.4% for import, and 4.7% for craft beer.

The general rise in demand for high-end beer can be attributed to growing affluence in the US. The sub-premium or discount-priced brands of American lager are inferior goods in the sense that demand decreases (increases) as consumer income rises (falls).[4] Examples of brands in this category include Busch, Pabst Blue Ribbon, and Miller High Life. In contrast, demand for higher-priced normal or luxury goods will increase during economic booms and contract during recessions. Figure 8.2 plots US per-capita income in real terms, 1970 to 2009. It confirms that the trend in the share of the high-end category tracks the trend in consumer income, which is consistent with the hypothesis that high-end beer is a normal good.[5] Recessionary decreases in

---

[4] For example, the sub-premium brand Pabst Blue Ribbon saw a 25% sales increase in the recession of 2009.

[5] A formal test of the hypothesis that a particular style of beer is a normal good requires an estimate of the income elasticity of demand for that style. Although there are many studies that have estimated the income elasticity of demand for beer generally (see Tremblay and Tremblay 2005), to our knowledge no one has estimated it for any particular style or category of beer.

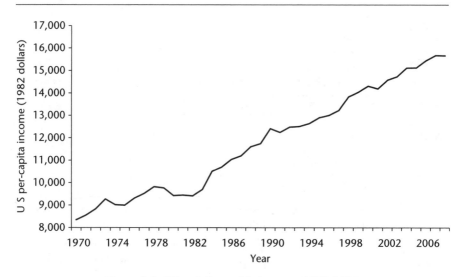

Figure 8.2. US real disposable income, 1970–2008

demand at the high end appear to be driven by declines in imports, as sales of craft beer held strong.

Other factors may explain why demand for craft beer did not decline during recessions. For example, demand for locally produced goods may increase during periods of economic stress if consumers want to keep local and regional businesses from failing (Carroll and Swaminathan 2000).[6] If this is the case, a recession has two effects: (1) it causes income to fall, which puts downward pressure on demand for normal goods such as import, craft, and super-premium beer; (2) it puts upward pressure on demand for craft brands because they are generally produced locally. This may explain why the share of imports, but not the share of crafts, fell during recessions.

Table 8.1 provides additional information concerning the influence of income and demographic factors on demand for several leading domestic premium, import, and craft brands of beer.[7] These include a variety of styles: Budweiser (American lager), Coors Light (American light lager), Corona (imported lager, Mexico), Guinness (imported stout, Ireland), Heineken (imported lager, Netherlands), Samuel Adams (domestic craft), and Sierra Nevada (domestic craft). Table 8.2 lists the average price of imported beer and several categories of domestic beer: craft, super-premium, and premium. It confirms that imported and craft beer sell for substantially higher prices

---

[6] Paul Gatza, Director of the Brewers Association, argues that craft beer also began to catch up with the reputation of imported brands (Theodore 2009). This too may have bolstered craft beer demand during the last decade.

[7] No super-premium brand was sampled.

Table 8.1. Demographics and US beer consumption for a sample of leading domestic, import, and craft brands, fall 2009

Percentage of consumers who purchase various brands of beer by gender, age, income, and region

	Budweiser	Coors Light	Corona	Guinness	Heineken	Sam Adams	Sierra Nevada
All	10.4	6.2	6.9	2.4	5.7	5.2	1.7
Male	15.0	7.9	9.1	3.9	8.2	7.6	2.4
Female	6.1	4.6	4.8	1.1	3.4	3.0	1.1
Age							
18–24	15.5	8.4	9.2	3.0	7.9	6.4	1.9
25–34	13.5	8.2	10.7	5.0	8.3	7.6	2.9
35–44	10.4	6.6	8.1	2.7	6.3	6.2	2.4
45–54	10.0	6.4	6.9	1.9	5.4	4.9	1.5
55–64	7.9	5.0	4.8	1.2	3.8	4.0	0.8
65+	6.1	2.7	1.7	0.6	2.6	2.1	0.3
Income							
150+	9.7	9.6	10.9	4.2	9.2	10.9	4.1
75–149.9	9.2	8.4	8.6	3.6	6.7	8.1	2.3
60–74.9	12.2	6.6	6.9	3.3	5.2	5.2	2.1
50–59.9	12.3	5.6	7.7	2.2	6.1	4.4	1.0
40–49.9	10.5	5.5	5.6	1.4	4.7	3.6	0.7
30–39.9	10.9	4.0	4.6	1.3	4.9	2.1	0.8
20–20.9	10.0	3.3	3.8	0.5	3.9	1.2	0.2
<20	10.9	3.0	4.5	0.9	3.6	1.5	1.0
Region							
Northeast	12.3	9.7	9.0	3.5	8.4	8.8	1.7
South	9.9	5.0	5.4	2.0	4.3	3.6	1.1
Midwest	9.7	4.5	5.5	1.8	4.5	4.9	1.1
West	10.6	6.9	9.1	2.9	7.0	5.2	3.3

Note: Income is measured in $1,000s. Budweiser is a premium American lager, Coors Light is an American light lager, Corona is an imported lager, Guinness is an imported stout, Heineken is an imported lager, Samuel Adams is a domestic craft ale, and Sierra Nevada is a domestic craft ale.

Source: Mediamark Research Inc. as reported in *Beer Industry Update* (2010).

Table 8.2. Average supermarket price per case by beer category

Beer Category	2006	2007	2008	2009
Import	25.68	26.75	27.02	27.26
Craft	27.20	28.11	29.64	30.63
Super-premium	20.51	21.62	23.09	23.90
Premium	16.71	16.91	17.35	17.91

Note: Values are in nominal dollars per case of 24 (12 oz) containers. Categories do not include light beer.

Source: Beer Industry Update (2010: 145).

than premium beer and that the price of super-premium beer falls between these extremes. Consistent with our discussion of normal and luxury goods, Table 8.1 shows that the largest proportion of consumers of high-end beer earn in excess of $75,000 a year. In contrast, the largest percentage of consumers who buy Budweiser earn between $50,000 and $75,000 a year.

Table 8.1 reveals other interesting differences among consumers who purchase different styles of beer. The percentages of women purchasing lighter lagers (Budweiser, Coors Light, and Corona) are higher than for the darker beers (Guinness, Samuel Adams, and Sierra Nevada). Similarly, consumers in the South, where the climate is warmer, are generally less likely to drink a darker beer than consumers in other regions. Location differences can be quite pronounced. In 2009, the market share of import and craft beer was approximately 17% in the US, 33% in California, and only 6% in Mississippi (*Beer Industry Update* 2010).

Several factors besides income and demographics have had an important effect on the sales trends of the import and craft segments of the high-end category. Because many of them affect import and craft beer consumption differently, we discuss them separately in the next two sections of the chapter.

Imports

Figure 8.3 plots the market share of the seven leading countries that export beer into the US for 1990–2009. In descending order from their 2009 shares, they are Mexico, the Netherlands, Canada, Germany, Ireland, Belgium, and the United Kingdom. Since World War II, the top four countries have remained the same, and their combined market share has grown from 67.2% in 1990 to 70.9% in 2009.

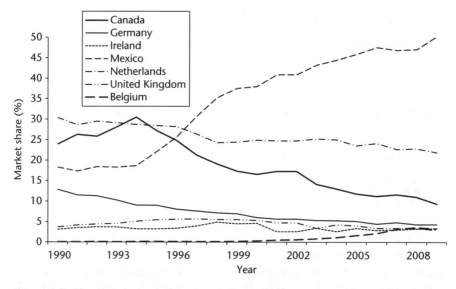

Figure 8.3. The domestic market share of the leading seven importing countries, 1990–2009

Table 8.3 lists the leading imported brands, their styles, and their countries of origin. The top 20 brands represent a variety of styles, including pale lagers, amber lagers, pale ales, brown ales, and stouts. As one might expect, most originate from the leading import countries. The success of Mexican beer is sustained by Corona, the leading imported brand and the sixth most popular brand of beer in the US in 2009. However, recent share growth of Mexican beer is attributable to the increased popularity of other brands, including Modelo Especial, Tecate, Corona Light, and Dos Equis. Five of the leading seven imported beers are now from Mexico.

Location gives Mexico a transportation cost advantage. Beer is expensive to ship given its high weight to value ratio. Also, shipping beer long distances can diminish freshness because of travel time and greater risk of exposure to light and heat. Given these limitations, some European brewers built production facilities in Canada, allowing them to cut transportation costs but still legally market their beer as an 'import'.[8]

Returning to Figure 8.3, the market share growth of beer from Mexico has come at the expense of beer from Germany, Canada, and the Netherlands,

Table 8.3. Import share (%) of the top 20 brands of beer imported into the US

Brand (beer style, country of origin)	2000	2005	2009
1. Corona (pale lager, Mexico)	27.8	30.7	27.7
2. Heineken (pale lager, Netherlands)	19.6	18.7	17.3
3. Modelo Especial (pale lager, Mexico)	1.9	4.3	7.6
4. Tecate (pale lager, Mexico)	4.1	4.6	5.5
5. Corona Light (pale lager, Mexico)	1.5	2.8	3.7
6. Guinness (stout, Ireland)	3.7	3.6	3.5
7. Dos Equis (pale lager, Mexico)	1.6	1.8	3.4
8. Stella Artois (pale lager, Belgium)	0.1	1.2	3.1
9. Labatt (pale lager, Canada)	5.2	3.8	3.0
10. Heineken Light (pale light, Netherlands)	—	—	2.3
11. Labatt Light (pale lager, Canada)	1.2	1.7	1.9
12. Newcastle (brown ale, UK)	1.3	1.8	1.9
13. Beck's (pale lager, Germany)	3.2	2.1	1.8
14. Amstel Light (pale lager, Netherlands)	2.6	2.8	1.7
15. Foster's (pale lager, Australia)	3.2	1.8	—
16. Pacifico (pale lager, Mexico)	1.9	1.3	1.4
17. Bass Ale (pale ale, UK)	2.7	1.7	1.0
18. Molson (pale lager, Canada)	1.4	1.1	0.9
19. Red Stripe (pale lager, Jamaica)	0.5	0.7	0.9
20. Negra Modelo (amber lager, Mexico)	0.5	0.8	0.9
Total	91.1	87.3	89.5

Note: Firms are ordered by the 2009 rank in import share.

Sources: Beer-style information obtained from Campbell and Goldstein (2010). Market share information for 2005 and 2009 obtained from *Beer Industry Update* (2010); for 2000 the sources are *Modern Brewery Age* (2001: 9) and *Beer Industry Update* (2005).

---

[8] Although somewhat deceptive, country-of-origin effects can be preserved if consumers are uninformed about the true brewing location.

although as Table 8.3 shows, Heineken still ranks second. Canada has three brands in the top 20, Labatt, Labatt Light, and Molson. Ireland's share is sustained by a single brand, Guinness. Beer from Belgium has gained share in the last decade, primarily due to the success of Stella Artois, which is distributed by Anheuser-Busch.

The US is a leading importer of beer and although beer exports have grown since 1990, the US continues to run a trade deficit in beer (see Figure 8.4). One way to describe a trade balance is with an Intra-Industry Trade Index (ITI), defined as $(IM - EX)/(EX + IM)$, where IM measures imports and EX measures exports (Karrenbroch 1990; Thompson 2001, chapter 7). With this definition, ITI = 1 when the product is imported and not exported, and ITI = −1 when it is exported and not imported. When imports equal exports, there is perfect trade balance, and ITI = 0. Figure 8.5 plots ITI for US brewing from 1990 to 2009. It shows that the index fell in the early 1990s as exports grew more rapidly than imports. Since 1995, the trade imbalance increased until the recession of 2007–9 which caused imports but not exports to decline.

It is unclear whether the success of imports slowed the growth of the craft beer segment, but there is evidence that it eroded the position of the super-premium brands (Tremblay and Tremblay 2005). Most brands from Mexico and Canada are light lagers, making them relatively close substitutes to American super-premium brands. Given their close proximity to the US, transportation costs are low and their prices are relatively competitive with super-premium brands.

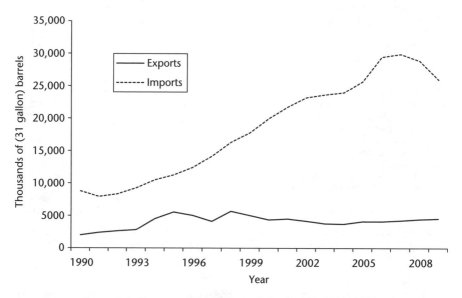

Figure 8.4. Beer exports and imports in the US, 1990–2009

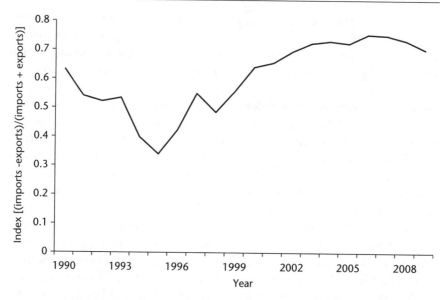

Figure 8.5. Intra-industry trade index for US beer, 1990–2009

Why has the import sector overall performed so well relative to domestic beers? Changes in both demand and supply conditions have contributed to the rapid growth in import beer consumption in the US over the last two decades. We have seen that import brands are normal goods, such that demand grows with economic prosperity. Another explanation derives from Veblen's (1899) theory of the influence of wealth and status. According to Veblen, an increase in income and wealth will cause some consumers to purchase more high status goods to impress others. These would include goods that command a high price and have a reputation for quality.[9] Through the conspicuous consumption of a high status good, consumers can signal to others that they are rich. Imports sell at a substantially higher price than domestic premium lager (Table 8.2), in part because of the high cost of shipping beer to the US. Thus, imported brands fulfil an important requirement of a high status good.

Quality is also important. On the demand side, consumers will pay more for high quality goods. Quality is a normal good and enhances status, so greater affluence should raise demand for high quality goods over time. On the supply side, higher quality goods generally sell for higher prices given that they are

---

[9] Various blind taste tests of beer show that beer drinkers generally receive higher utility when consumers believe that the beer they are drinking is high priced or when given positive information about the beer before tasting it. For example, see Allison and Uhl (1964), Lee et al. (2006), and Campbell and Goldstein (2010).

more expensive to produce. This begs the question: are import brands successful because they are of higher quality? Whether a higher price reflects higher quality is an important welfare issue. If consumers are continuously fooled into believing a high-priced brand is of higher quality when it is not, correcting this false belief will generally improve consumer welfare. On the other hand, if producers market both low- and high-priced brands of like quality to serve consumers with different attitudes about status, then this outcome is of less social significance. In such a setting, Wolinsky (1987) shows that consumers who care little about status are better served by low-priced brands, and consumers who value goods with a high prestige factor are better served by high-priced brands. Of course, there is unlikely to be social concern when a higher price reflects higher quality.

Some beer connoisseurs claim that traditional American lager lacks flavour and is inferior in quality to import and craft beers. A common argument is that import and craft brewers make better beer because they use a larger proportion of malted barley. Malted barley is more expensive than adjuncts, and beer made with a larger proportion of malted barley is darker and heartier. According to Goldammer (1999), American lager typically contains 25 to 65% adjuncts, while most European and craft style beers contain less than 30% adjuncts.[10]

In reality, consumers disagree over which style of beer they prefer, all-malt brands versus those made with adjuncts. Just as some consumers prefer red wine and others prefer white wine, some consumers prefer a darker beer and others a lighter beer. We saw in Table 8.1 that women generally prefer Coors Light to Guinness Stout. Michelob Ultra is a low carbohydrate beer that appeals to consumers on a special diet. Even Beck's, the famous German brand, sells both a regular and a light version in the US. When consumers disagree over one or more product characteristics such as the lightness of a beer, differentiation is said to be horizontal. In contrast, vertical differentiation exists when all consumers prefer the product with more of the vertical characteristic, ceteris paribus. Product quality is a good example of a vertical characteristic. In the case of beer, however, it appears that there is no consensus regarding which beer is better. Thus, a beer's lightness or the proportion of malted barley used in the brewing process is a horizontal rather than a vertical characteristic.

When products are differentiated horizontally, an increase in consumer income may generate greater demand for variety (Silberberg 1985). This

---

[10] Germany's Reinheitsgebot (meaning 'commandment of purity'), which required that beer be brewed from only malt, hops, and water, may have contributed to the perception that beer made from adjuncts is inferior in quality. For a more detailed discussion of the German beer purity law, see Mayer (1987), Jackson (1988), Glover (2001), and van Tongeren (Chapter 3 in this volume).

appears to be a contributing factor to the growing success of European-style beer in the US. After World War II, there was a general increase in consumer demand for light, low calorie foods (Tremblay and Tremblay 2005). In response, many processed foods and beverages became lighter and lower in calories. In the US beer industry, American lager had become so light by the 1970s that one brand was nearly indistinguishable from another.[11] As personal income increased over time, some consumers began to desire greater product variety and novelty. Foreign brewing companies were poised to fill this void. They were already making a variety of styles and were producing at efficient scale. All they needed to do was ship their products to the US. In addition, if consumers perceive product quality to be associated with a particular country or if products from distant places are viewed as exotic, then country-of-origin effects may also contribute to an imported brand's prestige factor and success.

Import success may also have been boosted by the greater advertising effort of the leading import brewers. As Table 8.4 shows, advertising per (31 gallon) barrel of the leading import brands (Corona, Guinness, and Heineken) generally exceeded the industry average and that of the leading super-premium brand, Michelob. This intensive advertising effort may have also contributed to the prestige factor of these brands.

Dos Equis provides an excellent example of how successful advertising, its 'Most Interesting Man in the World' campaign, can increase sales.[12] These ads feature a fictitious gentleman, the world's most interesting man, in an adventurous setting or bar environment, with a narrator describing his (frequently absurd) accomplishments. Examples include: 'He can speak French . . . in Russian' and 'He once had an awkward moment, just to see how it feels.' These ads typically close with the gentleman saying 'I don't always drink beer, but when I do, I prefer Dos Equis.' First introduced in 2006, analysts say that it is now the most recognizable advertising campaign in the beer industry (Fuhrman 2010). Its effectiveness is evident from the fact that Dos Equis sales rose 88.5% from 2005 to 2009, a period when import sales rose by only 1.2%.

In summary, the success of imported beer in the US is due to the increase in demand for high-end products that has been caused by long-run economic prosperity. It is also due to the ability of foreign suppliers to appeal to consumer demand for variety and prestige that is associated with rising income. On the cost side, many foreign brewers produce enough beer to reach scale efficiency but face high transportation costs relative to domestic brewers. The

---

[11] Blind taste tests demonstrate that most consumers cannot distinguish one brand of American lager from another and one brand of pale European lager from another. For example, see Allison and Uhl (1964), Lee et al. (2006), and Campbell and Goldstein (2010).

[12] For additional information and a montage of commercials, see <http://dosequis.com> and <http://www.youtube.com/watch?v=QI58wj4b4g0>.

Table 8.4. Advertising per barrel of the leading domestic and imported brands, 2000–2009

Beer category brand	2000	2001	2002	2003	2004	2005	2006	2007	2008	2009
Domestic Premium										
Budweiser	4.57	3.94	4.29	3.89	4.48	4.66	2.91	3.12	5.07	4.43
Coors	23.25	20.98	22.15	14.71	7.20	2.82	5.91	13.10	13.59	5.35
Miller GD	4.70	9.69	5.29	6.41	15.39	3.26	10.23	9.69	5.29	6.41
Domestic Light										
Bud Light	3.42	2.75	3.09	3.46	3.97	3.87	3.53	3.12	5.07	4.43
Coors Light	7.21	7.80	8.35	8.18	7.76	9.06	8.16	7.55	6.28	7.23
Miller Lite	5.61	6.45	7.76	7.52	7.42	8.53	5.95	5.10	6.14	7.22
Domestic Super-premium										
Michelob	7.96	9.16	5.72	7.28	2.63	1.81	0.07	16.94	2.92	1.01
Craft										
Boston	11.90	4.42	20.22	28.77	25.67	20.46	16.78	5.71	15.71	14.11
Import										
Corona (Modelo)	6.57	5.33	4.34	5.28	5.21	4.91	4.96	5.91	5.08	5.63
Guinness (Diageo)	5.87	14.71	23.68	18.25	12.27	12.14	12.74	6.61	6.59	8.79
Heineken	12.48	14.44	13.15	14.13	9.61	14.02	8.89	12.01	8.57	9.48
Industry average	4.54	4.80	5.71	5.28	5.63	5.69	4.87	4.56	4.72	4.88

Note: Advertising is measured in $1,000s.

Source: TNS Media Intelligence/CMR as reported in *Beer Industry Update* (various issues).

craft segment of the brewing industry, discussed next, shares some of the same features as the import segment.

Craft Brewers

Although there is some debate over the exact origins of the craft beer movement, early entrants in the 1970s and 1980s started out as very small enterprises.[13] Thus, they were originally called microbreweries or boutique breweries. Over time, successful ones outgrew the 'micro' name. Today, the Brewers Association defines the craft segment to include three subgroups: microbreweries, brewpubs, and regional craft breweries.[14] Each must produce primarily all-malt lagers and ales. A microbrewery is defined as a brewery that produces less than 15,000 barrels annually, with at least 75% of its beer sold off-site. A brewpub is a restaurant–brewery that sells less than 15,000 barrels a year and less than 75% of its beer off-site. A regional craft brewery is a microbrewery that has outgrown the 15,000 barrel limit.[15]

---

[13] See Tremblay and Tremblay (2005) for a more complete discussion of the origins of the US microbrewery movement.

[14] See <http://www.brewersassociation.org>, accessed 6 August 2010.

[15] The upper limit is debatable. For example, the Brewers Association sets it at 2 million barrels. This definition would exclude the Boston Beer Company, as its sales exceeded 2 million barrels for the first time in 2009. On the other hand, the definition in *Beer Industry Update* (2010), a

Figure 8.6 plots the total number of craft brewers (microbreweries, brew-pubs, and regional craft brewers) in the US from 1980 to 2009. Their numbers have risen from a handful of enterprises in 1980 to over 1,700 by 2009. The figure shows an increasing rate of entry from the mid-1980s through the mid-1990s. Entry continued, although at a slower rate, until over-exuberance led to a shakeout in the late 1990s. The number of craft brewers declined by over 10% from 1998 to 2001, but has returned to prior levels and stabilized since then. Figure 8.7 graphs the profit-to-sales ratios for three publically traded craft brewers, Boston, Pyramid, and Redhook.[16] It reveals that profit rates of the smaller craft brewers fell during the shakeout of the late 1990s. These rates had not yet recovered by 2006. Boston's profit-to-sales ratio was unaffected by the shakeout and has been relatively constant except for the drop in 2008, which is due to a product recall.[17]

The early success of the Boston Beer Company and several other craft brewers is at least partially attributable to their decision to be contract

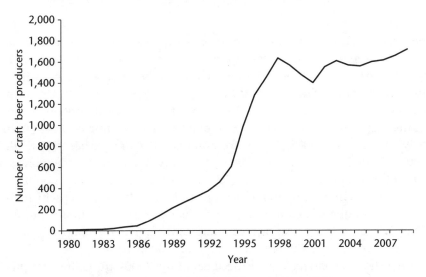

Figure 8.6. Number of craft brewers, 1980–2009

publication of annual industry reports, includes Boston. Throughout this chapter, we include Boston as a craft brewer.

[16] Profit data are limited because most craft brewers are privately owned. In 2008, the Redhook Brewing Company merged with the Widmer Brothers Brewing Company to form Craft Brewers Alliance (CBA). In addition, CBA owns 20% of the Kona Brewing Company of Hawaii and 40% of the Goose Island Brewing Company of Chicago. CBA benefits from the distribution system of Anheuser–Busch, as Anheuser–Busch owns 36% of CBA. For further discussion, see Fuhrman (2008b).

[17] The recall cost the company $14.90 per barrel or 8.8% of net revenue (*Boston Beer Company First Quarter Report* 2009).

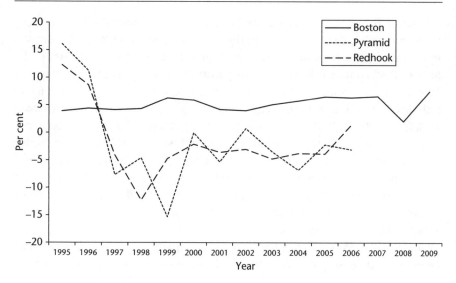

Figure 8.7. Profit-to-sale ratios for three craft brewers, 1995–2009

brewers,[18] that is, they contracted to have their beer brewed by established macrobrewers that had excess capacity. In the 1980s and 1990s, contract brewing was advantageous because there was substantial excess capacity in the beer industry. Such contracts not only benefited the macrobrewer by reducing its excess capacity, but they also benefited the craft brewer because of the high sunk costs associated with building new brewing facilities (Tremblay and Tremblay 2005). Today, for example, all craft style beer sold by the Pete's Brewing Company (e.g. Pete's Wicked Ale) is brewed under contract with other breweries.[19] A firm like Pete's, a 'virtual brewer', focuses on brand development, marketing, and strategic planning. As the excess capacity in the industry has diminished in recent years, however, so has contract brewing. Over 22% of craft beer was brewed under contract in 2000, but only 4% was brewed this way in 2009 (*Beer Industry Update* 2005, 2010).

Even though contract brewing declined in the 2000s, the craft sector prospered overall. Some of the same forces that drove up sales for imports also drove up sales for domestic craft beer. As discussed previously, economic prosperity led to an increase in demand for variety during a period when the macrobrewers were producing an increasingly homogeneous good. In addition, because craft beer sells for a higher price than traditional American lager

[18] Boston's brands had been brewed by several beer companies in the past, including High Falls (Genesee) Brewing Company in Rochester, New York and the Hudepohl–Schoenling Brewing Company in Cincinnati, Ohio (Tremblay and Tremblay 2005).

[19] The macros can also be contract brewers. For example, MillerCoors brews all of the beer marketed by the Pabst Brewing Company.

(Table 8.2), craft beer has a high prestige factor. Thus, demand for craft beer grew with increasing consumer income and as traditional American lager became lighter and lighter.

At the same time, craft brewers are located close to their customers, unlike import suppliers. This lowers transportation costs and allows them to deliver a fresher product. In contrast to the macrobrewers and import suppliers, however, most craft brewers are inefficiently small. Tremblay and Tremblay (2007) estimate that the average cost of production declines substantially until annual production reaches 1.2 million barrels and then falls slightly until almost 40 million barrels are produced. Of the craft brewers, only Boston exceeds the 1.2 million mark. The second largest brewer, Sierra Nevada, sold 724,000 barrels in 2009.

In spite of this cost disadvantage, there are some advantages to being small. First, it allows the craft brewer to be more flexible and responsive to the changing tastes of its customer base.[20] Offering a new brand or changing the formula of an existing brand takes less time for a small brewer. In addition, some consumers have a strong preference for local products and shun items produced by large corporations and sold using mass-market advertising campaigns (Carroll and Swaminathan 2000). This may be one reason why smaller craft brewers spend little or nothing on advertising. To compete with the extensive array of macro and import brands that are available today, small craft brewers put most of their sales efforts into gaining shelf space in supermarkets and tap access at bars. Marketing efforts of craft brewers generally target local customers by sponsoring community events, providing displays in local establishments, and distributing bar coasters, for example.

This illustrates the classic tradeoff that firms face when consumers demand variety, while efficiency requires large-scale production. Lower costs and prices are attained by producing large quantities of a relatively homogeneous product. Yet, greater consumer satisfaction is reached when a wide variety of styles are produced in small quantities. Under these conditions, it is common for firms to pursue different niche strategies (Porter 1980; McAfee 2002). In brewing, the macrobrewers pursue a low-cost strategy. Import and regional craft brewers offer greater variety, but import brewers face higher transportation costs and craft brewers are less scale efficient. Finally, small microbreweries are high-cost producers that offer a wide variety of products and are in a better position to serve the changing tastes of consumers in their local markets.

---

[20] For example, to meet the unique preferences of beer drinkers in the Northwest, the Deschutes Brewing Company has recently experimented with 'extreme beers' which have very high alcohol and hop content (Barnard 2008).

Changes in government regulations have also contributed to the growth of craft brewing. First, cuts in federal taxes for smaller brewers went into effect in 1977, just before the microbrewery movement took off. For brewers that sold at least 2 million barrels per year, the excise tax rate was $9 per barrel. For brewers that were below this threshold, the tax rate was $7 per barrel on the first 60,000 barrels and $9 on each additional barrel sold beyond 60,000.[21] Fifteen states currently give tax breaks to smaller brewers (*Brewers Almanac* 2009).[22] For example, the excise tax rate in Minnesota is $4.60 for each barrel sold in the state for brewers with total sales exceeding 100,000 barrels. For smaller brewers, the tax rate is $0 on the first 25,000 barrels and $4.60 on each additional barrel. Tremblay and Tremblay (2005) find that these tax differences have a sizeable effect on brewer costs: taxes account for about 5% of the cost of goods sold for small craft brewers and almost 30% for the macrobrewers.

Two other legislative acts encouraged craft brewing. First, in 1979 President Carter signed a bill to legalize home brewing. Second, beginning in the mid-1980s individual states began to make brewpubs legal. They were legal in only six states in 1984, but became legal in every state of the nation by 1999. These changes are beneficial because many of the early entrepreneurs who built successful craft breweries began as home brewers or brewpub owners.

Craft Consolidation

As is common in many maturing industries, a handful of firms have come to dominate the craft beer sector. By 2000, the four largest craft brewers produced over 39% of US craft beer. This number has changed very little over the last decade, standing at 41% in 2009. Sales trends over the last five years for the leading craft brewers are listed in Table 8.5. Although the share of the top four has remained relatively stable over this period, there has been some turnover among firms. Over the last decade, the Alaskan and Anchor brewing companies have dropped out of the top ten. A merger between the Widmer and Redhook brewing companies formed the Craft Brewers Alliance in 2008.[23]

---

[21] Since 1991, brewers that sell greater than or equal to 2 million barrels per year pay an excise tax rate of $18 per barrel. Smaller brewers continue to pay $7 per barrel on the first 60,000 barrels, but $18 on each additional barrel sold beyond 60,000.

[22] These include Alaska, Iowa, Kentucky, Michigan, Minnesota, Montana, New Mexico, New York, Ohio, Pennsylvania, Rhode Island, Texas, Washington, Wisconsin, and Wyoming.

[23] Sales figures in Table 8.5 for Craft Brewers Alliance include the sum of sales from Widmer, Redhook, and Kona for 2000–7. Widmer and Redhook were among the top ten craft brewers in 2000.

Table 8.5. Output of leading craft brewers

Brewer (year co. began)	2005	2006	2007	2008	2009
Boston (1985)	1,353	1,581	1,848	1,992	2,021
Sierra Nevada (1980)	613	637	663	670	724
Craft Brewers Alliance (2008)[1]	454	511	554	571	583
New Belgium (1992)	370	438	476	495	583
Pyramid (1984)	175	188	201	208	192
Deschutes (1988)	146	159	162	182	187
Magic Hat (1994)	61	79	103	128	154
Boulevard (1988)	104	117	130	138	139
Full Sail (1987)[2]	86	96	122	134	137
Harpoon (1986)	90	105	116	117	131

Notes: Output is measured in 1,000 barrels.
[1] Includes sales of Widmer (1984), Redhook (1982) and Kona (1995).
[2] Output includes contract production.
Source: *Beer Industry Update* (2010: 267).

This merger and the relative decline in Alaskan and Anchor sales opened the door for Magic Hat, Boulevard, and Full Sail to enter the top ten.

The Boston Beer Company is the largest producer in the craft beer sector. It has experienced remarkable growth since its start in 1985. In the last decade, Boston's market share of craft beer has grown from 17% in 2000 to over 22% in 2009 and its profit rate has remained steady. Part of Boston's rapid growth can be attributed to its successful advertising campaigns. Boston is the first craft brewer to heavily invest in advertising, in contrast to most craft brewers that typically shun traditional advertising media. Boston often outspends leading import suppliers (see Table 8.4). As discussed previously, another reason for Boston's early success is its decision to start out as a contract brewer. With continued growth and diminished excess capacity in the industry, however, Boston began to rethink this strategy. In 1997, it purchased a Cincinnati brewery from the Hudepohl-Schoenling Brewing Company, and in 2008 it purchased what once had been the Schaeffer Brewery in Pennsylvania from Diageo North America, which used it to make Smirnoff Vodka. With these mergers, Boston now brews all of its own beer and produces beer under contract for other brewers. Its growth in size has enabled it to gain scale efficiency. Today, Boston is the largest American-owned brewery in the US as a result of continued consolidation and internationalization of the beer industry.[24]

---

[24] In the last decade, the largest brewers have been Anheuser-Busch, Miller, Coors, and Pabst. In 2002, Miller was purchased by South African Breweries to form SABMiller. In 2008, Coors and SABMiller established a joint venture called MillerCoors. Pabst is now solely a marketing entity, with all of its beer brewed by MillerCoors. Finally, in 2008 Anheuser-Busch was purchased by Belgium's InBev to form Anheuser-Busch InBev.

Reaction from the Macrobrewers

The continued success of the import and craft beer categories has caused the leading macrobrewers to take notice. Today, the major macros have contracts to distribute imported brands in the US. For example, in 2010 Anheuser-Busch distributed 13 different imported brands of beer, including Bass Ale, Beck's Lager, and Stella Artois.[25] The macros have also purchased partial interest in smaller craft brewers, which gives the smaller brewers instant access to the macrobrewers' distribution networks. For example, Anheuser-Busch has partial ownership of the Craft Brewers Alliance, and MillerCoors purchased the regional craft brewer, Leinenkugal, in 1988.

In addition, the macrobrewers have introduced their own brands of craft-style beer. In the last decade, Anheuser-Busch has marketed craft-style beer under the Elk Mountain name, Miller under Road Plank, and Coors under Blue Moon. To help create the illusion that these brands are produced by small craft brewers, their labels do not carry their macrobrewery name. Hence, they are frequently called 'phantom', 'stealth', or 'microclone' brands (Tremblay and Tremblay 2005). Another response pursued by Anheuser-Busch has been the expansion of its Michelob line, with the marketing slogan—'Crafting a Better Beer' (Fuhrman 2008a). In 2010, it offered 12 different craft styles of its super-premium brand, including Michelob Pale Ale, Porter, Rye P.A., and Dunkel Weisse.[26] The Michelob line accounts for most of the sales in the super-premium category.[27]

In summary, the craft sector has benefited from growing consumer demand for variety, novelty, and high prestige goods. Craft brewers have also benefited from government policies that favour small-scale beer producers. The main strengths of small craft brewers is that they face relatively low transportation costs, bring a fresh product to market, and are in a position to respond quickly to changing consumer preferences. Their main weakness is that most are too small to take advantage of the substantial scale economies in brewing.

Conclusion

Import and craft brewers have made an impressive mark on the US brewing industry. Despite selling at higher prices, sales growth of import and craft beer has outpaced growth of traditional American lager. Presently, the import and

[25] From the Anheuser-Busch webpage, <http://anheuserbusch.com/s/>, accessed 13 August 2010.

[26] This was obtained from the Anheuser-Busch web site, <http://www.anhueser-busch.com/beerverified.html>.

[27] For example, *Beer Industry Update* (2005) reports that Michelob had a 71.5% share of the super-premium category in 2005.

craft segment accounts for 17% of beer sales in the US, compared with less than 1% in 1970. Traditional macrobrewers have responded to import and craft competition by creating their own versions of craft-style beer.

The import and craft brewers bring a variety of beers to consumers. Their price premium and image of quality generate prestige effects that are particularly appealing to some consumers. These factors positively correlate with income. As would be expected, import and craft beers gained market share as income rose over time, and imports fared poorly in recessions. Craft beers tied to local communities may be somewhat insulated from economic downturns, but the future success of imports, at least in the short term, may be hindered by hard economic times.

It is difficult to project the fate of the craft beer category and the small microbrewery, in particular. Given the substantial scale economies in brewing, unit costs fall as they increase their size. The irony is that as successful micros grow, they lose their ties to local communities and can no longer be called microbreweries. A case in point is the Boston Beer Company, now producing over 2 million barrels per year. Like the macros, Boston is large enough to exploit most scale economies and advertise in conventional media, a sharp departure from the microbrewery philosophy. The challenge for brewers such as Boston is to maintain their flexibility and small craft brewer image as they expand in size.

An important difficulty facing individual craft brewers as well as import suppliers is limited shelf space in supermarkets and number of taps in bars. Nevertheless, the established popularity of import and craft beer bodes well for their future. Overall, we expect the import and craft segments to continue to grow and capture a larger share of the US beer market in the future.

References

Allison, R. I., and K. P. Uhl (1964). 'Influence of Beer Brand Identification on Taste Perception'. *Journal of Marketing Research*, 1/3: 36–9.

Anheuser-Busch, <http://www.anheuserbusch.com/s/>, accessed 13 August 2010.

Barnard, J. (2008). 'Golden Goblet Runneth Over—A Very Good Year for High-End Beers'. *The Commercial Appeal*, Bend, Oregon, 27 July. Available at <http://www.highbeam.com>.

Beer Industry Update (2005, 2009, 2010). Nanuet, NY: Beer Marketer's Insights.

Brewers Almanac (2009). Washington: US Brewers Association.

Brewers Association, <http://www.brewersassociation.org>, accessed 6 August 2010.

Boston Beer Company First Quarter Report (2009). 29 March 2009, <http://www.boston-beer.com>.

Campbell, S., and R. Goldstein (2010). *The Beer Trials*. New York: Fearless Critic Media.

Carroll, G. R. and A. Swaminathan (2000). 'Why the Microbrewery Movement? Organizational Dynamics of Resource Partitioning in the American Brewing Industry after Prohibition'. *American Journal of Sociology*, 106/3: 715–62.

Consumer Reports (2001). 'Which Brew for You?' August: 10–16.

Fuhrman, E. (2008a). 'The Craft'. *Beverage Industry*, 1 January. Available at <http://www.highbeam.com>.

—— (2008b). 'Craft Brewers Alliance: Combined Passion for Great Beer'. *Beverage Industry*, 1 November. Available at <http://www.highbeam.com>.

—— (2010). 'Let's Hear it for Beer'. *Beverage Industry*, 1 March. Available at <http://www.highbeam.com>.

Glover, B. (2001). *The World Encyclopedia of Beer*. London: Lorenz Books.

Goldammer, T. (1999). *The Brewers' Handbook: The Complete Book to Brewing Beer*. Clifton, VA: KVP Publishers.

Jackson, M. (1988). *The New World Guide to Beer*. Philadelphia: Courage Books.

Karrenbroch, J. D. (1990). 'The Internationalization of the Beer Brewing Industry'. *Federal Reserve Bank of St Louis Review*, 72/6: 3–19.

Lee, L., S. Frederick, and D. Ariely (2006). 'Try It, You'll Like It: The Influence of Expectation, Consumption, and Revelation on Preferences for Beer'. *Psychological Science*, 17/12: 1054–8.

Mayer, K. J. (1987). 'The Verdict—Beer Purity on Trial'. *Brewers Almanac*, June: 32–5.

McAfee, R. P. (2002). *Competitive Solutions: A Strategist's Toolkit*. Princeton: Princeton University Press.

Modern Brewery Age (1999). 'Boston Beer's Jim Koch Talks to "Boston Globe" about Future of Company', 8 February.

—— (2001). 'Imports on a Roll'. 23 July.

Porter, M. E. (1980). *Competitive Strategy: Techniques for Analyzing Industries and Competitors*. New York: The Free Press.

Silberberg, E. (1985). 'Nutrition and the Demand for Tastes'. *Journal of Political Economy*, 93/5: 881–900.

The High End: 2007 (2008). Nanuet, NY: Beer Marketer's Insights.

Theodore, S. (2009). 'Beer Defies the Odds: Category Continues to Pick Up Steam, Despite Economic Challenges'. *Beverage Industry*, 1 April. Available at <http://www.highbeam.com>.

Thompson, H. (2001). *International Economics: Global Markets and International Competition*. London: World Scientific.

Tremblay, V. J. and C. Horton Tremblay (2005). *The U.S. Brewing Industry: Data and Economic Analysis*. Cambridge, MA: MIT Press.

—— —— (2007). 'Brewing: Games Firms Play', in V. J. Tremblay and C. Horton Tremblay (eds.), *Industry and Firm Studies*. Armonk, NY: M. E. Sharpe.

Tremblay, V. J., C. Horton Tremblay, and N. Iwasaki (2005). 'The Dynamics of Industry Concentration for U.S. Micro and Macrobrewers'. *Review of Industrial Organization*, 26/3: 307–24.

Veblen, T. (1899). *The Theory of the Leisure Class*. New York: Macmillan.

Wolinsky, A. (1987). 'Brand Names and Price Discrimination'. *Journal of Industrial Economics*, 35/3: 255–68.

9

Culture and Beer Preferences

Jill J. McCluskey and Sanatan Shreay

Introduction

> An intelligent man is sometimes forced to be drunk to spend time with his
> fools.
>
> (Ernest Hemingway, *For Whom the Bell Tolls*)

Beer is the oldest and the most widely consumed alcoholic beverage in the
world (Arnold 2005). In the United States, beer is the most consumed alcoholic beverage, with roughly $50 billion in annual sales. Beer drinking is
associated with social traditions such as beer festivals, as well as a rich pub
culture, and friendships. Although preferences for types of beer may be
regional, sharing beer with friends is universal. Friends might meet to socialize
over pitchers of beer every Friday night to end the work week. Many social
traditions and activities are associated with drinking beer, such as watching
sporting events. While specific types of beer and social attitudes towards
drinking beer vary around the world, the basics of brewing beer are shared
across many cultural boundaries.

Since beer is often consumed socially with a group of friends, social groups
often consume the same style of beer. This may lead to possible habit formation and peer effects. A new group member may buy a pitcher of beer that does
not conform to the social group's tastes. The pitcher may be consumed only
by the purchaser. The new group member will likely consider this feedback
when he or she makes the next purchase for the group.

The macrobrews dominate the beer market in the United States. US consumers' first (and sometimes only) contact with beer will likely be the macro
lagers that are designed to sell at a low cost. However, microbrews and
craft beers are gaining ground. Regional differences exist in preferences for
microbrews versus macro lagers. Microbrew pubs and microbrewed beer have

been growing in popularity in the United States for the past few decades, with greater growth in the West. However, in parts of the US Midwest and South, it is difficult to buy a microbrew, even in some urban centres. In other words, there is limited to no availability of certain beers. Borchgrevink and Susskind (1998) found that their respondents had preferences for microbrew beers compared to the widely available national brands.

Of course, differences in regional beer preferences are not just an American phenomenon. Germany has a long history and culture of beer drinking. Different regions of Germany have developed different beer styles, and certain styles of beers are more available in their region of origin. Correspondingly, many German consumers have preferences for the styles of beer from their own regions of origin and there is a great deal of variation across regions. For example, the blond *Kölsch* is the most popular beer in the Cologne region in northern Germany, and *Weissbier* has a large market share in Bavaria, but not in the country as a whole (German Beer Institute 2008).

There has been a great deal of recent interest in the economics of identity (Akerlof and Kranton 2000), social interaction, and peer effects. At the same time, there is a line of research on changes in preferences. This chapter discusses the intersection of these ideas and how they shape preferences for beer within the context of culture.

Previous Literature on Effects of Culture, Availability, and Peers

Many influential researchers have examined how tastes, habits, and preferences affect consumption. Gorman (1967) integrates tastes in his model, as a function of past behaviour. Peston (1967) presents a model that includes a taste parameter which is influenced by habits. Pollak (1970) creates a model of consumer behaviour based on habit formation. In an application, Gao et al. (1997) utilize an Almost Ideal Demand System (AIDS) method, with a single latent variable to model consumer taste determination and taste change for beef and complex carbohydrates. Following Pollak (1970), Gao et al. (1997) argue that taste differences are mainly determined by differences in household characteristics.

Recently economists have included identity—a person's sense of self—in economic models of preferences. Akerlof and Kranton (2000) include identity in the utility function. Identity was introduced into the utility-maximizing framework in an analysis which draws directly from social psychology's social identity approach and self-categorization theory. The power of social groups can often be explained with psychology that results in social comparison and imitation. Numerous approaches have been used to investigate such social processes in economic models. Duesenberry (1949) argues that an individual's utility from consumption depends not only on the absolute level of consumption, but also on one's consumption relative to others. This line of research provides a rationale for why one's peers' consumption patterns matter.

Psychological research posits that the qualities that affect consumer preferences exist not only in the products, but also in the social setting in which the products are being used. In other words, the preference for a given product may partly depend on who else uses the product. We may observe that one's peers' consumption has two effects. First, the consumer may experience a sense of belonging from purchasing the same products as their friends, peers, and family. Second, the effects of observing the consumption of others are called socialization effects. As a result of interpersonal contact, consumers may change their preferences. These socialization effects hold that personal preferences change in the direction of the characteristics of the product that is consumed by friends, peers, family, and other people. Hayakawa and Vinieris (1997) and Hayakawa (2000) find empirically that people with equal or higher status generally have an effect on one's consumptive behaviour.

One can think about how these ideas apply to immigrants who are living in a new culture. In a descriptive analysis, Mehta and Belk (1991) examine how Indian immigrants to the United States change their consumption patterns and adapt to US culture. These immigrants retain a strong preference for Indian foods, but to varying degrees they all also eat 'American' foods. Their sample of immigrants is more likely to include American food if they are entertaining American friends out of concern that their guests will not like Indian foods.

In addition to socialization, consumer preferences may also change as a result of repeated consumption of a product. Zajonc (1968) shows that mere exposure to a stimulus increases consumers' enjoyment of these stimuli. Zeller (1991) argues that processes of exposure, social factors, and conditioning can explain the strong shift in preferences for foods that are initially disliked. Stevenson and Yeomans (1995) experimentally demonstrate that consumer's preferences for the taste of chili burn increased after consuming food that produced this sensation, without affecting the preferences for other foods. These results suggest that consumption that is initially disliked may become more satisfying after repeatedly experiencing and consuming it. This process is called the exposure effect.

The exposure effect and the socialization effects should be jointly considered in modelling preferences for beer. In this chapter, we discuss how preferences for beer can incorporate consumers' own past consumption experiences, their peers' consumption patterns, availability of consumer goods, and their consumer's identity. In sum, we will argue that culture affects beer preferences.

Issues in Modelling Preferences for Beer

Empirically, most economists agree that past consumption patterns are important factors in explaining present consumption patterns. Thus, it is reasonable to assume that the quantity of a good should depend at least partly on past consumption or experience of that good. With beer, experience is more important. It is commonly understood that beer has an acquired taste. Most consumers do not like their first taste of beer. This makes beer an interesting good because preferences for it change with experience. We would expect preferences to increase to a higher level of utility with beer experience. Utility for beer could be modelled with a non-decreasing, non-linear function of past experience.[1]

At the same time, there are regional differences in the availability of beer. In the United States, macro lagers, such as Budweiser, are available everywhere, but microbrews are more available in specific regions. In Northern Europe, many pubs offer only two or three local beers, which limits availability. One can argue that availability can limit the experience. Thus, in turn, availability through the 'exposure effect' influences preferences.

Further, beer is usually consumed socially, so that one's peers influence one's experience. Hence, peers' experiences affect preferences. It is reasonable to assume that consumption of beer depends not only on past consumption, but also on other people's consumption behaviour. Following Akerlof and Kranton (2000), we argue that identity could be included as an argument in the utility for beer. For example, a US consumer who identifies with his or her Irish ancestry might choose to drink Guinness and develop a taste for stout beers.

An interesting addition to the literature would be to allow identity to change over time. Identity could be included in the model as a state variable that changes with time. Empirically, this dynamic identity function could be estimated as a dynamic latent variable. A possible estimation strategy is the dynamic multiple-indicator multiple-cause (DYMIMIC) modelling approach (Engle et al. 1985).

Based on the preceding discussion, several empirical predictions can be made. Availability will affect both experience and preferences for type of beer (e.g. the level of hops, microbrew versus macro lager). Consequently, one would expect consumers who immigrate to the United States to start to prefer US beers partly because they are available. Past experience will be an important factor in type and amount of beer consumption. Peers' consumption will be a significant factor in choice of beer. The consumer's identity will

---

[1] This is true as long as consumption is below the level that makes one ill. If the consumer tries to violate this physical constraint, then it will likely have a negative effect on preferences for beer.

be a function of many things, likely including the following factors: location and duration of stay in a region, peers, availability of products, education, and income. We expect all of these factors to be statistically significant in predicting consumer preferences for beers.

Case Study: Survey of International Students in the United States

For the purpose of this study, in-person interviews were conducted with international students in March 2009 in the university town of Pullman, Washington, USA. All participants were required to be at least 21 years of age, which is the legal drinking age in the United States. The objective of the survey was to investigate how beer consumption and preferences change as international students experience US influences and product availability. A total of 50 participants were interviewed, so this exercise constitutes a pilot study. Summary statistics about the participants and their responses to the survey are presented in Table 9.1. The largest group of respondents by region is from Asia with 42%, including those from China, India, Singapore, and Nepal. The next biggest group is from the Middle East, followed by Africa, North America, and Europe. The majority of respondents were male (64%), married (70%), and between 21 and 30 years of age (66%). Since the sample contains mostly international students, the majority (64%) had a household income of less than $20,000 (USD). The mean duration of time spent in the United States was 4.5 years.

We examined the availability of US beer in the participants' home country and their consumption habits. Just over half (54%) of participants could buy US beers in their home countries. Forty-six per cent reported that their beer drinking increased during their stay in the United States, 32% said beer consumption remained the same, and 22% reported that their beer consumption declined. In Figure 9.1, we compare preferences for beers before and after coming the United States. In terms of preferences for beer by country of origin, the respondents reported a major shift. Preferring one's homeland beers decreased from 40% to 6%. This supports our hypothesis that consumers who immigrate to the United States start to prefer US beers. Only 34% of respondents said that they could buy their homeland beer in their community stores. Among the respondents, those who preferred US beers jumped from 12% before coming to the United States to 66% after coming to the United States. Those who preferred beers from countries other than their home country or the United States fell from 48% to 28%.

Figure 9.2 presents the respondents' reported most important reasons for changes in their beer consumption habits. The largest category (31%) of

Table 9.1. Summary statistics

Variables	Percentage of respondents (n = 50)
Consumption of beer after coming to the US	
Decreased	22%
Remained the same	32%
Increased	46%
Availability of US beer in the respondent country	
Yes	54%
No	46%
Gender	
Male	64%
Female	36%
Age	
21–22	18%
23–29	48%
30–35	20%
36+	14%
Marital status	
Married	70%
Income	
Less than $20,000	64%
$20,000–$40,000	26%
$40,000 or more	10%
Native Region	
Canada & Mexico	8%
Africa	10%
Asia (East)	42%
Middle East	22%
Europe	8%

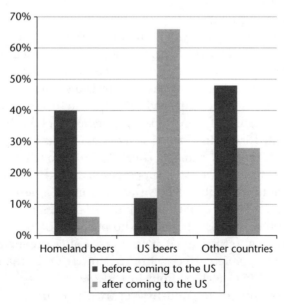

Figure 9.1. Preferences for beers, based on origin

reason is that their tastes changed. In a close second, at 29%, is the availability of their previously consumed beers. Since we had a significant number of Asian respondents, one would expect this. Asian beers are generally not available in standard US grocery stores. Next, at 24%, is peers' influence. Price only accounts for 10% of the change. The US macrobrews are less expensive, but microbrews are comparable to imported beers in price. Consequently, price is probably only a reason to switch if the respondent switched to a macrobrew.

We use a logit model in order to analyse the international students' preferences for US beers with the following equation:

$$y = \beta' x + \varepsilon, \tag{9.1}$$

where $y = \left\{ {1 \text{ if the subject prefers U.S. beers} \atop 0 \text{ otherwise}} \right\}$, β is a vector of coefficients to be estimated, and ε is an error term, which is assumed to have a logistic distribution. The vector of explanatory variables (x) includes years living in the US, an indicator for being male, whether the respondent's homeland beers are available to purchase locally, whether the respondent's consumption of beer has increased since coming to the US, whether peer influence is the most important factor in the subject's choice of beer, whether price is the most important factor in the subject's choice of beer, whether taste is the most important factor in the subject's choice of beer, and student status (graduate or undergraduate student).

The estimation results are presented in Table 9.2. As expected, the number of years living in the United States has a positive and statistically significant effect on positive preferences for US beers. This result supports the arguments about

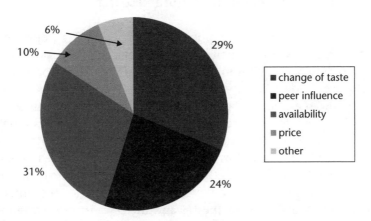

Figure 9.2. Most important reason for changes in beer consumption habits

Table 9.2. Model estimates: preferences for US beers

Variable	Coefficient	Standard error	P-value
Constant	1.56	1.88	0.40
Years in the US	0.27	0.16	0.09*
Male	1.51	0.92	0.04**
Increased Consumption in US	0.46	0.83	0.08*
Availability of homeland beers	−0.65	0.92	0.47
Peers most important	0.26	0.84	0.75
Price most important	−2.72	1.56	0.07*
Taste most important	−2.58	1.36	0.05**
Undergraduate	1.82	1.36	0.17
Graduate student	2.70	1.34	0.04**
Log-likelihood	−27.14		
Sensitivity	61%		
Specificity	82%		
Predictive value	72%		

Notes: *Statistically significant at the 10% level **Statistically significant at the 5% level.

culture affecting beer preferences. The intuition is that, as the duration of stay in the United States increases, the respondent develops a taste for US beers. If price or taste is the most important factor in choosing which beer to purchase, then the subject is less likely to prefer US beers. If price is the most important factor, then the subject is likely to drink the bland US macrobeers. If taste is the most important factor, then one can hypothesize that the subject may already have established strong preferences about taste in his/her home country. In terms of the demographic variables, being male and being a graduate student both have positive effects on preferences for US beers. The coefficients on the remaining variables have the expected signs, but are not statistically significant.

Conclusions and Directions for Future Research

The effect of culture on consumption and preferences is an open area for research. It includes behavioural and psychological aspects of economics. A next step in this research is to quantify how culture, in the form of habits, peer influences, and availability affect preferences for beer. In this chapter, we discussed how preferences for beer could be modelled with these effects included. We presented empirical findings from a pilot survey of international students in order to begin to understand how their preferences and consumption habits for beer changed as they spent time in the United States. The results of this pilot study support many of the hypotheses that come out of the discussion about modelling preferences for beer. The most interesting results are that years spent in the US and increases in beer consumption since coming to the US have positive effects on preferences for US beers.

Areas for future research include the dynamics of peer effects on preferences and willingness to pay for beer. Chen and Li (2009) apply an experimental approach to measure the effects of induced group identity on participant social preferences. Following Chen and Li (2009), we would like to use a laboratory experiment to measure the effects of induced group identity on participants' consuming preferences for beer. Since the identity is not observable, a latent variable model can be applied to analyse the effects of identity on beer preferences. One can envision an economic experiment in which a participant drinks a beer with a group who prefer a particular type of beer (the group is in on the experiment) and then the subject participates in an auction in which the group's favourite beer is offered. A related topic is how these socialization and exposure effects interact. This area of study could have implications for international marketing and trade of beer. How can a premium beer penetrate a non-traditional beer-drinking market, such as China?

Another potential area for future research is to understand whether the exposure effect is unidirectional. That is, we know that consumers who drink macro beers can develop a taste for microbrews, but can this go the other way? The beer industry argues that consumers do not shift from microbrews to macrobrews. It would be interesting to estimate a product characteristic model to understand how different beers substitute for each other. In the pilot study, we found that those who consider taste as the most important factor in choosing their beer are less likely to prefer US beers. It may be that some preferences become entrenched.

References

Akerlof, G. A., and R. E. Kranton (2000). 'Economics and Identity'. *Quarterly Journal of Economics*, 115/3: 715–39.

Arnold, J. P. (2005). *Origin and History of Beer and Brewing: From Prehistoric Times to the Beginning of Brewing Science and Technology*, repr. edn. Cleveland, OH: Beer Books.

Borchgrevink, C. P., and A. M. Susskind (1998). 'Micro-Brewed Beer and the Patrons of Mid-Priced, Casual Restaurants'. *Journal of Hospitality & Leisure Marketing*, 5: 115–29.

Chen, Y., and S. X. Li (2009). 'Group Identity and Social Preferences'. *American Economic Review*, 99/1: 431–57.

Duesenberry, J. S. (1949). *Income, Savings, and the Theory of Consumer Behavior*. Cambridge, MA: Harvard University Press.

Engle, R. F., D. M. Lilien, and M. Watson (1985). 'A DYMIMIC Model of Housing Price Determination'. *Journal of Econometrics*, 28: 307–26.

Gao, X. M., E. J. Wailes, and G. L. Cramer (1997). 'A Microeconometric Analysis of Consumer Taste Determination and Taste Change for Beef'. *American Journal of Agricultural Economics*, 79: 573–82.

German Beer Institute (2008). *German Beer Styles: Variety, Quality, Complexity, and Versatility*. Available at <http://www.germanbeerinstitute.com/styles.html>.

Gorman, W. M. (1967). 'Tastes, Habits and Choices'. *International Economic Review*, 8/2: 218–22.

Hayakawa, H. (2000). 'Bounded Rationality, Social and Cultural Norms, and Interdependence via Reference Groups'. *Journal of Economic Behavior and Organization*, 43/1: 1–34.

—— and Y. P. Vinieris (1997). 'Consumer Interdependence via Reference Groups'. *Journal of Political Economy*, 85: 599–615.

Mehta, R., and R. W. Belk (1991). 'Artifacts, Identity, and Transition: Favorite Possessions of Indians Immigrants to the United States'. *Journal of Consumer Research*, 17: 398–411.

Peston, M. H. (1967). 'Changing Utility Functions', in M. Shubik (ed.), *Essays in Honor of Oskar Morgenstern*. Princeton: Princeton University Press.

Pollak, R. (1970). 'Habit Formation and Dynamic Demand Functions'. *Journal of Political Economy*, 78: 745–63.

Stevenson, R. J., and M. R. Yeomans (1995). 'Does Exposure Enhance Liking for the Chili Burn?' *Appetite*, 24/2: 107–20.

Zajonc, R. B. (1968). 'The Attitudinal Effects of Mere Exposure'. *Journal of Personality and Social Psychology*, 9/2: 1–27.

Zeller, D. A. (1991). 'How Foods Get to be Liked: Some General Mechanisms and Some Special Cases', in R. C. Bolles (ed.), *The Hedonics of Taste*. Hillsdale, NJ: Lawrence Erlbaum.

Part III
Industrial Organization

10

Competition Policy towards Brewing: Rational Response to Market Power or Unwarranted Interference in Efficient Markets?[1]

Margaret E. Slade

Introduction

The brewing industry has been heavily scrutinized by competition authorities in the EU and in many member nations.[2] It is not clear, however, whether such attention is warranted. Is the brewing industry very different from, say, the fast-food industry? In both, there are large firms that sell worldwide as well as smaller local firms, and there are many retail establishments with different sorts of contractual relationships with their upstream suppliers. In spite of perhaps superficial similarities with other sectors, however, beer brewing and retailing appear to be more closely monitored.

In my chapter, I ask if this scrutiny is a natural response by competition authorities to the threat of market power at some level of the vertical chain (i.e. input procurement, brewing, wholesaling, or retailing), or if it is an unnecessary interference in markets that are workably competitive and are functioning efficiently. If the former is true, then consumers can be made better off by government intervention that lessens market power and leads to lower markups and retail prices, whereas if the latter is true, consumers can be harmed by higher costs that will be, at least partially, passed on to them in the form of higher retail prices.

---

[1] I would like to thank my coauthors Francine Lafontaine and Joris Pinkse for joint work and Johan Swinnen for helpful comments.

[2] To illustrate, the decades of the 1970s and 1980s witnessed 28 reviews of the UK industry by EU and UK authorities.

As with so many economic problems, the question is complex and does not lend itself to a simple yes or no answer. In particular, any attempt to come to grips with the question must consider the structure of the specific market, or really markets, since there are large differences across geographic regions, as well as the more general issues that a beneficent competition authority must confront. In my chapter, I attempt to do just that. Specifically, I start by discussing some general issues that authorities must take into account in designing a policy towards the industry. This analysis considers both horizontal and vertical issues (i.e. interaction in the same product market versus interaction between links in the vertical chain). After that, since the answer to the question that I propose depends on the setting in which the firms interact, rather than paint a broad-brush picture, I review some case studies that illustrate UK policy towards the brewing and retailing industry. Finally, I attempt to draw some conclusions based on the analysis, both general and specific to the industry.

Before looking at general policy issues, I would like to highlight a number of issues that I do not cover. First and perhaps most important, I do not describe or contrast competition policy and legal enforcement in the EU and in its member nations. In fact, my discussion is relatively free of legal detail. I have chosen to ignore these issues because, unlike the general considerations upon which the design of policy should be based, the policies and laws themselves change periodically, causing any in-depth analysis of antitrust enforcement and legal stances to become fairly quickly outdated. Moreover, the structure of the industry in each market is to a large extent shaped by decisions that were taken in periods when policies were different from those that prevail today.

Second, my discussion of the pros and cons of horizontal concentration and vertical arrangements does not attempt to be comprehensive. I do this because, although there are many theories that address these issues, from a practical point of view, some of them have proved more productive than others. Moreover, some are more relevant to brewing than others. I therefore emphasize what I feel to be the most important considerations, which often turn out to be those that antitrust authorities are most concerned with.

Finally, I do not consider relationships between brewers and their suppliers (e.g. sellers of hops and malting barley). This was done primarily because authorities have been less interested in these relationships than in those between brewers and their wholesalers and retailers. Perhaps for this reason, it is also true that there appears to be less data on brewer/supplier interactions.

General Policy Issues

Almost all markets have horizontal and vertical aspects, where the former refers to interactions among firms in the same product market and the latter to interactions among firms that buy from or sell to one another (i.e. input/output relationships). Not surprisingly then, competition authorities have been concerned with possible anticompetitive consequences of both sorts of arrangements. In what follows, I discuss possible pro and anticompetitive impacts of changes in the structure of vertical and horizontal markets from a general point of view. By this I mean that I consider time-invariant economic issues that underlie competition policy rather than the practical details of that policy as it manifests itself in different countries, industries, and time periods.

Before discussing possible impacts, however, it is useful to consider how one might define a market.

Market Definition

Market definition is an important aspect of many cases that authorities are asked to consider. This is true because it is not possible, for example, to say that a market has few firms if we don't know what that market is. Economists generally agree that a market has both a product and a geographic dimension. To illustrate, one can ask if the relevant product market is draught beer, beer, alcoholic beverages, or drinks and if the geographic market is local, regional, national, or worldwide. The way in which one chooses to define a market will determine the number of firms in that market, with broader definitions leading to more firms. One normally presumes that, unless proven otherwise, firms that operate in markets with few rivals have more market power than firms in markets with many competitors.

A product market is usually determined by the ease of substitution among products (e.g. brands of beer), with those that are in the same market being close substitutes and those that are outside being very imperfectly substitutable with those that are inside. Of course, this is rarely a cut-and-dried issue. For this reason, any choice will almost surely be disputed by some. In particular, the firms in the industry usually argue for a broad definition, whereas competition authorities often argue for a narrower choice.

A geographic market is also determined by the ease of substitution among products that are inside and outside the market, and some of the same considerations apply. However, with geography, substitution is spatial (i.e. within and across geographic regions). Furthermore, whereas product-market substitution often depends on product characteristics (e.g. alcohol content and product type—lager, ale, and so forth), geographic-market substitution often depends on transport costs relative to value. For this reason, for example, the geographic market for spirits is apt to be larger than that for 'real' or cask-conditioned ale.

Once one has chosen a market, which often pertains to the manufacturing stage (e.g. brewing), that choice also determines the suppliers, wholesalers, and retailers that are in the market. With respect to brewing, a convention that is often adopted is that the product market is beer and the geographic market is national. However, the choice is not clear cut, and some would argue, for example, that on- and off-licence trade constitute separate markets, and that, within on-licence, draught and packaged products are separate. Furthermore, others might argue that, due to differences in tastes across regions within a country, beer markets are not national but are regional or local. Finally, it is also possible that brewing is a national market, since products can easily be shipped throughout the country, whereas retailing is local, since consumers don't travel far to purchase a six pack of beer or to find a pub.

Vertical Practices: Efficiency Enhancing or Market Power Strengthening?

Firms are involved in a vertical relationship if they operate at different levels of the production/distribution chain.[3] All upstream/downstream or input/output relationships are vertical, and those relationships can take many forms. In this chapter, I am interested in the restrictions that one member of a vertical chain can impose on members of another link. Competition authorities mainly focus on a set of price and non-price restrictions known as vertical restraints (VR). The former refers to resale price maintenance (RPM), where a manufacturer either sets the price or sets a maximum or minimum price that retailers can charge, whereas the latter includes exclusive dealing—requiring that a retailer sell only the manufacturer's products, exclusive territories—dividing the geographic market into territories and assigning one reseller to each, quantity forcing—requiring that each retailer purchase a minimum amount of the manufacturer's product, and tying—selling one product to a retailer only if that retailer purchases another product from the manufacturer.

Vertical restraints most often arise in retail settings, with the upstream firm or manufacturer typically restricting its downstream firm or retailers' choices. For example, a brewer might limit a pub's product line to her own brands (exclusive dealing) or might set the retail price (RPM). In the UK when the former occurs, it is somewhat confusingly known as tying.

In what follows, I discuss some of the most important efficiency-enhancing aspects of vertical restraints and then go on to discuss possible market-power strengthening motives for adopting such restraints.

EFFICIENCY MOTIVES FOR ADOPTING VERTICAL RESTRAINTS
Many of the efficiency-enhancing motives for using VR are based on the idea of aligning incentives between manufacturer and retailer. Indeed, when those

---

[3] This subsection is based on Lafontaine and Slade (2008).

two links in the vertical chain are independent firms, each has its own objectives, and those objectives can diverge. Normally, inefficiencies result from the lack of agreement. Fortunately, this problem can often be overcome or lessened through the use of VR.

Dealer Services and Free-Riding Issues
Manufacturers who invest in improving retail outlets, promoting retail products, or training outlet managers might worry that retailers will free ride on those investments. For example, brewer investment in pubs enhances sales not only of own brands but also of the brands of rivals. Brewers might therefore worry that, for example, bartenders will encourage customers to switch to a rival brand that has a lower price—thereby making the sale easier—or that has a higher retail margin—thereby making the sale privately more profitable. Exclusive dealing resolves this problem by making it impossible for the bartender to propose an alternative brand. In this context, exclusive dealing is a mechanism that enables brewers to protect their investments against potential retailer opportunism. Furthermore, in its absence, potentially profitable investments might not be undertaken.

Alternatively, dealer services at the point of sale (e.g. keeping draught lines clean and maintaining carbon dioxide at appropriate levels) can enhance the demand for a brewer's product. However, the goodwill thus generated might cause some customers to purchase the brand from another pub. The brewer captures this externality or spillover but the retailer does not. The bartender might therefore provide a level of service that is suboptimal from the brewer's point of view. Furthermore, the problem worsens as the fraction of repeat business that pubs face falls. In other words, bartenders in tourist locations, for example, have less incentive to provide services.

In general, not only do retailers have incentives to free ride on the value of the brand and put in too little effort, a vertical externality, they also have incentives to free ride on services offered by other retailers (e.g. promotion), a horizontal externality. If service is important to the sale of a brewer's product, brewers will need to ensure that retailers provide it. Klein and Murphy (1988) proposed that manufacturers can use vertical restraints, such as minimum resale prices or exclusive territories, to ensure that their retailers earn above normal returns, which means that those retailers have something to lose if their contracts are terminated. Those returns, in combination with ongoing quality or service monitoring and the threat of termination, entice retailers to provide the desired level of quality or service. Since the quality and service levels in question are valued by customers—if it were otherwise brewers would not value them—quantities sold and consumer satisfaction should be enhanced.

Double Marginalization

The typical double marginalization or succession-of-monopoly problem arises when an upstream firm with market power sells a product to a downstream firm at a price above marginal cost. If the downstream firm also has market power, it is well known that it will choose a price that is higher, and a quantity that is lower, than the price and quantity that would maximize joint profits.[4]

In the retail context, it is well known that this problem can be overcome by the use of fixed fees (i.e. fees that retailers pay to manufacturers that are independent of the amount purchased). Indeed, the upstream firm can sell its product to the retailer at marginal cost, the retailer can take his profit downstream, and the manufacturer can then use the fixed fee to extract the downstream profit. In the brewing industry, however, retailers rarely pay fixed fees. Nevertheless, rental payments can serve the same function. For example, UK brewers often own pubs that they rent to retailers at rates that are independent of realized sales and need not equal market rates. Those rental payments can thus be used to extract profit or to subsidize operations. Vertical restraints can also overcome the problem. Maximum RPM is an obvious candidate. Alternatively, brewers can use a minimum quantity requirement.

When double marginalization is an issue, the imposition of vertical restraints will not only increase the overall efficiency of the vertical structure but also lead to lower prices for customers. In this context, therefore, restraints usually enhance well-being.

MARKET-POWER MOTIVES FOR ADOPTING VERTICAL RESTRAINTS
Vertical restraints (VR) are often viewed with suspicion because comparable horizontal practices are frowned upon. For example, resale price maintenance is vertical price fixing, exclusive territories can create monopoly power, and exclusive dealing can inhibit entry. Nevertheless, as we have just seen, real efficiencies can be associated with those restraints. Competitive harm, however, can also result. Competition authorities often focus on two anticompetitive motives for adopting VR—collusion and exclusion.

Collusion at Some Link of the Chain
It is often claimed that VR can strengthen retail cartels (e.g. minimum RPM can enforce a higher retail price). However, I have little to say about this since it does not explain why manufacturers would want a high retail price. VR can

---

[4] See Spengler (1950) for a discussion of the monopoly case, and Greenhut and Ohta (1979) for the oligopoly case.

also facilitate manufacturer cartels. For example, when RPM is adopted, upstream market rivals can infer that retail price changes signal manufacturer intent, and this reduction in uncertainty facilitates cartel stability.

Foreclosure and Raising Rivals' Costs
The main worry of antitrust authorities when it comes to vertical restraints is the possibility that their use will foreclose entry by competitors at some level of the vertical chain. In the context of brewing, a brewer that establishes an exclusive retail network (i.e. exclusive dealing) that involves most pubs might prevent competitors from gaining access to customers at a reasonable cost, if at all. This in turn could prevent entry of rival brewers and perhaps even lead rivals to exit.[5] Exclusive dealing, which has sometimes been referred to as vertical integration by contract, is the form of restraint for which foreclosure arguments are most frequently made.

In the end, if vertical restraints are used to lessen competition at some level of the vertical structure through foreclosing or disadvantaging rivals, prices to consumers should be higher, quantities sold smaller, and consumer choice more limited than they would be in the absence of such restraints. If restraints are adopted to increase efficiency, in contrast, costs in the vertical structure, and thus retail prices, should be lower.

Horizontal Practices: Efficiency Enhancing or Market Power Strengthening?

Horizontal practices involve firms that are in the same product market. Although there are many horizontal practices that competition authorities are concerned with (e.g. abuse of dominance, predation, and preemption), I emphasize mergers here for two reasons. First, unlike the above-mentioned practices, horizontal mergers are often efficient, and second, there have been many mergers in the brewing industry, and those mergers have been hotly debated.

Mergers are extremely common, and most of those mergers are not even considered by competition authorities. Indeed, most jurisdictions have 'safe harbours' or thresholds for market concentration and the value of assets involved in a merger such that, when the merging parties are below those thresholds, the merger is not challenged. Instead, since market-power motives are unlikely, it is assumed that the merger is undertaken for efficiency reasons. When mergers are investigated, they can still be allowed to go forward if it is established that there will be little competitive harm or if efficiencies will

---

[5] See e.g. Krattenmaker and Salop (1986), Aghion and Bolton (1987), and Comanor and Rey (2000).

outweigh the harm. It is therefore important to understand the motives for and consequences of undertaking a merger.

EFFICIENCY MOTIVES FOR MERGERS
Many aspects of efficiency must be considered when evaluating a horizontal merger. However, potential economies of scale and scope are perhaps the most important.

Economies of Plant Size and Scope
Economies of scale occur when costs fall more than proportionately with size, and many of those economies occur at the plant level. These include spreading up-front set-up costs over a larger number of units produced and longer production runs, both of which lower average costs.

Economies of scope are multi-product economies. For example, it might be cheaper to produce several brands of beer in one plant than it is to produce each brand in a separate plant, since those brands can share some equipment. Keeping plant size constant, however, joint production is not always efficient, since it results in shorter production runs.

Multi-plant Economies of Scale and Scope
It is often difficult to capture plant-level economies after a merger, since the configuration of plants can remain unchanged. Multi-plant economies, however, can still be very important. Those savings can occur at the procurement, production, and/or distribution stages. For example, a larger firm can bargain more effectively with suppliers and can often purchase inputs more cheaply. It can also coordinate production decisions over a larger number of plants and can thus control inventories and delivery times more efficiently, and it can facilitate closure of inefficient plants.[6] Finally, it can employ a larger but leaner distribution system.

Economies of scale and scope also include economies of shared facilities such as product development, marketing, and advertising. Furthermore, after a merger, the number and characteristics of brands can be rationalized, and those brands can be marketed and promoted more effectively.

In order to assess the costs savings associated with a particular merger, it is therefore necessary to determine what fraction of costs are due to each factor, as well as how those costs will change. To illustrate, whereas distribution costs constitute a large share of the total costs in the electricity and natural gas industries, they probably account for a much smaller share in the beer industry.

---

[6] Merging parties often claim plant closures as potential efficiencies. However, those parties should be required to demonstrate why closures could not have occurred absent the merger.

MARKET-POWER MOTIVES FOR MERGERS

Not all jurisdictions allow merging firms to claim efficiencies in defence of a merger, perhaps because it can be difficult to quantify efficiencies and to demonstrate that they are merger specific.[7] However, virtually all jurisdictions consider possible competitive harm as a reason for denying a merger. It is therefore natural to ask how competitive harm arises.

Increases in Market Concentration: Unilateral Effects

Market concentration refers to the number and size distribution of firms in the market. All else equal, concentration increases as the number of firms falls and as their shares become more asymmetric.

When a merger occurs, two or more firms become one. This reduces the number of decision makers in the industry and creates a firm that is larger than either of its constituents. Not only does a larger firm have a larger market share, its demand is usually less elastic. To see this, consider a dominant firm.[8] When such a firm increases its price, customers have few alternatives to choose from. The dominant firm therefore loses a smaller share of its customers and its demand is less elastic. A large firm thus has a unilateral incentive to raise its price relative to the prices that were charged by its (smaller) constituent firms, where, by unilateral, I mean it has that incentive even if rivals don't follow its price changes.[9] However, in equilibrium, smaller firms will also raise their prices. This is true because, when the dominant firm raises its price, it loses some of its customers to its rivals. The demands of the non-merged firms therefore shift out.

Increases in Market Concentration: Coordinated Effects

Coordinated effects refer to increased scope for collusion, tacit or otherwise, where by collusion I mean that firms adopt practices that allow them to realize higher profits than they would earn if they behaved in an uncoordinated fashion. Many economists believe that collusion is easier to sustain when firms are few, and a merger reduces the number of firms in the market. The possibility and effectiveness of collusion should therefore be enhanced. However, the situation is not quite so simple, since it is also claimed that collusion is more difficult to sustain when market shares are more asymmetric. This means that, if two of the largest firms merge, shares become more asymmetric, and a cartel might be less effective. However, if two small- to medium-sized firms merge, market shares can become more symmetric, thus facilitating a

---

[7] For example, the EU only introduced an efficiency defence in 2004.
[8] I discuss a dominant firm only as an example. The argument is the same for any oligopoly.
[9] For an analysis of unilateral and coordinated effects, see Slade (2004a).

cartel.[10] Before claiming that a merger in a concentrated market is detrimental to consumer interests, therefore, many factors must be evaluated. Moreover, competition authorities often consider coordinated effects to be less important than unilateral effects, since the theories that underlie the former are more fragile and more sensitive to the assumptions that underlie the models.[11]

UK Case Studies

To set the stage for an analysis of the case studies, it is helpful to place the UK industry in a European context. First, relative to many Western European nations, the UK is a large producer and consumer of beer, both absolutely and in per capita terms. Second, most of the beer consumed in the UK is also produced there. Guinness, however, which is Irish, is a notable exception. Third, a large fraction of UK consumption is 'on-licence', where on-licence refers to beer consumed in licensed premises. 'Off-licence', in contrast, refers to beer purchased in a store and consumed elsewhere. Finally, the UK is an outlier when it comes to consumption of draught beer, with a draught share of nearly 60%.[12]

Turning to competition policy, the analysis in the last section suggests that, even when there is a case to be made that competitive harm is likely, due to, for example, the use of exclusive dealing when entry is difficult or a merger when the market is concentrated, mechanical rules do not suffice. Instead, in most instances, the particulars of the case—the structure, practices, and culture of the market—must be carefully examined. In this section, I consider two cases that pertain to the UK brewing and retailing industry. The first case, which is vertical, involves restraints in contracts between brewers and pub operators, whereas the second, which is horizontal, involves mergers between large brewers.

One might ask if these UK cases are relevant for competition policy towards the beer industry in other countries. It should be clear that mergers occur in most regions and that the UK merger cases have relevance that extends well beyond the UK. The vertical case, in contrast, involves brewer ownership of pubs and exclusive dealing or 'tying', a practice that is not allowed in all countries. For example, in the US, brewer ownership of retailers is

---

[10] See e.g. Compte et al. (2002).

[11] This does not mean that, from a practical point of view, unilateral effects are easy to quantify and are not sensitive to assumptions. See Slade (2009) for a demonstration of this and an application to the brewing industry.

[12] Draught beer is a subset of on-licence consumption, since packaged products can also be consumed in bars.

prohibited.[13] The tie, however, is a common feature in other countries such as Germany and Belgium.[14] Moreover, in 2003 the EU forced the largest Belgian brewer, Interbrew, to break its ties with its Belgian retail establishments (see e.g. Atsma 2003). It should therefore be obvious that the tie is not just a peculiar UK practice.

A Vertical Case: Exclusive Dealing and Two-Part Tariffs

In 1989, the UK Monopolies and Mergers Commission (MMC) recommended measures that eventually led brewers to divest themselves of 14,000 public houses. The MMC claimed that their recommendations would lower retail prices and increase consumer choice. There is considerable doubt, however, that their objectives were achieved. This case study is based on Slade (1998), which contains an econometric analysis of the transition period. The analysis is based on a theoretical model of the relationship between retail price and retail organizational form that emphasizes how exclusive-dealing clauses and strategic factors interact.

The theoretical analysis in that paper suggests rankings of wholesale prices, retail prices, and brewer profits that differ by organizational form. Oligopolists should therefore prefer certain contractual arrangements over others. If instead the industry were monopolistic or perfectly competitive, brewers would be indifferent concerning many of those choices. In particular, when the retail sector is perfectly competitive, there can be no double marginalization; when the manufacturing sector is a monopoly, there is no role for exclusive-dealing contracts; and under both market structures, strategic behaviour is excluded.

THE MARKET AND THE CONTRACTS

Prior to the MMC report, most contractual relations between brewers and pub operators, which ranged from complete vertical integration to arm's-length transactions in a market, took one of four standard forms.

- Managed Houses: Managed houses were owned by the brewer. Moreover, the manager and the staff were the brewer's employees. The brewer set the retail price, bore all of the costs of operation, and received all of the profit.

- Tenanted Houses: Tenanted houses were also owned by the brewer. The tenant, however, was an independent entrepreneur who bought beer at a wholesale price and set the retail price. Furthermore, sales were subject to

[13] Even in the US, however, it is common for brewers to impose vertical restraints such as exclusive territories on their wholesalers (see e.g. Sass and Saurman 1993).

[14] For a discussion of tying in Germany, see Adams, Chapter 13 in this volume, and for a discussion of tying in Belgium, see Wauters and Van Passel (2009).

exclusive-dealing clauses, and rents were paid to the brewer for the use of the premises.

- Free Houses with Loan Ties: Free houses were owned by the operator. Brewers, however, provided capital to loan-tied houses at below-market rates in exchange for exclusivity for their products (exclusive dealing) or for a minimum throughput (quantity forcing).

- Free Houses without Loan Ties: With the final class of public houses, there were no legal ties between brewers and pub operators, and transactions were truly arm's-length.

The first two arrangements were known as the tied trade. With the tied trade, the brewer specified which beers might be sold and where they must be purchased, usually from the brewer himself. The third and fourth arrangements were known as the free trade, which is perhaps a misnomer, given that, for many of those houses, only ownership was 'free'.

A typical large brewer owned both managed and tenanted pubs. Managed pubs, which were often larger and newer, tended to place greater emphasis on non-beer amenities such as food service. Moreover, the manager was apt to be more loyal to the brewer than to the pub. Indeed, promotion often took the form of a move to a larger public house where a higher salary could be earned.

Tenanted pubs, which were often 'corner' houses, tended to be smaller. Moreover, they catered to a more regular crowd of beer drinkers. The tenant, who was a fixture in the pub, was apt to be more loyal to the neighbourhood and the regular customers than to the owner.

In the mid-1980s, just prior to the issue of the Monopolies and Mergers Commission report on the supply of beer, six national brewers accounted for 75% of total production. Fifty-two regional and local brewers controlled 17% of the market, and three brewers without tied estate were responsible for most of the remainder.[15] In addition, there were over 160 microbreweries operating on a very small scale. The market was thus moderately concentrated, particularly in certain regions. No single firm, however, had an overall market share of over 25%. This made brewing in the UK less concentrated than in most continental European and North American countries. Moreover, the largest brewers produced more than 100 brands each, ranging from ale and stout to lager. This large variety of products, coupled with strong differences in regional preferences, implied that even the largest breweries probably produced at a rate that was less than minimum-efficient scale.

In the same period, 75% of public houses were in the tied trade. Within the tied sector, approximately 30% of the houses were managed. Managed pubs,

---

[15] Brewers without tied estate are not vertically integrated into retailing.

however, which tend to be larger than tenanted, accounted for more than 30% of sales. Finally, approximately 25% of the free houses were tied to brewers through loans. The completely free sector was therefore small. Nevertheless, there existed a slow but steady trend towards a lessening of vertical integration and control.

THE MMC REPORT AND THE BEER ORDERS

In 1987, the Office of Fair Trading (OFT) began an investigation of the brewing industry. Its principal concerns seem to have been high prices, large price differentials across regions and products, and limited consumer choice. The OFT investigation led to a recommendation that an industry review be undertaken by the Monopolies and Mergers Commission. The product of this investigation was the 500-page MMC report entitled *The Supply of Beer*, which appeared in February 1989.

The MMC recommended that (i) A ceiling of 2,000 be placed on the number of on-licences that any brewer could own. This ceiling would require divestiture of 22,000 premises by the national brewers. No regional or local brewer would be affected. (ii) All loan ties were to be eliminated, with current loans subject to grandfather clauses. (iii) Tenants were to be allowed to purchase a minimum of one brand of draught beer from a supplier other than the landlord, the so-called 'guest' beer. (iv) Tenants were to be brought within the provisions of the Landlord and Tenant Act of 1954. (v) Brewers were to publish wholesale price lists.

The MMC believed that its recommendations, if adopted, would reduce prices and widen consumer choice. Those recommendations, however, were never implemented. Following the publication of the report, a period of intense lobbying ensued and a weaker set of regulations was put into place, the so-called 'Beer Orders'. The principal changes were (i) either divestiture or a release of ties on one half of the pubs in excess of 2,000 (11,000 pubs affected). (ii) Loan ties were subject to termination by the recipient, with three-months' notice upon repayment of the loan. (iii) Bartenders in tied premises of national brewers were allowed to serve at least one cask-conditioned ale from a supplier other than the owner, where a cask-conditioned ale is one that continues to ferment in the keg—a 'real' ale.

Changes in recommendation (i) considerably reduced the number of pubs affected. In addition, it allowed brewers to keep their pubs if they broke the tie. Few chose, however, to maintain ownership of pubs without ties. Loan ties remained, but were subject to what the government considered best market practice. Finally, the guest beer mandate was changed to a cask-conditioned product. This was done to avoid the prospect of tenants of regional and local brewers being allowed to sell one of the most popular national brands. In spite of these changes, however, the spirit of the recommendations remained.

It is not clear from the MMC report if any large interest group was in favour of the recommendations. Consumer organizations were principally concerned with local retail-market share and not with brewer ownership per se. Regional and local brewers were in favour of the tie, whereas brewers without tied estate had no strong views. The belief that there was something seriously wrong with the industry, therefore, seems to have been internal to the OFT. Moreover, since *The Supply of Beer* report contained little economics, it is difficult to understand the reasoning that lay behind the recommendations.

After 1989, the UK beer industry underwent radical changes. During the transition period, brewer ownership of on-licences fell from 53 to 37% of all licences held. Furthermore, total brewer ownership declined by more than 14,000, which is more than the mandated 11,000. This decline is partly a continuation of a gradual trend. However, sharp reductions occurred in 1991 and 1992. Since managed pubs tend to be larger and more profitable than tenanted, most of the pubs that were sold were tenanted houses. Moreover, many of the remaining tenanted pubs were converted from three-year to long-term leases. When this was done, the tenant became responsible for a much larger share of the capital improvements.

One of the major changes in ownership patterns that emerged is the formation of public-house chains. Many non-brewers, often in the hotel, food, or entertainment business, took advantage of the massive sales and bought large blocks of pubs. Most of those chains, however, signed long-term purchasing agreements with national brewers, and many of the agreements included exclusive-dealing clauses. When this change occurred, although exclusive dealing remained, the removal of rental payments to brewers was equivalent to the removal of two-part tariffs, where a two-part tariff is a payment of a fixed fee plus a price per unit purchased. Although the industry seems to have anticipated the emergence of pub chains, there is little analysis of its consequences in the MMC report.

The industry therefore had two new contractual arrangements in addition to those listed earlier. These are:

- Leased Houses: Leased houses were owned by the brewer and operated by the lessee under a long-term lease. The lessee or retailer purchased beer at a wholesale price and set the retail price. In addition the retailer was responsible for most capital improvements. The difference between tenanted and leased pubs is similar to that between rental and leasehold housing.

- Chain Houses: Chains are multi-establishment retail operations. Chains bargained with brewers over wholesale prices, but their retailers set retail prices. Since the chain owned the pub, no rent was paid to the brewer.

THE EFFECTS OF THE BEER ORDERS

The econometric analysis is described in Appendix A. That analysis revealed that, after the Beer Orders, prices in the formerly tied houses rose.[16] Moreover, they rose faster than those in the control group, the free houses. The analysis also showed that profits in the tied houses fell. These findings are consistent with the introduction of double marginalization after the tied houses were sold. As explained earlier, although pub operators did not pay fixed fees, they paid rental rates that were determined by the brewers, not by conditions in the real estate market. Such rental rates can play the same role as fixed fees and, when those fees are removed, double marginalization can be reintroduced.[17]

What about the effects of the tie (i.e. the exclusive-dealing clauses)? Unfortunately, that issue is impossible to evaluate for this case. The problem is that, to a large extent, the pubs were acquired by pub chains and those chains continued to operate under exclusive-dealing clauses, at least for the first few years. This means that the MMC remedies had the unexpected effect of removing the two-part tariffs but allowing the ties.

The MMC predicted that their remedies would lower retail prices and increase consumer choice. We have seen that their hopes concerning prices were disappointed. Their desire for greater consumer choice, however, fared better. In particular, many retailers took advantage of the right to serve a 'guest' cask-conditioned ale. In addition, the number of lagers with foreign trademarks increased substantially.

Should the Commission be chastised for its decision? That is a difficult question to answer. In practice, it is virtually impossible to anticipate all of the ramifications of mandated changes. Nevertheless, the situation in beer suggests that more attention should have been paid to recent theories of vertical restraints before far-reaching measures were advocated. In particular, the analysis suggests that the restraints were probably imposed on retailers for efficiency reasons. Specifically, whereas exclusive dealing protected brewers' investments in retail facilities, two-part tariffs aligned incentives between brewers and retailers.

---

[16] Price changes after the Beer Orders were modelled as a one-time break in trend (slope and intercept), with unknown break point.

[17] Of course, vertical restraints can also overcome double marginalization. However, brewers had less control over pub chains than over individual retailers and were in a weaker position to impose restraints.

A Horizontal Case: Mergers in the UK Brewing Industry

After the Beer Orders were adopted, large changes in the structure of the market occurred. Historically, the UK brewing industry was relatively unconcentrated. More recent years, however, have witnessed a succession of successful mergers that have increased concentration in the industry, as well as proposed mergers that, if successful, would have added to that trend. It is thus natural to ask how those mergers changed both product pricing and product offerings. In particular, the mergers could have resulted in higher prices, a reduction in the number of brands, an increase in brand uniformity, and a move towards competition through national advertising.

This case study is based on Pinkse and Slade (2004). In that paper, we attempted to assess the effects of actual mergers and to predict how unsuccessful mergers would have affected the industry. The formal analysis was limited to price changes, but other consequences were analysed informally.

Merger simulations were used to assess the price effects of the mergers. The goal of a merger simulation is to predict the equilibrium prices that will be charged and the quantities of each brand that will be sold under the new, post-merger market structure, using only information that is available pre-merger. The advantage of such an approach is that, if the simulation can forecast accurately, it is much more efficient to perform an ex ante evaluation than to wait for an ex post assessment. In particular, competition authorities are reluctant to impose costly divestitures once a merger has been approved, and it is much more difficult to impose an ex post remedy under the legislation.

THE MARKET AND THE MERGERS

In 1990, there were six national brewers: Bass, Allied Lyons, Scottish & Newcastle, Grand Metropolitan (Grand Met), Courage, and Whitbread. Moreover, those six firms had dominated the market for decades. Since 1990, however, a sequence of mergers increased concentration in brewing. First, three large mergers were approved by UK competition authorities: Courage and Grand Met merged to form Courage, Allied Lyons and Carlsberg merged to form Carlsberg-Tetley, and Courage and Scottish & Newcastle merged to form Scottish Courage. Although the cases were horizontal, with all three mergers the remedies restricted vertical relationships between brewers and retailers.

After 1995, however, horizontal-merger policy became less lenient. Indeed, a proposed merger between Bass and Carlsberg-Tetley was denied, and still more recently, when the Belgian firm Interbrew acquired the brewing assets of Bass and Whitbread, it was ordered to sell its Bass breweries. We discuss the two mergers that we evaluate in greater detail.

The Courage/Scottish & Newcastle Merger

The third merger occurred in 1995, when the merged firm Courage combined with Scottish & Newcastle to form Scottish Courage. This event reduced the number of national brewers from five to four and created the largest brewer in the UK, with a market share of 28%. In spite of the fact that the majority of the groups that were asked to comment on the merger favoured a full investigation by the Monopolies and Mergers Commission, the Office of Fair Trading did not refer the matter to the MMC. Instead, it allowed the merger to proceed subject to a number of undertakings, all of which involved relationships between brewers and their retailers.

The Bass/Carlsberg-Tetley Merger

A fourth merger was proposed in 1997 but not consummated. This involved the numbers two and three brewers, Bass and Carlsberg-Tetley, and would have created a new firm, BCT, with a market share of 37%. The MMC estimated that, after the merger, the Hirshman/Herfindahl index of concentration (HHI) would rise from 1,678 to 2,332, where the HHI is the sum of the squared market shares of the firms in the market multiplied by 10,000. Furthermore, it noted that the US Department of Justice's 1992 Merger Guidelines specify that a merger should raise concerns about competition if the post-merger HHI is over 1,800 and the change in the HHI is at least 50 points. Nevertheless, the MMC recommended that the merger be allowed to go forward.[18] In spite of the MMC's favourable recommendation, however, the BCT merger was not consummated because the president of the Board of Trade did not accept the MMC's advice.

UK competition authorities' views towards horizontal concentration in brewing seemed to change over the decade of the 1990s. In particular, early on, the Commission was more concerned with vertical relationships, even though they claimed that market power resided in brewing. By the end of the decade, however, a concern with horizontal concentration assumed prominence. Was increased concern with horizontal-market power justified? As a first cut to answering that question, we examined the market shares of the firms before and after each merger. That exercise revealed that, with all three consummated mergers, a few years after the merger the merged firm's market share was less than the sum of the pre-merger shares of its constituents. This suggests that increased efficiency did not overwhelm increased market power. While it is suggestive, a more formal analysis of specific mergers is required.

---

[18] The one economist on the Commission, David Newbery, wrote a dissenting opinion.

ANALYSIS OF THE MERGERS

Brewers either transfer beer internally to establishments that they operate, in which case the brewer sets the retail price, or they sell beer at wholesale prices to independent or affiliated retailers, in which case the retailer sets the retail price. In the former situation of vertical integration, the joint surplus, brewing plus retailing, is maximized. In the latter situation, the transaction between brewer and retailer is usually not arm's-length. Indeed, fixed rental fees are involved that can be used to distribute the surplus. We assumed that non-integrated brewers and retailers bargain efficiently to maximize the total surplus, given rival prices.[19] The division of that surplus, however, which determines the wholesale price, will depend on the relative bargaining strengths of the two parties. Furthermore, those strengths can change over time.[20] Our assumption is equivalent to having a single party choose the retail price optimally from the firm's point of view.

Our analysis was based on the simulation model that is described in the Appendix. We assumed Bertrand competition (unilateral effects) in a game among brewers. Mergers and divestitures were modelled as games with different numbers of players or decision makers. In other words, a merger involves a game with a smaller number of players, whereas, after a divestiture, there are more players.

The formal analysis indicates that, whereas the (consummated) merger between Courage and Scottish & Newcastle had little effect on prices, the proposed merger between Bass and Carlsberg-Tetley would have raised prices by a more substantial amount. This conclusion relies heavily on our findings about the structure of demand. Indeed, the local market shares of the post-merger firms would have been similar, so that, if competition had been symmetric, the effects of the two mergers would also have been similar. With localized competition, in contrast, the identity and product mix of each merging partner is key in determining whether a merger will be anticompetitive.

Conclusions

What should we conclude from this analysis? There are a number of things. First, antitrust cases, both horizontal and vertical, that involve large firms with substantial market shares are rarely straightforward and should be carefully considered on a case-by-case basis. In particular, with both horizontal and

---

[19] In other words, the vertical game between retailer and brewer is cooperative with side payments, whereas the horizontal retail game among brewers is non-cooperative.

[20] For example, on average, the retail price of beer in the UK increased faster than the wholesale price, implying that retailers received a larger fraction of the total, a fact that is consistent with a change in bargaining power.

vertical cases, the possibility of competitive harm must be balanced against the potential for realizing production, distribution, and organizational efficiencies. However, the two sorts of cases—horizontal and vertical—are not the same. Indeed, in my opinion, vertical issues should be treated more leniently, not for a lack of theories that predict that harm will occur, but because the empirical evidence of harm is at best weak (see Lafontaine and Slade 2007 and forthcoming).

Second, whereas market definition, market shares, and indices of market concentration can be reasonable indicators of the potential for harm when the products of the merging firms are homogeneous,[21] they can be very misleading when products are differentiated, as is the case with beer. In particular, when a merger simulation is used, there is no need to define the market. Instead, the entire matrix of cross-price elasticities is estimated, and that matrix is used to assess substitutability among products or brands of the merging firms.[22]

Finally, while it is true that market shares, and indices of market concentration, are highly imperfect indicators of the potential for damage, they can be useful for screening purposes. In particular, they can help determine which mergers should be investigated but are less useful for determining which should be prohibited. Moreover, merger simulations are not a panacea either, as they can also lead authorities to draw incorrect conclusions (see Slade 2009). In fact all quantitative measures of market power and increases in that power should be used with caution and should be considered complementary to more informal assessments.

Turning to the two UK cases, I believe that the attack on brewer ownership of public houses was misguided. Specifically, when two-part tariffs were removed, double marginalization was introduced. Moreover, the potential for double marginalization was exacerbated by the formation of public-house chains. Indeed, those large multi-establishment retail enterprises were in a better position to bargain with brewers and, as a consequence, a shift in power from brewers to retailers occurred. That shift led in turn to retail prices that increased faster than wholesale prices. The shift in itself would have been of little concern to public policy makers. However, increased market power on the part of retailers led to markups at the retail level that were higher than what would have been chosen if each brewer had maximized joint (brewing plus retailing) profits. The removal of the two-part tariffs, therefore, probably made both consumers and firms worse off.

The MMC report is unclear about the economic reasoning that led to its decision to force divestiture. Moreover, its proposals do not seem to have

---

[21] See e.g. Slade (2004b).

[22] The new US FTC/DOJ Proposed Horizontal Merger Guidelines (2010) agree with this position.

stemmed from external pressures. Nevertheless, with one exception, the Commissioners alleged that brewer ownership of public houses protected the upstream position of the firms. In my opinion, however, it was a mistake to attack the vertical structure if, as they alleged, market power resided upstream in brewing. In fact, it is almost always better to attack the source of a problem rather than to opt for indirect solutions.

With respect to the two mergers that I discuss, the decisions that were eventually made seem to have been sensible. In particular, although the market shares of the merged firms after the two mergers that we considered would have been similar, product substitutability across merging firms was quite different. This fact in turn led us to conclude that the first merger (Scottish Courage) should have been allowed, whereas the second (BCT) should have been prohibited: the decisions that ultimately prevailed. Nevertheless, the MMC originally recommended that the BCT merger be allowed to go forward. It was the president of the Board of Trade who overruled that decision and stopped the merger.

Earlier in the decade, merger decisions were less sensible. Indeed, almost all remedies that the MMC proposed as preconditions for allowing a horizontal merger to proceed involved vertical relationships between brewers and their affiliated retailers, in spite of the fact that the alleged problem was horizontal. Fortunately, however, the Commission's thinking has changed over the years, and I believe that it is unlikely that the current Competition Commission would advocate such indirect remedies today.

APPENDIX A: THE DATA AND ECONOMETRIC MODEL FOR THE VERTICAL CASE

The econometric analysis of the vertical case involves a detailed assessment of prices and brewer profits during the transition period. The data that I used to assess the mandated changes consist of three panels: two on retail prices by product type and ownership arrangement and the third on firm profitability.

I obtained price and volume data by product and public-house type. The product categories, all of which are draught beers, are bitter, lager, standard lager, premium lager, mild, and stout. The pub types are tied and free houses. These data are available at bimonthly intervals from StatsMR, a subsidiary of A. C. Nielsen Company. My data begin in January–February 1988 and end in March–April 1994. There are thus six cross-sectional and 38 time-series observations in each of the first two panels.

The profit data consist of accounting information from all of the brewing firms that were incorporated in the UK and traded publicly during the 1985–1993 period. These data came from the World Equities (formerly Euro Equities) financial database. There are 14 firms or cross-sectional units and nine years or time-series observations.

In addition to the dependent variables, I collected data on demand variables such as unemployment and a house-price index[23] and supply variables, such as the prices of the major inputs to brewing.

A preliminary analysis of the data revealed that, after the Beer Orders, retail prices rose and brewer profits fell. It is not clear, however, if those trends were due to the Beer Orders or to other factors. An econometric model is needed to distinguish between the two.

The equations that were estimated are reduced-form price and profit equations. The dependent variables are (i) the price of beer sold in tied houses, (ii) the price of beer sold in free houses, and (iii) company net profit divided by sales revenue. The explanatory variables are the supply and demand variables mentioned earlier. In addition, draught type (lager, ale, stout, etc.) and firm fixed effects were included.

The effects of the Beer Orders were modelled as a one-time exogenous break in trend (intercept and slope). The date when the Orders were published is well documented. Nevertheless, a great deal was known about their content prior to publication. In addition, the brewers were given three years to comply. If a regime shift occurred, therefore, it is not obvious when it began. For this reason, the break point was estimated in addition to the model parameters. A difference-in-difference specification was also estimated, with the free houses as the control group, since those houses were not affected by the Beer Orders.

APPENDIX B: THE DATA AND ECONOMETRIC MODEL FOR THE HORIZONTAL CASE

The horizontal case makes use of merger simulations that are based on a structural model of demand, cost, and market equilibrium. The equilibrium assumption must be carefully chosen. We assumed a static pricing game (Bertrand competition), which is a model of unilateral effects. Before calculating the equilibrium, however, one must estimate the building blocks—demand and cost. We estimated a very flexible specification of the demand for brands of a differentiated product (beer) and we used our estimated demands, together with engineering data on costs, to predict equilibrium prices and margins under the ownership structure that prevailed in the period of the data (1995). We then assessed the effects of the mergers by solving for equilibria of games with different numbers of players. In other words, changes in market structure—mergers and divestitures—were modelled as changes in the number of decision makers, where each decision maker controls the prices of some set of brands. This means that when two firms merge, some pricing externalities are internalized. Moreover, since brands of the differentiated product are substitutes and price competition was assumed,[24] all prices should rise after a merger or at least should not fall. The question is: by how much will they rise?

---

[23] The period surrounding the Beer Orders was one of declining real estate prices. It is therefore important not to attribute the trend in profits that was due to this factor to the Beer Orders.

[24] Formally, prices are strategic complements.

To build the simulation model, we first considered demand. With a differentiated product, market shares alone are not very informative, and substitutability among brands is key. To illustrate, suppose that two large firms merge, but each firm's brands are very imperfect substitutes for those of the other firm. In those circumstances, prices should change little. On the other hand, if the firms' brands are highly substitutable, prices should increase. It is therefore necessary to estimate cross-price elasticities for each brand pair.

Estimation of flexible demand for brands of beer, one that does not constrain the cross-price elasticities, requires very disaggregated data. Such data were obtained from StatsMR, a subsidiary of A. C. Nielson. The data are for 63 brands, two bimonthly time periods—August–September and October–November 1995, two regions of the country—London and East Anglia, and two types of establishments—multiples and independents, where multiples are pubs owned by a large retailer, usually a brewer or an independent pub chain. The 63 brands were owned by ten brewers: the four nationals, Bass, Carlsberg-Tetley, Scottish-Courage, and Whitbread; two brewers without tied estate, Guinness and Anheuser-Busch; and four regional brewers, Charles Wells, Greene King, Ruddles, and Youngs. The data also include brand and market characteristics.

Our data were collected in a period after the Courage/Scottish & Newcastle merger had occurred, but before the Bass/Carlsberg-Tetley merger was proposed. We began by solving for the pricing equilibrium under the market structure that prevailed when the data were collected. When we were satisfied that the simulation model predicted the observed prices well, we evaluated a divestiture and a merger. The divestiture was modelled as a breakup of the Courage and Scottish & Newcastle merger, whereas, with the merger, the proposed Bass and Carlsberg–Tetley merger was allowed to go forward. In other words, we modelled the first (second) as an increase (decrease) in the number of decision makers.

References

Aghion, P., and P. Bolton (1987). 'Contracts as Barriers to Entry'. *American Economic Review*, 77: 388–401.

Atsma, K. (2003). 'European Commission Opens Up Interbrew's Belgian Horteca Outlets to Competing Beer Brands'. *Antitrust*, 2: 58–9.

Comanor, W. S., and P. Rey (2000). 'Vertical Restraints and the Market Power of Large Distributors'. *Review of Industrial Organization*, 17: 135–53.

Compte, O., F. Jenny, and P. Rey (2002). 'Capacity Constraints, Mergers, and Collusion'. *European Economic Review*, 46: 1–29.

Greenhut, M. L., and H. Ohta (1979). 'Vertical Integration of Successive Oligopolists'. *American Economic Review*, 69: 137–41.

Klein, B., and K. M. Murphy (1988). 'Vertical Restraints as Contract Enforcement Mechanisms'. *Journal of Law and Economics*, 31: 265–97.

Krattenmaker, T., and S. C. Salop (1986). 'Anti-competitive Exclusion: Raising Rival's Costs to Achieve Power over Price'. *Yale Law Journal*, 96: 209–93.

Lafontaine, F., and M. E. Slade (2007). 'Vertical Integration and Firm Boundaries: The Evidence'. *Journal of Economic Literature*, 45: 631–87.

—— —— (2008). 'Exclusive Contracts and Vertical Restraints: Empirical Evidence and Public Policy', in P. Buccirossi (ed.), *Handbook of Antitrust Economics*. Cambridge, MA: MIT Press, 391–414.

—— —— (forthcoming). 'Contracting between Firms: Evidence' in R. Gibbons and J. Roberts (eds.). *Handbook of Organizational Economics*. Princeton: Princeton University Press.

Pinkse, J., and M. E. Slade (2004). 'Mergers, Brand Competition, and the Price of a Pint'. *European Economic Review*, 48: 617–43.

Sass, T. R., and D. S. Saurman (1993). 'Mandated Exclusive Territories and Economic Efficiency: An Empirical Analysis of the Malt-Beverage Industry'. *Journal of Law and Economics*, 36: 153–77.

Slade, M. E. (1998). 'Beer and the Tie: Did Divestiture of Brewer-Owned Public Houses Lead to Higher Beer Prices?' *Economic Journal*, 108: 1–38.

—— (2004a). 'Market Power and Joint Dominance in UK Brewing'. *Journal of Industrial Economics*, 52: 133–163.

—— (2004b). 'Competing Models of Firm Profitability'. *International Journal of Industrial Organization*, 22: 289–308.

—— (2009). 'Merger-Simulations of Unilateral Effects: What Can We Learn from the UK Brewing Industry?' in B. Lyons (ed.), *Cases in European Competition Policy: The Economic Analysis*. Cambridge: Cambridge University Press.

Spengler, J. (1950). 'Vertical Integration and Anti-trust Policy'. *Journal of Political Economy*, 58: 347–52.

UK Monopolies And Mergers Commission (1989). *The Supply of Beer*. London: Her Majesty's Stationery Office.

US FTC/DOJ Proposed Horizontal Merger Guidelines (2010). Washington.

Wauters, E., and S. Van Passel (2009). 'The Pub Tie: An Examination of the Impact of Exclusivity Contracts on Pub Level Beer Diversity'. Paper presented at the Beeronomics Conference, Leuven, Belgium, 27–9 May.

11

Developments in US Merger Policy: The Beer Industry as Lens[1]

Kenneth G. Elzinga and Anthony W. Swisher

Introduction

The beer industry in the United States has been marked by massive change over the last 60 years. Few, if any, American industries have undergone such a remarkable structural shakeup in the post-World War II period. During this time frame, many mergers and acquisitions were consummated and, in the process of its structural transformation, the beer industry was the subject of several prominent antitrust decisions, including two Supreme Court opinions that interpreted the new anti-merger law, the Celler-Kefauver amendment to Section 7 of the Clayton Act. More recently, the acquisition of Anheuser-Busch by InBev and the joint venture between SABMiller and Molson Coors have further transformed the industry.

The structural shakeup of the beer industry has been due to a combination of economic forces: economies of scale, superior skill, foresight and industry (on the part of some brewers), rising income-supporting forms of product differentiation, mergers and acquisitions, and, more recently, the emergence of a craft segment consisting of hundreds of new entrants (see Elzinga 2009. Also Greer 1998; Lynk 1984; Ornstein 1981; Tremblay 1985; and Tremblay and Tremblay 1988, 2005).

Running alongside the structural transformation of this prominent American industry has been the transformation of federal anti-merger enforcement. Indeed, changes in the beer industry's structure provide a lens for understanding changes in federal anti-merger enforcement. Revised enforcement

---

[1] This chapter extends the paper by Elzinga and Swisher (2005).

principles have been the result of the development of economic thinking and the implementation of new economic principles through the Department of Justice (DOJ)-Federal Trade Commission (FTC) Horizontal Merger Guidelines. The role of the Hart-Scott-Rodino pre-merger notification process also represents a fundamental change in merger analysis and enforcement, although we do not discuss the impact of this legislation on mergers (Symposium 1997). Economic analysis in mergers has advanced to the point at which the early beer industry cases before the Supreme Court have been superseded by the Merger Guidelines and the exegesis of these Guidelines by the enforcement agencies.

After a review of the changing structure of the American beer market, we review the early Court opinions that fashioned amended Section 7 of the Clayton Act, explain the context of these opinions, and then show how anti-merger enforcement adopted a more sophisticated economic analysis as manifested in the Merger Guidelines. We then show, again through the lens of the beer industry, that notwithstanding the different paradigm of anti-merger enforcement, the original merger doctrines had little effect on the recent major beer mergers, or the current shape of the beer industry.

The Changing Structure of the US Beer Market

During 1947–95, the number of beer companies dropped over 90% (although beer sales doubled). Beer analyst Robert S. Weinberg counted 421 'traditional brewers' operating in 1947; by 2002, this number had fallen to only 22 firms. In 1947, the top five beer producers in the United States accounted for only 19% of the industry's barrelage; in 2001 their share was 87%. In 2002, three firms met almost 80% of domestic demand: Anheuser-Busch (49.0%), Miller (19.1%), and Coors (10.9%). In 1947, the Herfindahl-Hirschman Index (HHI) for the US beer industry was 140; in 2001, the HHI was over 2,900 (Elzinga 2004: 76–7). (The HHI for a given market is the sum of the squares of the market shares of the sellers in the market.)

Recently, due to the growth of the craft beer segment, there has been a noticeable increase in the number of new plants and independent companies—though these new entrants are at the small end of the industry size spectrum. The number of craft brewers went from one in 1965 to over 1,400 in 2002, achieving a critical mass in 1995 by producing over 1 million barrels of beer. Some craft brewers can no longer claim 'micro' status since they now sell lots of beer (current examples would be Boston Brewing and Sierra Nevada). In 2002, craft brewers numbered around 1,000 brewpubs (most of these produce less than 1,000 barrels of beer annually), more than 400 microbreweries (producing less than 15,000 barrels per year), and over 40 regional specialty brewers (with 15,000+ barrels capacity). Even with the growth of the craft segment, the decline in the number of major brewers has been dramatic. In recent years, beer drinkers also have chosen imported beers in increasing numbers. In 2002, imports held over 11% of the US beer market; craft brewers held 3%. Thus, while concentration has increased among the largest sellers, craft brewing and imports have caused an explosion in new beer brands that offer consumers different taste signatures.

Mergers in the American Beer Industry

During the period 1950–83, about 170 horizontal mergers were consummated in the beer industry. But only recently have mergers had a significant effect on the growth of the three firms (Anheuser-Busch, Miller, and Coors) that drove much of the industry's volume. If the anti-merger law affected industry structure, it should be most manifest in the experience of these three firms.

The first anti-merger action in the beer industry was taken by the Antitrust Division in 1958 against the industry's leading firm, Anheuser-Busch. Anheuser-Busch had purchased the Miami brewery of American Brewing Company. The government successfully argued that this merger would eliminate American Brewing as an independent brewer and end its rivalry with Anheuser-Busch in Florida. The impact of this early anti-merger action was profound. Anheuser-Busch had to divest itself of this brewery and refrain from buying any others without court approval for a period of five years. As a result, Anheuser-Busch forsook horizontal mergers and instead began an extensive programme of building large, efficient plants in Florida and at other locations around the United States. Anheuser-Busch deviated only once from its no-merger, internal growth policy in 1980 when it acquired the Baldwinsville, New York brewing plant of the Schlitz Brewing Company. Schlitz's sales had declined so much that it did not need the brewery; the plant's capacity was so huge that only an industry leader could absorb its 5.4 million barrel capacity. Since 1958, the anti-merger law restrained Anheuser-Busch from making any major acquisitions, but this did not prevent the firm from retaining the market leader status it attained in 1957.

Miller Brewing Company, the second largest brewer, also grew primarily by internal expansion. In 1966, Miller purchased breweries in Texas and California but acquired no other breweries until 1987, when it acquired Leinenkugel, a small family-run brewery in Wisconsin. Miller Brewing Company itself was the subject of a conglomerate acquisition by Philip Morris in 1970. From that point, Miller, unlike Anheuser-Busch, had a large corporate parent. In 2002, Philip Morris sold Miller to South African Breweries, a London-based firm that is the second largest brewer in the world behind Anheuser-Busch. SAB markets such brands as Pilsner Urquell and Castle Lager. The venerable Miller Brewing Company became SABMiller.

In 1972, just after being acquired by Philip Morris, Miller purchased three brand names from Meister Brau, a defunct Chicago brewing firm. The Meister Brau trademarks included one called Lite. Hardly anyone noticed at the time, but out of this acquisition came the low-calorie or 'light beer' phenomenon. Lite had been marketed locally by Meister Brau to weight-conscious consumers. The Miller management noticed that Lite had sold fairly well in Anderson, Indiana, a town with many blue-collar workers. In what became a marketing classic, Miller zeroed in on 'real' beer drinkers, claiming that Lite's fewer calories allowed them to drink their beer with even less of a filled-up feeling. Lite became the most popular new product in the history of the beer industry. While Lite enjoyed great commercial success as the first mover in the light beer category, Miller has not been able to maintain Lite's leadership position in the low-calorie market segment the company first pioneered. In 2001, Bud Light became the leading US brand of beer, outselling Budweiser. In 2002, Bud Light and Coors Light outsold Miller Lite. First-mover advantages do not ensure long-run leadership.

In 1974, Miller bought the rights to brew and market Lowenbrau, a prominent German beer, in the United States. Miller was never able to develop this brand into an important US product. (Labatt, a Canadian brewer, currently is attempting to revive the Lowenbrau name in the US beer market.) After this event, mergers played no role at Miller until 1993 when it acquired the marketing rights in the United States for the brands of Molson, a Canadian brewer. In 2001, Miller sold these rights back to Molson, which sold them to Coors.

In 1999, Miller, Stroh (then the no. 4 brewer), and Pabst (then no. 5) consummated a complex acquisition associated with Stroh's exit from the industry. Miller acquired four brands (Henry Weinhard, Mickey's, Hamm's, and Olde English 800) and Pabst acquired all other Stroh brands (including, in addition to Stroh, Old Milwaukee, Schlitz, Schaefer, Old Style, Schmidt's, Lone Star, Special Export, Schlitz Malt Liquor, and Rainier). Miller also acquired Pabst's Tumwater, Washington brewery (which it closed in 2003) and Pabst acquired Stroh's Lehigh Valley, Pennsylvania brewery. This facility was then acquired by Guinness-Bass Import Co. (GBIC), the US branch of the British firm Diageo, in part to produce Smirnoff Ice, GBIC's best-selling flavoured malt beverage. Miller agreed to produce some of Pabst's beer on a contract-brewing basis. Most of the remaining Stroh breweries were to be sold as real estate for non-brewing purposes. Yuengling acquired Stroh's 1.6 million barrel capacity Tampa brewery to meet demand in the Northeast and for geographic expansion in the Southeast. Stroh's Portland, Oregon brewery (the former Blitz-Weinhard plant) has ceased operations. Despite the deal's magnitude in terms of brand ownership rearrangement, it resulted in only a small increase in industry concentration and had no antitrust consequence.

Third-ranked Coors long had a policy of brewing its Coors brand only in one location, Golden, Colorado. This policy itself restrained Coors' expansion by merger. Coors then began shipping beer in bulk to Elkton, Virginia, where it was bottled and canned for sale in the East. In 1990, Coors acquired the Memphis brewery of Stroh. There, as in Virginia, the company only *packages* the Coors brand (but brews the company's lower-priced Keystone brand). One reason Coors has been a high-cost producer relative to Anheuser-Busch is because its beer historically travelled an average of 1,000 miles; Anheuser-Busch, with its dispersed breweries, shipped its beer an average of 200–250 miles. In 2002, Coors acquired Carling, Britain's best-selling brand, from Interbrew, marking Coors' first major acquisition outside North America. In 2005, Coors and Molson (a Canadian brewer) merged to create Molson Coors Brewing Company, the world's fifth largest brewer. In 2008, as discussed later in this chapter, SABMiller and Molson Coors formed a joint venture: the new firm is called MillerCoors.

Stroh had been a prominent brewer since 1850 and was itself an acquirer until its demise. In 1980, when it was the seventh largest brewer in the country, Stroh acquired the F. M. Schaefer Brewing Company. In 1982, Stroh acquired the Joseph Schlitz Brewing Company, itself in a sales tailspin, but at the time the fourth largest brewer. (In 1950, Schlitz was the leading seller of beer in the USA, with a 7% share of the market.) This acquisition catapulted Stroh to number three in the industry, but also shackled the firm with debt and set the stage for its demise. In 1996, Stroh made another sizable acquisition: the G. Heileman Brewing Company. But its size did not insulate the firm from market competition. In 1999, then the fourth-ranking firm in the beer industry, Stroh exited the market.

Until recently, then, the numerous mergers in the beer industry did not make much of an imprint on the structure of the brewing industry, and did not result in market power for merging partners. Indeed, the most active merging firms, Stroh and Heileman, eventually failed. Prior to the transactions involving SABMiller/Molson Coors and InBev/Anheuser-Busch, much of the increase in concentration in the past three decades was due to the internal growth of Anheuser-Busch, Miller, and Coors.

US v Pabst and US v Falstaff

The Supreme Court issued its beer market decisions in *US v Pabst* (1966) and *US v Falstaff* (1973) during a period of aggressive anti-merger enforcement. Other successful early challenges to beer mergers include *US v Lucky Lager* (1958) and

US v Joseph Schlitz Brewing Co. (1966). The DOJ's challenge in 1965 to the proposed merger of Pittsburgh Brewing Company and Duquesne Brewing Company and to the proposed merger of Molson Limited (of Canada) and Hamm Brewing Company led to these combinations being dropped. The DOJ was unsuccessful in thwarting Heileman from acquiring Associated Brewing Company in 1973 (*US v G. Heileman Brewing Company* 1972).

Pabst came shortly after the Court's 1962 decision in *Brown Shoe v US* (1962). *Brown Shoe* was the Court's first treatment of Section 7 of the Clayton Act, as amended in 1950. Section 7 of the Clayton Act is the principal US statute governing the competitive aspects of mergers and acquisitions. Originally, as passed in 1914, Section 7 covered only acquisitions of the stock of one corporation by another corporation. The 1950 amendments to Section 7 expanded its coverage to assets acquisitions as well as stock acquisitions.

The *Brown Shoe* decision established the principles of merger enforcement that would guide the Supreme Court's future decisions. These principles, which would be further developed in cases like *Pabst* and *Falstaff*, reflected a zealous approach to anti-merger enforcement designed to protect small competitors and halt trends towards concentration in their 'incipiency'. As the Court stated,

> [I]t is apparent that a keystone in the erection of a barrier to what Congress saw was the rising tide of economic concentration, was its provision of authority for arresting mergers at a time when the trend to a lessening of competition in a line of commerce was still in its incipiency. Congress saw the process of concentration in American business as a dynamic force; it sought to assure the Federal Trade Commission and the courts the power to brake this force at its outset and before it gathered momentum. (*Brown Shoe v US* 1962: 317–18)

Other cases from that era also discussed the need to address concentration in its incipiency. For example, in *US v Von's Grocery Co.* (1966: 278), the Court stated 'a market marked at the same time by both a continuous decline in the number of small businesses and a large number of mergers would slowly but inevitably gravitate from a market of many small competitors to one dominated by one or a few giants, and competition would thereby be destroyed'. Similarly, in *US v Penn-Olin Chemical Co.* (1964: 170–1), the Court noted '[t]he grand design of the original § 7 ... was to arrest incipient threats to competition which the Sherman Act did not ordinarily reach'.

During this period the Court often declined to entertain elaborate economic reasoning, viewing virtually all concentration as potentially harmful to competition. For example, in *US v Philadelphia National Bank* (1963: 321), the Court held that the 'intense congressional concern with the trend toward concentration warrants dispensing, in certain cases, with elaborate proof of market structure, market behavior, or probable anticompetitive effects'.

It was against this backdrop that in 1966 the Supreme Court decided *US v Pabst Brewing Co. Pabst* involved the merger of Pabst Brewing Company and Blatz Brewing Company. Pabst, the nation's tenth largest brewer, acquired Blatz, the nation's eighteenth largest brewer, in 1958 (*Pabst* 1966: 550) and the DOJ sued to challenge the merger in 1959 (*Pabst* 1966: 547). The Antitrust Division alleged that '[t]he effect of this acquisition may be substantially to lessen competition or to tend to create a monopoly in the production and sale of beer in the United States and in various sections thereof, including the State of Wisconsin and the three state area encompassing Wisconsin, Illinois and Michigan. . . .' (*Pabst* 1966: 548)

The trial court in *Pabst* dismissed the matter after the DOJ had presented its case, finding that the government had failed to prove that the state of Wisconsin and the three-state area of Wisconsin, Illinois, and Michigan constituted relevant markets within which to evaluate the competitive effects of the merger. The trial court also found that as to the United States as a whole—the sole remaining relevant geographic market—the DOJ had failed to prove that the merger would tend substantially to reduce competition (*Pabst* 1966: 548). The Supreme Court reversed the district court on both holdings.

First addressing relevant geographic market, the Court found that the district court had held the government to too strict a standard, finding that, '[p]roof of the section of the country where the anticompetitive effect exists is entirely subsidiary to the crucial question in this and every § 7 case which is whether a merger may substantially lessen competition anywhere in the United States' (*Pabst* 1966: 549–50). Turning to the merger's competitive effects, the Court noted that the 'merger took place in an industry marked by a steady trend toward economic concentration', and that 'the leading brewers were increasing their shares of sales' (*Pabst* 1966: 550–1). The Court expressed its concern that this trend towards concentration should be stopped 'in its incipiency' before competition was diminished (*Pabst* 1966: 551–2).

Commentators at the time recognized the Court's emphasis on halting a trend towards concentration as a significant development. Austin (1969: 772) noted that 'In his treatment of the merits of the case, [Justice] Black avoided the problems of competitive effect analysis. Neither theory nor effort at effect ascertainment was employed to bridge the gap between facts and antitrust decisional principles. Primary statistical facts, reflecting a trend toward concentration, were extended into a proscriptive holding.' Agata (1966: 638) commented that '*Von's Grocery* and other language in *Pabst* suggests that the Court will make no further inquiry concerning anticompetitive effects if the government can establish some trend toward concentration. . . . In the light of

Von's Grocery, a trend towards concentration may have become more than a "highly relevant factor" and may now be a conclusive presumption of anti-competitive effect'. The concentration the Court feared transpired anyway, notwithstanding the *Pabst* decision. The Blatz brand was acquired by Heileman in 1969, and the Blatz brewery was closed.

Seven years following *Pabst* the Supreme Court again addressed a beer industry merger in *US v Falstaff Brewing Co* (1973). In 1965, Falstaff, then the fourth largest brewer in the United States, acquired the Narragansett Brewing Co., a regional brewer accounting for roughly 20% of the beer sold in New England (*Falstaff* 1973: 526, 528). Falstaff was a brewing pioneer in geographic market extension; it was the first American brewer to attach the same brand (Falstaff) to beer brewed at different locations (McGahan 1991: 243). The parties in *Falstaff* stipulated that the relevant geographic market for evaluating the competitive effects of the merger included six New England states: Maine, New Hampshire, Vermont, Massachusetts, Connecticut, and Rhode Island (*Falstaff* 1973: 527). The relevant product market, as in *Pabst*, was the production and sale of beer (*Falstaff* 1973: 527). After a full trial on the merits, the district court found that Falstaff did not compete in New England prior to the merger, and that it had no plans to enter the New England market except through an acquisition. Accordingly, the trial court found that the DOJ had failed to prove the merger would substantially lessen competition for the production and sale of beer in New England (*Falstaff* 1973: 532).

Once again, the Supreme Court reversed the trial court's ruling, finding that the lower court should have 'give[n] separate consideration to whether Falstaff was a potential competitor in the sense that it was so positioned on the edge of the market that it exerted beneficial influence on competitive conditions in that market' (*Falstaff* 1973: 532–3). The Court noted that Falstaff would have been a significant competitor in the New England market if it had chosen to enter the market *de novo*. The Court's approach was criticized by commentators at the time as being superficial and not supported by the facts. For example, Snider and Trier (1974: 853) commented that the Court 'was satisfied to consider only whether Falstaff was perceived as a potential entrant and would not go further to enquire whether its existence on the edge of the market actually had a beneficial influence'.

Development of a More Sophisticated Analysis

The mid-1970s saw the beginnings of a major shift in anti-merger enforcement doctrine. In response to the work of Robert Bork and others, the Chicago School of economics gained ground, and its focus on economic rigour in legal reasoning and an emphasis on consumer welfare as the goal of antitrust enforcement had a significant influence on antitrust law (Bork 1978; Elzinga 1977). The emphasis shifted from the theme in *Brown Shoe, Pabst,* and *Falstaff* on the protection of small business and thwarting a trend to concentration. Market concentration still mattered, but only in the service of consumer welfare protection. Moreover, the Court began to engage in more sophisticated economic analyses when considering the competitive effects of mergers.

For example, in 1974 the Supreme Court decided *US v General Dynamics Corp.* (1974), a case often heralded as ushering in a new era in merger analysis. Then-judge, now-Justice Thomas commented that '*General Dynamics* began a line of decisions differing markedly in emphasis from the Court's antitrust cases of the 1960s. Instead of accepting a firm's market share as virtually conclusive proof of its market power, the Court carefully analyzed defendants' rebuttal evidence' (*US v Baker Hughes* 1990: 990). As one commentator noted,

> Federal enforcement in the 1970s operated against a backdrop of a judicial loosening of restrictions on mergers. Key developments included the Supreme Court's decisions in cases such as United States v General Dynamics Corp. and United States v Marine Bancorporation and court of appeals decisions that emphasized the importance of supply substitution in defining relevant markets and measuring market power. In selecting cases in the 1970s, the federal agencies retreated from the more intervention-oriented approaches that had guided DOJ and FTC merger policy in the 1960s. (Kovacic 2003: 434–5)

In the *Hospital Corporation of America v FTC* case (1986: 1386), Judge Posner, a noted antitrust scholar, commented that,

> The most important developments that cast doubt on the continued vitality of such cases as Brown Shoe and Von's are found in other cases, where the Supreme Court, echoed by the lower courts, has said repeatedly that the economic concept of competition, rather than any desire to preserve rivals as such, is the lodestar that shall guide the contemporary application of the antitrust laws, not excluding the Clayton Act.... Applied to cases brought under Section 7, this principle requires the district court... to make a judgment whether the challenged acquisition is likely to hurt consumers, as by making it easier for the firms in the market to collude, expressly or tacitly, and thereby force price above or further above the competitive level.

The DOJ-FTC Horizontal Merger Guidelines

As profound as any change in Supreme Court doctrine was the adoption by the federal enforcement agencies of the DOJ-FTC Horizontal Merger Guidelines. The joint Merger Guidelines were first published in 1982 and have been revised several times since then. On 19 August 2010, the DOJ and FTC issued the latest version of the Merger Guidelines. This chapter discusses the 1992 revisions to the Guidelines, as this was the version in effect during the DOJ's review of the Anheuser-Busch/InBev and SABMiller/Molson Coors transactions. As stated in the 1992 Merger Guidelines (US DOJ and FTC 1992: § 0.1), '[t]he unifying theme of the Guidelines is that mergers should not be permitted to create or enhance market power or to facilitate its exercise. Market power to a seller is the ability profitably to maintain prices above competitive levels for a significant period of time.' The Guidelines reflect the fundamental shift in anti-merger enforcement that has accompanied advancements in the economic understanding of mergers and acquisitions (even if the Court did not recant its approach to mergers in *Brown*, *Pabst*, and *Falstaff*). For useful discussions of the ways in which the Guidelines represent the progression of economic understanding, see generally, for example, Baker and Blumenthal (1983) and Werden (1983).

In almost every way, a Guidelines analysis would look at the prominent beer merger cases differently. The last decade has seen two major transactions in the beer industry that amply demonstrate the modern approach to anti-merger enforcement reflected in the Merger Guidelines: the acquisition of Anheuser-Busch by InBev and the joint venture between SABMiller and Molson Coors.[2] Below we will look at the elements of a Guidelines merger analysis, followed by a discussion of the DOJ's analysis in these two transactions.

Elements of Analysis under the Merger Guidelines

The Guidelines state '[a] merger is unlikely to create or enhance market power or to facilitate its exercise unless it significantly increases concentration and results in a concentrated market, properly defined and measured' (US DOJ and FTC 1992: § 1.0). Thus, merger analysis under the Guidelines begins with a definition of the relevant product and geographic markets. The agencies look only at demand-side substitution—i.e. potential consumer responses to a price increase—to determine which products or services belong in the relevant geographic market and how large a geographic area comprises the relevant geographic market (US DOJ and FTC 1992: §§ 1.1, 1.2).

After the agencies identify the relevant product and geographic markets, they attempt to identify the competitors in those markets and assign market shares.[3] Calculating market shares allows the agencies to measure concentration

---

[2] These are but two examples. The mergers that brought together Molson and Coors and SAB and Miller, respectively, are themselves examples of beer industry transactions that might have had far different outcomes under the Supreme Court's *Pabst* and *Falstaff* paradigm.

[3] 'The Agenc[ies] normally will calculate market shares for all firms (or plants) identified as market participants... based on the total sales or capacity currently devoted to the relevant

levels and determine whether the merger at issue will take place in a market that is unconcentrated, moderately concentrated, or highly concentrated (US DOJ and FTC 1992: § 1.5). The Guidelines use the HHI to measure concentration in a relevant market. Contrary to the precepts of *Pabst* and *Falstaff*, under the Guidelines (US DOJ and FTC 2003: 2), '[a]lthough large market shares and high concentration by themselves are an insufficient basis for challenging a merger, low market shares and concentration are a sufficient basis for not challenging a merger'.[4]

After the agencies have defined the size, scope, and concentration of the relevant markets involved, they generally will consider two broad categories of potential competitive effects: 'coordinated effects' and 'unilateral effects'. A merger may potentially result in 'coordinated effects' when it increases concentration in a market with a small number of relatively large players who may find it easier to coordinate their behaviour—either explicitly or tacitly—after the merger.[5] 'Unilateral effects' are those that occur when a merger results in a single firm that is large enough profitably to raise price on its own, regardless of the reaction of other firms in the market (US DOJ and FTC 1992: § 2.2).

If the agencies determine that a proposed merger likely will not result in significant anticompetitive effects, the analysis ends there. If a merger raises competitive concerns, however, the agencies will then consider other factors that may ameliorate those concerns. These other factors were absent in the anti-merger calculus of the *Pabst* and *Falstaff* era. Specifically, the agencies now will consider potential entry, efficiencies, and the 'failing firm' defence.

When evaluating entry, the agencies will consider whether entry by new competitors in the relevant market would be 'timely, likely, and sufficient in

---

market together with that which likely would be devoted to the relevant market in response to a "small but significant and nontransitory" price increase' (US DOJ and FTC 1992: § 1.41).

[4] Although the 2010 Guidelines generally employ fewer bright-line rules regarding market definition and market shares, they still recognize that '[m]ergers resulting in unconcentrated markets are unlikely to have adverse competitive effects and ordinarily require no further analysis' (US DOJ & FTC, 2010: § 5.3).

[5] 'Coordinated interaction is comprised of actions by a group of firms that are profitable for each of them only as a result of the accommodating reactions of the others. This behavior includes tacit or express collusion, and may or may not be lawful in and of itself' (US DOJ and FTC 1992: § 2.1). Coordinated effects analysis has sometimes been explained through use of a 'dinner party' analogy:

> [F]ewer firms make tacit collusion more likely or more effective for much the same reason that friends arranging a restaurant get-together will likely find it easier to coordinate the calendars of four people than five, and will more likely notice if one person accepts but does not show up. Under this view, coordination may technically not be inevitable when a market becomes highly concentrated, but the odds of success are high and those odds grow as concentration increases. (Baker 2002: 139)

its magnitude, character and scope to deter or counteract the competitive effects of concern'.[6] The consideration is more sophisticated than the premise in *Falstaff* that the acquiring firm might have entered New England *de novo*; therefore the merger should be disallowed.

As to efficiencies, the agencies will consider whether 'cognizable efficiencies' (i.e. merger-specific efficiencies that have been verified and do not arise from anticompetitive reductions in output or service) are of a character and magnitude such that the merger is not likely to be anticompetitive in any relevant market (US DOJ and FTC 1992: § 4). At the time of *Pabst* and *Falstaff*, if anything, efficiencies from amalgamation were viewed negatively when accompanied by an increase in market concentration.

Finally, the agencies can consider whether the target of the proposed acquisition meets the 'failing firm' defence. The Guidelines impose a high standard for the defence, requiring both that the firm be on the brink of failure, and that there be no less anticompetitive alternative available to it than the proposed acquisition (US DOJ and FTC 1992: § 5.1). By today's standards, *Pabst* and *Falstaff* would not have been decided differently because of the failing firm doctrine.

The Merger Guidelines Approach: SABMiller/Molson Coors and Anheuser-Busch/InBev

The DOJ's review of the SABMiller/Molson Coors and Anheuser-Busch/InBev transactions—both of which it allowed to proceed—demonstrates the significant advances in economic thinking and competitive effects analysis that have taken place since the Supreme Court's early beer decisions.

The SABMiller/Molson Coors transaction involved a joint venture that would combine their US brewing operations. Effectively merging the two firms' US operations, the deal brought together the number two and number three US brewers. Miller and Coors were each smaller than industry leader Anheuser-Busch, but considerably larger than any other domestic brewer. Critics of the two transactions referred to the industry becoming a duopoly (Johnson 2009). If the Supreme Court's analysis in *Pabst* still held sway and mergers reflecting an incipient trend towards concentration could be blocked in their entirety, then one would expect the DOJ to make short work of the proposed Miller/Coors merger. Yet, the DOJ allowed the deal to close without

---

[6] Regarding entry, the Guidelines state '[a] merger is not likely to create or enhance market power or to facilitate its exercise, if entry into the market is so easy that market participants, after the merger, either collectively or unilaterally could not profitably maintain a price increase above premerger levels' (US DOJ and FTC 1992: § 3.0).

obtaining any relief. In its closing statement, the DOJ explained its reasoning in declining to challenge the transaction. The DOJ stated that it had 'verified that the joint venture is likely to produce substantial and credible savings that will significantly reduce the companies' costs of producing and distributing beer', and that these cost savings were 'of the type that are likely to have a beneficial effect on prices' (Statement of the Department of Justice's Antitrust Division 2008).

The parties had argued that the joint venture, despite bringing together two major US brewers, would result in significant synergies, resulting in lower costs. These included cost savings from brewing Coors beer, which previously had been brewed exclusively in Golden, Colorado, at Miller breweries, and the resulting transportation and supply chain savings (Investor Presentation 2007). The parties estimated that the cost savings flowing from reduced transportation costs, more complete utilization of the parties' brewing capacity, and other efficiencies would result in cost savings of over $500 million per year (Investor Presentation 2007: 23).

The DOJ's decision not to challenge the Miller/Coors joint venture reflects a far more sophisticated approach to merger enforcement than the Supreme Court's *Pabst* decision. Unlike *Pabst*, in which the Court viewed any merger that increased concentration as inherently suspect, the DOJ engaged in a detailed analysis of efficiencies the joint venture could capture, as called for by the Merger Guidelines, in concluding that the combination would improve the competitive position of the two firms, despite enhanced market shares and increased industry concentration. The DOJ's analysis amply demonstrates just how far economic analysis has progressed in the last 40 years and the substantial effect it has had on merger enforcement.

Another revealing example of the development of US merger policy is the DOJ's review of the merger of InBev and Anheuser-Busch (AB). That transaction brought together under one roof InBev's strong European brands, many of which are sold in the United States (such as Stella Artois and Becks), and AB's iconic Budweiser and Bud Light brands in the United States. Although Anheuser-Busch already was the largest brewer in the United States, accounting for roughly 50% of US beer sales, InBev's brands added about a 2% US share.

Despite AB's position as the leading US brewer, and InBev's status as a major European brewer, the DOJ allowed the transaction to proceed with only a limited divestiture of the Labatt brand in upstate New York.[7] The combination

---

[7] The DOJ alleged that in Buffalo, Rochester, and Syracuse, NY, beer markets were highly concentrated, with AB and InBev (through its Labatt brand) together holding a greater than 40% share. *US v InBev et al.* (2008). The transaction also faced a challenge from private plaintiffs who sought to enjoin it, but the district court denied their motion for a preliminary injunction. *Ginsberg v InBev* (2008).

got a green light in large part because the DOJ did not consider InBev to be a perceived potential large-scale entrant in the United States.

InBev's *de novo* large-scale entry into the United States was unlikely in part due to the substantial capital costs that would have been required, and the need to establish a large-scale distribution network. Evidence about the US brewing industry suggests that the optimal size for a brewery to achieve economies of scale is a capacity of approximately 4 million barrels of beer per year (Elzinga 2009: 138–9). The cost of constructing such a plant would have been over $250 million (Elzinga 2009: 140). Similarly, building out a nationwide distribution network would not only be costly, it would be unlikely, given InBev's existing distribution agreement with AB. In 2006, InBev entered into an agreement to distribute its European brands in the USA, taking advantage of AB's extensive national distribution network (Anheuser-Busch Inbev 2008). *De novo* entry presumably would have required foregoing the benefits of that established relationship.

History also suggests that InBev was not likely to enter the US *de novo*. There is no precedent for successful, large-scale *de novo* entry into the US beer market by a foreign brewer. Historically, entry into the US market by a foreign brewer has been through shipments into the United States, not the construction of a new brewery in the US. Indeed, no entrant in the US beer market, whether foreign or domestic, has penetrated the ranks of the top three US brewers since World War II (Elzinga 2009: 140–1). The recent history of the beer industry indicates that a foreign brewer, one with a small share of the US market, would not build new, large-scale domestic brewing capacity, establish a new US distribution network, and generate consumer demand sufficient to make profitable investments in manufacturing and distribution. For example, Heineken, which had a much larger share of the US market than did InBev prior to the AB transaction, does not have any production facilities in the United States (Beer Marketer's Insights 2008: 203, 210).

The contrast between the DOJ's lack of further action in the InBev/AB transaction—it did not block the deal in its entirety—and the Supreme Court's decision in *Falstaff* is striking. In *Falstaff*, the Court relied on Falstaff's status as a potential entrant into the Northeast to block the merger. By contrast, in allowing the InBev/AB deal to proceed, the DOJ was likely aware of the low probability of InBev's independent entry into the United States, and that InBev had actually sold off its Rolling Rock brand just a few years earlier (Press Release 2006). By employing a more sophisticated analysis, informed by the Merger Guidelines, which took into account more than simply InBev's status as a potential entrant, the DOJ reached a very different conclusion than did the Court in *Falstaff*.

Conclusion

The beer industry has seen massive structural changes over the last six decades, resulting in increasing concentration in the industry. But although several recent high-profile mergers have changed the beer industry's landscape, so have other market forces such as the exploitation of scale economies and the demise of suboptimal capacity; new or superior products; changes in packaging and marketing methods; poor management on the part of some firms; the strategic use of product differentiation; and the emergence of the craft beer segment.

Equally as striking has been the development of US merger enforcement policy, as reflected in a comparison of the early Supreme Court beer cases with the modern DOJ beer industry enforcement efforts. The view espoused by the Supreme Court in cases such as *Pabst* and *Falstaff* was wooden and mechanical, viewing all increases in market concentration with suspicion. Over the last 30 years economic thinking has advanced significantly, recognizing that other factors in addition to market shares and concentration play a role in the competitive effects of a transaction. The modern government antitrust enforcement efforts reflect this advancement in thinking, as reflected in the Merger Guidelines, and utilize a sophisticated, multi-factor analysis that considers potential efficiencies that the merger might enable, entry conditions in the market, and the strength of the merging firms, among many other factors. This has enabled consolidation among the largest brewers that would not have been permitted in an earlier enforcement era.[8]

References

Agata, B. C. (1966). 'Antitrust'. *Annual Survey of American Law*, 629–48.

Anheuser-Busch Inbev (2008). 'Creating the Global Leader in Beer'. InBev investor presentation, 14 July. Available at <http://www.globalbeerleader.com/documents/Final_Investor_Presentation.pdf>.

Austin, A. D. (1969). 'A Priori Mechanical Jurisprudence in Antitrust'. *Minnesota Law Review*, 53: 739–84.

Baker, J. B. (2002). 'Mavericks, Mergers and Exclusion: Proving Coordinated Competitive Effects under the Antitrust Laws'. *New York University Law Review*, 77: 135–203.

Baker, D. I., and W. Blumenthal (1983). 'The 1982 Guidelines and Preexisting Law'. *California Law Review*, 71: 311–47.

---

[8] This consolidation has not, thus far, enhanced the portfolio of the industry's leading brands. For the 12-month period July 2009–June 2010, Anheuser-Busch and MillerCoors were down 6.5 million barrels compared to the prior 12 months. The two firms have never before sustained such losses (Beer Marketer's Insights 2010).

Beer Marketer's Insights (2008). Beer Industry Update. Suffern, NY.
—— (2010). 16 August: 41/15.
Bork, R. H. (1978). *The Antitrust Paradox*. New York: Basic Books, Inc.
Brown Shoe v US, 370 US 294 (1962).
Elzinga, K. G. (1977). 'The Goals of Antitrust: Other than Competition and Efficiency, What Else Counts?'. *University of Pennsylvania Law Review*, 125: 1191–213.
—— (2004). 'The Beer Industry', in W. Adams and J. Brock (eds.), *The Structure of American Industry*, 11th edn. Upper Saddle River, NJ: Prentice Hall, 72–95.
—— (2009). 'The Beer Industry', in J. Brock (ed.), *The Structure of American Industry*, 12th edn. Upper Saddle River, NJ: Prentice Hall, 128–54.
—— and A. W. Swisher (2005). 'The Supreme Court and Beer Mergers: From *Pabst/Blatz* to the DOJ/FTC Merger Guidelines'. *Review of Industrial Organization*, 26: 245–67.
Ginsberg v InBev SA/NV, 2008-2 Trade Cases 76,400 (ED Mo. 18 November 2008).
Greer, D. F. (1998). 'Beer: Causes of Structural Change', in L. L. Duetsch (ed.) *Industry Studies*, 3rd edn. New York: M. E. Sharpe, Inc., 27–58.
Hospital Corporation of America v FTC, 807 F.2d 1381 (7th Cir. 1986) (Posner, J)
Investor Presentation (2007). 'A Stronger, More Competitive U.S. Brewer', 9 October. Available at <http://www.sec.gov/Archives/edgar/data/24545/000110465907073971/a07-26272_1ex99d3.htm>.
Johnson, J. (2009). 'Beer: State of the Industry Report'. *Beverage Dynamics*. Available at <http://www.beveragedynamics.com/ME2/Audiences/dirmod.asp?sid=&nm=&type=MultiPublishing&mod=PublishingTitles&mid=6EECC0FE471F4CA995CE2A3E9A8E4207&tier=4&id=02B7A302802042A7918B03948F59E7B2&AudID=6150A311BC5647F1A7892E5AC71F2AD9>.
Kovacic, W. E. (2003). 'The Modern Evolution of U.S. Competition Policy Enforcement Norms'. *Antitrust Law Journal*, 71: 377–478.
Lynk, W. J. (1984). 'Interpreting Rising Concentration: The Case of Beer'. *Journal of Business*, 57/1: 43–55.
McGahan, A. M. (1991). 'The Emergence of the National Brewing Oligopoly: Competition in the American Market, 1933–1958'. *Business History Review*, 65: 229–84.
Ornstein, S. I. (1981). 'Antitrust Policy and Market Forces as Determinants of Industry Structure: Case Histories of Beer and Distilled Spirits'. *Antitrust Bulletin*, 26: 281–313.
Press Release (2006). 'InBev USA sells Rolling Rock brands to Anheuser Busch'. 19 May. Available at <http://www.inbev.com/go/media/global_press_releases/press_release.cfm?theID=37&theLang=EN>.
Snider, D. L., and D. L. Trier (1974). 'Note, *United States v. Falstaff Brewing Corporation: Potential Competition Re-Examined*.' *Michigan Law Review*, 72: 837–68.
Statement of the Department of Justice's Antitrust Division on its Decision to Close its Investigation of the Joint Venture Between SABMiller PLC and Molson Coors Brewing Company (2008). 5 June. Available at <http://www.justice.gov/atr/public/press_releases/2008/233845.htm>.
Symposium (1997). 'Twenty Years of Hart-Scott-Rodino Merger Enforcement'. *Antitrust Law Journal*, 65: 825–927.
Tremblay, V. J. (1985). 'A Reappraisal of Interpreting Rising Concentration: The Case of Beer'. *Journal of Business*, 58: 419–31.

Tremblay, V. J., and C. H. Tremblay (1988). 'The Determinants of Horizontal Acquisitions: Evidence from the U.S. Brewing Industry'. *Journal of Industrial Economics*, 37: 21–45.

—— —— (2005). *The U.S. Brewing Industry*. Cambridge, MA: The MIT Press.

Werden, G. J. (1983). 'Market Delineation and the Justice Department's Merger Guidelines'. *Duke Law Journal*, 514–79.

US DOJ and FTC, *Horizontal Merger Guidelines* (1992). Available at <http://www.justice.gov/atr/public/guidelines/hmg.pdf>.

—— (2003). *Merger Challenges Data, Fiscal Years 1999–2003*, 18 December. Available at <http://www.ftc.gov/bc/mergerenforce/index.html>.

—— (2010). *Horizontal Merger Guidelines*. Available at <http://ftc.gov/os/2010/08/100819hmg.pdf>.

US v Baker Hughes Inc., 908 F.2d 981 (DC Cir. 1990) (Thomas, J).

US v Falstaff, 410 US 526 (1973).

US v G. Heileman Brewing Company, 345 F. Supp. 117 (ED Mich. 1972).

US v General Dynamics Corp., 415 US 486 (1974).

US v InBev et al., Competitive Impact Statement, No. 1:08-cv-01965 (DDC, 14 November 2008).

US v Joseph Schlitz Brewing Co., 253 F. Supp. 129 (ND Cal.), *aff'd*, 385 US 37 (1966).

US v Lucky Lager, 1958 Trade Cas. (CCH) 69, 100.

US v Pabst, 384 US 546 (1966).

US v Penn-Olin Chemical Co., 378 US 158 (1964).

US v Philadelphia National Bank, 374 US 321 (1963).

US v Von's Grocery Co., 384 US 270 (1966).

12

The Growth of Television and the Decline of Local Beer

Lisa M. George

The product using TV most successfully to date is beer.

(Sponsor Magazine 1948)

The angel of death for the brewing industry was the television tube. It changed the whole nature of the beer industry. You had Pabst coming in with their Friday night fights, all kinds of stuff like that, and the little guys were just overwhelmed.

(Interview with William Coors, *Modern Brewery Age* 13 September 1999)

Introduction

The brewing industry has in many ways functioned as a research laboratory for the field of industrial organization, providing a platform for the study of technological innovation, government regulation, strategic behaviour, and merger activity. Fuelling this debate was a massive shift from local brewing of local beers to a consolidated national market, dominated by a handful of firms. The process of change began after World War II and continued for several decades. The change was dramatic, with the number of brewers decreasing from over 350 in 1950 to 24 in 2000. The share of production by the four largest brewers increased from 20% to over 90% during this period.

Yet despite extensive study, the reasons for a 30-year period of consolidation long remained unresolved. Two competing explanations have been offered for the shift from local to national beer in the US. Greater economies of scale brought about by technological innovations in packaging, automation, and water treatment almost certainly played a role, and a large literature explores changes in efficient scale in the industry. But others argued that strategic advertising expenditures by the largest brewers were a more important driver of concentration, and there is empirical evidence that national brewers reaped larger economies of scale in advertising than smaller producers.[1]

The dialogue in the literature long centred on welfare and antitrust implications of higher industrial concentration. But the controversy obscured the underlying link between the two arguments, namely that fundamental changes in the market for advertising, brought about by the invention of television, contributed to changing costs in the industry that advantaged large brewers. This chapter describes how the changing nature of advertising brought about by television advantaged large brewers over smaller local brewers, then documents the relationship between the spread of television and the decline of local breweries, both across markets and over time.

Industry Background

Brewing

The number of independent, mass-producing brewers began a sharp decline after World War II. Figure 12.1 illustrates the trend from 1950, mapping the number of independent producers in the US over this period. Figure 12.2 shows the resulting industry concentration. The solid line in the figure shows changes in ownership concentration, measured as the share of the

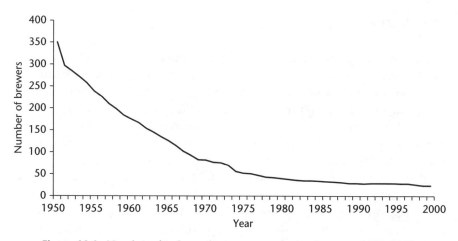

Figure 12.1. Number of independent mass-producing brewers, 1950–2000
Source: Tremblay and Tremblay (2005).

[1] Tremblay and Tremblay (2005) summarize the debate and supporting evidence.

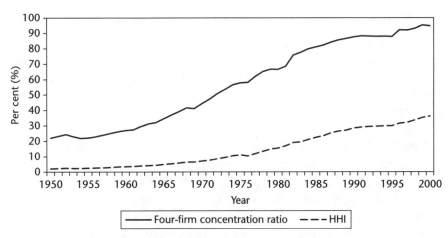

Figure 12.2. Brewing industry concentration, 1950–2000
Source: Tremblay and Tremblay (2005).

market supplied by the top four producers, which increased from 20% to over 90% during this period. The dashed line shows the Hirshman-Hirfendahl index, which increased from close to zero to over 30%. Per capita beer consumption was relatively flat from 1950–70 at about 23 gallons annually before expanding through the 1970s to about 30 gallons per year.[2]

In order for television advertising to have contributed to higher ownership concentration in brewing, it is important that the spread of beer advertising closely follow the spread of television. Historical evidence shows this to be the case. Beer advertising was present at the inception of television in the 1940s, with Narragansett's sponsorship of Boston Red Sox telecasts in 1945. Early beer commercials appeared in St Louis in 1947 with Hyde Park Brewery's 'Albert the Stick Man'. By the end of 1947, Griesedieck Beer was sponsoring a sports program in St Louis and Goebel Beer was sponsoring Tigers' baseball games in Detroit. Other breweries broadcasting pre-recorded spots or sponsorships in the 1940s included National Bohemian Beer in Baltimore, Maryland, Sunshine Beer in Reading, Pennsylvania, and three competing breweries in Chicago (Keeley, Peter Fox, and Canadian Ace). Beer advertising expenditures also increased steadily from 1950 through 1965 as television reached smaller markets.[3]

---

[2] Figures 12.1–12.2 are reconstructed from data in Tremblay and Tremblay (2005), which extensively documents trends in beer production and consumption.
[3] Miller (2002) offers an engaging summary of early beer advertising.

Television

The spread of television was rapid but uneven, with wartime scarcity, technical limits, and policy arguments injecting unanticipated shocks into the startup of stations in many markets. Although commercial television broadcasting officially dates from 1 July 1941 when the Federal Communication Commission (FCC) issued the first commercial broadcast licences, wartime policies curtailed the initial expansion. At the end of World War II, commercial stations broadcast in only four cities: New York, Philadelphia, Chicago, and Schenectady. The true spread of television began after World War II, with 71 stations broadcasting in 42 cities by the end of 1948 (FCC 1949). However, the expansion of television was abruptly halted again in September 1948 by an FCC freeze on station licensing. Although intended to last for a few months while the Commission studied signal interference, colour standards, and spectrum allocation, the outbreak of the Korean War and controversy over channel assignments kept the freeze in place until 1952. Licensed stations not yet operating were allowed to complete construction and begin broadcasting, but as a result of the freeze no new stations were authorized until the end of 1952. After the freeze ended, television spread rapidly, with 440 VHF stations reaching about 96% of the US population by 1960. TV ownership lagged only slightly, with close to 90% of households owning a television by that time.[4]

The wartime construction ban and the FCC freeze created three distinct sets of markets: markets with stations licensed before Pearl Harbor which were able to resume commercial broadcasts immediately after the war; markets with stations licensed after the war but before the freeze; and markets with stations licensed after the freeze. Set ownership expanded rapidly in markets with licensed stations, magnifying the effects of licensing delays.[5] The idiosyncratic nature of the expansion aids empirical study of the effect of television, as the expansion of television can be viewed as exogenous to the market for local beer.

Figure 12.3 shows the spread of television from 1945–60. The top line shows the fraction of the US population within broadcast range of at least one television station each year. The bottom line shows television ownership. The impact of the war and the freeze are evident in the station data, which show steep increases, interrupted by a flat period of minimal growth. With ownership data, the impact is muted, as set ownership in markets with television continued to expand even as the number of TV markets remained constant.

---

[4] Licensing policy and licensing statistics are described in FCC annual reports, available at <http://www.fcc.gov/mb/audio/decdoc/annual_reports.html>. See especially FCC (1949, 1952, and 1953). Armstrong (2007) offers a more extensive narrative on the controversies of the freeze period.

[5] For example, during the FCC freeze, television ownership expanded from an estimated 250,000 in 1948 to more than 17 million in 1952.

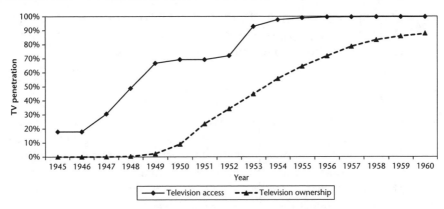

Figure 12.3. Television penetration, 1945–1960

Source: Television Digest (1957–70).

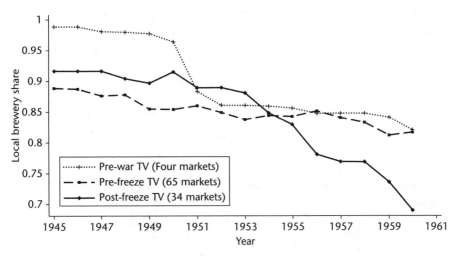

Figure 12.4. Average local brewery share by television group, 1945–1960

To illustrate the effect of television on local breweries, it is helpful to plot the share of local breweries in three sets of markets, those with television before World War II (pre-war markets), those acquiring television after the war but before the FCC licensing freeze (pre-freeze markets), and those acquiring television after the FCC freeze (post-freeze markets). Results are shown in Figure 12.4. A few features are readily apparent in the graph. The local brewery share in markets acquiring television after the freeze, shown with a solid line, remains relatively flat until 1953, at which point it begins a steep decline. Both sets of markets with television before the freeze (dotted and dashed lines) see the local brewery share decline at the beginning of the sample, levelling off in the early 1950s. Markets with television before the war see steeper declines

217

than those acquiring television after the war, but it is not clear from the graph whether the decline begins sooner in pre-war television markets. The patterns in the graph can be shown to hold in a controlled regression analysis.[6]

Advertising

How did the expansion of television alter the market for local beer? A central effect of television was to dramatically lower the cost of transmitting information across regional or national markets. However, small firms did not obtain the same cost reductions as large firms. The primary reason was that the geographic *product market* for local breweries was smaller than the *media markets* created by television. A competitive advertising environment leads to equilibrium prices per *viewer*. But if a firm can serve only a fraction of the viewing population, the effective price per *customer* can be much higher. In markets where all firms operate on the same local scale, advertising prices might increase, but not advantage particular firms. However, in markets where some firms can service larger geographies than others, advertising prices rise for small firms compared to large firms. The 'indivisibility' of the television market thus creates large price differences for large and small firms.[7]

Large producers took full advantage of this change in relative costs, increasing advertising expenditure dramatically during the television expansion period. Advertising expenditure per barrel roughly doubled from 1950–60, from about $100 to $200 per barrel. Figure 12.5 plots advertising spending per barrel from 1950–2000, illustrating the change.[8]

Through this process, television lowered the cost of advertising for large regional and national brewers relative to local counterparts. The actual price difference would depend on the fraction of the audience for local media such as newspapers who switch to television, differences in the per-viewer advertisement price across media, and the productivity of local versus national advertising in generating sales. However, as long as some viewers switch from local media to television and television advertising is no less productive than newspaper advertising, television is likely to increase economies of scale in advertising and hasten the spread of national relative to local products.

---

[6] See George (2009) for regression estimates of the effect of television on local breweries by television group.

[7] A substantial literature documents the effects of new media technology on economies of scale within media markets (George and Waldfogel 2006; George 2008) and the consequences of these changes for consumer and voter behaviour beyond media markets (Gentzkow 2006; George and Waldfogel 2008).

[8] Advertising expenditure dropped off rapidly after the expansion period, then increased again during the 'Brewer Wars' among national brewers in the 1970s and 1980s. See Tremblay and Tremblay (2005) for details.

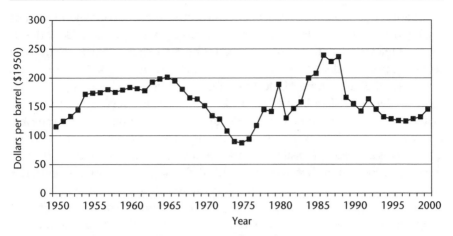

Figure 12.5. Beer advertising expenditure, 1950–2000
Source: Tremblay and Tremblay (2005).

Empirical Analysis

The goal of this section is to measure the extent to which television penetration in a market led to declines in local relative to non-local breweries and to a decline in the production of local beer. Because television stations began broadcasting at different times, markets with faster and steeper increases in television penetration should see faster and steeper declines in local breweries. The analysis will exploit the idiosyncratic spread of television across markets to evaluate whether television played a causal role in the decline of local breweries or was simply correlated with unobserved market factors responsible for the decline.[9]

The analysis relies on two sets of data to estimate the effect of television on the market for local beer. The first is a market-level panel of the number and share of local and non-local breweries, along with television penetration, from 1945–60. The second set of data is a firm-level panel of locally produced beer production, combined with television penetration at the market level from 1950–60.[10]

Television penetration at the market level is measured as the number or fraction of individuals in a market within range of a broadcast television signal. The market-level measures of television population and television

---

[9] The analytical results in this section represent a condensed version of work in George (2009). Readers seeking more comprehensive analyses and discussion are referred to that paper for results.

[10] The market definition used throughout is the Designated Market Area (DMA), which is similar to a Metropolitan Statistical Area but encompasses all suburban and rural areas. DMAs are defined by Nielsen Media Research and are the standard market measure in the television industry.

population fraction are constructed from county-level data on whether or not the county receives a television signal from an operating station. Counties in range of television stations are recorded in the *Television Factbook*, an industry reference published since the 1950s (see Television Digest 1957–70).

The number and share of local and non-local breweries is compiled from *American Breweries II*, published by the Eastern Coast Brewers Association (Van Wieren 1995). *American Breweries II* documents dates of operation, locations, and owners of all breweries in the US. For the analyses presented here, a brewery is considered local to a market in a given year if the parent brewery that year is located in that market. By this definition, even national breweries are local to some location. For example, Anheuser-Busch breweries are considered local in the St Louis market and non-local elsewhere. The number of local and non-local breweries is summed to create a market-level total and market-level local share for use in the regressions.

Firm-level production data for the 100 largest brewers from 1950 to 2001 were originally compiled by Robert S. Weinberg as part of the R. S. Weinberg & Associates Brewing Industry Research Program. The Weinberg data are used extensively in Tremblay and Tremblay (2005) and are generously made available by the authors for other research. Production data are only available by firm each year, with no breakdown by market. However, by assigning all output for local breweries to the home market and eliminating national and major regional breweries from the data, it is possible to construct a sample of local brewery output by market. This panel can be used to estimate the effect of television on local production.

The Effect of Television on Local Breweries

Figure 12.4 showed the average local brewery share over time in three classes of television markets: those with television before World War II (pre-war markets), those acquiring television after the war but before the FCC licensing freeze (pre-freeze markets), and those acquiring television after the FCC freeze (post-freeze markets). Markets with early access to television saw earlier and steeper declines in the share of local breweries than markets with late access to television.

To measure the effect in the graph more formally, it is useful to start with ordinary least squares regressions of the number of non-local and local breweries across markets over time, estimating:

$$N_{Mt} = a_0 + a_1 TV_{Mt} + bX_M + e_{Mt}, \tag{12.1}$$

where N_{Mt} is the number of non-local or local breweries and TV_{Mt} is the population with access to television in market M at time t. The X_M are time-constant market observables and e_{Mt} is a random error term.

Although ordinary least squares estimates provide a useful baseline, coefficient estimates will be biased if unobserved factors influence both television penetration and the market for beer. To account for unobserved heterogeneity, market and year fixed effects can be added to equation (12.1), producing:

$$N_{Mt} = a_0 + a_1 TV_{Mt} + bX_M + g_M + v_t + e_{Mt}. \tag{12.2}$$

Market fixed effects allow a different intercept for each market, with the effect of television identified from deviations from average television penetration and the average number of non-local or local breweries in a market. The effect of time-constant unobservables is captured in the fixed effect and thus cannot be estimated directly. A set of year dummies controls for shocks that are common across markets, but vary over time.

Table 12.1 reports estimates of equations (12.1) and (12.2). Columns (1) and (2) show results for non-local breweries and columns (3) and (4) show results for local breweries. The first column in each set reports pooled ordinary least squares estimates. The second column includes both market and year fixed effects.[11] Standard errors are clustered by market. In all columns, the results indicate that a greater television population is associated with more non-local breweries and fewer local breweries. Estimates with market fixed effects and time dummies are somewhat smaller than those without, although it is likely that the time dummies absorb some effects of television, especially FCC decisions.

How large are the estimated effects? It is useful to consider an increase of 0.2 million viewers, which is approximately the average increase in television population in the sample markets from 1950–5. Using the coefficient estimates in columns (2) and (4), an increase in the television population of 0.2 million increases the number of non-local breweries by $0.101 \times 0.2 = 0.02$, an increase of 5% from an average of 0.4. An increase in the television population of 0.2 million reduces the number of local breweries by $0.596 \times 0.2 = 0.12$, a decrease of 5% from an average of 2.1. A larger increase in the television population of 0.7 million, equivalent to the increase in television population from 1945–50, increases the number of non-local breweries by $0.101 \times 0.7 = 0.07$ (an increase of 18% from an average of 0.4) and decreases the number of local breweries by $0.596 \times 0.7 = 0.42$ (a decrease of 20% from an average of 2.1).

The estimates above show that increases in the television population are associated with increases in the number of non-local breweries and decreases in the number of local breweries. Equations (12.1) and (12.2) can also be estimated in terms of the fraction of the population with access to television

---

[11] The four markets with television before World War II are not included in the regression sample because they differ from markets with later access in systematic ways and thus might bias results. See George (2009) for a discussion of market attributes for each television group.

Table 12.1. The effect of television on the number of non-local and local breweries

	Non-Local Breweries		Local Breweries		Local Brewery Share	
	(1)	(2)	(3)	(4)	(5)	(6)
TV Population or Share	0.146	0.101	−1.139	−0.596	−0.070	−0.032
	(0.057)*	(0.052)+	(0.184)**	(0.166)**	(0.024)**	(0.024)
DMA Pop 1950	0.246	—	2.305	—	−0.073	—
	(0.166)	—	(0.623)**	—	(0.036)*	—
Fraction Age≥60	0.531	—	50.257	—	1.940	—
	(3.960)	—	(21.151)*	—	(2.335)	—
Fraction Age<25	1.524	—	41.724	—	0.650	—
	(3.548)	—	(22.597)+	—	(1.941)	—
Fraction Low Education	−3.229	—	−0.823	—	1.505	—
	(2.272)	—	(11.550)	—	(1.214)	—
Fraction High Education	0.636	—	−20.440	—	−0.466	—
	(1.713)	—	(8.458)*	—	(0.733)	—
Fraction High Income	−0.862	—	6.179	—	2.803	—
	(2.754)	—	(18.562)	—	(1.498)+	—
Fraction Low Income	1.715	—	−17.974	—	−0.144	—
	(2.005)	—	(6.784)**	—	(0.764)	—
Fraction Urban	−0.510	—	2.313	—	0.160	—
	(0.530)	—	(2.261)	—	(0.229)	—
Fraction Non-White	−0.521	—	−1.320	—	−0.071	—
	(1.082)	—	(3.423)	—	(0.410)	—
Fraction Foreign Born	0.140	—	3.310	—	0.145	—
	(0.593)	—	(2.949)	—	(0.254)	—
Population Growth 1940–50	0.600	—	−2.859	—	−0.140	—
	(0.532)	—	(2.152)	—	(0.276)	—
Population Growth 1950–60	0.520	—	−0.538	—	−0.486	—
	(0.528)	—	(1.855)	—	(0.282)+	—
Population Growth 1960–70	0.130	—	3.881	—	−0.137	—
	(0.825)	—	(3.527)	—	(0.411)	—
Fixed Effects	None	Market, Year	None	Market, Year	None	Market, Year
Constant	−0.956	0.414	−14.279	2.134	0.191	0.788
	(1.525)	(0.059)**	(11.435)	(0.213)**	(0.983)	(0.030)**
Markets	99	99	99	99	99	99
Observations	1,384	1,384	1,384	1,384	1,384	1,384

Notes: Dependent variable in columns (1) – (4) is the number of local or non-local breweries in the DMA. Dependent variable in columns (5) and (6) is the local brewery share. Television population in columns (1)–(4) is the number of people in range of a television station each year. Columns (5) and (6) use the television population share. See text for details. Standard errors in parentheses:
+ significant at 10% level;
* significant at 5% level;

and the fraction of local breweries. This specification provides a closer analogue to Figure 12.4.

Columns (5) and (6) of Table 12.1 repeat the estimates of equations (12.1) and (12.2), replacing television population with the television population fraction and the number of breweries with the local brewery share. Results are consistent with those in the first four columns, although the standard errors are larger. Using the coefficient estimates in column (6), an increase in television penetration of 0.4, approximately the average increase in penetration from 1950–5, reduces the fraction of local breweries by $0.032 \times 0.4 = 0.0128$ on an average of 0.788, or about 2%. Moving from 0 to 100% television penetration reduces the share of local breweries by $0.032 \times 1.00 = 0.032$, or 4%. With the total fraction of local breweries in the sample dropping from 0.90 in 1945 to 0.78 in 1960, the spread of television explains about 27% of the total decline.

The Effect of Television on Local Brewery Output

The results above indicate that the expansion of television and associated changes in advertising scale economies contributed to the decline of local breweries. However, the link between the number of local breweries and sales of local beers remains indirect. One concern with studying breweries alone is that, while the share of local breweries declines with the spread of television, local breweries might be expanding output. If this is the case, the local brewery share would underestimate the actual market share of local producers.

Historical information on the brewery industry indicates that local breweries were not, in fact, expanding output faster than non-local breweries. National and large regional brewers were adding capacity faster than local ones, and even larger regional brewers were losing market share in years before failure.[12] The relationship between local brewery production and television penetration can be tested, though in a limited way, with output data by brewery. Production data are available by firm, but not by market, for large brewers during most of the television expansion period. With this data, it is possible to estimate whether increased television penetration is associated with lower local beer production, but not the relationship between television expansion and the local production share.

The output of local breweries can be written as:

$$Q_{iMt} = b_0 + b_1 TV_{Mt} + k_i + v_t + e_{iMt}, \qquad (12.3)$$

[12] See Tremblay and Tremblay (2005), Chapter 8, especially pp. 218–24; also Elzinga (1986). Active antitrust enforcement played a role in limiting the expansion of national brewers through mergers, driving capacity growth among top-tier brewers toward internal expansion.

Table 12.2. The effect of television on local brewery output, 1950–1960

	Local Brewery Output Per Capita (Barrels/1950 Pop.)			
	(1)	(2)	(3)	(4)
TV Pop. Fraction	−0.131	−0.123	0.013	0.008
	(0.079)	(0.082)	(0.013)	(0.015)
TV Pop. Fraction Lag			−0.152	−0.125
			(0.060)*	(0.061)*
TV Pop. Fraction Lead			−0.016	−0.034
			(0.056)	(0.058)
Fixed Effects	Brewery	Brewery, Year	Brewery	Brewery, Year
Constant	0.362	0.386	0.384	0.400
	(0.077)**	(0.085)**	(0.104)**	(0.107)**
Markets	46	46	46	46
Breweries	99	99	99	99
Observations	809	809	809	809
Combined Effects				
Current + Lag			−0.140	−0.117
			(0.058)*	(0.061)$^+$
Lead			−0.016	−0.034
			(0.056)	(0.058)

Notes: Dependent variable is barrels per capita output by local breweries. Television population fraction is the fraction of the DMA population in range of a television station each year. See text for details. Standard errors in parentheses:
+ significant at 10% level;
* significant at 5% level;
** significant at 1% level. Constants in fixed effects regressions represent the average value of the fixed effects. Standard errors clustered by market.

where Q_{iMt} is per capita output from brewery i in year t in market M. TV measures the fraction of the market population with access to television each year. kt and vt are brewery and time fixed effects, and e_{iMt} is an individual error term. A negative estimate for b_1 would suggest that an increase in television penetration reduces local brewery output. The final production sample includes 99 breweries in 46 markets from 1950–60.

Table 12.2 presents estimates of equation (12.3). The first column estimates a pooled ordinary least squares model. The second column includes brewery fixed effects and year dummies. Greater television penetration is associated with lower local beer production, though the estimates do not reach standard significance levels. If the model is re-estimated with lagged television penetration, which allows the effect of television access to accumulate over time, the cumulative effects are statistically significant. The lead term in the specification serves as a robustness check. Its insignificance indicates that the decline in local beer production did not precede the introduction of television.

In terms of magnitude, the smallest cumulative effects are in column (4). An increase in television penetration of 0.4 reduces local brewery output by about $0.117 \times 0.4 = 0.0468$ barrels per capita, a decline of 12% from an average output of 0.4 barrels per capita. Increasing television access from 0 to 100% reduces local production by 0.117 or 29%. Since locally produced beers were generally consumed locally, the results in Table 12.2 suggest that television played a role in the decline of local production. Considered along with historical evidence that national brewers were expanding output, these results further support the hypothesis that television hastened the decline of local beer.

Conclusion

The evidence presented here indicates that the spread of television contributed to the decline of local breweries. However, the role of television appears to be modest, with full television penetration reducing the fraction of local breweries by 4% overall, which constitutes about 27% of the decline from 1945–60. Television penetration reduces local brewery output by about 29% over this period. Also, because industry concentration continued through the 1970s, well after television penetration had reached close to 100%, television access cannot account for all of the post-war trend in industry concentration.

How should we think about the benefits and costs of this consolidation? In markets with identical products, the number of products and their prices are the only factors relevant for evaluating the effect of market changes on consumers. In this context, replacing local with national brands that have lower advertising costs and lower prices would unambiguously benefit consumers. However, with differentiated products, the welfare balance is more nuanced. Consumers who switch to national brands would generally be better off, either because of a taste preference for the new products or because lower prices made the switch worthwhile. It would only be individuals with a strong taste for the particularly local product that might be harmed as national brands replaced local products.

However, if the dimensions of taste are not actually dependent on geography, but rather replicable product characteristics, then the larger markets made possible by lower advertising costs might also serve to support national products along these taste dimensions as well. The brand proliferation among national brewers that emerged in the 1970s, introducing light beers, ice beers, etc., may perhaps be viewed as a realignment from geographic to taste-based product differentiation.

What do these results imply for current media innovations? In a general sense, advances in information technology continue to lower the cost of distributing information over large areas. The results here suggest that these lower costs will further enable the spread of national over local brands. As internet penetration spreads internationally, it is perhaps likely that large international brands will see new marketing advantages over smaller national ones. But at the same time, the internet and expanded channel capacity in television both offer opportunities for better targeting of individuals with particular tastes. As technology lowers the cost of aggregating individuals based on preferences, more targeted consumer products may emerge as well. Thus information technology might also play a role in both industry concentration and 'mass customization' emerging in markets for consumer products.

References

Armstrong, J. S. (2007). 'Constructing Television Communities: The FCC, Signals, and Cities, 1948–1957'. *Journal of Broadcasting & Electronic Media*, 51/1: 1–18.

Elzinga, K. G. (1986). 'The Beer Industry', in W. Adams (ed.), *The Structure of American Industry*, 7th ed. New York: Macmillan.

FCC (Federal Communications Commission) (1949). *Fifteenth Annual Report*. Washington: FCC.

—— (1952). *Eighteenth Annual Report*. Washington, DC: FCC.

—— (1953). *Nineteenth Annual Report*. Washington, DC: FCC.

Gentzkow, M. (2006). 'Television and Voter Turnout'. *Quarterly Journal of Economics*, 121/3: 931–72.

George, L. M. (2008). 'The Internet and the Market for Daily Newspapers'. *The B.E. Journal of Economic Analysis & Policy (Advances)*, 8/1: Article 26.

—— (2009). 'National Television and the Market for Local Products: The Case of Beer'. *Journal of Industrial Economics*, 57/1: 85–111.

—— and J. Waldfogel (2006). 'The New York Times and the Market for Local Newspapers.' *American Economic Review*, 96/1: 435–47.

—— —— (2008). 'National Media and Local Political Participation: The Case of the *New York Times*', in R. Islam (ed.), *Information and Public Choice: From Media Markets to Policymaking*. Washington: World Bank.

Miller, C. H. (2002). 'Beer and Television: Perfectly Tuned In', *All About Beer Magazine*, 80. Available at <http://www.beerhistory.com/library/holdings/beer_commercials.shtml>.

Modern Brewery Age (1999). 'A Talk with the Chairman', 13 September: 8–16.

Sponsor Magazine (1948). July: 75.

Television Digest (1957–70). *Television Factbook*. Washington: Television Factbook, Inc.

Tremblay, V. J., and C. H. Tremblay (2005). *The U.S. Brewing Industry: Data and Economic Analysis*. Cambridge, MA: MIT Press.

Van Wieren, D. P. (1995). *American Breweries II*. West Point, PA: Eastern Coast Breweriana Association.

13

Determinants of the Concentration in Beer Markets in Germany and the United States: 1950–2005

William James Adams

Introduction[1]

Between 1950 and 2000, the four-firm producer-concentration ratio for beer increased from 22 to 95 in the United States; and Anheuser-Busch's share of domestic output ballooned from 6 to 54 per cent (columns 1 and 4 of Table 13.1). This metamorphosis has attracted considerable attention (Elzinga 2005; Greer 2002; Scherer 1996; Sutton 1991; Tremblay and Tremblay 2005), and a consensus interpretation has emerged: during the third quarter of the twentieth century, technological progress enabled the automation of brewing and the acceleration of packaging (Keithahn 1978; Scherer et al. 1975). The scale-augmenting properties of this progress induced a shakeout, in which a few national brewers grew, while most regional and local brewers disappeared. The success of the nationals resulted from their advantages in television advertising (Greer 2002; Porter 1976). After their triumph, the national brewers were largely invulnerable to entry and mobility, because large sunk investments in television advertising created large advantages for first-movers (Sutton 1991). The

[1] This chapter is a revised version of Adams (2006). For magnificent data, I thank Anja Branz, Erich Dederichs, Birte Kleppien, Carol Tremblay, Victor Tremblay, and Robert S. Weinberg. For excellent research assistance, I thank Christian Siller, Ronald Alquist, and Annika Mueller. For true colleagueship, I thank Richard Caves, Gunter Dufey, Kenneth Elzinga, Daniel Halberstam, James Hines, Ulrich Hommel, Kai-Uwe Kühn, Richard Porter, Stephen Salant, F. M. Scherer, Eric Stein, Timothy Taylor, and Michael Waldman. Special thanks to Louis Gimbel, George Kuehn, Nadine Mouy, Philippe Nasse, Anne Perrot, Barry Seeskin, and John Stroh III.

Table 13.1. Producer concentration in the beer industry, Germany and the United States

| | 1950 | | 1958 | | | | 2000 | | | | 2005 | |
| | USA (1) | | USA (2) | | Germany (3) | | USA (4) | | Germany (5) | | Germany (6) | |
Rank	Share	Firm	Share	Firm	Share	Firm	Share	Firm	Share	Firm	Share	Firm
1	6	Schlitz	8	AB	3	DUB	54	AB	9	Holsten	17	Oetker
2	6	AB	7	Schlitz	3	Oetker	22	Miller	9	Binding	15	InBev
3	5	Ballantine	5	Falstaff	3	Schultheiss	12	Coors	6	B&B	9	Carlsberg
4	5	Pabst	5	Ballantine	2	Dresdner	6	Pabst	5	Beck	8	Schörghuber
5	3	Rheingold	4	Carling	2	Hypo-Bank	1	Boston	5	Warsteiner	5	Warsteiner
6	3	Schaefer	4	Hamm	2	DAB	1	Genesee	5	Bitburger	5	Bitburger
7	3	Falstaff	3	Rheingold	2	Carl Funke	1	Latrobe	4	Krombacher	4	Krombacher
8	3	Miller	3	Schaefer	2	Holsten	1	Yuengling	4	BBH	4	Oettinger
Top 4	22		25		12		95		29		49	
Top 8	34		40		20		97		48		67	

Notes: 'Share' is per centage of domestic shipments, measured by volume. A 'firm' is all affiliated companies, as determined by the source in columns 1–5 and by the author in column 6. AB = Anheuser-Busch, BBH = Bayerische BrauHolding, B&B = Brau und Brunnen, DAB = Dortmunder Actien Brauerei, Dresdner = Dresdner Bank, DUB = Dortmunder Union Brauerei. In column 6: company affiliations on 1 November 2005; shipments data for 2002; Schörghuber includes all of Brau Holding International and Karlsberger, even though both are controlled jointly by Schörghuber and Heineken; the parent companies are Dr August Oetker KG, InBev SA (Belgium), Carlsberg A/S (Denmark), Schörghuber Stiftung & Co. Holding KG, Warsteiner Brauerei Haus Cramer KG, Bitburger Getränke Verwaltungsgesellschaft mbH, Krombacher Brauerei Bernhard Schadeberg GmbH & Co. KG, and Oettinger Brauerei GmbH.

Sources: Columns 1, 2, and 4: Tremblay and Tremblay (2005, appendices A, A.1). Column 3: Schwalbach and Müller (1984, table 4). Column 5: DBB (2001, table 4). Column 6: DBB (2003, table 4). Dun And Bradstreet (2003–4), company websites, <http://www.ratebeer.com/beer/breweries/brewers-directory/brewers-directory-0-79.htm>, <http://www.calsky.com/lexikon/de/txt/l/li/liste_von_brauereien.php, amadeus.bvdep.com/ip>.

subsequent proliferation of microbreweries had not reduced concentration significantly at the national level by 2005.

How relevant is the consensus interpretation to other countries? In Germany, concentration has risen, but it remained low by 2005 (columns 3, 5, and 6 of Table 13.1).[2] In 2000, the four-firm producer-concentration ratio was just 29; and the *eight*-firm ratio in Germany was smaller than the *one*-firm ratio in the United States. In 2005, after five years of important mergers involving big brewers, the German beer industry was still much less concentrated than its American counterpart.

Within Germany itself, the consensus interpretation faces another challenge: The scale of breweries and the concentration of brewing are much greater in the north than in the south. In 2000, Bavaria had 12.2 million inhabitants and 667 breweries, while North Rhine–Westphalia had 18.0 million inhabitants and 114 breweries. Clearly, minimum efficient scale and market size are not the only determinants of Germany's beer landscape.

In this chapter, I discuss several candidate explanations for the failure of producer concentration to rise as much in Germany as in the United States: the relevance of the new technologies to German brewers, the preferences of German consumers, the rules for advertising on German television, and factors largely absent from the consensus interpretation of American experience. I find that market structure depends on a remarkably broad range of factors, extending well beyond the technological opportunity and market size emphasized by Bain (1966).

Technological Change in Brewing and Packaging

Product mix, packaging mix, and transport costs can affect technological choice. Can they explain the differences in scale between German and American brewers?

Product mix

Beer is a physically heterogeneous product. The individual raw materials, the recipes, and the production process are all differentiated; so beers differ in appearance, odour, and taste (Jackson 1998). Customarily, beers are classified as bottom-fermented lagers or top-fermented ales. Pilsener (dry and hoppy) and Export (less hoppy, more alcohol) are two lagers. Alt (dark amber and hoppy), Kölsch (pale and hoppy), and Weizen (wheat beer) are traditionally

---

[2] International comparisons of concentration can be quite misleading. In many countries, government data ignore corporate affiliations, so true concentration is understated (Adams 1980).

top fermented. In both countries, the leading seller is Pilsener; but other beers appear more commonly in Germany than in the United States (Tremblay and Tremblay 2005: 132; Sutton 1991: 521; DBB 2001: 70–1). Currently, devotees distinguish between 'craft' and 'mass' beers. 'Craft' connotes both 'small scale' and 'high quality', with 'quality' usually meaning no 'adjuncts' (like rice or corn) and no artificial ingredients; but scale and quality are not synonymous. Sam Adams and Pete's Wicked Ale, two American beers of craft quality (Van Munching 1997: 152, 259; Tremblay and Tremblay 2005: 120), are produced under contract in large breweries; and every domestic lager in Germany, however large the brewery that produced it, is free of adjuncts and artificial ingredients.

The new scale economies affect packaging more than brewing, so national-level differences in product mix shouldn't affect technological choices. Also relevant, however, are firm-level differences in breadth of product line. If setup costs are large, then firms producing many different beers, and packing them in many different types and sizes of container, might not gain much from adopting the new technologies. According to Scherer et al. (1975: 51, 305), setup costs are not especially important in brewing, but they can be significant in packaging. Thus, the product-mix explanation of technological choice boils down to the claim that, at the firm level, product mix is broader in Germany, and a broader product mix entails a broader packaging mix.

Packaging mix

In 2000, beer consumed in the United States was packaged 51 per cent in aluminum cans, 40 per cent in glass bottles, and 9 per cent in half-barrels or kegs (Tremblay and Tremblay 2005: 4). That same year, beer produced in Germany was packaged 20 per cent in cans, 60 per cent in bottles, and 20 per cent in barrels or kegs (DBB 2003, table 26). Bottling and kegging are faster today than in 1950, but canning has accelerated even more. By 2005, bottle lines could fill 1,100 containers per minute, while can lines could fill 2,000 containers per minute (Elzinga 2005: 81–2). The German-American difference in brewery scale is qualitatively consistent with the German-American difference in packaging mix.

Transport costs

Beer is quite costly to transport (Scherer 1996: 394), but is it more costly to transport in Germany than in the United States? Germany has higher population density, smaller distances between major cities, and not-worse systems of freight transport. As a result, one might surmise that the ratio of transport to production cost is lower in Germany than in the United States. Nevertheless, high transport-like costs might have discouraged German brewers from building large breweries.

First, the United States allows beers to contain preservatives, while Germany prohibits lagers produced and sold domestically from containing any ingredients other than malted barley, yeast, hops, and water (BMF 1993a, 1993b). One effect of Germany's 'purity' requirements is to increase the perishability of domestic beer—increasing the cost of transport and counteracting the cost advantages of large-scale brewing.

Second, recall that American beer is sold primarily in cans, while German beer is sold primarily in bottles. Bottled beer is the more costly to transport, especially when the bottles are reusable and returned to the brewery for refilling. In the United States, the disposal of used containers is regulated by the states. Overall, the system induces the recycling of cans, not the reuse of bottles (Porter 2002: 31–7, 92–101). In Germany, the relevant national rules (BMU 1998) date from 1991, and the relevant rules of the European Union (EPC 1994, 2004) date from 1994. Between 1982 and 2002, the importance of cans grew dramatically—from 5 to 29 per cent of all beer sold in food and liquor stores (DBB various editions); but Germany's rules ultimately tilted its beer container mix back toward reusables—the containers most costly to transport and hence least conducive to adoption of the new scale-augmenting technologies.

Implementation of the German rules constitutes a fascinating story of political economy. Rather than accept the German legislation and plan a deposit-return system for non-reusable containers, firms in the beer supply chain challenged the German rules in German court. During the legal proceedings, neither the firms nor the government developed the necessary infrastructure for handling returned containers and transferring deposit money from net receivers of deposits to net payers of refunds. As a result, when the legal challenge failed (in 2002) and the compulsory deposit system for non-reusable containers took effect (1 January 2003), many stores refused to refund a deposit unless the consumer could prove that the beverage had been purchased in that very shop. Sales of canned beer decreased by 70 per cent that year! Meanwhile, foreign beverage producers and the European Commission complained that the German system discriminated de facto against non-reusable containers and hence against imported beverages. After two adverse judgments of the European Court of Justice (ECJ 2004a, 2004b), Germany amended its packaging rules (BMU 2005). Still unknown is how much the new rules will weaken the incentive to package beer locally and hence how much they will strengthen the incentive to adopt scale-augmenting technologies.[3]

---

[3] An obligation to reuse containers does not necessarily blunt the incentive to adopt scale-augmenting technologies. If secondary markets exist for used (but refillable) bottles, then such containers need not be transported back to the original packaging plant. Moreover, in principle,

Preferences

Is the preference for 'local' beer stronger in Germany than in the United States?[4] If so, then small, locally oriented German brewers might have survived the appearance of scale-augmenting technologies even if their American counterparts did not.

One indication that Germans prefer local beers is the variation across Germany in the types of beer consumed. In 2000, for example, Pilsener accounted for 33 per cent of 'Off'[5] sales in Bavaria, but 67 per cent in North Rhine–Westphalia; Alt accounted for 0.2 per cent in Bavaria, but 11 per cent in North Rhine–Westphalia; Weizen accounted for 18 per cent in Bavaria, but 3 per cent in North Rhine–Westphalia (DBB 2001, table 26). Major differences exist within German states as well (DBB 2001, table 21).

Consumer *choices* should not be equated with consumer *preferences*, though. Given the importance of transport costs (discussed above), local beers might be chosen for their prices rather than their attributes.

One way to disentangle the effects of tastes from those of transport costs is to ask the experts. Germany's competition authority has argued that German beer markets are smaller than national in scope, largely because German preferences are local in nature (BKA 2000). The European Union's competition authority concurs, observing (EC 2002a, para. 12): 'The large majority of German beers are "Pilsner" beers and other possible regroupings vary considerably according to German regional preferences'. Academic experts also agree. After studying the beer industry in six countries, Scherer et al. (1975: 142) concluded: 'Whatever the causes, strong brand loyalties permit hundreds of small [German] breweries to survive serving very limited local markets and simultaneously make penetration by regional and national brewers difficult'.

Even if many German consumers behave today as if they prefer local beers, an understanding of how market structure evolves over time requires an understanding of how preferences are formed.

---

distant brewers can enlist local licensees to produce and package their beers. In Germany, however, licensing can be problematic, even though many German brewers suffer from chronic excess capacity. First, since 1987, Germany allows a beer that is produced and sold legally in another country to be sold in Germany, even if the beer fails to satisfy Germany's 'purity' rules; but Germany still requires domestically produced beers to be 'pure'. Most foreign beers fail to satisfy the German rules, so they cannot be supplied to the German market from breweries inside Germany. Second, many German brand names include the town or area in which the brand is traditionally produced. Warsteiner was sued for misleading labelling when it shifted some production of 'Warsteiner Pils' from its brewery in Warstein to its (own) brewery in Paderborn, just 40 kilometres away (ECJ 2000).

[4] Does 'local' mean (1) brewed from local raw materials? (2) brewed in a local brewery? (3) packaged in a local plant? (4) brewed and packaged by a locally owned company? (5) associated by name or advertising with a particular locale? For many German beers, these criteria yield conflicting geographic classifications.

[5] 'Off' and 'On' refer to where the beer is consumed—off or on the premises of the retailer.

The preference for local beer depends partly on exposure to beers associated with 'other' places. The European Court of Justice (ECJ 1980, 1983, 1987) believes in the importance of such exposure, contending that the integration of European markets for alcoholic beverages will augment consumer valuations of foreign products. The Court's arguments apply when goods move freely and when consumers travel frequently. What about the changes in tastes that might result from permanent changes in residential location? After all, the Third Reich and the Cold War occasioned two major reshufflings of the German population.

During the mid-1940s, large numbers of refugees converged on West Germany from the east. In addition, many uprooted individuals migrated from one West German state to another. Thus, in the population census of 1950, 24 per cent of all West Germans reported that their place of residence in 1938 was outside their state of residence in 1950 (STBA 1952, table 7a). The experiences of these migrants served sometimes to preserve their pre-existing tastes and sometimes to develop new ones. Favouring the preservation of tastes was the spatial and social isolation of the displaced (Berghoff 1996: 41–2): 'Housing estates for refugees were deliberately built well outside existing residential areas, and for quite some time their inhabitants felt somewhat out of place'. Unsurprisingly, the resulting '... state of mind led ... to a ... reluctance to ... make a genuine effort to integrate. Instead many ... socialized primarily with people from their own native region, and intensified the maintenance ... of their traditions and customs'. On the other hand (p. 49), '... the integration of millions of expellees and refugees contributed to the decline of traditional attitudes and lifestyles as well as to the dissolution of hermetically closed milieux'.

During this period, several German regions experienced heightened demand for non-traditional beers. One example involved sweet beer (Sußbier) in Bavaria (Speckle 2001: 67, 91, 203). Recipes for sweet beer complied with Germany's 'purity' requirements, but failed to satisfy the stricter Bavarian requirements. From 1949 until 1965, the Bavarian Brewers' Association frequented both the corridors of state government and the courts to militate against the production and sale of sweet beer inside Bavaria. In response, brewers' associations in other states, individual brewers, and even the government of Berlin complained to the federal government and challenged Bavaria in court. One brewery deliberately violated the Bavarian ban by shipping sweet beer into Bavaria from its facilities near Frankfurt. Ultimately, Germany's Federal Court of Justice held that sweet beer could be sold in Bavaria, but not as 'beer'. By that time, the provocative brewery was calling its beverage a 'nutritional' drink.

The residential dislocations of this period affected northern brewers, too. During the 1950s, North Rhine–Westphalia experienced increased demand for Pilsener. Given the traditional local taste for beers like Alt, Export, and Kölsch, the region's largest brewers dismissed this demand as transitory and allowed the pubs they controlled to buy Pilseners from any brewer (Kemmer 1984). This gave Warsteiner its start. In 1950, Warsteiner produced just 18,000 hectolitres of beer; today, it is the fifth largest brewer in Germany, producing 5.7 million hectolitres in 2002.

When the Iron Curtain rose, Germany experienced another population shift and new disturbances in the beer market. For example, during the 1990s, a brewery in the former East Germany was initially denied the right to call its beverage 'beer', even though it was using a centuries-old recipe. Ultimately, the Federal Administrative Court decided in its favour, but on a technicality (BVerwG 2005). In addition to battling before administrative authorities and courts in various German states, the brewery in eastern Germany had to contend with 'fellow' brewers who sided with the authorities and wanted to expel it from a trade association (Fritsche 2004). The brewery also had to fend off a suit, initiated by a small brewer in Bavaria, who argued that the eastern brewery was engaging in unfair competition.

Four final clues regarding German tastes:[6] each runs counter to expectations based on conventional descriptions of German preferences. First, Pilsener-style beer is growing in popularity throughout the country. Between 1981 and 2002, its share of 'Off' sales increased from 49 to 69 per cent (DBB various editions). German Pilseners are not perfect substitutes, but the rise of Pilsener marks the decline of physical heterogeneity and hence the decline of an important source of local preference. Second, private-label beer sells better in Germany (Winston et al. 2002: 9) than in the United States (Elzinga 2005: 88). Third, at the brand level, German consumers (Winston et al. 2002: 7), like American consumers (Elzinga 2005: 75), are price sensitive. Fourth, individual German consumers tend to consume multiple brands of beer. In 2001, among 25 heavily advertised consumer goods, beer ranked *last* in terms of consumer loyalty to a few brands; moreover, between 1993 and 2001, brand loyalty declined more for beer than for any sample product except yoghurt (Bauer Media 2001).

Television

In the United States, regional and local brewers were dealt a fatal blow by national television advertisements. Large national brewers bought exclusive

---

[6] In the United States, scientifically designed blind tastings show: (1) perceived brand quality and actual brand price are not highly correlated, and (2) brands are difficult to identify by taste (Greer 2002; and Tremblay and Tremblay 2005). For Germany, I have seen neither experimental nor econometric evidence on brand loyalty.

network rights to major sporting events (Van Munching 1997: 67), and local spots entailed significant cost disadvantages in comparison with national spots (Scherer 1996: 408–9). Was television as lethal a weapon in the German beer market as it was in the American?

Before 1990, German television (Humphreys 1994) was unlikely to advantage national brewers vis-à-vis local brewers. First, television was not an attractive advertising medium (RStV 1991). Commercial time was scarce and inelastically supplied (a small number of channels, limited amount of time per channel). Little if any commercial time was available during evenings, Sundays and holidays—and most of it was available only within large groupings of advertisements. Thus television advertising was expensive, poorly suited to reaching drinking males, and unlikely to leave a lasting impression. Second, German television did not offer decisive advantages to national advertisers. Until 1984, only two channels showed advertisements; and, commercially speaking, one of them operated more as a collection of regional stations than as a network. Between 1984 and 1990, the number of national cable channels was small, cable packages were unavailable in many parts of the country, and few households subscribed.

By 1990, however, the situation was changing; and many of the changes favoured national brewers. In 2005, most advertising was shown on truly national channels. Several of these channels attracted large national audiences, while others targeted national audiences of special interest to brewers. Given the (relative) latitude of private channels regarding quantity and timing of commercials (European Council 1989; EPC 1997), the appeal of television to national advertisers was considerable. But given the paucity of regional spot time on the national channels (even in 2005, none of the leading private channels offered regional spots), the price of commercial time per potential customer was unlikely to be attractive to regional brewers.[7]

This change is apparent in how brewers advertise. In 1990, German brewers allocated less than one-third of their advertising budgets to television (Bauer Media 2005a); but, during the 1990s, the importance of television to the brewers grew dramatically. By 1999, when television accounted for 26 per cent of all advertising spending in Germany (WARC 2004: 129), it accounted for two-thirds of all advertising spending on beer (Bauer Media 2005a). Large brewers invested disproportionately heavily in television (Bauer Media

---

[7] On the other hand, the European Commission (2005) has endeavoured to ensure that professional soccer is available on many channels and in multiple formats. This makes it difficult for a few brewers to lock up all soccer advertising. It also contrasts sharply with American policy. Van Munching (1997: 66–7) describes a 1980s exclusivity contract, between Anheuser-Busch and ESPN, that affected 'everything the network covered. Though such a contract would seem like restraint of trade, the Justice Department rejected the 1985 challenge to exclusivity clauses brought by Stroh.'

2005b). In 2000, for example, when television accounted for 65 per cent of all beer advertising in Germany, it accounted for 84 per cent of advertising by the top ten advertisers of beer. These ten companies accounted for 76 per cent of all beer advertising on German television. Smaller brewers tend to rely on media other than television. In 2000, radio, daily newspapers, and billboards accounted for 10 per cent of the advertising of the top ten beer advertisers, but 58 per cent of the advertising of other beer advertisers.

In sum, only since 1990 has television advertising become an important commercial weapon of Germany's largest brewers. The timing of the decline in brand loyalty (Bauer Media 2001) is quite consistent with the chronology of commercial television, but I have not seen any systematic, brand-level calculations of advertising elasticities of demand or market-share instabilities. Until they appear, remember that television became an important advertising medium under very different circumstances in these two countries. In the United States, it occurred during the golden age of triopolistic network television. In Germany, it occurred contemporaneously with the proliferation of channels on cable and satellite. The fact that concentration and mean output per brewery remain low in Germany—even by European standards and even though national brewers have tilted their media mix heavily toward television—might reflect the declining importance of television in a shakeout. Or it might simply reflect the newness of commercial television in Germany.

Other Shakeout Scenarios

In this section, I consider several other possible explanations of why concentration has risen less in Germany than in the United States between 1950 and 2005.

Horizontal Collusion and Merger

The rigour of competition policy might affect the reactions of existing sellers to scale-augmenting technological change. For example, if horizontal collusion is tolerated (and barriers to entry exist), then established sellers might adopt a live-and-let-live pattern of conduct, retarding the rise of concentration. The effects of horizontal merger policy are less clear-cut: On the one hand, tolerance of mergers could speed concentration insofar as mergers facilitate the sharing between brewers of the gains from closing inefficiently small facilities. On the other hand, prohibition of mergers could speed concentration insofar as it hastens a bellicose shakeout.

During the relevant period, American antitrust authorities attacked horizontal collusion forcefully, and they prevented several important mergers between brewers (Elzinga and Swisher 2005; Tremblay and Tremblay 2005: 234–47 and table C1). In Germany, brewers are subject to both German and European Union rules of competition. The European Commission (2004b) has uncovered and attacked collusion in several European beer markets, but it has never alleged collusion in the German beer market. On the other hand, both Germany and the European Union are quite tolerant of mergers affecting the German beer market (BKA 2000; EC 2001a, 2001b, 2002a, 2002b, 2003a, 2004a), and German brewers have grown primarily by acquisition (Brouwer 1988: 165; Müller 1976; Schwalbach and Müller 1984).

Vertical Integration and Restraints

The evolution of concentration might depend on whether or not some brewers have privileged access to wholesalers and retailers.

One might think that all brewers have good access to distributors in the United States. After all, most American states prohibit brewers from integrating forward, by ownership or subsidy, into wholesaling and retailing (Elzinga 2005: 88). Nevertheless, wholesaling is concentrated (Elzinga 2005: 88; Scherer 1996: 409), exclusive dealing contracts between wholesalers and the largest brewers are apparently compatible with antitrust law (Van Munching 1997: 256–7; Tremblay and Tremblay 2005: 248–50), and space-constrained distributors are naturally reluctant to stock all of the brands proffered by brewers. No wonder Redhook, a microbrewery based in Seattle, was willing to become 25 per cent owned by Anheuser-Busch (Tremblay and Tremblay 2005: 74–5): Redhook performs its own brewing, packaging and promotion; but it relies on Anheuser-Busch's wholesalers to distribute its beer. More generally, the high level of concentration in American brewing is quite consistent with the difficulties experienced by small and new brewers in attracting and retaining distributors.

In Germany, too, wholesaling is concentrated and distributors are space constrained. In addition, however, German brewers are allowed to integrate forward into distribution. One might think, therefore, that large national brewers enjoy at least as many distribution advantages in Germany as they do in the United States. Historically, however, the German distribution system has offered one important advantage to regional brewers, and this advantage has probably reduced the likelihood of an American-style shakeout. The distribution of beer to some of Germany's 'On' retailers involves a 'tied-house' system (Brouwer 1988; Dumez and Jeunemaître 1994; Slade 1998): the brewer supplies the retailer with commercial equipment and/or financial credit at below-market prices. In return, the retailer buys beer almost exclusively from that brewer. In most American states, the tied-house system disappeared by law after Prohibition was repealed. Under the German legislation in effect before 1984, exclusive purchasing contracts between retailers and brewers could last as long as 20 years. Under European Union legislation, the maximum duration of the tie (before it must come up for renewal) has been shortened in stages (EC 1967, 1983, 1999). Since 1999, it is normally five years.

To a large regional brewery in Germany, the tied-house system offers an alternative to television as a means of burnishing its brands. Many of Germany's most prominent and popular 'On' retailers are tied to established local brewers. The signs, glassware, beer mats, and ambiance of these tied retailers all reinforce the images associated with the brewer's beers. As long as consumers buy beers promoted in this manner, the local brewers usually succeed in getting local 'Off' retailers to stock their brands as well (MMC 1989: 19). In sum, the tied-house system might help local and regional brewers to attract and retain distributors—not merely by foreclosure in the short run (which definitely occurs; see EC 2003b), but by development of brand image for the medium and long run.

The Profit Motive

Most American breweries, including those associated with particular families, have enough outside owners to guarantee a preoccupation with profit. In Germany, as recently as 2000, limited partnerships (KGs) accounted for half of all beer sales; and limited liability corporations (GmbHs), which are usually closely held, accounted for another 12 per cent (DBB 2003, Table 30). Although most of Germany's so-called abbey breweries (Klosterbrauerei) by 2005 belonged to commercial brewers, a few remained authentically insulated from extra-monastery motives. Given their history, organizational form, and current ownership structure, some German breweries might be managed with objectives other than profitability in mind. In a shakeout, these breweries might not exit quickly, even if they lose money regularly (Brouwer 1988: 172).

Excise Taxes

In both Germany and the United States, beer is subject to excise taxes. If their rates depend on brewer size, such taxes might affect market structure.

In the United States, in 1977, the federal excise tax on beer was $7.67 per hectolitre. Between 1977 and 1991, brewers producing less than 2.35 million hectolitres paid only $5.97 per hectolitre on the first 70,400 hectolitres of output. In 1991, the standard rate doubled to $15.34 per hectolitre, while the treatment of small brewers remained unchanged. The birth rate for small breweries displays an unmistakable increase right after the change (Tremblay and Tremblay 2005, figure 5.6).

In Germany, the excise tax on beer is governed primarily by two Directives of the European Union (European Council 1992a, 1992b; see also BMF 1993a,

1993b, 1994). These allow a country to reduce its tax rate by up to 50 per cent for breweries producing less than 200,000 hectolitres per year. Germany offers a reduction of 25 to 50 per cent, depending inversely on brewer size (DBB 2003: 147). In 2002, 61 per cent of all German breweries qualified for the maximum reduction, and only the largest 6 per cent qualified for no reduction (DBB 2003, table 2). The advantage to the small brewer is limited, though. Among European Union countries, Germany has the lowest 'standard' rate of excise tax on beer (DBB 2003, table 86).

Lessons

What are the ultimate determinants of market structure? Neoclassicists emphasize production technologies and consumer preferences, while institutionalists emphasize community cultures and public policies. What are the lessons of this enquiry for studies of market structure in other industries and countries?

First, regarding technological determinism: most observers of the American beer industry attach great importance to brewing and packaging technologies. In the US setting, scale-augmenting technological change boosted concentration substantially. In Germany, it did not. Nevertheless, beer in Germany *is* partly a technological story. The technology in question, however, involves the transmission of television signals. Germany experimented with commercial television only after new satellite and cable technologies made it very difficult, politically if not technologically,[8] to impede German households from receiving foreign signals.

Second, regarding tastes, most observers of the German beer industry attach great importance to the local nature of consumer preferences, but the significance of this geographic specificity must be clarified. Bavarian brewers have been fighting for more than a century to ban certain types of German beer from their region, and they have tried to impose Bavaria's own, relatively stringent 'purity' rules on the whole country (BBB 2005). Would these efforts have been worth the trouble if Bavarian consumers shunned the beers produced elsewhere in Germany? Beer in Germany *is* partly a story of preferences, but the story differs from the one usually told. The demographic dislocations of the Third Reich and the Iron Curtain would not have created new patterns of demand at the regional level if all migrants had abandoned quickly the preferences typical of the places they had left. In a mobile society, locally

---

[8] West Germany would not have wanted to confer legitimacy on the political signal-jamming in East Germany.

formed preferences cannot explain by themselves the survival of small breweries and spatially fragmented markets.

Third, the importance of seemingly unrelated public policies: beer market structure is influenced by a remarkably broad array of public policies, administered by a multiplicity of public authorities. Given the lags, interdependencies, and political economy, it can be tricky to identify the effects of individual policies on market structure.

Fourth, the distinction between policy mandates and policy impacts: many policies are fashioned by courts, and courts often lack the authority and/or willingness to deploy the carrots and sticks that alter market behaviour (Rosenberg 1991). In 1987, the European Court of Justice told Germany to open its borders to beers produced and marketed legally in other European Union countries. Germany complied; but the French brewer who had triggered this legally successful proceeding failed to collect damages in German court (BGH 1996; see also ECJ 1996). The brewer was then acquired by Heineken (CC 1996); and imported beers have been unable to increase their share of the German market by 2005 (see also van Tongeren, Chapter 3 in this volume).

Convergent Market Structures after All?

In the United States, two strategic groups (in the sense of Newman 1978) occupy the seller's side of the beer market: mass brewers, who sell nationwide and differentiate their products primarily by advertising on television; and craft brewers, who sell locally or regionally and differentiate their products primarily with raw materials. After World War II, craft production nearly disappeared. Since the mid-1980s, however, it has rebounded. In 2003, craft production (the output of brewers producing less than 17,600 hectolitres annually) accounted for just 3.2 per cent of domestic output (Tremblay and Tremblay 2005, table A-1); but, unlike their mass-production counterpart, the craft group is growing—in membership, in output, and in share of domestic shipments. Meanwhile, mass producers have consolidated their position vis-à-vis a third, virtually extinct group: regional brewers who lacked the physical products to rival craft brewers and the television advertising to rival mass brewers.

In Germany, craft brewing never approached extinction, but it has waned (DBB various years). By 1992, small breweries (producing no more than 20,000 hectolitres annually) accounted for just 3.2 per cent of domestic shipments— the very share associated with American craft brewing in 2003!

The most important differences between Germany and the United States do not involve craft brewers. Large regional brewers have virtually disappeared in the United States, but not in Germany. The survival of such brewers in

Germany might be attributable to the later introduction of nationwide commercial television, the later weakening of the tied-house system, and/or the stronger policy penchant for reusable bottles. If so, recent German policy changes in these areas might presage attrition in this group. The current tolerance of beer mergers in Germany might facilitate such attrition, but the German market for corporate control is dampened by the scarcity of broadly held companies (Winston et al. 2002).

More interesting is the difference within mass brewing. In the United States, mass production was a triopoly in 2005, dominated increasingly by Anheuser-Busch; Germany's mass brewers are scaled more symmetrically (as shown in Table 13.1). As television is increasingly available as a weapon, Germany's mass producers might engage in warfare similar to the 1970s hostilities between Anheuser-Busch and Miller. Those hostilities caused considerable collateral damage to regional mass producers in the United States.

If the German and American beer industries do converge, with a small group of mass producers and a large group of craft producers in each, then the vigour of competition in both countries will depend importantly on the structure of distribution (CC 2004, 2005; OFT 2000: 36). In the United States (Sass and Saurman 1993, 1996), since Prohibition, many states have mandated both a 'three-tier' system of distribution (which requires brewers to sell only to wholesalers and wholesalers to sell only to retailers) and a system of exclusive territories for wholesalers (inside a specified geographic area, a brewer's beers are available from only one wholesaler). In *Granholm v Heald* (2005), however, the Supreme Court challenged the protected position of the wholesalers. Specifically, it held that a state cannot prohibit internet purchases of wine from out-of-state wineries (which bypass in-state wholesalers) if it authorizes such purchases from in-state wineries. In his majority opinion, Justice Kennedy mentions concentration in wholesaling—the challenges it poses for small out-of-state wineries as they attempt to attract wholesalers. He also mentions the cost disadvantage of out-of-state wineries when, unlike in-state wineries, they must use the three-tier system of distribution. These are precisely the distribution difficulties confronting craft brewers. Insofar as *Granholm* applies de facto to beer, the Supreme Court might have laid the groundwork for increased competition in beer distribution—but only if the political clout and monopsony power of the new mass retailers (like Wal-Mart and Costco) is also controlled. Big mass retailers already figure prominently in the distribution of German beer, so the future structure of the beer market may be surprisingly similar in Germany and the United States.

References

Adams, W. J. (1980). 'Producer-Concentration as a Proxy for Seller-Concentration: Some Evidence from the World Automotive Industry'. *Journal of Industrial Economics*, 29/2: 185–202.

—— (2006). 'Beer in Germany and the United States'. *Journal of Economic Perspectives*, 20/1: 189–205.

Bain, J. S. (1966). *International Differences in Industrial Structure: Eight Nations in the 1950s*. New Haven, Conn.: Yale University Press.

Bauer Media (2001). VerbraucherAnalyse 2001. Available at <http://www.bauermedia. com/studien/markt_media_studien/verbraucheranalyse/verbraucheranalyse.php>.

—— (2005a). Mediensplit: S + P 10 Jahresvergleich: Alkoholische Getränke: Bier. Available at <http://www.bauermedia.com/pdf/studien/branchen/food/bier_sp10.pdf>.

—— (2005b). Mediensplit: Top 10 nach Bruttowerbeinvestitionen: Alkoholische Getränke: Bier. Available at <http://www.bauermedia.com/pdf/studien/branchen/food/bier_top10.pdf>.

BBB (Bayerischer Brauerbund) (2005). 'The Long Struggle for Quality'. Available in English at <http://www.bayerisch-bier.de/>.

Berghoff, Hartmut (1996). 'Population Change and its Repercussions on the Social History of the Federal Republic', in Klaus Larres and Panikos Panayi (eds.), *The Federal Republic of Germany since 1949: Politics, Society and Economy before and after Unification*. London: Longman, 35–73.

BGH (Bundesgerichtshof) (1996). Zum Gemeinschaftsrechtlichen Staatshaftungsanspruch. Judgment of 24 October 1996, III ZR 127/91. BGH Press Release 62/96, 'Keine Haftung der Bundesrepublik Deutschland in Sachen Brasserie du Pecheur'. Available at <http://www.jura.uni-sb.de/Entscheidungen/pressem96/BGH/zivil/eu_1.html>.

BKA (Bundeskartellamt) (2000). Holsten/König. Case B2-15963-U-8/00, 26 April. Available at <http://www.bundeskartellamt.de/wDeutsch/download/pdf/Fusion/Fusion00/B2_8_00.pdf>.

BMF (Bundesministerium der Finanzen) (1993a). Biersteuergesetz 1993 (BierStG) of 21 December 1992. Available at <http://bundesrecht.juris.de/bundesrecht/bierstg_1993/index.html>.

—— (1993b). Vorläufiges Biergesetz (VorlBierG) of 29 July 1993. Available at <http://www.rechtliches.de/info_VorlBierG.html>.

—— (1994). Biersteuer-Durchführungsverordnung (BierStV) of 24 August 1994. Available at <http://www.rechtliches.de/info_BierStV>.

BMU (Bundesministerium für Umwelt, Naturschutz und Reaktorsicherheit) (1998). Ordinance on the Avoidance and Recovery of Packaging Wastes—Third Amending Ordinance. Available in English at <http://www.bmu.de/english/waste_management/downloads/doc/35132.php

—— (2005). Questions and Answers on the 'Drinks Can Deposit'. Available in English at: <http://www.bmu.de/english/waste_management/downloads/doc/3386.php>.

Brouwer, M. (1988). 'Evolutionary Aspects of the European Brewing Industry', in H. W. de Jong, (ed.), *The Structure of European Industry*. Dordrecht: Kluwer Academic Publishers, 157–82.

BVerwG (Bundesverwaltungsgericht) (2005). Judgment of 24 February 2005, BVerwG 3 C 5.04. Available at <http://www.bverwg.de/enid/505521679b644c1f7421fb68c3284ce3, a34f177365617263685f646973706c6179436f6e7461696e6c6572092d0935333933/En-tscheidungssuche/Entscheidungssuche_8o.html>.

CC (Conseil de la Concurrence, France) (1996). Avis n° 96-A-09 du 9 Juillet 1996 Relatif à la Prise de Contrôle de la Société Brasserie Fischer et de sa Filiale Grande Brasserie Alsacienne d'Adelshoffen par la Société Sogebra in Conseil de la Concurrence, *Dix-ième Rapport d'Activité*. Paris: Direction des Journaux Officiels, 886–900.

—— (2004). Avis n° 04-A-08 du 18 Mai 2004 Relatif à Plusieurs Acquisitions d'Entrepôts Réalisées par le Groupe Scottish&Newcastle-Kronenbourg dans le Secteur de la Distri-bution de Bières dans le Circuit CHR. Available at <http://www.conseil-concurrence. fr/user/avis.php?avis=04-A-08>.

—— (2005). Décision n° 05-D-50 du 21 Septembre 2005 Relative à la Plainte de la Société SCOB à l'Encontre de Pratiques Mises en Oeuvre par la Société Brasseries Kronenbourg dans le Secteur de la Distribution de la Bière. Available at <http:// www.conseil-concurrence.fr/user/avis.php?avis=05-D-50>.

DBB (Deutscher Brauer-Bund) (2001). *23. Statistischer Bericht, Mai 2001*. Bonn: Deutscher Brauer-Bund.

—— (2003). *24. Statistischer Bericht, 2003*. Bonn: Deutscher Brauer-Bund.

Dumez, H., and A. Jeunemaître (1994). 'Competition in the European Beer Industry: An Enquiry into the Economics of Exclusive Purchasing'. Special Report. Paris: Centre de Recherche en Gestion, Ecole Polytechnique.

Dun And Bradstreet (2003–4). *Who Owns Whom: Continental Europe*. High Wycombe: Dun and Bradstreet.

EC (European Commission) (1967). Regulation No. 67/67/EEC of 22 March 1967 on the Application of Article 85(3) of the Treaty to Certain Categories of Exclusive Dealing Agreements. OJ L 57, 25 March: 849–52.

—— (1983). Regulation (EEC) No. 1984/83 of 22 June 1983 on the Application of Article 85(3) of the Treaty to Categories of Exclusive Purchasing Agreements. OJ L 173, 30 June: 5–11.

—— (1999). Regulation (EC) No. 2790/1999 of 22 December 1999 on the Application of Article 81(3) of the Treaty to Categories of Vertical Agreements and Concerted Practices. OJ L 336, 29 December: 21–5.

—— (2001a). Heineken/Bayerische BrauHolding. Available at <http://europa.eu.int/ comm/competition/mergers/cases/decisions/m2387_en.pdf>.

—— (2001b). Interbrew/Beck's. Available at <http://europa.eu.int/comm/competi-tion/mergers/cases/decisions/m2569_en.pdf>.

—— (2002a). Interbrew/Brauergilde. Available at <http://europa.eu.int/comm/compe-tition/mergers/cases/decisions/m3032_20021219_310_en.pdf>.

—— (2002b). Karlsberg/Brau Holding International/Karlsberg International. Available in German at <http://europa.eu.int/comm/competition/mergers/cases/decisions/ m2877_de.pdf>.

—— (2003a). Interbrew/Spaten-Franziskaner. Available at <http://europa.eu.int/comm/ competition/mergers/cases/decisions/m3289_en.pdf>.

—— (2003b). 'European Commission Opens Up Interbrew's Horeca Outlets to Competing Beer Brands'. Press Release IP/03/545, 15 April. Available at <http://europa.eu.int/ rapid/pressReleasesAction.do?reference=IP/03/545&format=HTML&aged=1&language=EN& guiLanguage=en>.

—— (2004a). Carlsberg/Holsten. Available at <http://europa.eu.int/comm/competition/mergers/cases/decisions/m3372_en.pdf>.

—— (2004b). 'Cartel Fine in the French Beer Market'. Press Release IP/04/1153, 29 September. Available at: <http://europa.eu.int/rapid/pressReleasesAction.do?reference=IP/04/1153&format=HTML&aged=1&language=EN&guiLanguage=en>.

—— (2005). 'Competition: German Football League Commitments to Liberalise Joint Selling of Bundesliga Media Rights Made Legally Binding by Commission Decision'. Press Release IP/05/62, 19 January. Available at <http://europa.eu.int/rapid/press-ReleasesAction.do?reference=IP/05/62&format=HTML&aged=1&language=EN& guiLanguage=en>.

ECJ (European Court of Justice) (1980). *Commission v United Kingdom*. Case 170/78, ECR 417.

—— (1983). *Commission v United Kingdom*. Case 170/78, ECR 2265.

—— (1987). *Commission v Germany*. Case 178/84, ECR 1227.

—— (1996). *Brasserie du Pêcheur v Germany and The Queen v Secretary of State for Transport, ex parte Factortame*. Joined Cases C-46/93 and C-48/93, ECR I-1029.

—— (2000). *Schutzverband gegen Unwesen in der Wirtschaft v Warsteiner Brauerei Haus Cramer*. Case C-312/98, ECR I-9187.

—— (2004a). *Commission v Germany*. Case C-463/01, ECR I-11705.

—— (2004b). *Radlberger Getränkegesellschaft and Spitz v Land Baden-Württemberg*. Case C-309/02, ECR I-11763.

Elzinga, Kenneth (2005). 'Beer', in W. Adams and J. W. Brock (eds.), *The Structure of American Industry*. Upper Saddle River, NJ: Pearson Education, 72–95.

—— and A. W. Swisher (2005). 'The Supreme Court and Beer Mergers: From Pabst/Blatz to the DOJ-FTC Merger Guidelines'. *Review of Industrial Organization*. 26/3: 245–67.

EPC (European Parliament and Council) (1994). Directive 94/62/EC of 20 December 1994 on Packaging and Packaging Waste. OJ L 365, 31 December: 10–23.

—— (1997). Directive 97/36/EC of 30 June 1997 Amending Council Directive 89/552/ EEC on the Coordination of Certain Provisions Laid Down by Law, Regulation or Administrative Action in Member States Concerning the Pursuit of Television Broadcasting Activities. OJ L 202, 30 July: 60–70.

—— (2004). Directive 2004/12/EC of 11 February 2004 Amending Directive 94/62/EC on Packaging and Packaging Waste. OJ L 47, 18 February: 26–32.

European Council (1989). Council Directive 89/552/EEC of 3 October 1989 on the Coordination of Certain Provisions Laid Down by Law, Regulation or Administrative Action in Member States Concerning the Pursuit of Television Broadcasting Activities. OJ L 298, 17 October: 23–30.

European Council (1992a). Council Directive 92/83/EEC of 19 October 1992 on the Harmonization of the Structures of Excise Duties on Alcohol and Alcoholic Beverages. OJ L 316, 31 October: 21–7.

—— (1992b). Council Directive 92/84/EEC of 19 October 1992 on the Approximation of the Rates of Excise Duty on Alcohol and Alcoholic Beverages. OJ L 316, 31 October: 29–31.

Fritsche, H. (2004). *Der Bierkrieg: Im Fadenkreuz der Bürokratie*. Husum: Verlag der Nation Ingwert Paulsen Jr.

Granholm v Heald (2005). United States Supreme Court, No. 03-1116, Slip Opinion. Decided 16 May 2005. Available at <http://a257.g.akamaitech.net/7/257/2422/16may20050800/www.supremecourtus.gov/opinions/04pdf/03-1116.pdf>.

Greer, D. F. (2002). 'Beer: Causes of Structural Change', in Larry L. Duetsch (ed.), *Industry Studies*. Armonk, NY: M. E. Sharpe: 27–58.

Humphreys, P. J. (1994). *Media and Media Policy in Germany: The Press and Broadcasting since 1945*. Oxford: Berg.

Jackson, M. (1998). *Ultimate Beer*. New York: DK Publishing.

Keithahn, C. F. (1978). *The Brewing Industry*. Washington: Federal Trade Commission.

Kemmer, H.-G. (1984). 'Der Preis Macht den Durst Erst Schön', *Die Zeit*. 1 June: 16

MMC (Monopolies and Mergers Commission, United Kingdom) (1989). *The Supply of Beer*. Cm 651. London: Her Majesty's Stationery Office.

Müller, J. (1976). 'The Impact of Mergers on Concentration: A Study of Eleven West German Industries.' *Journal of Industrial Economics*. 25/2: 113–32.

Newman, H. H. (1978). 'Strategic Groups and the Structure-Performance Relationship'. *Review of Economics and Statistics*. 60/3: 417–27.

OFT (Office of Fair Trading, United Kingdom) (2000). *The Supply of Beer: A Report on the Review of the Beer Orders by the Former Director General of Fair Trading*. OFT317, December. Available at <http://www.oft.gov.uk/nr/rdonlyres/34960586-5561-468f-adb7-1a0eb8a6f367/0/oft317.pdf>.

Porter, M. E. (1976). 'Interbrand Choice, Media Mix and Market Performance'. *American Economic Review*, 66/2: 398–406.

Porter, R. C. (2002). *The Economics of Waste*. Washington: Resources for the Future.

Rosenberg, G. N. (1991). *The Hollow Hope: Can Courts Bring About Social Change?* Chicago: University of Chicago Press.

RStV (Rundfunkstaatsvertrag) (1991). Rundfunkstaatsvertrag, 31 August. Version of 1 April 2005. Available at <http://www.lfk.de/gesetzeundrichtlinien/rundfunkstaats-vertrag/main.html>.

Sass, T. R., and D. S. Saurman (1993). 'Mandated Exclusive Territories and Economic Efficiency: An Empirical Analysis of the Malt-Beverage Industry'. *Journal of Law and Economics*, 36/1: 153–77.

—— —— (1996). 'Efficiency Effects of Exclusive Territories: Evidence from the Indiana Beer Market'. *Economic Inquiry*, 34/3: 597–615.

Scherer, F. M. (1996). *Industry Structure, Strategy, and Public Policy*. New York: Harper-Collins College Publishers.

Scherer, F. M., Alan Beckenstein, Erich Kaufer, and R. D. Murphy (1975). *The Economics of Multi-Plant Operation: An International Comparisons Study.* Cambridge, MA: Harvard University Press.

Schwalbach, J., and J. Müller (1984). 'Brauereiindustrie', in P. Oberender (ed.), *Marktstruktur und Wettbewerb in der Bundesrepublik Deutschland: Branchenstudien zur Deutschen Volkswirtschaft.* Munich: Verlag Franz Vahlen, 421–54.

Slade, M. E. (1998). 'Beer and the Tie: Did Divestiture of Brewer-Owned Public Houses Lead to Higher Beer Prices?' *Economic Journal,* 108/448: 565–602.

Speckle, B. (2001). *Streit ums Bier in Bayern: Wertvorstellungen um Reinheit, Gemeinschaft und Tradition.* Münster: Waxmann.

STBA (Statistisches Bundesamt) (1952). *Statistisches Jahrbuch für die Bundesrepublik Deutschland.* Stuttgart: W. Kohlhammer.

Sutton, J. (1991). *Sunk Costs and Market Structure: Price Competition, Advertising, and the Evolution of Concentration.* Cambridge, MA: MIT Press.

Tremblay, V. J., and C. Horton Tremblay (2005). *The U.S. Brewing Industry: Data and Economic Analysis.* Cambridge, MA: MIT Press.

Van Munching, P. (1997). *Beer Blast: The Inside Story of the Brewing Industry's Bizarre Battles for Your Money.* New York: Random House.

WARC (World Advertising Research Council) (2004). *World Advertising Trends, 2004.* Henley on Thames: NTC Publications.

Winston, C., A. Spielman, and N. Schäufele (2002). 'Thirst Impressions: How to Access Growth in the German Beer Market'. Mimeo, London: Schroder Salomon Smith Barney.

14

How the East was Won: The Foreign Takeover of the Eastern European Brewing Industry

Johan F. M. Swinnen and Kristine Van Herck

Introduction

Eastern Europe is an important player in the European, and even in the world, beer market. In 2008, the whole of Europe accounted for 32% of total beer production in the world and Eastern Europe accounted for more than half of this (17%). Within Eastern Europe, Russia, Ukraine, Poland, and the Czech Republic are the major beer producers. Russia, by itself, is the third largest producer of beer in the world and accounted for more than 6% of world beer production in 2009.

The beer market, like all markets in the former communist countries, has been strongly affected by the economic reforms at the beginning of the 1990s. Beer production and consumption were high, and strongly regulated under the communist system, but since the 1990s, the Eastern European beer market has undergone dramatic changes.

The economic and political reforms in the early 1990s led to major disruptions in the economic system. Consumption fell with declining incomes and high inflation. On the production side, the combination of price liberalizations, subsidy cuts, the introduction of hard budget constraints, and a weak legal environment caused a substantial decline in the production of barley, malt, and beer in the first years after transition.

However, the brewery sector soon attracted much interest from foreign investors. The combination of a substantial beer consumer market, privatization of the brewing companies, liberalization of the investment regimes, and closeness to the (West) European home market induced a massive inflow of foreign investment by mostly Western European brewing companies. In fact, in a few years time, all the main breweries in Eastern Europe were taken over by foreign brewing companies.

When foreign breweries invested in the Eastern European beer industry, they faced a problem sourcing sufficient high quality malt in order to produce high quality beer. The local financially distressed malting companies and farms were not able to produce the high quality malt and barley that was needed. Therefore, foreign brewers initially imported malt from their traditional Western European suppliers. However, soon afterwards, they started investing in innovative contracts with local malt producers and, further upstream, with barley farms and seed companies. In doing so, they reintroduced vertical coordination in the supply chain to obtain malt and barley that consistently met their quality requirements. Contracts often included assistance programmes to barley farms, such as the provision of inputs, technical assistance, and credit.

Since the late 1990s, economic growth and later the accession to the EU led to substantial improvement of incomes, better functioning market institutions, and subsidies to farms in the new EU member states. In combination, these factors reduced constraints in the supply chains. This, in turn, reduced the need for brewers and malting companies to provide credit or inputs to farms, and hence led to a decrease in vertical coordination.

This chapter describes and analyses this dramatic restructuring of the beer industry and its supply chain over the past two decades. First, we analyse changes in consumption and production in the region. Next, we discuss how different factors have affected the supply chain in the Eastern European beer market and document these general changes with comparative data and detailed case study evidence from the Slovakian beer and malting industry. Finally, we draw some conclusions.

The Eastern European Beer Market

Communist Period

In 1989, before the reforms started, beer consumption and production were highest in Russia, followed by the Czech Republic (see Tables 14.1 and 14.2). The main driver for high consumption and production in Russia was not so much high per capita consumption, but rather its large market size. In contrast, in the Czech Republic, consumption per capita was very high (Figure 14.1). In the Czech Republic, per capita consumption of beer was the highest in Eastern Europe and even in the world. In 1989, the average Czech citizen consumed around 170 litres beer per capita. In Hungary and Slovakia, beer consumption per capita was respectively 103 and 94 litres per capita. These consumption levels are comparable with per capita consumption in traditional beer-loving

Table 14.1. Beer consumption (in billion litres)

	1989	1992	1995	1998	2007	Total Change (%) 1992–2007	Annual Change (%) 1992–2007
CEE	n.a.	6.18	6.07	6.75	8.23	33%	2.2%
Bulgaria	0.67	0.38	0.42	0.37	0.40	5%	0.4%
Czech Republic	1.61	1.54	1.61	1.65	1.63	6%	0.4%
Estonia	n.a.	0.05	0.05	0.07	0.13	160%	10.7%
Hungary	1.07	0.97	0.77	0.70	0.74	−24%	−1.6%
Latvia	n.a.	0.09	0.07	0.08	0.16	78%	5.2%
Lithuania	n.a.	0.12	0.11	0.16	0.30	150%	10.0%
Poland	1.21	1.45	1.51	2.11	2.93	102%	6.8%
Romania	1.12	1.00	0.89	1.00	1.33	33%	2.2%
Slovakia	0.45	0.44	0.45	0.45	0.44	0%	0.0%
Slovenia	n.a.	0.15	0.18	0.15	0.16	7%	0.4%
FSU	n.a.	4.26	3.19	4.36	10.61	149%	9.9%
Belarus	n.a.	0.28	0.14	0.22	0.22	−21%	−1.4%
Moldova	n.a.	0.04	0.03	0.03	0.05	25%	1.7%
Russia	n.a.	2.85	2.33	3.43	8.41	195%	13.0%
Ukraine	n.a.	1.10	0.69	0.69	1.93	75%	5.0%

Note: CEE = Central and Eastern Europe; FSU = Former Soviet Union.
Source: FAOstat (2010).

Table 14.2. Beer production (in billion litres)

	1989	1992	1995	1998	2008	Total Change (%) 1992–2008	Annual Change (%) 1992–2008
CEE	n.a.	6.32	5.96	6.97	9.79	55%	3.4%
Bulgaria	0.67	0.47	0.15	0.38	0.55	17%	1.1%
Czech Republic	1.88	1.69	1.77	1.83	1.99	18%	1.1%
Estonia	n.a.	0.04	0.05	0.07	0.14	226%	14.1%
Hungary	0.97	0.92	0.77	0.72	0.48	−48%	−3.0%
Latvia	n.a.	0.09	0.07	0.07	0.13	44%	2.8%
Lithuania	n.a.	0.12	0.11	0.16	0.30	150%	9.4%
Poland	1.21	1.41	1.41	2.10	3.55	152%	9.5%
Romania	1.15	1.00	1.00	1.00	2.08	108%	6.8%
Slovakia	0.45	0.41	0.44	0.45	0.37	−10%	−0.6%
Slovenia	0.19	0.18	0.21	0.19	0.19	6%	0.3%
FSU	n.a.	4.20	3.03	4.33	15.03	258%	16.1%
Belarus	n.a.	0.27	0.15	0.26	0.35	30%	1.9%
Moldova	n.a.	0.04	0.03	0.03	0.07	75%	4.7%
Russia	n.a.	2.79	2.14	3.36	11.40	309%	19.3%
Ukraine	n.a.	1.10	0.71	0.68	3.20	191%	11.9%

Note: CEE = Central and Eastern Europe; FSU = Former Soviet Union.
Source: FAOstat (2010).

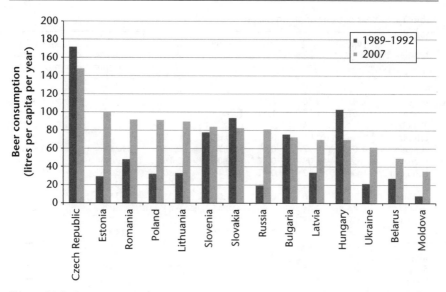

Figure 14.1. Beer consumption in Eastern Europe, Belgium, and Germany in 1989–1992 and 2007 (litres per capita per year)

Notes: 1989 per capita consumption data for Bulgaria, the Czech Republic, Hungary, Poland, Romania, and Slovakia. 1992 per capita consumption data for Estonia, Latvia, Lithuania, Slovenia, Belarus, Moldova, Russia, and Ukraine.

Source: FAOstat (2010).

countries in the EU15, such as Belgium and Germany, where per capita consumption in 1989 was respectively approximately 120 and 140 litres per capita. In Poland and Russia, these figures were considerably lower, around 30 litres per capita in Poland and 20 litres per capita in Russia.[1]

Reform and Transition

The beer market, like all markets in former communist countries, has been strongly affected by the economic reforms in the beginning of the 1990s. However, the reforms did not affect the beer markets in the different Eastern European countries in the same way. We can distinguish several patterns (Larimo et al. 2006) (see Tables 14.1 and 14.2).

First, there are countries in which consumption and production decreased slightly in the first years of transition, but recovered rapidly and remained relatively stable at the pre-transition levels. Examples are countries with high per capita consumption, such as the Czech Republic and Slovenia.

---

[1] Per capita consumption was 20 litres in the USSR in 1989 and 19 litres in Russia and 21 litres in Ukraine in 1992—the first year for which data are available for the ex-USSR countries.

Second, in some countries, consumption and production declined strongly during transition. For example, in Hungary, beer consumption has declined annually by 1.6% and beer production by 3.0% since the beginning of the 1990s. In Bulgaria, too, consumption and production decreased sharply, although recently there have been some signs of recovery.

Third, in some countries, consumption and production increased strongly, sometimes even dramatically. For example, Polish beer consumption more than doubled. In 1989, it was 1.2 billion litres, while in 2007, it was 2.9 billion litres. Also Polish beer production strongly increased: in the past two decades, beer production tripled. A similar pattern is found in Estonia, where production and consumption also tripled compared to the beginning of the 1990s.

In many countries of the Former Soviet Union (FSU), including Latvia, Lithuania, Russia, and Ukraine, consumption and production increased strongly in recent years, but after a temporary decline in the mid-1990s. For example, in Russia, beer consumption in 1992 was 2.9 billion litres and, after an initial decline in the mid-1990s, consumption started to increase rapidly. By 2007, consumption was three times higher than the 1992 level. Russian beer production shows a similar pattern: in 1992, production was approximately 2.8 billion litres and, after an initial decline, production started to increase by more than 19% per year. In 2008, production was approximately four times higher than the production in 1992. Similar results hold for Latvia, Lithania, and Ukraine, but consumption and production growth were more moderate compared to Russia.

The Current Situation

Despite a small decline compared to 1989, beer consumption per capita in the Czech Republic is still the highest in all of Europe, in the range of 145 litres per capita in 2007 (see Figure 14.1).[2] In the other high income countries in the region, such as Slovenia, Slovakia, Hungary, and Poland, per capita consumption ranges between more than 80 litres per capita in Slovenia and 70 litres per capita in Hungary. In Russia and Ukraine, consumption per capita more than tripled compared to consumption in 1992 and currently, consumption in Russia and Ukraine exceeds respectively 80 and 60 litres per capita. In Belarus and Moldova, the poorest countries in the region, per capita consumption is low and ranges between 50 litres per capita in Belarus and only slightly more than 35 litres per capita in Moldova.

---

[2] This is considerably more than in Belgium and Germany, where consumption per capita is currently approximately 100 litres per capita.

Table 14.3. Beer sales as a percentage of the total volume of alcoholic drinks sales and as a percentage of total sales of alcoholic drinks in 2008

	Share in volume (%)	Share in sales (%)
CEE		
Bulgaria	85.0	43.6
Czech Republic	85.5	44.7
Estonia	66.9	36.3
Hungary	70.4	42.3
Latvia	74.7	29.0
Lithuania	70.1	24.6
Poland	86.2	54.1
Romania	86.1	58.0
Slovakia	80.7	32.4
Slovenia	64.0	31.6
FSU		
Belarus	55.5	28.9
Moldova	n.a.	n.a.
Russia	75.8	43.7
Ukraine	72.3	34.8

Note: CEE = Central and Eastern Europe; FSU = Former Soviet Union.
Source: Euromonitor (2009b).

The sales of beer represented more than half of the total volume of alcoholic drinks that are sold in all countries in 2008 (see Table 14.3). However, there were important differences between countries. In Poland, the Czech Republic, Slovakia, Romania, and Bulgaria, this percentage exceeds 80%. In the Russia and Ukraine, where strong spirits such as vodka are the traditional alcoholic drinks, beer represents respectively 76% and 72% of the total sales volume of alcoholic drinks. Also in the Baltic states, the share of beer is relatively low due to the popularity of strong spirits (Euromonitor 2009b).

The share of beer sales in the total sales value of alcoholic drinks is lower than its share in volume (see Table 14.3). In Romania and Poland, beer sales represent more than 50% of the total value of alcoholic drinks sales. In Lithuania and Latvia, the share of beer sales in the total value of alcoholic drinks sales is the lowest in Eastern Europe, namely 25% and 29% respectively.

Russia is an interesting case, since there has been a dramatic shift from consumption of vodka to beer over the past 15 years (see Chapter 16 by Deconinck and Swinnen in this volume). The share of beer is now around 75% in volume terms and 45% in value terms, much higher than in the Communist period. The sharp increase of beer consumption has turned Russia into one of the largest beer markets in the world.

Privatization and Disintegration of the Beer Chain in the 1990s

Before 1989, beer production, like all agricultural and food production systems in the former communist countries, was fully integrated and state controlled (Rozelle and Swinnen 2004). Every step in the supply chain, from barley production to malting and brewing, and to retailing, was organized by the central command system. In general, barley production was organized in large cooperative or state farms, except for Poland and former Yugoslavia. Central planning organized the provision of inputs to these farms and they sold the produced barley to state-owned malting and brewing enterprises which had a monopoly position in beer sales in the region.

At the beginning of the 1990s, the former communist countries liberalized their economies. This had a substantial impact on the entire supply chain as the industrial organization of the supply chain underwent tremendous changes (Gow and Swinnen 1998).

First, with privatization of the industry, the previous vertically integrated supply chains were split into autonomous enterprises, which were independent in setting production targets and were free to decide with whom they exchanged inputs and outputs. In a second stage, these firms were privatized, for example through voucher privatization programmes or by selling them off (OECD 1997). For example, in Slovakia, the privatization process resulted in the establishment of 13 independent Slovakian malting and brewing companies.

Second, prior to the reforms, companies and farms were directly and indirectly subsidized. As a consequence, price liberalization, subsidy cuts, and hard budget constraints caused dramatic price adjustments. For example, the terms of trade in agriculture fell between 30% in Hungary and 70% in Russia in the 1990s (Macours and Swinnen 2002).

Third, in the first years after transition, the legal system was not adjusted to a market economy. In addition, legal actions were not commonly used because of high costs associated with going to court, ineffective contract law, and the potential loss of a trading partner.

The combination of these reforms caused major contract enforcement problems, which often took the form of delayed payments along the supply chain (Cungu et al. 2008; Van Herck et al. forthcoming). Gorton et al. (2000) find that in 1998 late payments by customers were the most important obstacle to the growth of food-processing companies in Eastern Europe.

In combination with the 'normal' credit market constraints and macroeconomic instability, contract enforcement problems constrained companies' and farms' access to credit. In the short run, this reduced access to inputs. In the long term, it reduced investments in fixed assets and affected the long-term

Table 14.4. Barley production (in thousand tons)

	1989–1991	1992–1994	1995–1997	1998–2000	2001–2003	2004–2006	2007–2009
CEE	n.a.	12,579	12,023	10,178	10,256	11,004	11,255
Bulgaria	1487	1090	813	682	889	795	719
Czech Republic	2934	2496	2296	1953	1942	2141	2047
Estonia	n.a.	372	303	269	258	321	393
Hungary	1421	1473	1220	1082	1052	1226	1183
Latvia	n.a.	457	338	278	247	319	308
Lithuania	n.a.	1085	1087	902	849	851	947
Poland	4128	2920	3527	3265	3177	3438	3870
Romania	3022	1788	1604	1041	1094	1086	974
Slovakia	998	866	794	665	704	766	742
Slovenia	n.a.	32	41	41	44	61	72
FSU	n.a.	43,124	27,519	19,453	29,720	29,606	n.a.
Belarus	n.a.	3037	2172	1394	1663	1909	208
Moldova	n.a.	404	256	177	170	227	n.a.
Russia	n.a.	26,962	17,502	11,493	18,759	17,003	18,863
Ukraine	n.a.	12,721	7589	6389	9128	10,467	10,142

Note: CEE = Central and Eastern Europe; FSU = Former Soviet Union.
Source: FAOstat (2010).

profitability of the sector. This resulted in the decline of input use and consequently a decrease in the quantity and quality of production.

These problems affected the production of beer both directly and indirectly. An important direct effect was on the supply of malt and barley. Barley production and yields decreased substantially in the first years of transition. In the 1990s, barley production decreased by 10% to 30% in the Baltic states, Czech Republic, Slovakia, Hungary, and Poland, and by 50% to 60% in the other countries (see Table 14.4).

The Foreign Takeover of the Brewing Industry

The opening of East European markets and the privatization of breweries attracted huge interest from foreign investors. The rich beer tradition, high consumption levels, relatively high incomes, and geographic and cultural proximity to the EU made Eastern Europe a very attractive market for Western brewers once the system opened up. The privatization and liberalization of foreign investment regulations, the need to upgrade production facilities and marketing strategies, combined with strong capital market constraints on domestic investors resulted in a massive inflow of foreign capital into the East European beer industry.

In fact, the beer industry was one of the first economic sectors to attract substantial foreign direct investment (FDI). In 1991, Interbrew (now AB

InBev) became the first foreign company to invest in the Eastern European brewing industry when they bought the brewery Borsodi Sörgyar in Hungary (Hübner 1999). In the years that followed, Heineken, SABMiller, and Carlsberg also invested heavily in the Eastern European malting and brewing industry.

There are several reasons why foreign investors entered the Eastern European markets via FDI rather than by exporting or licensing (Arnold et al. 2000; Marinov and Marinova 2001). First, initially, there was only limited demand for foreign beer because of the consumer preference for local brands and the reduced purchasing power of the majority of the population. Second, there was only limited scope for exports to Eastern Europe because of the restrictive import taxes in some countries.

Hence, the main drivers of foreign investments in the beer industry were market-seeking motives and strategic asset-seeking motives (the ownership of local brands) (Hübner 1999; Larimo et al. 2006). In addition, efficiency motives also played an important role as production costs in Eastern Europe were substantially lower than in their West European home markets and some countries also had an interesting investment climate in the early years of transition (Marinov and Marinova 2002).

In the early and mid-1990s, investments were concentrated in the more economically advanced countries, such as Hungary, Czech Republic, Slovakia, and Poland. Interbrew and Heineken were the first to invest in the Czech, Hungarian, and Slovakian markets. Later SABMiller too became active in these countries. For example, in Slovakia, foreign investments in the malting and brewing industry started in 1995 when the Dutch brewer Heineken took over the Zlatý Bažant brewery. Later they also bought Corgoň (1997), Martiner (1999) and Gemer (1999). SABMiller was the second foreign investor that entered the Slovakian market when it bought Pivovar Šariš in 1997 and Pivovar Topolčany in 2006. Together these two foreign companies now control almost 80% of the Slovakian malt and beer market.

When the economic and institutional environment improved in the less advanced countries, foreign investors started to invest also in Romania, Bulgaria, Russia, and Ukraine. An exception to this was the Baltic Beverages Holding (BBH), established in 1991 as a joint venture between the Swedish-Norwegian Pripps Ringnes and Finnish Hartewell breweries, which entered the Russian market in 1992.[3] By comparison, Interbrew and Heineken entered

---

[3] These investments aimed to create an entry barrier for low-cost imports from the Baltic states and Russia. Initially, these protectionist motives were the main drivers for investments by BBH in the Eastern European beer industry and market-seeking reasons were of only secondary importance. However, from the mid-1990s, market-seeking motives became also the main driver of investments by BBH (Arnold et al. 2000).

Table 14.5. Market share of the leading breweries in selected countries in 2000 (%)

	AB InBev	Carlsberg	Heineken	SABMiller	Other
CEE					
Bulgaria	37	0	23	0	40
Czech Republic	10	0	1	37	52
Estonia	1	50	0	0	49
Hungary	25	0	9	25	41
Latvia	1	28	0	0	71
Lithuania	0	41	0	0	59
Poland	0	8	33	22	37
Romania	13	4	36	12	34
Slovakia	0	0	37	24	39
Slovenia	0	0	1	0	99
FSU					
Belarus	0	0	0	0	100
Moldova	n.a.	n.a.	n.a.	n.a.	n.a.
Russia	9	24	0	0	67
Ukraine	29	23	0	0	52

Note: CEE = Central and Eastern Europe; FSU = Former Soviet Union.
Source: Euromonitor (2009a).

the Russian market in 1998 and 2002 respectively.[4] In Ukraine, the first multinational breweries that entered the local market were BBH and Interbrew, which both started their investments in 1996.

Between 1990 and 2005, the worlds' four largest multinational brewing companies—AB InBev, SABMiller, Heineken, and Carlsberg—invested heavily in the region by purchasing domestic breweries and the combined market share of these four breweries rapidly increased in all countries. In 2000, the market share represented by these four breweries was already more than 50% in six out of the 13 countries in Eastern Europe for which we have data, and in 2009 the number of countries with a combined market share of more than 50% increased to nine (see Tables 14.5 and 14.6). In all countries in Eastern Europe, expect for Slovenia and Belarus, the market leader is a foreign investor. Heineken and Carlsberg are each market leader in four out of 13 countries, SABMiller is market leader in two countries, and AB InBev is market leader in one country. The strong concentration is illustrated by the market shares in Tables 14.5 and 14.6. For example, in Estonia, Carlsberg alone has a market share of 53% in 2009 and in Latvia and Lithuania, the market share of Carlsberg is also very high (41%). In the Czech Republic and Poland, the South African brewer, SABMiller, has a market share of respectively 44% and 41%.

---

[4] For a detailed discussion on FDI in the Russian beer market, see Chapter 16 by Deconink and Swinnen in this volume.

Table 14.6. Market share of the leading breweries in selected countries in 2009 (%)

	AB InBev	Carlsberg	Heineken	SABMiller	Other
CEE					
Bulgaria	29	24	31	0	16
Czech Republic	12	0	10	44	34
Estonia	1	53	1	0	45
Hungary	22	0	24	24	30
Latvia	2	41	0	0	57
Lithuania	0	41	0	0	59
Poland	0	14	33	41	12
Romania	17	9	29	27	18
Slovakia	0	0	40	37	23
Slovenia	0	2	4	0	94
FSU					
Belarus	0	0	0	0	100
Moldova	n.a.	n.a.	n.a.	n.a.	n.a.
Russia	15	38	13	5	29
Ukraine	37	26	0	4	33

Note: CEE = Central and Eastern Europe; FSU = Former Soviet Union.
Source: Euromonitor (2009a).

Quality Demands and Vertical Coordination in the Beer Chain

After foreign investors entered the market, they were faced with the problem of obtaining a sufficient quantity of high quality malt and barley to produce high quality beer. In general, in the 1990s, the quality of the malt that was locally produced did not meet the quality standards of the foreign investors.

In response, foreign investors initially imported malt and barley from their traditional channels in Western Europe (Cocks and Gow 2003). In the long run, however, the development of a local supply base was more beneficial because of tariffs and exchange rate fluctuations, and for logistical and operational reasons. Therefore they invested in long-term relationships with malting companies and producers and reintroduced vertical coordination along the supply chain (World Bank 2006).

Besides increasing the quality of malt and barley, there is a second reason why vertically coordinated supply chains emerged in the brewing industry. While brewing and malting companies in the West tend to work together under contractual relationships, but as separate companies, brewing and malting companies in Eastern Europe were often privatized as a single 'package'. Hence, foreign brewery companies often ended up owning malting companies as they took over the Eastern brewing (cum malting) companies (Cocks and Gow 2003; Gits 2006). In the beginning, foreign investors were not interested in malting or farming activities, since this was not their 'core business'. However, quality problems with their raw materials forced them

Table 14.7. Elements of assistance programmes offered by malt processors and breweries to supplying farms

	Malt processor 1	Malt processor 2	Brewery 1	Brewery 2	Brewery 3
Support to production and storage	X	X	X		
Support to improving quality	X	X	X		X
Support to management	X				
Credit provision	X	X	X		
Advice on investments	X				
Support on purchase of farm inputs	X	X			

Note: 'X' means 'yes' or 'applicable to'.
Source: Survey carried out by RIAFE Bratislava (World Bank 2006).

to engage not just in solving the malting company problems, but even further up the supply chain in farming and the provision of seeds.[5]

Brewing companies developed vertical coordination mechanisms to build up long-term relationships with farms and seed suppliers. Part of these relationships includes sophisticated contracts with assistance to farms.[6] Examples of such assistance programmes were seed selection and supply schemes, credit provision, investment loans, technical assistance, and advance payments. By reducing farms' credit constraints and improving their access to quality inputs and credit, these assistance programmes were targeted at improving the supply of high quality malt and barley production. Table 14.7 documents how in Slovakia, in 2003, support in improving quality, support for production and storage, and credit provision were the three most commonly used assistance programmes for suppliers in the Slovakian beer chain.

These vertically coordinated programmes have been very important, both generally and in the beer chain specifically (World Bank 2006). Besides having an effect on quality, the farms' improved access to input markets had also an effect on efficiency. For example, companies in the Slovakian beer and malting industry, such as Heineken, stated that barley producers with a contractual relationship with the company had higher yields than the Slovak average

---

[5] Later, a typical strategy of Western brewing companies was to sell the malting division to Western malting companies and to engage in traditional Western-style purchasing contracts with these malting companies.

[6] Case studies show that throughout the food industry such FDI introduced vertical integration and contributed to an improvement in access to credit or inputs and to their suppliers' productivity growth (Gow et al. 2000; Dries and Swinnen 2004, 2010). Among the main drivers of improved credit access were farm assistance programmes offered by the processor. These programmes included input supply programmes, credit and investment assistance programmes, bank loan guarantees, and extension services.

Table 14.8. Comparison of the average barley yield in Slovakia and the average barley yield of primary producers delivering to Heineken in Slovakia (tons per hectare)

	Barley yields in Slovakia	Barley yields in Heineken
1998	3.51	4.21
1999	3.06	4.13
2000	1.99	2.77
2001	3.49	4.88
2002	3.72	4.58
2003	3.02	3.67

Source: Heineken Slovensko Sladovne (World Bank 2006).

(World Bank 2006). This is illustrated in Table 14.8. Partly, these differences reflect selection: Heineken mostly deals with producers from the more productive regions in Slovakia, but Heineken also confirmed that its farm assistance programmes—such as assistance in selecting the appropriate seed variety, plant protection and nutrition, and advising on post-harvest storage and treatment—enhanced quality and productivity.

Even more striking is the evolution of the supply of malt in Russia. In 2001, only 0.5 million tons malt or 49% of the total domestic demand for malt was purchased locally, while in 2007, this increased to more than 1 million tons or 85%. This change was mainly driven by large, foreign investors who invested in their own malting activities and introduced malting barley breeding programmes to enhance the quality of locally produced barley (FAO 2009).

However, vertical coordination has reduced in intensity and extent over time. Gradually, when the institutional and economic situation improved, brewing companies started to disassociate themselves from barley and malt activities and returned to their core business, brewing and selling beer. They started buying malt from the malting companies via more traditional contracts and the malting company became responsible for the quality of the malt. For example, in Hungary, Interbrew bought the brewery and malting company Borsodi Sörgyar in 1991. Initially, Interbrew participated in the malting company and offered contracts and assistance to the farmers who were producing high quality malting barley. However, at the end of the 1990s, Interbrew sold its malting activities to the German malting company, Weissheimer, and engaged in a traditional, 'Western style' contract with Weissheimer.

There are similar developments in Romania, Russia, and Ukraine, where currently malting companies are investing heavily in expanding their malting capacity. International malting companies have become increasingly active. A number of projects have been successfully implemented by Soufflet, Champagne Céréals, and other multinational malting companies. In many cases,

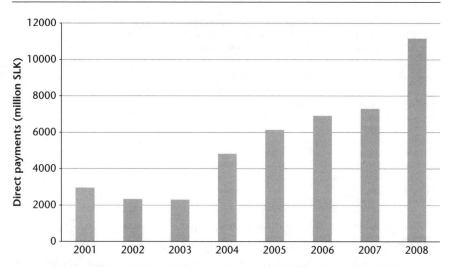

Figure 14.2. Evolution of direct payments in Slovakia (in million SLK)
Source: National statistics.

they continue to work with farms through interlinked contracts. For example, in Russia, Group Soufflet invested heavily in extension services to improve local malting barley varieties and in Ukraine, Champagne Céréals helped farms to finance the input provision of farms (seeds and fertilizer) through interlinked contracts (FAO 2009).

Overall economic growth and the benefits from EU accession also contributed to a reduction in vertical coordination, and to industrial organization of the supply chain which is closer to the West European model, with independent companies producing malt and beer—albeit with contracting—and more spot market transactions in the barley and seed markets.

Between 2004 and 2007, ten Eastern European countries joined the European Union. The accession process implied a lot of changes and economic effects. As a consequence, these countries now receive substantial farm subsidies from the EU's Common Agricultural Policy (CAP). These subsidies have a significant effect on farmers' income and credit constraints. Figure 14.2 presents the evolution of the most important form of subsidies, i.e. direct payments to farms, in Slovakia before and after accession to the EU.

Accession to the EU has both direct and indirect effects on the beer supply chain. Directly, the CAP subsidies not only increase farms' income, but also improve farms' access to credit. Financial institutions are more willing to give loans to farmers because direct payments can be used as loan collateral (Ciaian and Swinnen 2009). Indirectly, accession to the EU improved institutions and the general working of input markets. Both effects reduced the need for vertically coordinated farm assistance programmes.

Table 14.9. Recent developments in farm assistance programmes offered by malt processors

	Company I		Company II		Company III	
	2002	2008	2002	2008	2002	2008
Monetary credit—(short term; variable inputs)	X		X			
Advance payments	X		X		X	
Recommendation for a bank loan						
Technical assistance/agronomic support/ field days	X	X	X	X	X	X
Provision of seeds					X	
Use of a truck during the delivery season	X	X	X	X		
Premium for quality	X	X	X	X	X	X

Note: 'X' means 'yes' or 'applicable to'.
Source: Own survey results.

In 2008, we interviewed three Slovakian malting companies[7] on the evolution of farm assistance programmes before and after accession to EU. The results, summarized in Table 14.9, show that all companies stopped providing credit assistance programmes after EU accession. In 2002, two companies offered monetary credit for the purchase of variable inputs, while another company offered seeds. In addition, one company offered bank loan guarantees. The malting companies indicated that at the end of the 1990s, when they started their activities, they needed to introduce these programmes, because at that time the majority of the farmers were not able to produce the requested quality of barley. In general, farmers did not have access to bank loans and they had not enough pre-harvest income to buy variable inputs such as seeds, fertilizer, pesticides, and fuel. The malting companies indicate that the credit programmes were successful as they were an important driver behind quality improvements at the beginning of the 2000s. However, in 2004, the year of EU accession, two companies stopped their credit programmes, while the third processor stopped offering its credit programme in 2007.[8] The latter is located in the east of Slovakia, which is a relatively poor region of Slovakia. All three companies indicated that the most important reason for halting these programmes was that farms now have better access to commercial loans due to the fact that financial institutions accept direct payments as collateral. The malting companies still offer extension services to guarantee and improve the quality of the production.

---

[7] Two of the malting companies are completely foreign owned, while the third is domestically owned. They represent a market share of more than 80%.

[8] The processors stopped providing these credit programmes first for larger producers and later also for smaller ones.

Conclusion

In Eastern Europe, economic and institutional reforms had an important impact on barley, malt, and beer production and consumption. In most Eastern European countries, beer production and consumption decreased in the first few years after transition, but recovered in the second half of the 1990s and the beginning of the 2000s. In Russia, for example, after an initial decline in beer production, production increased by more than 19% per year and by 2008, production was approximately four times higher than in 1992. Russian beer consumption tripled over the same period. This pattern reflects important changes that have affected the supply chain of all food products, including beer, since the economic reforms at the beginning of the 1990s.

In the early 1990s, economic reforms led to major disruptions in beer production and consumption. Beer production declined due to a combination of privatization, price liberalization, and poor legal enforcement systems. Also, further upstream, these factors influenced the production of barley and malt, since, in combination with 'normal' rural credit constraints, farms produced less (high quality) barley and consequently, malting companies produced less (high quality) malt. At the same time, demand for beer decreased because of lower disposable consumer incomes and high inflation.

Soon after the start of liberalization, the Eastern European brewery industry attracted foreign investors. The first countries to attract investments were those with the highest incomes and most advanced reform processes, such as Hungary, the Czech Republic, Slovakia, and Poland. Later, foreign investors went further east and south and invested in the less economically advanced countries, such as Romania, Russia, and Ukraine. Foreign investors ended up regionally dividing the Eastern European beer market among the four largest international beer companies, AB InBev, SABMiller, Heineken, and Carlsberg. Currently, these four foreign investors have a market share of more than 50% in almost all Eastern European countries, except for Slovenia and Belarus, where local producers still dominate the market.

When foreign breweries started their activities in Eastern Europe, they faced a problem sourcing sufficient high quality malt in order to produce high quality beer. The local financially distressed malting companies and farms were in many cases not able to produce the high quality malt and barley that was needed. In order to avoid the higher costs associated with importing malt, foreign brewers invested in the supply chain and introduced innovative contracts with malting companies and farms to help them produce malt and barley that met their quality requirements. These contracts led to important improvements in efficiency and quality in the production of barley and malt.

Since the late 1990s, rapid economic growth and later the accession to the EU led to a substantial improvement in disposable income, better functioning markets and institutions, and the introduction of subsidies to farms. This resulted in a reduction of farms' credit constraints and, hence, a decline in the need to offer assistance to malting companies and farms. This is illustrated by case study evidence from Slovakia, where vertical coordination in the beer supply chain fell as the three largest malting companies stopped providing credit programmes to barley farms after EU accession. The industrial organization of the supply chains is thus gradually moving towards that of developed market economies.

References

Arnold, S., Larimo, J., Miljan, M., Virvilaite, R., Frize, E., and N. Starshinova (2000). 'A Comparative Analysis of the Beer Market in Selected European Countries: Estonia, Finland, Lithuania, Russia and the UK', in P. Chadraba, and R. Springer (eds.), *Proceedings of the 8th Annual Conference on Marketing Strategies in Central and Eastern Europe*. Vienna: Wirtschaftsuniversität, 7–25.

Ciaian, P., and J. F. M. Swinnen (2009). 'Credit Market Imperfections and the Distribution of Policy Rents'. *American Journal of Agricultural Economics*, 91/4: 1124–39.

Cocks, J., and H. R. Gow (2003). 'Supplier Relationship Development in the Food Industry of Transition Economies: The Case of Interbrew'. *Journal of Food Distribution Research*, 34/1: 63–8.

Cungu, A., H. R. Gow, L. Vranken, and J. F. M. Swinnen (2008). 'Investment with Weak Contract Enforcement: Evidence from Hungary during Transition'. *European Review of Agricultural Economics*, 35/1: 75–91.

Dries, L., and J. F. M. Swinnen (2004). 'Foreign Direct Investment, Vertical Integration, and Local Suppliers: Evidence from the Polish Dairy Sector'. *World Development*, 32/9: 1525–44.

—— —— (2010). 'The Impact of Interfirm Relationships on Investment: Evidence from the Polish Dairy Sector'. *Food Policy*, 35/2: 121–9.

Euromonitor (2009a). Market reports on beer, various CEE and FSU countries. Euromonitor International.

—— (2009b). Market reports on alcoholic drinks, various CEE and FSU countries. Euromonitor International.

FAO (Food and Agricultural Organization of the United Nations) (2009). *Agribusiness Handbook: Barley, Malt and Beer*. FAO Investment Centre Division, cooperation between FAO and EBRD. Rome: FAO.

FAOstat (2010). Online Database of the Food and Agricultural Organization of the United Nations. Accessed September 2010. Rome: FAO.

Gits, K. (2006). 'Vertical integratie in de Centraal-en Oost-Europese brouwerijsector: Case study Inbev'. Master's thesis at the Faculty of Business and Economics. Leuven: KULeuven:.

Gorton, M., A. Buckwell, and S. Davidova (2000). 'Transfers and Distortions along the CEEC Food Supply Chains', in S. Tangermann and M. Banse (eds.), *Central and Eastern European Agriculture in an Expanding European Union*. Wallingford: CABI Publishing, CAB International.

Gow, H.R., D. H. Streeter, and J. F. M. Swinnen (2000). 'How Private Contract Enforcement Mechanisms can Succeed where Public Institutions Fail: The Case of Juhocukor A.S.'. *Agricultural Economics*, 23/3: 253–65.

—— and J. F. M. Swinnen (1998). 'Up- and Downstream Restructuring, Foreign Direct Investment, and Hold-Up Problems in Agricultural Transition'. *European Review of Agricultural Economics*, 25/3: 331–50.

Hübner, S. (1999). 'Impact van buitenlandse investeringen in de bierbrouwerijsector in Centraal- en Oost Europa'. Gevalstudie: Interbrew. Master Thesis at the Faculty of Bioscience Engineering. Leuven: KULeuven.

Larimo, J., M. Marinov, and S. T. Marinova (2006). 'The Central and Eastern European Brewing Industry since 1990'. *British Food Journal*, 108/5: 371–84.

Macours, K., and J. F. M. Swinnen (2002). 'Patterns of Agrarian Transition'. *Economic Development and Cultural Change*, 50/2: 265–94.

Marinov, M., and S. T. Marinova (2001). 'Foreign Direct Investments in the Emerging Markets of Central and Eastern Europe: Motives and Marketing Strategies'. *Advances in International Marketing*, 10: 21–52.

—— —— (2002). 'Internalization of Interbrew in Eastern Europe', in M. A. Marinov (ed.), *Internalization in Central and Eastern Europe*. Aldershot: Ashgate Publishing, 204–32.

OECD (Organisation for Economic Co-operation and Development) (1997). *Review of Agricultural Polices: Slovak Republic*. Centre for co-operation with economies in transition. Paris: OECD.

Rozelle, S., and J. F. M. Swinnen (2004). 'Success and Failure of Reforms: Insights from Transition Agriculture'. *Journal of Economic Literature*, 42/2: 404–56.

Van Herck, K., N. Noev, and J. F. M. Swinnen (forthcoming). 'Institutions, Exchange and Firm Growth: Evidence from Bulgarian Agriculture'. *European Review of Agricultural Economics*.

World Bank (2006). 'Market Linkages in the Slovak Agri-Food Sector'. Working Paper No. 43. Environmentally and Socially Sustainable Development Unit Europe and Central Asia Region. Washington: World Bank.

Part IV
The New Beer Markets

15

Beer Battles in China: The Struggle over the World's Largest Beer Market

Junfei Bai, Jikun Huang, Scott Rozelle, and Matt Boswell

Introduction

Throughout history, China has revered men of the bottle. One of the most famous of all poems from the greatest cultural epic in the nation's history, the Tang Dynasty (written in AD 761) pays tribute to the spirits, the liquid ones, that is:

> How many great men are forgotten through the ages?
> Great drinkers are better known than sober sages.
> I only want to drink and never wake up.

Li Bai, the poem's author, is perhaps China's most famous poet and drinker. According to legend, he drowned himself in a river while drunkenly trying to embrace the moon (Owen 1997).

China arguably has one of the world's oldest beer cultures. Some historians suggest that beer-like beverages were consumed in China as long ago as 7000 BCE. Oracle bone characters referring to a primitive form of beer (called *li* in modern Chinese) have been found inscribed on tortoise shells dating from the Shang Dynasty over 3,000 years ago (Xu and Fa n.d.). Although China had not yet become the cohesive civilization we know today, it is quite possible that early Chinese people living on the banks of the Yellow River were sipping beer out of pre-porcelain ware.

China's lead in beer brewing, however, did not last. By the Han Dynasty, *c.*200 BC, distilled rice wine had risen to prominence. The earliest forms of millet and sorghum-based *baijiu* (a type of highly distilled, highly alcoholic spirit) were making their way onto the tables of soldiers, farmers, gentry, and royalty. Meanwhile, beer had disappeared from the menus of taverns and the shelves of stores until the Russians opened the first modern brewery in Harbin, a city in China's cold northeast, at the end of the nineteenth century. Not long after, groups of Germans and Czechs also set up breweries, primarily to serve the growing numbers of their merchants, officials, and soldiers stationed in China.

Large-scale political tumult throughout the first half of the twentieth century meant that beer would not have had a chance to really catch on in China. However, once stability was established in the late 1970s, consumption really began to ramp up. In 1978, China's rank in the world beer market in terms of quantity produced and consumed was somewhere around 100 (Chen 2009). By 2006, China was the largest beer market in the world.

This chapter is divided into three parts. The first describes the development of beer consumption and production in China over the three decades since economic reforms began. The second describes the intense competition for China's beer market that has ensued in the past three decades. A third section offers some concluding thoughts.

The Development of China's Beer Industry

In the 1970s, beer was a luxury. By the time economic reforms began in 1978, there were only 90 breweries in all of China (Guo and Yang 2006), and the vast majority were small and local. All beer was produced and distributed through the central plan. During a time when China was struggling to provide sufficient calories for its population, planners apparently did not give too much weight to beer consumption.

In the late 1970s, reform came to China's economy. China's leaders gradually unlocked the handcuffs of farmers and entrepreneurs, first in agriculture and later in industry. The economy began to boom in almost all sectors.

It was during this time that the beer industry bloomed like hops in the spring. Literally hundreds of small breweries emerged from the rice paddies (Guo and Yang 2006). Most were state owned at the county level. A county's beer factory frequently was its status symbol. Breweries also provided employment, tax revenues, and, of course, new forms of mealtime fun. Consumption began to grow markedly (Chen 2009).

In the 1990s, as China became richer, consumers—especially those in the cities—began to have greater amounts of disposable income. Dining out rose (Ma et al. 2006) and bars emerged (Diao 2007). In relative terms, beer consumption soared (Chen 2009).

Beer Consumption and its Drivers

Annual per capita consumption of beer in China continued to rise steadily over the next three decades (Figure 15.1). In the late 1970s and early 1980s, the average consumer in China drank less than 2 litres (less than 1 litre in 1979 and 1980; and only 3 litres in 1985). After the mid-1980s, the trend in beer consumption per person rose—faster between 1985 and 1988, 1992 and 1997, and 2003 and 2007 and relatively more slowly between 1989 and 1991, and 1998 and 2002. In 2007, per capita beer consumption reached 30 litres per capita, more than 30 times the level in 1979–80.

Along the way, China passed a number of milestones in world rankings. In 1979, total beer consumption was less than 400,000 tons—less than 100th in the world (Chen 2009). However, by 1995, China had surpassed Germany to become the second largest beer consumer in the world. In total, in 1995, China's consumers (1.2 billion of them) drank about 16 billion litres (1.2 billion times 13 litres per capita) or 34 billion pints. In 2006, China became number one in global beer consumption, surpassing the US's 30 billion litre (63 billion pint) level. Rapid growth between 2006 and 2007 meant that, by the last year of our data, 2007, China's consumers were drinking about 10 billion more pints per year than consumers in the US.

There are many drivers of this growth. Over the past 30 years China has seen rapid growth in average household income—especially in the urban sector, but, also in the rural economy (Figure 15.2).

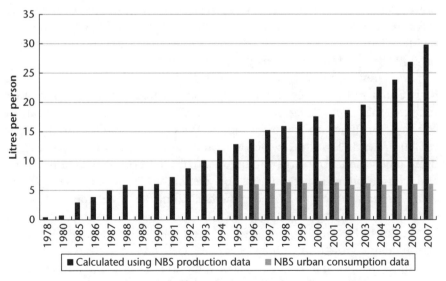

Figure 15.1. Annual per capita beer consumption in China

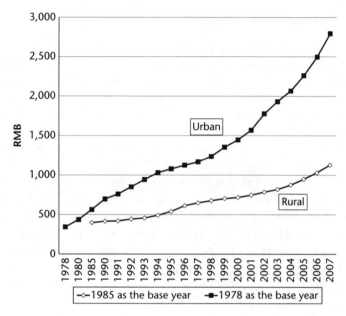

Figure 15.2. Average per capita disposable income in urban and rural China

Migration is also rising rapidly (Zhao 2003). Huang and Rozelle (1998) and Huang and Bouis (1996) demonstrate how, even at constant incomes, migration will raise consumption of most goods from the rural average up towards (though not all the way to) the urban average. During this time of rapid growth and migration (at least during the past decade), the price of beer has stayed relatively constant in real terms, although consumption has been rising rapidly (Figure 15.3). Finally, the sharp rise in eating away from home during the 1990s and 2000s has also played a role (Figure 15.4).

It is interesting to note, however, that despite this trend, on a per capita basis China still consumes a relatively modest amount of beer. Figure 15.5 indicates that China is far down the list at 30 litres per person per year. In contrast, consumers in countries such as the Czech Republic (156 litres per capita), Ireland (130 litres per capita), and Germany (116 litres per capita) drink much more. The large gap between consumption per capita in China and consumption per capita in the champion European beer-drinking countries, raises the question of whether China will ever approach these levels. If it does, the potential growth for global beer consumption is still tremendous. However, several factors suggest that, while there is still significant potential growth in China's beer market, it will not increase by three or four times. As shown in Figure 15.5, consumption in China's wealthier neighbouring countries in East Asia, Japan and Korea (towards which China is converging in income terms), is only 51 and 38 litres per capita, respectively.

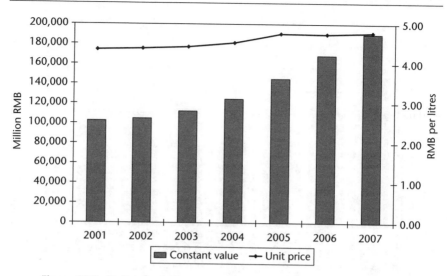

Figure 15.3. Unit price for beer compared with rising beer consumption

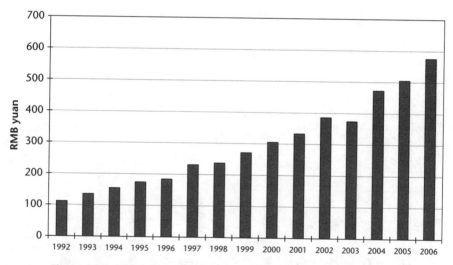

Figure 15.4. The rising incidence of dining out in China, 1992–2006

Hence, if China's consumers end up having tastes and preferences closer to those of Japan and South Korea, rather than those of Europe, China's beer economy could still nearly double, but not quadruple.

In understanding beer consumption, it is worth examining the consumption of competing alcoholic beverages. Figure 15.6 indicates that per capita consumption of spirits in China remained the same for the most part during the period when consumption of beer was increasing gradually and

271

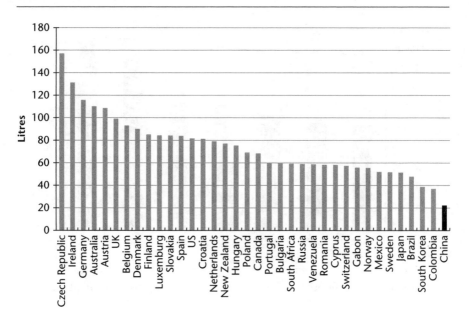

Figure 15.5. Per capita beer consumption by country, 2004
Source: Kirin Holdings Company, Ltd.

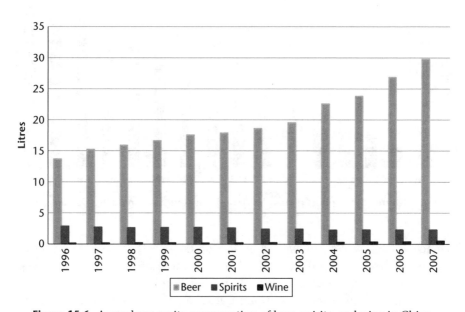

Figure 15.6. Annual per capita consumption of beer, spirits, and wine in China

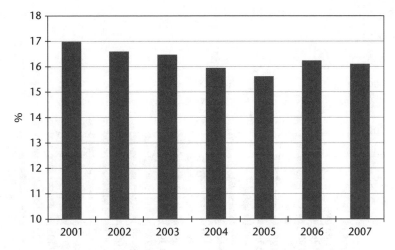

Figure 15.7. Beer's share of alcoholic drinks (constant after 2001)

dramatically. Interestingly, per capita wine consumption has also experienced notable growth over the period, although it is still very low relative to that of beer or spirits.

Figure 15.7 demonstrates, at least in value terms, that the rapid growth in beer consumption is matched by that of spirits. According to data from China Statistics Yearbooks, published by NBS, between 2001 and 2007, the share of beer's value in the total value alcoholic beverages is constant. This, coupled with Figure 15.6, suggests either increasing prices of spirits or decreasing beer prices or both, implying that the rapid growth in consumption in China's beer market in the 2000s was also experienced in the spirits market. Hence, it is clear that, at least if past trends of consumption are somewhat indicative of future trends, China's beer market will face stiff competition from spirits. Because of this, future consumption of beer will likely top out long before the typical Chinese beer consumer drinks much more than 50 litres per capita.

Who is Producing China's Beer?

As we have seen, beer has become a well-nigh indispensable part of everyday life in China over the past 30 years. But where has this growing volume of beer come from? Who is brewing it? Before tackling this question it is important to note that trade plays a minimal role in China's beer economy. On the import side, while China produced nearly 40 billion litres in 2007, total imports amounted to only 0.2 billion litres. This means that only one-half of 1% of China's beer is imported. On the export side, the negligible role of trade can best be seen from the books of Tsingdao, the nation's largest exporter and the

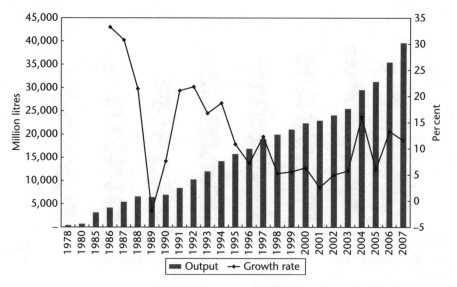

Figure 15.8. Beer production and annual growth rate in China, 1978–2007

nation's only global brand. In 2007, foreign sales accounted for only 0.15% of Tsingdao's total sales volume, according to *Beer in China 2008*, a market report conducted by Access Asia Limited (2008). Certainly, the share of exports of other breweries is far less than this. Hence, from these figures, it is clear that, in China, the picture of beer production over time (Figure 15.8) is the same as the picture of beer consumption.

When the production trends are graphed alongside growth rates (Figure 15.8), it is clear that China has seen high and sustained rates of growth in beer production over the past three decades. However, the other defining trend in production growth is that, as total volume has risen, the rate of growth has trended downwards. In the 1980s, annual growth rates, while variable, average well over 15%. In the 2000s, annual growth rates average between 5 and 10%.

Industrial Structure

As noted earlier, this growth in beer production has occurred almost entirely in China—trade has not played a significant role. Some of the most interesting facets of beer production in China can be understood by examining the number of firms that are producing beer and the market share of the top firms. In 1978, there were very few breweries in China. In fact, we have done extensive interviews with scores of respondents aged over 60. Almost no one can remember ever drinking beer during the 1960s or early 1970s. There were around 90 breweries producing beer in 1978. By 1985, there were over 500. By 1990, the apex of brewery expansion, there were nearly 900 (Guo and Yang 2006; Sun et al. 2006).

In the 1980s and early 1990s, almost half of China's counties had a beer brewery. In 1992, for example, Zhejiang province had 117 breweries and only 90 county-level divisions (Wang 1992). In the same year, Heilongjiang province had 90 breweries and 130 county-level divisions (Heilongjiang 1998). Beer production provided localities with employment, tax revenues, and prestige. Beer began to appear on the banquet tables of officials during their business dinners. Average citizens, especially those in the cities, remember beginning to drink beer on a fairly regular basis during this time. Almost all of the breweries were owned and operated by township, county, or other government units.

The high-water point for brewery numbers was the early 1990s, at about 900. Many were poorly managed and operated at a loss. There followed a period of stagnation in which a flurry of mergers and foreign investment occurred. In 1996, there were 741 breweries operating at an estimated average loss of 30% (Guo and Yang 2006). Some breweries grew on account of rising consumer appetite, while others declined, stagnated, or were acquired by competitors (Lu et al. 2007). The government also shut down particularly egregious loss makers. In addition, private breweries emerged across China; Yanjing Brewery in Beijing remains the most prominent of these (Access Asia Limited 2008). In short, the first half of the 1990s was a time of jockeying for position, experimentation, and nascent structural change, without a precipitous decline in brewery numbers.

Between 1998 and 2007 the story changed. In 2007, there were fewer than 400 breweries left in China (Access Asia Limited 2008). In other words, more than 50% of breweries had stopped functioning—at least as independent enterprises. This reduction in the number of breweries, however, was happening during a time when overall beer production more than doubled.

The fall in the number of breweries and rise of production necessarily means that China's beer industry was becoming more concentrated (Figure 15.9). In 1998, the top three breweries accounted for only 10% of China's beer production, while the top ten accounted for 21%. However, between 1998 and 2007, the concentration ratio of the top three breweries rose to nearly 40%; and the concentration ratio of the top ten breweries rose to more than 60%.

While the rise in concentration ratios was quite rapid in China, in 2006 the beer industry was less concentrated than in many countries (Figure 15.10). For example, in Mexico, Brazil, Poland, and Japan, the top three brewing companies account for at least 80% of domestic production. The top three (ten) concentration ratios of the US, Spain, Russia, and the UK, while somewhat lower, are also relatively high. In fact, with the exception of Germany,

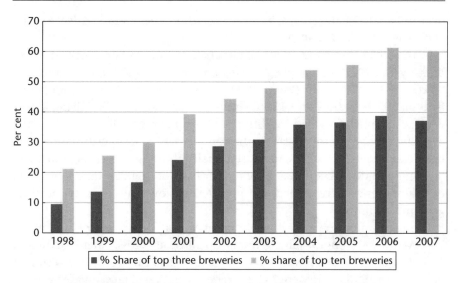

Figure 15.9. Leading breweries' market volume shares in China
Source: Access Asia Limited (2008).

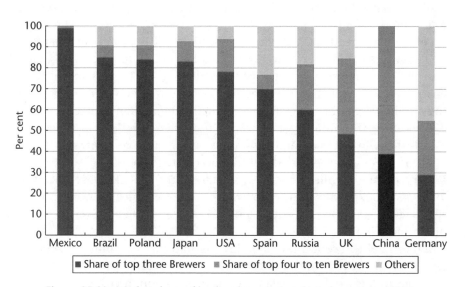

Figure 15.10. Market share of leading brewers in selected countries, 2006
Source: Euromonitor; China Light Industry Association; Gao Hua Securities.

a country that has a notably low concentration ratio, China has the least concentrated beer sector of any of the major beer-producing nations. If the trends of the past decade continue, concentration ratios could look like most other major producing countries within another decade.

In summary, it is possible to argue that no major beer industry in the history of the world has changed so dramatically in a single decade (from 1998 to 2007). In the 1990s, most breweries were (local) state owned, and almost all were domestic, small, and (technologically) backward. By 2007, the industry was being driven by private firms. Foreign firms were becoming active. Conglomerates were emerging. The new firms were highly capitalized and growing rapidly. Many new breweries were using state-of-the-art brewing technology.

Multinational Beer Corporations and the China Beer Market

Perhaps naïvely, the world outside China, looking in, said of many industries: 'If every Chinese would only buy one . . . ' The beer industry was no different. In the 1990s, multinational beer corporations rushed into China. In the 1990s, Foster's, Heineken, Asahi, Anheuser-Busch, InBev, and more were trying to get into the China market (*China Beer Industry Development Research Report* 2008). The problem was that, while brand names like Budweiser and Carlsberg had high recognition globally outside of China, such names meant nothing in the Middle Kingdom. It was as if Chinese beer firms had rolled out their top brand names in Brussels, Munich, or London. Nobody would recognize, much less be influenced by, marketing campaigns for beers with names like Cloudy Lake, Clock Tower, or Dragon-and-Elephant. To sell beer in China, the strategy was simple: capture a well-known Chinese brand.

Multinational companies endeavouring to sell beers throughout China had a problem, however. There were only a few national brands. Tsingtao was erstwhile premier Zhou Enlai's favourite. In the 1970s, Tsingtao was perhaps the best-known beer in China, and small volumes of it were exported. Beijing Beer was a cheap and more available alternative—although its market was mostly restricted to the nation's capital. Five Star was the Chinese beer of choice in the 1970s and 1980s. Then, and also today, it is known as the 'beer on the banquet table of the Great Hall of the People'. Multinationals saw Five Star as a prime route into the fabled China market.

The First Skirmish in the Domestic–Foreign Beer Market Battle

The story of the takeover of Five Star illustrates well the clash of corporate culture and government interference that has defined the attempts of foreign companies to play a major role in China's beer market. When reforms got under way in China in the 1980s, Five Star was among China's largest and highest profile breweries. It was also the most geographically dispersed. Five Star owned three brewing facilities. They had built their two older facilities during the period of Socialist construction. One of the breweries was built with a soft loan from the Belgium government (an appropriate piece of foreign aid from one the world's pre-eminent beer-producing and consuming countries). Five Star Beer was also produced by 48 small breweries across China. In 1996, Five Star produced close to 1 million tons of beer per year (that is, for readers who find it difficult to conceive of the notion of a ton of beer, about 1.25 billion litres). Five Star was by far the largest brewery in China at that time. This made Five Star the ultimate prize for the foreign investor.

But there were weaknesses even in China's best brewery. The brewing technology was ancient. One of the early wannabe investors described the equipment in Five Star's No. 3 brewery as 'something akin to Frankenstein's cauldron'. A lot of the beer was flat. There were exploding bottles in every case. Poor management on the factory floor left broken glass and leaking beer on seemingly every square metre of factory floor space. The breweries—even China's largest—were small by global standards.

Foreign investors were not deterred, however. Their strategy was clear. If they could get their hands on a Chinese brewery, the foreign firm would bring in new capital and new brewing technologies, as well as a new way of doing business. The foreign firm would introduce branding and advertising. A relatively small market share was not a concern. New business practices, including ambitious investment schemes and a merger and acquisition strategy, would grow their market share. All of the major players were in the bidding: Foster's, Anheuser-Busch, Asahi, and others.

So, who won? According to the book, *Mr China*, Jack Perkowski won. Jack, who in the roaring 1980s on Wall Street had risen to become the head of investment banking at Paine Webber, put in the winning bid. His assistant, Tim Clissold, known as Mr China, helped Jack put the bid package together. The result of the winning bid was the emergence of a new Joint Venture (JV) between AISMCO Technologies (the US partner) and the Beijing City Government (the main shareholder on the China side).

Although it should have been 'easy', according to the description in the book, *Mr China*, JVs were never easy in the 1990s—especially mergers in the beer industry (Heracleous 2001). There were many problems. The new JV factory manager had no experience of brewing beer. His main business experience in the beverage industry was brewing second-class *Erguotou*, a brand of distilled Chinese liquor. Workers and management in the JV enjoyed an 'iron rice bowl' and could not be fired. Accountants were not bound by generally accepted accounting principles (GAAP). There were 'little treasure troves' (or *xiao jingku*—pots of money squirrelled away in various bank accounts and safety deposit boxes) everywhere. The Beijing government allowed the Chinese side of the JV to use US$67 million of JV liquid assets to be transferred to a Beijing bank in order to settle the debts of the Chinese side's predecessor. The US side of the JV was not consulted.

There were many other problems. The US side of the JV delivered on their promise. They installed new, state-of-the-art equipment. They introduced new bottling technology to reduce breakage. But the technology never worked. Theft stalled the roll out of the new bottling process. While waiting for the new bottles to be produced, much of the raw material was sold for scrap.

Marketing problems exemplify the problems. The main innovation on the US side of the JV was to introduce branding and advertising, a concept that was still new in China. But there was trouble with this, too. Logos changed constantly (almost certainly confusing consumers). The colour schemes also shifted back and forth. There was trouble with delivering a message that could capture the imagination of Chinese consumers. Some ads were silly (and certainly made no sense to a Chinese audience). Others played on emotions and preferences of consumers in foreign markets and were clearly confusing to Chinese consumers.

At the very time that the JV was implementing one stop-and-start business plan after another, time was passing. Potential domestic competitors were keenly observing beer marketing overseas and inside China. Technologies and turnkey operations were becoming available for domestic investors. The inevitable occurred. A new, fully owned domestic brewery, Yanjing Brewery, opened their doors—right across the street from one of the Five Star beer factories. Yanjing was private, nimble, entrepreneurial, and ambitious.

In part because of the new competition, the main, planned channel to higher revenues became clogged. The pricing strategies of the JV never materialized. Advertising was supposed to create a perception of high quality and allow the marketing department to raise prices. But even after all of the early ad campaigns and marketing ploys, the price of beer in China was much cheaper than water. Even as late as 2007, the price of a 600 ml bottle of beer was about 1.5 yuan per bottle. At that time, the exchange rate was 7.5 yuan per dollar. If 600 ml is the equivalent of about two 12-ounce cans or bottles, this means that China's beer was selling for about 63 (US) cents per six pack.

The burdens were too big, even with penetration of the elusive China market on the line. In 1998, the Five Star JV went bankrupt. Tsingtao, China's export beer enterprise and a company fully backed by the Qingdao Municipal State-Owned Asset Supervision and Administration Committee (SASAC), bought the JV and its assets for US$20 million. The US side of the JV had invested more than US$100 million.

Significantly, during the time that Tsingtao was buying Five Star back from its (partly) foreign-based owners, there were other buy-backs. Tsingtao invested heavily in the operation backed by Carlsberg to keep the ailing company afloat. Fearful that a foreign beer company could not make money in China (obviously influenced by the experiences of Five Star), the Japanese beer conglomerate, Asahi, sold a large share of its JV to a domestic buyer.

The cash infusion from the reverse FDI buyouts was not enough. Foster's Brewery, an Australian brewing giant, was the first of a string of foreign beer firms to leave in the late 1990s and early 2000s. Bass, Carlsberg, and Asahi followed. The sales of the building and removal of the Foster's logos from their Tsingtao location signified the downfall of the foreign firms. The new building projects of Tsingtao—in addition to its new acquisitions—signified the rise of a strong domestic China brewing industry.

Round one of the beer battles clearly belonged to China.

Beer Battles, Round Two

So who is producing (and who will be producing—at least in the near future) China's beer? Domestic or foreign firms? Shopping in the supermarket, doing the rounds of restaurants, bars, and nightclubs, and watching television, it is clear that domestic and foreign firms are competing to produce and grow in China's beer market. The question asked here is: who is the greatest contributor? And why?

According to Access Asia Limited (2008), the market shares of the top twelve breweries in China from 1998 to 2007 show several insights. First, the three largest domestic brewers are CR Snow, Tsingtao, and Yanjing. The three largest foreign-owned (or partially foreign-owned/foreign-controlled) breweries are InBev, Anheuser-Busch (AB), and Heineken. All of these beers have very high name recognition and can be found in almost every supermarket and in many restaurants. Almost all of them have a national presence. In addition, the market shares of all of these major breweries have grown fairly steadily.

A clearer picture emerges when we combine and graph the market shares of foreign and domestic firms in the top ten breweries. Figure 15.11 (which shows this) illustrates that, although the market share of both foreign and domestic firms (in the top ten firms) grew almost equally fast between 1998 and 2007, because the initial share of domestic firms was higher, large domestic firms have been able to gain a larger share of the Chinese beer market during this time period. In short, domestic firms can be said to have won round two of China's beer battles.

Table 15.1. Top beer brewers and their market shares in China, 1998–2007

Brewer	1998	1999	2000	2001	2002	2003	2004	2005	2006	2007
CR Snow	2.95	4.44	5.92	7.41	8.89	10.38	11.93	12.96	15.39	16.07
Tsingtao	2.8	5.2	6.7	11.62	14.11	14.04	13.5	13.38	13.16	11.70
Yanjing	3.3	3.6	3.9	5.04	5.63	6.42	10.37	10.23	10.20	9.31
Zhujiang (InBev)	3.18	3.9	4.02	4.83	4.03	4.03	3.97	3.54	5.80	6.26
Budweiser (AB)	1.3	1.5	1.7	1.73	2.36	2.85	3.17	3.58	3.99	4.39
Harbin (AB)	1.55	1.76	1.97	2.35	2.19	2.49	2.95	3.30	3.38	3.45
Sedrin (InBev)	0.48	0.6	0.72	0.85	1.85	2.69	2.62	2.76	2.96	3.11
Chongqing	0.61	0.71	0.77	1.03	1.58	1.77	2.26	2.43	2.78	2.34
Reeb	1.8	0.6	1	1.4	1.8	1.56	1.64	1.72	1.80	1.88
Kingway	1.31	1.35	1.39	1.43	1.47	1.51	1.42	1.74	1.85	1.71
Heineken	0.3	0.5	0.7	0.9	1.1	1.3	1.4	1.52	1.54	1.57
Liquan (Yanjing)	1.32	1.32	1.33	1.41	1.26	1.26	1.43	1.35	1.36	1.41
Huiquan (Yanjing)	1.6	1.76	1.92	2.08	1.84	1.65	1.46	1.44	1.42	1.18
Other brewers	77.5	72.76	67.96	57.92	51.89	48.05	41.88	40.05	34.37	35.62

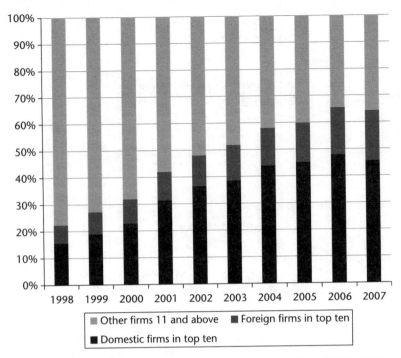

Figure 15.11. Market share of leading beer brewers in China, 1998–2007
Source: Access Asia Limited (2008), company data, and trade press.

Branding, Advertising and M&A

Systematic data on the business strategies of major firms in China's beer industry unfortunately do not exist. Therefore, an analysis of the business practices that have been the foundation of the rise of successful breweries has to be based on observation and anecdote. The analysis in this section, where possible, is supplemented with as many numbers as we could find.

Branding has been at the heart of the business practices of larger breweries during the 2000s. Beer logos and trademarks are among the most recognizable of all enterprises—for both domestic and foreign breweries. CR Snow's Harbin Brewery uses a panda. Yanjing Brewery uses sheaves of wheat and a symbol that looks a bit like a red patriotic sickle (the worker's beer?). Tsingtao's distinctive red logo stands out in hypermarkets, restaurants, and on television ads. Even children can recognize the brands, offering assurance that the next generation at least recognizes the firm's product lines.

To make sure a brand is even more recognizable (and not forgotten) and that the message of the breweries is heard, companies have also begun to turn to advertising and promotional campaigns. Unfortunately, industry-wide information on advertising is not available for any year and certainly not over time. However, there are bits of information through which it is possible to see the rising commitment of firms to advertising. For example, Tsingtao has reported in its last three annual reports that advertising expenditures rose from less than 200 million yuan in 2005 to more than 525 million yuan in 2007. In fact, in 2007 Tsingtao alone (with its 525 million yuan expenditure) nearly outspent the entire beer industry expenditure on advertising in 1999. Clearly billions are being spent on promotion. Advertising spans the entire range of possibilities. Television ads for beer are as pervasive in China as they are in the US. Billboards, text messages, radio spots are all full of beer promotions. And the advertising materials have become increasing sophisticated, trying to produce an emotional response in consumers.

Promotional efforts have also targeted newly emerging food and beverage business ventures. Most noticeable is the effort that beer enterprises are putting into merchandising in supermarkets. Their displays are flowery, noisy, and innovative. They have to be to compete against each other as well as against their arch alcoholic rivals, the spirit firms. Rising competition means that merchandising fees are becoming more popular. Beer companies also work hard to get their beer products displayed prominently and served in bars and restaurants.

But to support the huge investments in brand building and promotion, firms need to be large. Small firms are unable to compete because their volumes of sales are unable to provide enough revenue to be reinvested in large advertising budgets. It is for this reason that companies began to worry about market share and growth. Firms had to get large. To do so they had two choices: build their own capacity, or buy it in the merger and acquisition market.

Firms in China—both domestic and foreign—have mainly chosen to take the M&A route. As a result, they have gone down the acquisition road with a vengeance. Twenty years ago Tsingtao was a firm producing mostly in Tsingtao, Shandong Province. Today the Tsingtao Brewery itself has grown from four breweries in 1996 to 48 today. With 35 breweries, CR Breweries has over 30 leading beer brands in its portfolio, including its flagship Snow Beer. Beijing Yanjing Brewery Company now has 20,000 employees, almost 3,800 of whom are engineers and technicians, producing Yanjing Beer in 29 breweries across China. Domestic firms that were once the acquisition target of foreign firms are now doing the acquiring. Foreign firms are trying to do the same, but domestic firms are doing it as well or better—as the market share analysis shows.

So why is it that domestic firms can do so well—and appear to be outcompeting (or at least competing toe-to-toe with) foreign breweries? Part of the reason may be that foreign firms, with their expertise honed in other markets, just do not 'get' the China beer market.

It is, after all, a beer market with Chinese characteristics. And what a market it is. A place where beer is often chugged, in a series of *ganbei* (dry-the-glass) drinking games. This makes super light, lightly carbonated beers in demand. Who needs microbrewery quality? Beer in China is drunk in large quantities and quickly, so low price is nice—especially in many of the drinking venues where people are relatively poor.

In fact, China's beer is fairly undifferentiated. We ran a blind-taste test of the top ten beers and found that almost no one could identify what they believed was their favourite beer. So if beer is an undifferentiated product, it needs to compete on price. Therefore a strategy that depends on a willingness to make a small profit in a huge market for many years is needed. It may be that domestic producers are more willing and used to participating in such markets. Strategies based on high-priced premium quality products just will not work—even though this is how many foreign firms earn their highest profits elsewhere in the world.

China is China. Perhaps it is because of this that only Chinese firms can fully grasp China's beer market. It is possible that only Chinese firms could imagine that pineapple beer would sell. Who would ever have thought that clam-juice beer would be a consumer favourite? One of the most successful promotion campaigns was run by a domestic firm that gave away aromatic gel candles in a cup of beer. The candle's slogan: 'It looks like beer but smells like vanilla!' A Budweiser marketing expert could never have come up with such a scheme. It may be that domestic Chinese firms know better and this has made them more successful . . . so far.

Conclusions: Beer Battle Round Three Brewing?

In this chapter, we have shown the remarkable evolution of China's beer industry. Its growth has been unprecedented. But its transformation has been equally noteworthy: from a state-owned and backward industry to one that is able to compete with the largest, most sophisticated brewery conglomerates in the world. Domestic brewing firms learned fast and are now able to implement an effective business strategy, based on brand building, promotion, advertising, and merger-led growth.

This new-found expertise and steadfastness has been the driving force behind the success of domestic firms. Despite the few inroads made by international brewing giants, domestic firms have held their own. They started the last decade with a higher market share and their lead has been maintained. Their understanding of China's beer market—the penchant of consumers for low-priced beer with quality that is consistent with Chinese tastes and preferences—has been behind this success.

So will China's domestic firms be able to keep their battle-winning streak going? In fact, it is not clear that future markets will be the same as past markets. Foreign beer makers specialize in quality beer. Almost certainly, the demand for quality will rise with incomes. As China gets richer (and as the beer market continues to mature), it is almost certain that the demand for quality beer will rise. As this happens, the competitive advantage of foreign firms will rise. Chinese firms will respond, and the battle will continue.

China's beer economy, like the rest of the economy, is subject to rapid changes. It is being driven by shifting drivers—rising incomes, migration, and changing habits. These may lead to surprising consequences. Given this, can we predict where China's beer market will be ten to twenty years from now? It will be bigger, no doubt. It will converge on the norms of the rest of the world. When this happens, will foreign conglomerates dominate? Or will China's domestic firms continue to be able to compete? Certainly China's beer drinkers will remain enigmatic, in their own special way, as they have for the past 9,000 years.

References

Access Asia Limited (2008). *Beer in China 2008: A Market Analysis*. Shanghai: Access Asia Limited.

Chen, J. (2009). 'Beer Demand in China, 1982–2004'. *Researches in Chinese Economic History*, 1: 138–45 (in Chinese).

China Beer Industry Development Research Report (2008). Beijing: China Light Industry Press.

Diao, Y. (2007). 'Dynamic Competition of Beer Industry in China'. Doctoral dissertation, University of International Business and Economics, Beijing (in Chinese).

Guo, C., and Z. Yang (2006). *Dynamic Barriers and Strategic Business Behavior*. Beijing: Management Economics Press (in Chinese).

Heilongjiang Almanac Editorial Committee (1998). *Heilongjian Provincial Almanac, 1998*. Harbin, Heilongjiang: Heilongjiang Almanac Press (in Chinese).

Heracleous, L. (2001). 'When Local Beat Global: The Chinese Beer Industry'. *Business Strategy Review*, 12/3: 37–45

Huang, J., and H. Bouis (1996). 'Structural Changes in the Demand for Food in Asia'. Food, Agriculture, and the Environment Discussion Paper 11. Washington: International Food Policy Research Institute.

—— and S. Rozelle (1998). 'Market Development and Food Demand in Rural China'. *China Economic Review*, 9: 25–45.

Lu, Y., G. Liu, and G. Dong (2007). *A Market Report of Beer Industry in China*. Donghai Securities, China.

Ma, H., J. Huang, F. Fuller, and S. Rozelle (2006). 'Getting Rich and Eating Out: Consumption of Food Away from Home in Urban China'. *Canadian Journal of Agricultural Economics*, 54: 101–19.

Owen, S. (1997). *Anthology of Chinese Literature: Beginnings to 1911*. New York: W. W. Norton & Company.

Sun, H., Y. Gong, and Z. Jun (2006). *Trade and Industry Organization Analysis*. Shanghai: Shanghai Finance and Economics University Press (in Chinese).

Wang, D. (1992). *Explorations of Contemporary Finance and Economics*. Beijing: Electronic Industry Press.

Xu, G., and B. Fa (n.d.). 'Wine Production in China: An Historical Survey'. Available online at: <http://www.sytu.edu.cn/zhgjiu/umain.htm>.

Zhao, Y. (2003). 'The Role of Migrant Networks in Labor Migration: The Case of China'. *Contemporary Economic Policy*, 21/4: 500–11.

16

From Vodka to Baltika: A Perfect Storm in the Russian Beer Market

Koen Deconinck and Johan F. M. Swinnen

> Russia is a riddle, wrapped in a mystery, inside an enigma.
>
> (Winston Churchill)

Introduction

Between 1996 and 2007, Russian beer production increased from 2.1 to 11.5 billion litres, making for an impressive annual growth rate of nearly 17%. Driving these changes in production is the spectacular change in beer consumption per capita in Russia. For more than 30 years, from the 1960s through the 1980s and the early 1990s, per capita beer consumption in the Soviet Union and Russia fluctuated between 15 and 25 litres per capita—much lower than in the rest of Europe.

However, since the mid-1990s, consumption has increased dramatically. In 1996, a creeping decline in beer consumption halted and made way for double-digit growth. Thanks to this impressive growth, Russian beer consumption is now at a level similar to the EU average, and Russia has become the world's third largest beer market, after China and the US, but ahead of Germany, the UK, or Brazil (see Colen and Swinnen, Chapter 7 in this volume), with Carlsberg's Baltika brand firmly dominating the Russian market.

These developments are remarkable since Russia was traditionally a 'vodka-drinking nation'. As recently as 1995, surveys showed that 78% of Russians identified themselves as vodka drinkers, whereas only 23% reported drinking beer. By 2003, the proportion of beer drinkers (57%) had overtaken the share of vodka drinkers (53%). Between 1994 and 2007, the share of beer in total

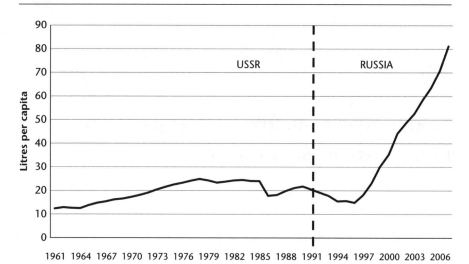

Figure 16.1. Beer consumption per capita in Russia, 1961–2007
Note: Data for the USSR until 1991; data for the Russian Federation from 1992 until 2007.
Source: FAOSTAT.

alcohol consumption increased from 51% to 79%, while the share of vodka decreased from 39% to 13% (Treml 1997; Euromonitor 2010b).

This chapter attempts to explain the causes of the Russian beer boom. After reviewing and discussing a series of hypotheses, we conclude that the dramatic increase in beer consumption in Russia is due to a 'perfect storm' in the Russian market for alcoholic drinks. In other words, a combination of factors between 1995 and 2005 reinforced each other to cause a disproportionate shift in consumer choice towards beer consumption.

The chapter is organized as follows. The following section documents the recent dramatic changes in the Russian beer market. Next, a series of possible causes are presented and discussed. Finally, we show how these causes combined to create a 'perfect storm' that transformed the Russian beer market.

Russia's Recent Love Affair with Beer

Historically, Russians followed the consumption pattern of other Nordic spirits-drinking countries, where alcohol is drunk irregularly but in large amounts and usually in the form of strong spirits (Popova et al. 2007). This contrasts with both the Mediterranean pattern, where traditionally alcohol is drunk regularly, in moderate amounts, and in the form of wine, and with the Central

European pattern, which is similar to the Mediterranean pattern, but where the traditional beverage is beer (Simpura et al. 2001).

In 1961, the average Russian consumed around 12 litres of beer annually. This figure gradually increased and reached a peak of 24 litres in 1985, when Gorbachev initiated his plan to decrease national alcohol consumption. According to official statistics, this policy was quite successful, and beer consumption fell to 18 litres per year in 1986, a decrease of 25%. Although there was a recovery afterwards, beer consumption remained quite low for some time. Interestingly, the collapse of the Soviet Union in 1991 did not lead to drastic changes in beer consumption. Statistics show a moderate decrease, reaching a low around 1996 (Figure 16.1).

At that point, however, the great transformation began. Between 1996 and 2007, consumption increased dramatically: in one decade, beer consumption grew from 15 litres per capita to around 80 litres—a level which is similar to the EU average (Figures 16.2 and 16.3). As a result, Russia is now the third largest beer market in the world, accounting for 6% of global beer consumption and production.[1]

In 2009, beer accounted for 77% of the total volume of alcoholic drinks sold (Figure 16.4). In terms of money spent, beer is now the most popular drink, occupying 44% of total sales in the alcoholic beverages market (Table 16.1).

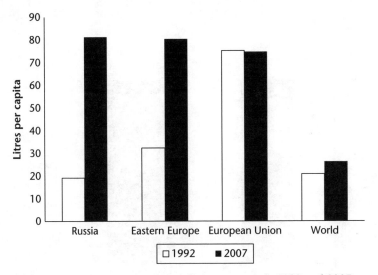

Figure 16.2. Beer consumption (litres per capita), 1992 and 2007
Source: FAOSTAT.

---

[1] Trade plays almost no role. In 2008, imports accounted for less than 3% of domestic consumption, while 2% of domestic production was exported.

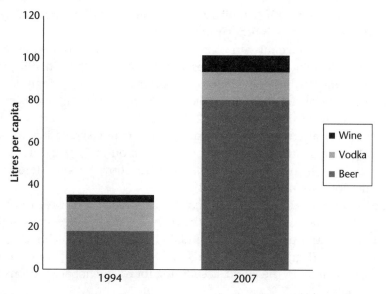

Figure 16.3. Consumption of alcoholic beverages by volume (litres per capita), 1994 and 2007

Source: Treml (1997) for 1994, Euromonitor (2010b) for 2007.

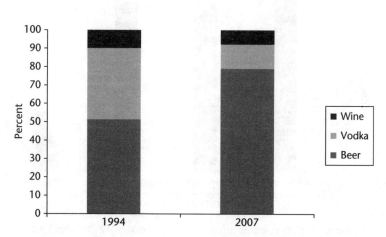

Figure 16.4. Volume shares of alcoholic beverages, 1994 and 2007
Source: Treml (1997) for 1994, Euromonitor (2010b) for 2007.

Table 16.1. Shares of volume and sales, 2009

	Volume	Sales
Beer	77%	44%
Spirits	12%	34%
Wine	8%	19%
RTDs/High-strength pre-mixes	3%	3%

Compared to 2004, the beer market grew annually by 16% in real terms. In recent years, beer has consistently outpaced other beverages (wine, spirits, and 'ready to drink' mixes), both in volume and in sales growth (Euromonitor 2010a).

Table 16.2 gives a breakdown of consumption, in volume, by type of beer, from which we see that imported lager and premium domestic lager have outperformed the market. Dark beer and low-alcohol beer also increased in importance. These figures demonstrate the trend towards 'premiumization' of the Russian beer market, with consumers increasingly buying special beers (dark beer, low-alcohol beer) or beer of higher quality.[2] Premium lager increased its market share from 43% in 2004 to 49% in 2009.

Privatization of the Russian breweries during economic transition in the 1990s coincided with a large inflow of foreign companies (see Swinnen and Van Herck, Chapter 14 in this volume). The first foreign companies to invest in the Russian beer industry were the Scandinavian joint venture BBH, which bought the formerly state-owned Baltika brewery in 1992, and the Indian SUN Group, which started its brewing activities in Russia in 1993, after an initial acquisition of five breweries. Other multinational firms entered the Russian market later. Interbrew (now AB InBev) entered the Russian market in 1998 after buying the Rosar brewery. In 1999, Interbrew and SUN combined their brewing activities in the joint venture SUN Interbrew. The Turkish brewer Anadolu Efes started a joint venture with the City of Moscow in 1997 to develop a maltery and a brewery, with support from the European Bank for Reconstruction and Development (EBRD). This brewery opened in 1999. SAB entered Russia in 1998, opening a new brewery close to Moscow, and Heineken only entered in 2002 through the acquisition of Bravo International.

The Russian beer market has seen increasing consolidation over the past decade, and the market is now dominated by five large international firms: Carlsberg Group (which is the market leader through its Baltika brand), AB InBev, Heineken, Anadolu Efes, and to a lesser extent SABMiller (Table 16.3). Usually, these 'global brand owners' operate through ownership of local

---

[2] In the Russian market, economy lager sells at around 30 Rubles per litre, standard lager at around 45 Rubles per litre, and premium lager ranges in price between 65 and 200 Rubles per litre (Euromonitor 2010b). The average exchange rate in 2009 was 1 Ruble = 0.023 euro.

Table 16.2. Sales of beer by subsector: total volume 2004–2009

	Total volume (in million litres)			Market share		Annual real sales growth
	2004	2009	CAGR[1], 2004–2009	2004	2009	2004–2009
Lager	8,735.5	10,048.4	2.8%	97.3%	97.0%	15.9%
Premium Lager	2,355.3	3,498.2	8.2%	42.8%	49.2%	19.3%
Imported	138.7	146.9	1.2%	6.9%	5.7%	11.7%
Domestic	2,216.6	3,351.3	8.6%	35.9%	43.5%	20.5%
Standard Lager	3,784.7	4,132.9	1.8%	37.4%	34.7%	14.2%
Imported	—	194.6	n.a.	—	2.9%	—
Domestic	3,784.7	3,938.3	0.8%	37.4%	31.7%	12.2%
Economy	2,595.5	2,417.3	−1.4%	17.1%	13.1%	9.9%
Imported Lager	138.7	341.5	19.8%	6.9%	8.7%	21.4%
Domestic Lager	8,596.8	9,706.9	2.5%	90.4%	88.3%	15.4%
Dark Beer	53.5	65.1	4.0%	1.1%	1.2%	18.9%
Stout	2.3	2.6	2.7%	0.0%	0.0%	14.1%
Low/Non- Alcohol Beer	159.6	206.4	5.3%	1.6%	1.8%	17.9%
Beer (Total)	8,950.9	10,322.5	2.9%	100%	100%	15.9%

Note: [1] CAGR: Continuously Compounded Annual Growth Rate.

Source: Euromonitor (2010b).

Table 16.3. Market shares by company, 2005–2009

% Total Volume	2005	2006	2007	2008	2009
Carlsberg	1.5	2.3	3.1	38.7	39.6
AB InBev	—	—	—	17.0	16.7
Heineken	12.0	12.7	12.7	13.8	13.0
Anadolu	6.0	8.4	8.7	9.2	9.7
SABMiller	3.8	4.8	4.8	4.9	5.2
BBH	33.5	33.2	34.4	—	—
InBev	16.2	18.0	18.6	—	—
Ochakovo	5.2	4.6	4.0	3.9	4.0
Others	21.7	15.7	13.5	13.0	11.8
Total	100	100	100	100	100

Source: Euromonitor (2010b).

brands, managed by 'national brand owners'. Hence Carlsberg, through its acquisition of Scottish and Newcastle in 2008, became the owner of Baltika, the strongest national brand on the Russian market.[3] Baltika now represents 40% of the Russian beer market (Euromonitor 2010b).

What Caused the Beer Boom?

In this section, we review a series of factors that could contribute to explaining the Russian beer boom. We discuss, consecutively, the possibility that Russians switched from vodka to beer because globalization led to a 'Westernization' of Russian preferences, including preferences for alcoholic drinks; that changes in relative prices or incomes induced the changing consumption pattern; that quality improvements made beer a more attractive beverage; that increasing health concerns led to a shift from vodka to beer; and that advertising regulations favoured beer over vodka. Finally, we discuss the potential role of network effects and generational shifts.

Cultural Convergence

As globalization leads to progressive integration of economies, we might expect it to lead to a convergence of cultural values, beliefs, and preferences. Surprisingly, this issue has not received much attention. The article by Konya and Ohashi (2007) is one of the few empirical investigations of convergence in consumption patterns. Analysing data for OECD countries between 1985 and

---

[3] In 2003, Carlsberg, together with Scottish and Newcastle, had bought BBH from its former owners. In 2008, Heineken and Carlsberg jointly acquired Scottish and Newcastle, splitting the assets between them. In this way, Carlsberg gained full ownership of BBH.

1999, they find consistent evidence for convergence in consumption patterns, and they show that bilateral trade and FDI flows contribute to this process.

In the specific case of preferences for alcoholic beverages, Aizenman and Brooks (2008) investigate a panel of 38 countries between 1963 and 2000, and find that the variation in consumption patterns has decreased over time. For instance, the share of wine in total consumption (here defined as the sum of wine and beer consumption) has been decreasing in wine-drinking countries, such as France, while it has been increasing in beer-drinking countries, such as Germany. However, convergence seems to be a rather slow process. Bentzen and Smith (2009), using OECD data and looking at three types of beverages (wine, beer, and spirits), develop a metric for the 'balancedness' of alcohol consumption, and show that this metric has been slowly increasing for nearly all the countries studied, signifying gradual convergence in alcohol consumption patterns.

Leifman (2001) offers further evidence on this homogenization process, studying 15 European countries (i.e. the member states of the EU as of 1998 and Norway). Not only does he find convergence in terms of absolute alcohol intake, he also shows there is convergence in drinking patterns. In the Nordic countries, this effect has been so strong that, in the European Comparative Alcohol Study (ECAS), the usual denomination for this group, 'spirits-drinking countries', was changed into 'former spirits-drinking countries', since beer is now the dominant drink. As noted by Leifman (2001), it seems implausible that this homogenization process is purely driven by changes in incomes and relative prices. With respect to cultural explanations, Leifman notes that there appears to be no direct connection between 'modernization' (e.g. urbaniza-tion rates, industrialization, female labour force participation, etc.) and the convergence in alcohol consumption.

As noted earlier, after more than a decade of strong growth, Russia now has a per capita level of beer consumption similar to the EU average. Moreover, the share of beer in total alcohol consumption increased strongly. Hence, Russian alcohol consumption patterns seem to conform to the homogenization pro-cess observed in other countries. On the other hand, while convergence may be an apt *description* of the phenomena observed, it is not an *explanation* of the changes in consumption patterns, unless we are able to clearly identify a channel through which consumer preferences or market circumstances con-verged. As we argue below, such channels can be identified, but a 'Westerni-zation' of preferences is not a plausible explanation.

There are several problems with assuming a convergence in Russian con-sumer preferences around 1996. First, if consumers in Russia came to prefer the Western way of life, one would expect this change to have been gradual. But even with a sudden change, it is hard to find a reason why this change would only have occurred in 1996–7 and not several years earlier (e.g.

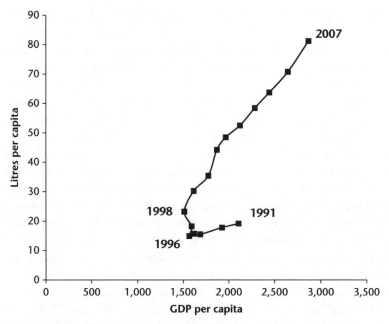

Figure 16.5. GDP and beer consumption, 1991–2007

Source: FAOSTAT (beer consumption); World Development Indicators (GDP per capita, in constant 2000 US dollars).

immediately after the collapse of communism), or after 1998, when Russian living standards finally recovered after years of economic hardship. A second problem with this explanation is that beer in Russia is not being sold as a 'Western' product at all. Morris (2007) analysed Russian television advertising for beer and found that these commercials overwhelmingly played on feelings of nationalism and nostalgia for the past (the Soviet-era and even pre-revolutionary times), especially during the Putin years (2000–8), which comprise the main part of the convergence period. Beer seems to have been actively marketed as a 'patriotic' beverage. Moreover, this nostalgia in Russian advertising was not limited to beer (Holak et al. 2007). Even if Russians were adopting a Western consumption pattern for alcoholic beverages, this was clearly not because of a conscious desire to adapt Western habits. Therefore, the cultural convergence hypothesis seems unable to explain the observed changes in Russia.

Changes in Relative Prices or Incomes

Figure 16.5 plots Russian per capita beer consumption against per capita GDP for the years 1991–2007. This graph clearly shows the decline in both beer consumption and income in the early years of the transition, and the increase in both, starting in 1998. Hence, the ups and downs of the beer market largely coincide with parallel movements in income. However, Figure 16.5 also constitutes prima-facie evidence against overreliance on the income effect. First of all, the turning points in the two series do not match. The decline in beer consumption is reversed around 1996, but the decline in GDP is only reversed in 1998. During this two-year interval, however, average beer consumption rises from 15 to 23 litres—an increase of more than 50% at a time when average income was decreasing. Second, during the income decline of the early 1990s there was only a moderate decrease in beer consumption, whereas income growth after 1998 was accompanied by rapid increases in beer consumption. In 2003, Russian GDP per capita was again at its 1991 level, while beer consumption was more than three times the 1991 level. Even if there are reasons to doubt the GDP figures for the early 1990s (Shleifer and Treisman 2005), changes in income are clearly not the sole determinant of changes in beer consumption.

It is possible that changes in relative prices, together with income changes, have produced the observed outcome. For instance, Treisman (2010) presents evidence that, in the 1990s, changes in real vodka prices influenced vodka

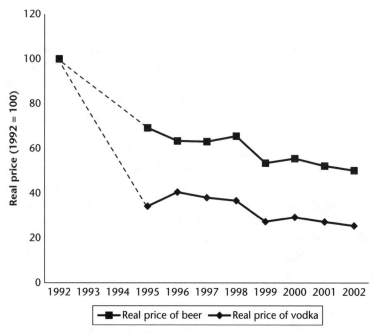

Figure 16.6. The real price of beer and vodka, 1992–2002

Source: Goskomstat (beer and vodka prices), World Development Indicators (CPI).

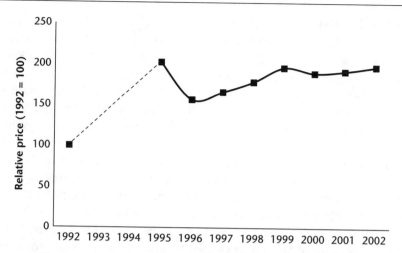

Figure 16.7. The relative price of beer versus vodka, 1992–2002
Source: Goskomstat.

consumption to such an extent that this price variation, both over time and across different regions, 'closely matched variation in mortality'. It seems plausible that relative price changes might also have affected beer consumption in such a significant way.

Figure 16.6 shows the evolution of the real price of beer. Between 1992 and 1995, the real price of beer decreased by 30%, at a time when beer consumption was constant or decreasing slowly. From 1995 to 1996, the decrease was 9%, while beer consumption fell by 3%; and, between 1996 and 1997, the real price of beer was constant, while beer consumption increased by 25%.

Figure 16.7 plots the relative price of beer and vodka (arguably the most important substitute) for 1992 until 2002. As is apparent from this graph, the price of beer doubled relative to that of vodka between 1992 and 1995. This change seems to have been accompanied by a strong increase in vodka consumption, from 3.8 to 7 litres of pure alcohol (World Drink Trends 2005). At the same time, there was a decrease in beer consumption from 19.1 to 15.7 litres of beer, according to FAO statistics. Hence, substitution effects seem to have been at work in the period from 1992 to 1995. But between 1995 and 1996, the relative price of beer decreased by 25% and reached a low in 1996, slowly increasing afterwards. While this change resulted in a decline in vodka consumption (from 7 to 5.5 litres of pure alcohol), beer consumption only started to grow one year later. Although there is some evidence for substitution effects between 1992 and 1995, changes in relative prices cannot by themselves fully account for the trend break in beer consumption.

The explanatory power of income and relative prices is also questioned by the results of Andriendko and Nemtsov (2005), who estimate the individual demand for alcohol based on the Russian Longitudinal Monitoring Survey (RLMS). Although their analysis gives correct signs for own-price and cross-price elasticities of beer, vodka, and wine, they are unable to explain the drastic changes in the structure of alcohol consumption between 1994 and 2002, in particular the falling number of vodka drinkers and the rising number of people consuming beer in the sample. In 1995, 78% of people who reported drinking alcohol drank vodka, and 23% drank beer (Table 16.4). In 1998, the proportion had changed to 68% vodka drinkers and 38% beer drinkers, and by 2002 the proportion of beer drinkers (57%) had actually overtaken the proportion of vodka drinkers (55%). Hence, although there is some evidence of substitution effects between vodka and beer, the spectacular increase in beer consumption cannot be fully explained by changes in income and relative prices.

Table 16.4. Popularity of beer and vodka

	1995	1996	1998	2000	2001	2002	2003
Percentage of beer drinkers	23%	29%	38%	49%	58%	57%	57%
Percentage of vodka drinkers	78%	73%	68%	62%	56%	55%	53%

Source: Based on RLMS survey data.

FDI and Quality Improvements

As foreign investors entered the Central and Eastern European beer markets, they discovered that locally produced malt was generally of poor quality. At first, foreign companies imported quality malt and barley from Western Europe. Later on, they adopted a strategy of vertical coordination in the supply chain to ensure a domestic supply of high-quality raw materials (see Swinnen and Van Herck, Chapter 14 in this volume). Between 2000 and 2005, Russian malt production increased spectacularly from 231,000 tons (49% of total domestic demand) to around 1 million tons (85% of total domestic demand). The driving force behind this evolution was the launch of malting facilities by large brewing companies (FAO 2009).

As argued by Belaya and Hanf (2010), quality management is one of several improvements in management techniques introduced in the Russian agrifood business by foreign investors. Since these foreign companies were more concerned about quality than local producers had been, the entry of multinational brewers into the Russian beer market raised the quality of beer. When BBH gained control of Baltika in 1993, the company embarked on a large-scale investment programme to modernize production, as part of the company's strategy to create a beer of European quality (Baltika 2008). In 1995, SUN Brewing (now Sun InBev) invested $11.7 million in upgrading machinery to improve beer quality and taste, since, according to then-chairman Shiv Khemka, 'the problem is not that [Russians] dislike beer...It's just that they don't have a first-rate national brand to choose from' (Russia Review 1996). Foreign companies' quality improvements made beer a more attractive drink to Eastern European, and Russian, consumers (Ebneth 2006).

The two pioneers (BBH and SUN) entered well before the turning point in the Russian beer market. Both companies consciously adopted a strategy of quality improvements, and subsequently became the two main players in the market, which suggests this strategy was successful. Quality improvements by foreign investors made beer more attractive to Russian consumers, thereby increasing demand. The entry of foreign companies into the Russian beer market thus seems to be one element contributing to the Russian beer boom.

Health Considerations

One possible explanation for the popularity of beer is that Russians have become increasingly concerned about the health impact of vodka consumption, and have decided to switch to less dangerous beverages. To evaluate this hypothesis, two tests are possible. First, we could verify whether there has indeed been a substitution away from vodka and towards beer. Second, increasing concerns about health would also affect other types of behaviour. Information on these other habits can indicate whether or not people are increasingly worried about their health.

The substitution away from vodka and towards beer has not been gradual and smooth, as one would expect if health concerns were a main force behind increased beer consumption. Figure 16.8 shows official data on per capita vodka consumption. While these numbers need to be treated with caution,[4] we may infer that vodka consumption peaked in 1995 and decreased in 1996. However, afterwards, vodka consumption remained at a high level for several years. Assuming health concerns are somewhat persistent, we would expect to see a continuing decrease in vodka consumption, not the one-time decrease found here. Although the decline in vodka consumption after 2003 (and, indeed, the growing popularity of alcohol-free beer in recent years) may be due to health concerns, these were probably not the driving force behind the first years of the beer boom.

---

[4] In fact, Treml (1997) cites the data in a paper discussing problems with official alcohol statistics like these. Moreover, although the World Drink Trends (2005) data also originate from government sources, the trends do not correspond perfectly. In any case, the data on beer consumption for later years, both in World Drink Trends and on the Goskomstat website, correspond with those found in other sources, e.g. Euromonitor (2010b).

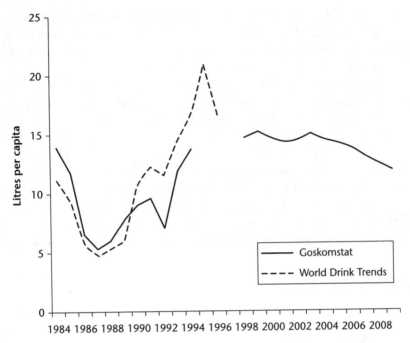

Figure 16.8. Vodka consumption (litres per capita), 1984–2009

Note: World Drink Trends data expressed in pure litres of alcohol have been reconverted into litres of vodka assuming a ratio of alcohol by volume of 33%.

Source: Treml (1997); Goskomstat; World Drink Trends 2005.

Table 16.5. Health habits

	1995	1996	1998	2000	2001	2002	2003
Percentage of smokers	31%	25%	26%	31%	30%	31%	32%
Percentage of people exercising	8%	8%	10%	11%	10%	12%	12%
Percentage of people jogging	5%	2%	3%	5%	4%	4%	4%

Source: Based on RLMS survey data.

Furthermore, if health concerns were the main driver, we might expect people to have changed other elements of their lifestyle as well. As explained by Cockerham (2000, 2007), the lifestyle of the average Russian is very unhealthy, and typically consists of heavy drinking, smoking, lack of exercise, and a fat diet. Table 16.5 provides data from the Russian Longitudinal Monitoring Survey (RLMS) on smoking and exercising. Although there appears to have been a drop in the number of smokers between 1995 and 1996, and there is some upward trend in the number of people exercising, in general these figures do not show a large shift in habits towards more healthy patterns. Hence, it seems unlikely that a significant change in health concerns explains increased beer consumption.

Advertising Regulations

In Russia, with its tradition of heavy vodka drinking, beer is commonly regarded as a soft drink, and this attitude is reflected in the law. When the first restrictions on alcohol advertising were adopted in 1995, these did not apply to beer. As a result of the law, vodka commercials were banned on television (*New York Times* 2004). Is it possible that this partial advertising ban shifted people's preferences from vodka to beer?

Nelson (2001), in a review of the literature on alcohol advertising and advertising bans, notes that there is little or no evidence that advertising bans reduce total alcohol consumption. Advertising expenditures do influence market shares of competing brands, but do not increase the total size of the market. However, only a few studies have analysed the impact of a partial ban. Those studies do find a significant effect. Young (1993) used data on 17 OECD countries between 1970 and 1983 and found that a ban on spirits advertising led to higher beer consumption. Nelson (2003), studying 45 American states over a 15-year period, finds evidence of substitution effects of beverage-specific alcohol policies. Specifically, a ban on price advertising for spirits reduces spirits consumption and increases beer consumption. Hence, there is evidence that a partial advertising ban can lead to substitution between beverages, even if total alcohol consumption is unaffected.

Advertising for beer is strong in Russia. In 2005, beer was the second-most advertised product on Russian television (Morris 2007). Expenditures for beer advertising are said to account for 10% of total advertising expenditures in Russia (*New York Times* 2004). Although it is difficult to find data for the 1990s, anecdotal evidence suggests that beer advertising was strong in the second half of the decade. Around the time vodka commercials were banned (1995), BBH, owner of the Baltika brands, started a major advertising and distribution campaign. The strategy of SUN Brewers, the market leader in the 1990s, was to 'buy up a host of smaller breweries, raise the quality and unite the improved beer behind a well-marketed national brand' (Russia Review 1996). Given the possibility of substitution following beverage-specific advertising bans, and given the conscious strategy of brewers to engage in an aggressive marketing campaign, advertising may well have played a role in luring consumers towards beer.

Shocks, Network Effects, and Generational Shifts

Crucial to understanding the changes in the Russian beer market is the fact that alcoholic beverages have important network effects on consumption. Alcoholic beverages are traditionally used as a way to facilitate social interactions, and as such, they fulfil an important social function. As noted by Skog (2006), alcoholic drinks are used to create an atmosphere different from that of everyday life. Beverages are used to emphasize the 'social content' of a meeting, and they are mostly consumed in groups. This is also true of some other beverages, such as tea and coffee in many Islamic societies.

Because of this social function, beverages are consumption goods with network externalities. The utility attached to different beverages will depend on what the majority of people in one's peer group usually drink. One implication is that the choice of beverage has the character of a coordination game, and hence we may expect persistence in beverage consumption patterns: even if prices and incomes change somewhat, the incumbent popular drink is still the focal point. This is consistent with the observation that the international convergence of drinking patterns is generally quite slow and seems to be unrelated to prices and incomes (Leifman 2001). On the other hand, once a new beverage gains popularity above a certain threshold, it can quickly become the new standard. Hence, temporary shocks in relative prices, preferences, or other circumstances can have 'lock-in' effects once a critical mass of people is persuaded to switch.

In his study of the growing popularity of coffee in nineteenth-century Norway, Skog (2006) shows how an initial decrease in alcohol consumption created a niche, ready to be taken over by another drink that could fulfil the social function of beverages. In the Norwegian case, coffee turned out to be the drink of choice. A similar mechanism was at work in Russia between 1995 and 1998, with some factors creating a 'push' out of vodka and others creating a 'pull' into beer.

From 1995 to 1996, the real price of vodka increased by 18%, while the real price of beer decreased by 8%. Moreover, vodka commercials were banned on television. The result was a decrease in vodka consumption from 7 to 5.5 litres of pure alcohol per capita (World Drink Trends 2005). At the same time, foreign direct investment in the brewing industry had led to quality improvements. Together with an aggressive advertising campaign on the part of brewers, and the absence of vodka advertising, this made beer a viable alternative to consumers. As a result, there was a 25% increase in beer consumption from 1996 to 1997. Once beer had gained momentum, the network effects of beverages led to further increases in the number of people consuming beer. Moreover, after 1998, rising incomes sustained the increase in beer consumption.

Table 16.6. Beer consumption in litres per capita

	1995	1996	1998	2000	2001	2002	2003
Over all respondents	15	16	21	26	31	34	32
Over all beer drinkers	69	56	56	54	53	59	56

Source: Based on RLMS survey data.

Table 16.7. Percentage of people drinking beer, by age group

	14–25	25–35	35–50	50+	Total population
All Years	68%	58%	43%	29%	47%
1995	36%	31%	22%	12%	23%
1996	43%	37%	28%	14%	29%
1998	56%	49%	37%	22%	38%
2000	71%	61%	47%	29%	49%
2001	82%	72%	54%	36%	58%
2002	77%	69%	54%	39%	57%
2003	79%	69%	53%	38%	57%

Source: Based on RLMS survey data.

Table 16.8. Percentage of people drinking vodka, by age group

	14–25	25–35	35–50	50+	Total population
All Years	42%	63%	69%	66%	62%
1995	67%	78%	79%	82%	78%
1996	58%	76%	77%	77%	73%
1998	51%	69%	72%	73%	68%
2000	44%	62%	70%	64%	62%
2001	35%	56%	64%	61%	56%
2002	34%	57%	63%	60%	55%
2003	33%	53%	63%	58%	53%

Source: Based on RLMS survey data.

This interpretation of events is consistent with RLMS survey data. Between 1995 and 2003, there were important shifts in the number of people drinking vodka or beer. As shown in Table 16.4, the proportion of people drinking beer increased from 23% to 57%. Furthermore, the increase in per capita consumption was not the result of existing beer drinkers consuming larger quantities; in fact, the average intake per beer consumer seems to have decreased over time (Table 16.6).[5] This implies that the Russian beer boom was not the result

[5] Survey data on alcohol consumption always need to be treated with caution, especially in Russia. It is often found that reported alcohol consumption is far below that implied by official sales statistics, which themselves probably underestimate the true extent of alcohol consumption. The RLMS data set contains the question 'how many grams of beer did you usually consume in a day?' When these figures are extrapolated, they result in yearly figures far higher than official beer consumption. We corrected for this using a different question, which asks respondents how many days each month they drank alcohol. Assuming people reported the average intake on days when alcohol was consumed, this procedure gives us a correct measure of implied beer consumption, as

of changes on the intensive margin (existing consumers drinking more beer), but of changes on the extensive margin (more people turning to beer), consistent with the hypothesis of network effects persuading consumers to switch to a new beverage.

Moreover, given our interpretation of the choice of beverage as a coordination game, we would expect a higher adoption of the 'new' beverage among younger age groups. Since habits have not been fully formed, and since their peer group has not yet settled on a beverage which can act as a focal point, younger people are more likely to adopt a new drink. In addition, younger people could also be more sensitive to advertising. Hence, we would expect a higher adoption of beer among younger people. This is confirmed by the data. As shown in Table 16.7, the proportion of beer drinkers is consistently higher among the younger age groups in all years of the survey. This is not the case for vodka, where the proportion of drinkers is higher in the older age groups (Table 16.8).

A different interpretation of these numbers is possible, however. It has recently been shown that shifts in the age distribution can influence total alcohol consumption (see Freeman, Chapter 6 in this volume). In the US, cohorts born before 1940 have a higher alcohol consumption than those born after 1946. Moreover, there are beverage-specific effects, as cohorts born before the 1930s consume more spirits, and those born between 1946 and 1965 drink more beer. Hence, generational shifts can be a source of variation in alcohol consumption over time (Kerr et al. 2004). However, based on the survey data presented here, generational shifts do not seem to be a main explanation for the Russian beer boom. The proportion of beer drinkers increased by several percentage points per year, while the share of vodka drinkers plummeted. Although beer is mostly consumed by younger generations and vodka is most popular among older cohorts, the observed changes are too large and too quick to be fully accounted for by generational shifts. Moreover, these rapid changes can be found in all age groups, which is not consistent with the hypothesis of a new generation of young beer drinkers replacing the older vodka-drinking generation. It does appear to be the case that younger generations adopted beer more quickly. The increase in percentage points in the share of beer drinkers is always higher among younger age groups, even though these already started from a higher level. Vodka also quickly fell out of grace with the youngest age groups, consistent with our hypothesis that since habits are not yet fully formed among younger generations, these will be more likely to shift to a new beverage. Hence, the available evidence appears consistent with our hypothesis that network effects are crucial to understanding the Russian beer boom.

given in Table 16.6. Interestingly, these figures match official data for the first few years, but underestimate consumption in later years by a wide margin.

Conclusion: A Perfect Storm

Between 1996 and 2007, beer consumption in Russia grew at an annual rate of 17%, bringing per capita beer consumption close to the European average. This change in the Russian consumption pattern cannot be explained by increasing health concerns or by a 'Westernization' of tastes, and it seems implausible that any of the other potential causes identified in the previous section has sufficient explanatory power on its own.

Rather, we propose that a focus on the network effects of alcohol consumption is crucial to understanding the changes in the Russian beer market. Since alcoholic beverages are usually consumed together with other people, an individual's choice of drink will be strongly influenced by the choice of his peer group. On the one hand, this may create persistence in alcohol consumption patterns. Once a group of people has settled on a drink of choice, this becomes the focal point for all members of the group. As a result, consumption may become insensitive to small changes in prices. In general, it will be difficult for a competing beverage to become popular. On the other hand, a new drink can quickly become the dominant beverage once a critical mass of consumers decides to switch. The growing popularity of the new drink may become self-accelerating due to these network effects, even if the factors causing the initial increase were only temporary.

The Russian beer boom fits this description. Temporary and structural factors combined around 1996 to persuade a critical mass of consumers to change their drinking habits. Improvements in the quality of beer were a structural factor making beer intrinsically more attractive to consumers. At the same time as vodka commercials were banned on television, Baltika and Sun both started an aggressive marketing campaign for their improved beers. Moreover, a strong increase in the real price of vodka had led to a sharp decline in vodka consumption, creating an opportunity for a new drink to gain dominance. This way, a 'perfect storm' of events led to a sharp increase in beer consumption from 1996 to 1997, leading to more and more people starting to drink beer during the following years because of network effects. Survey data support the claim that, through a combination of 'pull' and 'push' factors which combined into a 'perfect storm' around 1996, beer is now replacing vodka as the typical social drink in Russia.

References

Aizenman, J., and E. Brooks (2008). 'Globalization and Taste Convergence: The Cases of Wine and Beer'. *Review of International Economics*, 16/2: 217–33.

Andriendko, Y., and A. Nemtsov (2005). 'Estimation of Individual Demand for Alcohol'. Economics Education and Research Consortium Working Paper 05/10. Moscow: EERC.

Baltika (2008). *Baltika Annual Report 2007*.

Belaya, V., and J. Hanf (2010). 'Foreign Direct Investment as an Agent of Change in Russian Agrifood Business—Consequences of the Export of Chain Management Concepts by Foreign Investors'. *Post-Communist Economies*, 22/1: 55–72.

Bentzen, J., and V. Smith (2009). 'Developments in the Structure of Alcohol Consumption in OECD Countries'. Mimeo, Aarhus University, Denmark.

Cockerham, W. C. (2000). 'Health Lifestyles in Russia'. *Social Science & Medicine*, 51: 1313–24.

—— (2007). 'Health Lifestyles and the Absence of the Russian Middle Class'. *Sociology of Health and Illness*, 29/3: 457–73.

Ebneth, O. (2006). 'Review of the Central & Eastern European Beer Markets', in O. Ebneth, 'Internationalisierung und Unternehmenserfolg Börsennotierter Braukonzerne', Ph.D. Dissertation, Göttingen.

Euromonitor (2010a). 'Alcoholic Drinks in Russia', Country Market Insight Report.

—— (2010b). 'Beer in Russia', Country Sector Briefing.

FAO (2009). *Agribusiness Handbook: Barley, Malt and Beer*. Rome, Italy: FAO Investment Centre Division.

Holak, S., A. Matveev, and W. Havlena (2007). 'Nostalgia in Post-Socialist Russia: Exploring Applications to Advertising Strategy'. *Journal of Business Research*, 60: 649–55.

Kerr, W., T. Greenfield, J. Bond, Y. Ye, and J. Rehm (2004). 'Age, Period and Cohort Influences on Beer, Wine and Spirits Consumption Trends in the US National Alcohol Surveys'. *Addiction*, 99: 1111–20.

Konya, I., and H. Ohashi (2007). 'International Consumption Patterns among High-Income Countries: Evidence from the OECD Data'. *Review of International Economics*, 15/4: 744–57.

Leifman, H. (2001). 'Trends in Population Drinking', in Norström, T. (ed.), *Alcohol in Postwar Europe: Consumption, Drinking Patterns, Consequences and Policy Responses in 15 European Countries*. Stockholm: ECAS.

Morris, J. (2007). 'Drinking to the Nation: Russian Television Advertising and Cultural Differentation'. *Europe-Asia Studies*, 59/8: 1387–403.

New York Times (2004). 'Moscow Journal: As Russia Discovers Beer, Deputies Try to End the Binge'. 6 August.

Nelson, J. (2001). 'Alcohol Advertising and Advertising Bans: A Survey of Research Methods, Results, and Policy Implications', in M. Baye and J. Nelson (eds.), *Advances in Applied Microeconomics, Volume 10: Advertising and Differentiated Products*. Amsterdam: JAI Press & Elsevier Science.

—— (2003). 'Advertising Bans, Monopoly, and Alcohol Demand: Testing for Substitution Effects using State Panel Data'. *Review of Industrial Organization*, 22: 1–25.

Popova, S., J. Rehm, J. Patra, and W. Zatonski (2007). 'Comparing Alcohol Consumption in Central and Eastern Europe to European Countries'. *Alcohol and Alcoholism*, 42: 465–73.

Russia Review (1996). 'SUN's Golden Brew'. 21 October. SUN Group. Available at <http://www.sungroup-global.com/english/media-centre/details.asp?m_id=2&search_str=>.

Shleifer, A., and D. Treisman (2005). 'A Normal Country: Russia after Communism'. *Journal of Economic Perspectives*, 19/1: 151–74.

Simpura, J., T. Karlsson, and K. Leppänen (2001). 'European Trends in Drinking Patterns and their Socio-Economic Background', in T. Norström (ed.), *Alcohol in Postwar Europe: Consumption, Drinking Patterns, Consequences and Policy Responses in 15 European Countries*. Stockholm: ECAS.

Skog, O. J. (2006). 'Studying Cultural Change: Were the Changes in Alcohol and Coffee Consumption in the Nineteenth Century a Case of Beverage Substitution?' *Acta Sociologica*, 49/3: 287–302.

Treisman, D. (2010). 'Death and Prices: The Political Economy of Russia's Alcohol Crisis'. *Economics of Transition*, 18/2: 281–331.

Treml, V. (1997). 'Soviet and Russian Statistics on Alcohol Consumption and Abuse', in J. L. Bobadilla, C. A. Costello, and F. Mitchell (eds.), *Premature Death in the New Independent States*. Washington: National Research Council.

World Drink Trends (2005). World Advertising Research Center & Commissie Gedistilleerd, Henley-on-Thames, UK.

Young, D. (1993). 'Alcohol Advertising Bans and Alcohol Abuse: Comment'. *Journal of Health Economics*, 12: 213–28.

17

Opening the Beer Gates: How Liberalization Caused Growth in India's Beer Market

Abhimanyu Arora, Anjor Bhaskar, Bart Minten, and Anneleen Vandeplas

Introduction

The river of beer has flowed a long way in India. It all started off as a trickle of the famous India Pale Ale,[1] which was introduced at the beginning of the eighteenth century by the British for expatriates working for the East India Company. Nevertheless, over time and especially in the past decade, as we will document below, a variety of factors have contributed to a true deluge of beer being unleashed in India.

Traditionally, alcohol has an ambivalent place in India's culture and history. On the one hand, there are deities like Shiva who glorify the intake of intoxicating drinks in Hindu mythology. Tribal folklore of the Rathwa Bhils of Gujarat considers alcohol as a gift from God, meant to ease the inevitable sorrows on the path to death. Even Ayurvedic medicine prescribes the use of (small doses of) herbal wines to treat specific diseases.

On the other hand, there have been strong anti-alcoholism movements in India driven by different objectives. First, like Muslims, upper-caste Hindus—the Brahmins—traditionally do not consume alcohol and this tradition has sometimes been taken over by other castes as well. Second, throughout the Indian freedom struggle against the British, as well as under subsequent governments, alcohol came to be seen as one of the evils of society, with several attempts at a nationwide prohibition over the years. Anti-alcoholism

---

[1] India Pale Ale contained pale malt for its good preservative qualities, and a high proportion of hops. The latter ingredient was known to stabilize the beer on its long (and turbulent) voyage to India, and gave the beer its typical bitter taste (Pryor 2009).

gained special prominence in the early twentieth century, with the fierce advocacy of the 'Father of the Nation' Mahatma Gandhi. Because of this, the WHO estimated in 2000 that two-thirds of the Indian male population abstained from alcohol, against almost nine out of ten Indian women (WHO 2004).

Given the perception of alcohol in Indian society, stringent regulations (including high taxation) on alcohol distribution and consumption, and consumers' preferences for stronger drinks (such as rum and whisky), average per capita beer consumption in India is very low by international standards. Indians drink on average around 1 litre per capita per year, compared to 22 litres in China and around 75 litres in the US and Western Europe.[2] However, because of the sheer size of the country, this quantity still represented 12 million hectolitres in 2009, about the same as the size of the Spanish or French beer market.

In this chapter, we look at the structure and growth of the beer sector in India and potential determinants that might influence them. An important feature of the sector is the presence of a large number of regulations. The regulatory framework is perceived as a brake on growth, as frequently noted by locally established breweries that feel constrained in their operations, as well as on trade, as evidenced by the numerous complaints by foreign governments and beer companies that dispute the protectionist stand the Indian government has been taking, at central as well as at state level. Rules and regulations in the Indian beverage sector are quite complex, in an attempt to serve multiple purposes. On the one hand, Indian governments like to promote local production and to use the alcohol market as a means of generating tax revenues.[3] On the other hand, governments are pressured by lobby groups envisaging the prevention of social tragedies related to alcohol abuse and want to control consumption. This has led to a multitude of regulations involving licences, trade and marketing restrictions, and price controls. In recent years, this regulatory system has been relaxed to some extent, contributing to higher growth rates and modernization of the sector. In particular, the beer sector has experienced strong growth in recent years, at an average rate of about 11% annually between 1999 and 2009. The high growth rates and the relaxation of rules on foreign direct investment in the last decade have attracted foreign investment in the beer sector, and have led to a large differentiation in the market, with a greater emphasis on quality. This also has had important impacts on backward linkages of the brewery sector with farmers. Due to the

---

[2] While FAOSTAT estimates the 2005 per capita beer consumption in the US to be 86 litres, and in Western Europe 70 litres, Euromonitor (2009) data point to 61 litres for the US, and around 85 litres for Western Europe.

[3] Rahman (2003) estimates that excise revenues on average account for approximately 20–25% of total state revenue in India.

high variability in the quality of local barley and malt, a major problem in the Indian beer market has been to ensure a consistent quality of beer. In order to improve quality, contract farming schemes are being set up, mostly led by international firms that have only recently entered the market.

The structure of the chapter is as follows. We start with an overview of the major policies governing the alcohol and beer sector since the nineteenth century. The current characteristics and trends in market size, growth, and foreign investment are then discussed. Next, the focus is on the strategies that have been chosen in recent years to upgrade beer quality, followed by a discussion of future prospects for Indian beer markets.

Regulations in the Beer Market

Alcohol as a Source of Tax Revenues

Successive Indian governments have been strongly involved in the regulation of the Indian alcohol market. The first excise or 'abkari' regulations were introduced in India in 1790, during the era of the British East India Company in India (Hansard 1888; Singh 2003). Not only was alcohol taxed, as part of an 'excise on intoxicating liquors and drugs', but certain rules were also introduced to prevent illegal manufacture and sale of alcohol by restricting production to government-licensed contractors who managed sales through a small set of retailers (Cassels 2004). These excise regulations, also called 'farming systems' (Evans 1895), were pioneered by Lord Cornwallis, the Governor-General of India in Bengal, although it is argued that similar rules had been applied in earlier centuries by Mughal emperors in India (Buckland 1902: 825). The principles behind these excise regulations soon spread to Bombay and Madras at the beginning of the nineteenth century. Licences were sold to the highest bidder in a public auction, generating significant revenues for the government. The winner of the auction was allotted the monopoly right to the production and sale of alcohol within a demarcated area. However, excise rules were not very well enforced, and the government quickly realized that it was forgoing a substantial amount of tax revenues.

Consequently, in an attempt to further increase government control so as to more fully tap potential tax revenues, centralized government distilleries (so-called 'sudder' distilleries) were set up in 1813 (Buckland 1902: 825; Rose et al. 1929: 86). These were fenced-off areas where licensed contractors could produce alcohol and where guards were put in place to make sure no alcohol would leave the premises without the appropriate excise duties being paid (Evans 1895). Alcohol manufacturing outside the central distillery was banned. While the government would argue that increased control and higher prices were in place to avoid the negative impacts of illicit alcohol consumption, there were plenty of indications that increasing tax revenue was their main purpose (Cassels 2004; Evans 1895). The new Excise Policy that came into force in 1878 made this particularly evident. In that year, the government resumed the issuing of licences to alcohol manufacturers outside the central government distillery, mainly with a view to increasing their tax base. The establishment of these 'outstills' was very controversial, as the number of alcohol outlets multiplied quickly. In many of these outlets, low-quality alcohol was sold at giveaway prices (Evans 1895). The new market structure was blamed for driving up alcohol consumption, especially among the poor, and for aggravating alcohol-related social problems all over India (Hansard 1889). Nevertheless, it is estimated that alcohol excises were the largest contributor to public revenues under British colonial rule in India (1858–1947) after taxes on land use (Benegal et al. 2003). After widespread criticism of the outstill system, the Government of Bengal partially reverted to the central distillery system in 1889 (Buckland 1902: 861). This suspension was only temporary, however, as a sudden drop in state revenue soon encouraged reopening of the outstills (Evans 1895).

Prohibition

In the first half of the twentieth century, important anti-alcohol movements started in Gujarat. While, on the one hand, they were rooted in resentment over the colonial excise policies, on the other hand, adopting the values of the higher castes—including abstention from alcohol—was seen as a means to climb up the caste ladder (Benegal et al. 2003). One noteworthy initiative was the Devi movement in the 1920s, with its call to give up alcohol, meat, and fish, to wear domestically produced ('khadi') cotton clothes, and to follow the Gandhian ideology. For Gandhi, prohibition was an important element of his 'civil disobedience' campaign, and he supported public protests at liquor shops, as a result of which liquor consumption is said to have fallen by 19% in Bombay (Brown 1972; Gandhi 1954). His stance was that 'prohibition should be the first step for ameliorating the conditions of the poor masses who, in particular, had long been suffering from the evil effects of drinking' (GoI 1980). Under Gandhi's influence, the Constitution of India features a section advocating (but not imposing) prohibition: '... the State shall endeavour to bring about prohibition of the consumption except for medicinal purposes of intoxicating drinks and of drugs which are injurious to health' (Article 47 of the Constitution of India 1949).

As part of this drive for national austerity, prohibition was first introduced in 1937 in parts of Madras state (largely, present-day Tamil Nadu) and Bombay state (largely, present-day Maharashtra and Gujarat). Parts of Madhya Pradesh and Karnataka followed suit in 1938. During World War II, prohibition was provisionally suspended, but it was resumed and extended after the war and Independence. For instance, strict prohibition was enforced in Maharashtra from 1949 until 1963 (Government of Maharashtra 2008). From 1948 until 1971, the whole of Tamil Nadu was under prohibition (Reddy and Patnaik 1993). Also, other parts of India imposed complete or partial alcohol bans in the post-war years (Reddy and Patnaik 1993).

However, as alcohol is a state matter, effective prohibition had to be decided by each state separately.[4] Even when the second five-year plan, presented by the central government in 1956, sought nationwide implementation of prohibition by 1958 as part of its 'social welfare program' (Planning Commission 1956), the respective state governments largely refrained from undertaking concrete legislative action. In the third five-year plan, the Planning Commission further insisted on the necessity of prohibition for social welfare (Planning Commission 1961), and a 1964 report by the Justice Tek Chand Committee advocated complete prohibition by 1970, but again with little success: nationwide prohibition was never realized.

In fact, most states revoked their prohibition acts in the 1960s. Loss of state revenue, problematic implementation, lack of public backing, and the pervasiveness of illicit distillation and trading of alcohol that encouraged underground organizations to thrive are said to lie at the heart of such failure (GoI 1980). Only in Gujarat was complete prohibition still in force in 1970, and has continued in effect until today.[5]

Still, prohibition remains a vital part of many political campaigns. Three minor states in the north-east of India (Nagaland, Manipur, and Mizoram) introduced prohibition in 1989, 1991, and 1995, respectively (e.g. Government of Mizoram 2007). Andhra Pradesh and Haryana also experimented with prohibition. In Andhra Pradesh, alcohol was banned from 1995 to 1997, as a result of which the state treasury quickly ran out of resources (Benegal et al. 2003). The government consequently decided to resume alcohol sales. In Haryana, prohibition was in force from 1996 to 1998.

A number of states, such as Tamil Nadu (since 1991), maintain a ban on the production and sale of country liquor (Government of Tamil Nadu 2002), while sales of Western-style hard liquor (such as whisky and rum, whether

---

[4] The Ministry of Food Processing and Industries is part of central government and is responsible for the development of the beer and wine-processing sector. It may give some direction by designing model policies, but the state governments need to ratify these policies prior to implementation.

[5] The prohibition policy was proposed by Mahatma Gandhi to the British rulers in 1915. During British rule, the Congress Party had promised Mahatma Gandhi that it would implement prohibition in Gujarat, Gandhi's state of birth, after Independence. The policy was thus enacted in Gujarat from 1950 onwards and has not been changed since. While alcohol consumption is officially banned, there is however a thriving black market.

Indian-produced or not) are allowed. In other Indian states, such as Delhi, alcohol consumption is only banned on national holidays such as Republic Day, Independence Day, and the birthday of Gandhi, as well as at election time.[6]

Licences and Monopolies in Distribution

The result of each state government being at liberty to impose its own restrictions on the production, distribution, and consumption of alcohol has been very diverse licensing regulations concerning alcohol distribution among states.

The most liberal system is in force in states such as Goa and Maharashtra, where it is close to an open market system. In many other states, a licensing system is in vogue, implying that governments decide on the number of licences of each type (based on the kind of liquor to be stocked, the type of establishment, and whether for wholesale, export, or retail) and the period for which they are given out. The number of licences may be limited, in which case they may be allotted through an auction as in Haryana (Government of Haryana 2009) or a lottery as in Punjab (Government of Punjab 2009), in each case for Indian-Made Foreign Liquor (IMFL).[7] Alternatively, the number of licences may be unlimited, in which case licences are sold at a fixed price, as in Punjab and Haryana for beer, and in Chandigarh for any type of alcohol (Government of Chandigarh 2007; Government of Haryana 2009). Revenue components include licence fees (as a lump sum or a percentage of sales), as well as (various types of) taxes.

While auctioning of licences in theory increases the licence revenue earned by the government, the system's major drawback is the observed cartelization or collusion among bidders in those states which have implemented it. Such cartelization has in some states led to underbidding and reduction of state revenues, as well as to marking up of retail prices (Mehta 2006: 115). As a result, Punjab switched to a lottery system to allot its alcohol retail licences for country liquor and IMFL (and an unrestricted number of fixed-fee licences for beer sales); Tamil Nadu eventually took the opposite course. The state-owned Tamil Nadu Sales and Marketing Corporation (TASMAC), which initially had control only over wholesale trade, was also granted monopoly rights to retail of alcohol in Tamil Nadu in 2003 (Mehta 2006: 116).

[6] In fact, in New Delhi, there are more than 20 days a year when no alcohol can be sold in retail shops, but alcohol can still be served in bars, clubs, and hotels. There are three dry days on which alcohol cannot be served in bars, clubs, and hotels, except for room service (Government of NCT of Delhi 2010).
[7] The term 'Indian-Made Foreign Liquor' refers to Western-style hard liquor which is produced in India.

Like Tamil Nadu, there are other states where the government is in full control of their alcohol markets, implying that government-owned companies have a monopoly on wholesale and/or retail of alcohol. One example is Andhra Pradesh, where the state government founded the Andhra Pradesh Beverages Corporation (APBCL) in 1986 to bottle and distribute country liquor known as arrack. When the state banned arrack sales in 1993, APBCL's arrack-bottling units were transformed into wholesale trading centres for IMFL, beer, and lately also wine and ready-to-drink alcoholic mixes (APBCL 2010). APBCL procures beverages through open tenders from manufacturers all over the country; retail is licensed through a lottery system, and maximum retail prices are fixed by the state government.

Restrictions of Production and Foreign Investment

The creation of additional capacity in the distillery and brewery sector (building of new units or expansion of existing capacity) was legally banned from 1975 until 1989 (except for 100% export-oriented production) (MOFPI 2007a). To that end, all companies with existing non-licensed capacity received an ultimatum in November 1975 to obtain a 'Carry-on-business' licence within the following three months (Goyal et al. 1983). While the ban imposed on additional capacity was not well enforced, in the sense that most of the existing companies did effectively increase their capacity between 1975 and 1989, entry of new players into the market was deterred. The regulation could thus be seen as a protectionist measure for existing distilleries and breweries (Goyal et al. 1983). In fact, the limited data available suggest that the beer market was growing at 11% per year between 1970 and 1986 (see Figure 17.1).

Moreover, while in most industrial sectors, the requirement to obtain a government licence prior to production was abolished between 1985 and 1991, in a few sectors, licensing under the Industries (Development and Regulation) Act of 1951 remained compulsory. Examples include distilleries and breweries, tobacco manufacturers, the defence and arms industry, manufacture of hazardous chemicals, and the drugs and pharmaceutics industry— all sectors which are deemed to require 'special regulations' for social or security reasons. Obtaining these licences has not always been transparent, and unclear and protectionist rules have largely prevented foreign direct investment (FDI) in the sector until the late 1990s.

For example, it was not until 1997 that there was some clarification regarding the appropriate authority to grant industrial licences for potable alcohol production. In a 1997 lawsuit brought by Bihar distillery against the Government of India, the Supreme Court decided that state governments rather than central government should have full control over (and hence be the sole

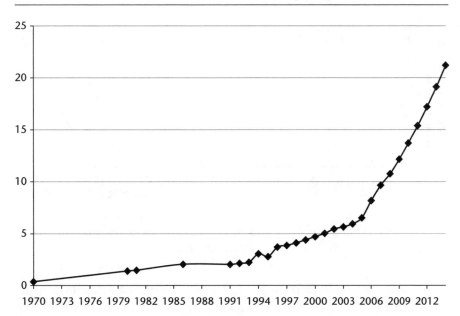

Figure 17.1. Growth of the Indian beer market (in million hectolitres per year)

Source: Compiled from various sources: Central Statistical Organization, India; Centre for Monitoring the Indian Economy, Rabobank, Euromonitor, Saxena (1999).

authority issuing licences for) the production of potable alcohol (Supreme Court of India 1997).

In 2006, the Government of India undertook a comprehensive review of its FDI policy which led to FDI being allowed, under the Reserve Bank of India (RBI)'s 'automatic route', in several industries, including the distilling and brewery sector (GoI 2006). This procedure does not require any prior approval by the government or by RBI. Investors are only required to notify the regional RBI office concerned within 30 days of receipt of inward remittances and within 30 days of issue of shares to foreign investors, the required documents must be filed. This change in the rules has given rise to a sudden leap in FDI, not only in the brewery industry in particular, with Carlsberg, Heineken, and AB-InBev entering the Indian market, but also generally across, sectors (see Figure 17.2).

Price Regulation

In some states, consumer prices are determined through market mechanisms, but maximum and/or minimum prices may be imposed (Government of Haryana 2009; Government of Punjab 2009). In other states, the government

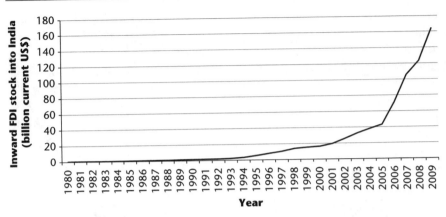

Figure 17.2. Inwards FDI stock in India, 1980–2008 (in billion US$)
Source: UNCTAD FDIStat.

fixes procurement and/or retail prices. Companies producing alcohol in the latter states need to apply for government permission whenever they want to change their prices. This recently led to a lawsuit by the two major breweries, SABMiller and United Breweries (UB), against the Andhra Pradesh government in 2008, indicting the government of not having adequately revised the beer procurement price (Unnikrishnan 2008). The breweries complained that, since 1997, the state procurement price had gone up by only 9%, while production costs had experienced manifold increases, and even consumer prices had quadrupled since 1997. This dispute led to a three month ban on UB and SABMiller beer sales in Andhra Pradesh, but eventually the requested revision of procurement prices by about 10% was agreed to (Jacob 2010).

National and International Trade Restrictions

The fact that potable alcohol is a state matter—and a heavily regulated one—seems to impose important additional constraints on the brewery sector, as production cannot be moved freely around India. While export fees are often levied on alcohol leaving a particular state, alcohol originating from other states is also subject to import duties.[8] This incites breweries to decentralize production, largely preventing the benefits of scale economies.

Moreover, the taxes imposed at the state level have recently been contested at the World Trade Organization (WTO). When India removed its quantitative import restrictions in 2001 as a result of WTO negotiations, a national

---

[8] For instance, in the state of Haryana, an import duty of Rs. 3 and an export duty of Rs. 0.25 per 650 ml bottle of beer have been levied, according to the 2009–10 Excise Policy (Government of Haryana 2009).

'additional duty' was imposed on foreign alcohol to avoid an uncontrolled influx of cheap imports. This additional duty was added to the existing basic customs duties of 100% on beers and wines, and 150% on spirits, resulting in a total import duty exceeding the bound tariff of 150% imposed by the WTO in 1995. After a complaint at the WTO by, among others, the European Union and the United States, India agreed to remove the 'additional duty' in 2007 (Central Board of Excise and Customs 2009; European Council 2006; World Trade Organization 2010).[9]

However, in January 2010, negotiations were still ongoing between the EU and India, as the EU was disputing a number of state-level taxes which (again) led to a composite duty exceeding the WTO bound tariff of 150%. Furthermore, it is argued that some of the Excise Acts of states where the alcohol market is state controlled (specifically, Tamil Nadu and Andhra Pradesh) do not provide for procurement of alcohol from foreign companies, thus ruling out sales of imported alcohol in practice.

Size and Growth of the Beer Market

Per capita beer consumption in India was estimated at 1 litre per year in 2009 (up from 0.5 litres in 2003) (Euromonitor 2009). As yet, beer only occupies a small share of the Indian alcoholic beverage market. The Indian market for beer is estimated at over 12 million hectolitres per year (Euromonitor 2009). Even if in volume terms this amounts to 43%, in terms of value, it represents not even 10% of Indian alcohol sales (Euromonitor 2009) (see Figure 17.3). There are estimates that two-thirds of the total volume of alcohol consumed is informal (e.g. home-made) and hence remains unreported (WHO 2004). The real share of beer in Indian alcohol consumption is therefore probably considerably less.

Among the various types of alcoholic drinks, indigenous beverages, also known as 'country liquor' or as 'desi sharab', are the most popular in India. The type of country liquor varies from region to region, such as 'toddy' (palm wine) or the further distilled version 'arrack' in south India, '(cashew) fenny' in Goa, or 'mahua' (made out of fermented Mahua tree flowers), which is prevalent across the tribal belts of India. In the north-east, a rice beer called 'hadia' is the traditional 'poor man's beer', while 'kacchi daru', made by fermenting and distilling sugar cane juice, is popular in the sugar-cane-growing regions.

---

[9] In return, India increased its applied basic duty on imported wine from 100% to 150%.

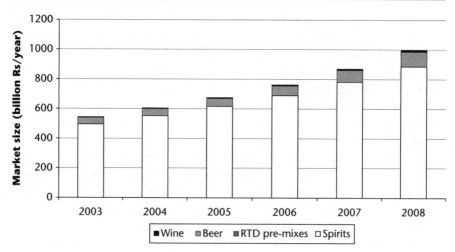

Figure 17.3. Indian alcohol market per sector (in billion Rs/year)
Source: Euromonitor (2009).

After country liquors, it is IMFLs, such as whisky and vodka, that are consumed most. In fact, India is reported to be the largest whisky market globally, estimated at nearly 9 million hectolitres per year in 2008 (Euromonitor 2009). As a consequence of the high import taxes levied by central and state governments, less than 1% of the whisky consumed in India is produced abroad (Euromonitor 2009). Wine is doing even worse than beer, with an average per capita consumption of only 4.6 millilitres per capita per year (Indiastat 2009).

However, the demand for beer, wine, and IFMLs seems to be rising at a fast pace. In fact, the market for beer has seen a tremendous rate of growth over the last decade with an annual average growth rate of 11% between 1999 and 2009 (see Figure 17.1), while the economy grew at 7% (IMF 2009). As such, India is the fastest-growing beer market, even outpacing other emerging markets such as China, Russia, and Brazil. The highest rate of growth was recorded between 2005 and 2006, when the Indian beer market grew by over 25%, seemingly due to increasing deregulation of the alcoholic beverage industry. As far as regional distribution is concerned, south and west India constitute the lion's share of the Indian alcohol market (see Figure 17.4).

Market Structure

In the first half of the nineteenth century, Edward Dyer (now Mohan Meakin) for the first time started to produce India Pale Ale locally, in Himachal Pradesh,

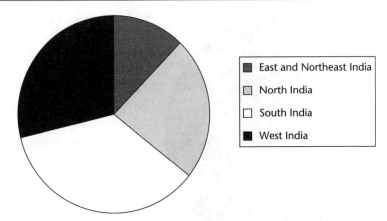

Figure 17.4. Regional distribution of the Indian alcohol market in value terms, 2008
Source: Euromonitor (2009).

under the brand 'Lion'. Over a century later, Mohan Meakin converted Lion into a (bottom-fermented) lager beer. Until then, Lion had been the number one selling beer in India. From 1960 until 1980, another Mohan Meakin beer, Golden Eagle, gained the status of top-selling beer in India. Yet by 2000, the beer market in India was largely shared between two Indian-owned companies: United Breweries Group, with its key brand Kingfisher—currently the number one beer in India (see Figure 17.5)—had 40% of the market share (Euromonitor 2009; Lakshman and Carter 2007), and Shaw Wallace, with its key brands Haywards and Royal Challenge—the number two and number three beers, respectively, in India—had 23% of the market share in 2000. They took over the reins in the 1980s from Mohan Meakin's Lion and Golden Eagle. Interestingly, each of these three breweries had been founded by Englishmen in the nineteenth century, with Indian management taking over eventually.

The landscape changed with the advent of SABMiller in 2000.[10] It entered the Indian market by acquiring a minor brewery (Narang breweries) in 2000, but quickly increased its market share by acquiring, among others, Mysore breweries (brand name 'Knock out') in 2001, Shaw Wallace in 2003, and Foster's India in 2006. With all its beer brands taken together, SABMiller had a market share of 34% in the Indian beer market in 2009 (see Figure 17.6). In the same year, United Breweries' market share reached almost 44%.

The Indian beer market is highly concentrated, as the joint market share of the two major companies amounted to 78% in 2009. The market has witnessed a trend of increasing concentration in the past ten years, as the joint

[10] SABMiller is essentially of South African origin, but it has a large stake in the European, North and South American, and even Chinese and Indian beer markets.

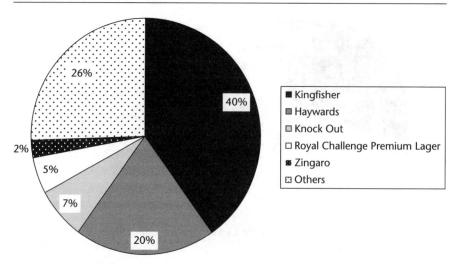

Figure 17.5. Market shares of major brands in the Indian beer market, 2009
Source: Euromonitor (2009).

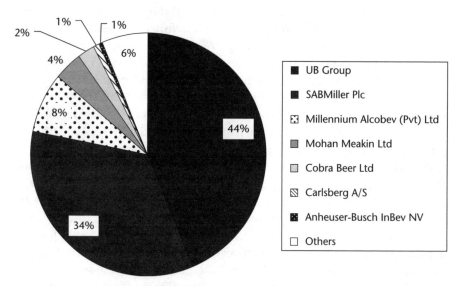

Figure 17.6. Market shares of major companies in the Indian beer market, 2009
Source: Euromonitor (2009).

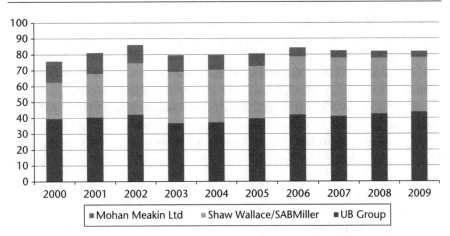

Figure 17.7. Trends in major breweries' market share of since 2000
Source: Euromonitor (2009).

market share of the two major companies was 62.4% in 2000 (see Figure 17.7). However, with 22% of the market still owned by smaller players, it seems that there is still scope for further consolidation.

Foreign Investment

All major global breweries have a keen interest in investing in India, owing to its great growth potential. Most of these brewers, including InBev, Miller, and Heineken, surveyed the market in the early 1990s before deferring entry plans. InBev had been negotiating with Mysore Breweries, while Miller explored Mohan Meakin as a potential joint-venture partner in the past. Anheuser-Busch had come close to finalizing a deal with Shaw Wallace as early as 1995. About the same time, Heineken (through its Singapore-based arm Asia Pacific Breweries) was in an advanced stage of talks with ITC (one of India's foremost private sector companies), when the latter thought of venturing into the food and beverage business. Carlsberg almost signed a memorandum of understanding with the UB Group (Kurian 2004). However, as has been mentioned before, strong government regulation of the beverages industry turned out to be a strong deterrent to FDI for most of the 1990s, as the procedure to apply for a brewery or distillery licence was only improved in 1997.

The first foreign beer company to enter the Indian market was Australia-based Foster's in 1998. SABMiller, currently one of the biggest players in the beer sector, entered India in 2000. In 2003, Scotland-based Scottish &

Newcastle (S&N) entered the Indian market through a joint venture with United Breweries called 'Millennium Alcobev', with Zingaro, Sandpiper, and Kingfisher in its brand portfolio.

The next move was by Carlsberg, who, in 2006, entered into a joint venture with its Sri Lankan partner, The Lion Brewery Ceylon. South Asia Breweries was set up to brew and sell Carlsberg in India, as well as selling Tuborg and the strong beer Palone. In the same year, Heineken entered the Indian market through its Singaporean affiliate Asian Pacific Breweries (APB), acquiring a local brewery in Aurangabad.[11] While APB's flagship brands are Tiger and Heineken, APB first started to produce Baron and Cannon in India. Only in 2008 did local production of Tiger commence.

In 2008, Heineken took over Scottish & Newcastle, through which Heineken became a joint-venture partner of UB. However, as Heineken was already involved in another Indian joint venture (APB India), UB claimed that competition between UB and APB India would rule out a smooth collaboration between UB and Heineken. The dispute was resolved at the end of 2009 when Heineken agreed to buy APB India from its partner Fraser and Neave,[12] and to bring it under the auspices of its joint venture with UB in 2010.

InBev and Anheuser-Busch (AB) have entered India as well. In May 2007, InBev entered into a joint venture with the RKJ Group, the main bottler for Pepsi in India, with a view to increasing the scale of InBev's export activities to India through RKJ's distribution network (AB InBev 2007). In 2008, a joint venture with the Dasappa and Sons brewery of Karnataka enabled InBev India to start brewing, among other products, its Beck's beer locally.

Simultaneously, AB entered into a joint venture with Crown Beers International. One year later, AB bought up its partner's stakes, such that Crown Beers India became a wholly owned subsidiary of AB. After the international merger of AB and InBev, Crown Beers India was integrated with AB InBev India. At the end of 2009, locally brewed Budweiser was launched in India.

The Drive for Quality and the Impact of Backward Linkages

The Indian beer market has traditionally been characterized by low-priced, high-alcohol content beer. The widespread use of inferior malts, as well as of malt substitutes such as rice flakes, and the use of glycerin as a preservative, reduces the quality of the beer, with inconsistencies in taste between different

---

[11] APB was set up in 1931 as Malayan Breweries Limited, a joint venture between Heineken International and the Singapore-based Fraser and Neave to serve as a gateway to 12 countries in the Asia Pacific region. Heineken is the majority (42.5%) shareholder.

[12] The latter agreed in return for Heineken's promise to sell its stakes in APB Indonesia and New Caledonia back to Fraser and Neave.

bottles of the same brand. Official food safety and quality standards with respect to beer are limited, and if they exist, they remain subjective with regard to quality: for example, the Karnataka Prohibition Act 1961 promises a penalty for mixing alcohol with any foreign ingredient 'likely to add to its intoxicating quality or strength', any 'ingredient whatsoever likely to render the intoxicant inferior in quality', as well as for selling alcohol 'which is not of the nature, substance and quality demanded by the purchaser' (Government of Karnataka 2007).[13] Even the latest draft of the Food Safety and Standards Regulations 2009 only mentions a maximum permissible concentration (70 ppm) of sulphur dioxide, which is used as a preservative in beer (FSSAI 2009).

With the advent of foreign investment, private food safety and quality standards are increasingly gaining ground, as observed in other food sectors (e.g. Henson and Reardon 2005). In general, foreign players are strict in terms of the safety and quality standards met, forcing domestic brewers to invest and keep up with competition. This is why domestic firms were seemingly eager to join hands when leading international breweries knocked at their door (even if later divestment was anticipated), as they looked forward to acquiring not only access to brands with global fame, but also knowledge of the latest trends in production and packaging techniques. As a spillover, investments by leading brewers triggered the entry of state-of-the-art equipment manufacturers, such as the German-based Ziemann Group, into India.

However, the major hurdle for achieving high-quality beer seems to be the low quality or lack of consistency in quality of raw materials. Barley produced in India is mostly used as cattle feed (or for human consumption), which allows for more laxity in moisture and nutrient composition and results in grains with variable kernel size and high moisture content (Genier et al. 2008). For beer production, however, a uniform composition (e.g. low protein content) of barley grain is required (FAO 2009). Moreover, Indian barley production has been on the decline (Figure 17.8), supporting claims that, in general, Indian farmers see barley as a non-profitable crop, because of low yields and the lack of price incentives to improve quality.

As a matter of fact the poor quality of domestically produced raw materials prompted APB Breweries to resort in the first instance to malt imported from Australia, hops imported from Europe, and yeast cultured in the Netherlands for the production of their Tiger beer (APB 2008). However, domestic malt production would always be the preferred option, as barley production costs in India

---

[13] Similarly, APBCL, the parastatal company charged with wholesale trade in alcohol, imposes the following quality conditions on purchased beer: (a) freedom from sediments or suspended particles, (b) freedom from any ingredients injurious to health, (c) freedom from added colouring matters except caramel, (d) possession of the relevant characteristic aroma and taste, (e) freedom from coliform bacteria and other pathogenic micro-organisms, and (f) pasteurization. In addition, packaging has to satisfy the Bureau of Indian standards requirements (APBCL 2010).

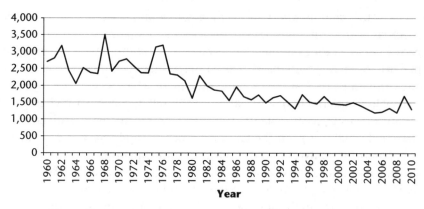

Figure 17.8. Barley production in India (1,000 million tons/year)
Source: United States Department of Agriculture.

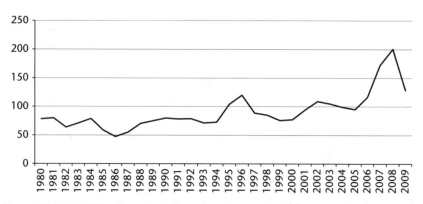

Figure 17.9. World barley prices (Canadian Western No. 1 Spot, US$/million tons)
Source: IMF Primary Commodity Prices.

are considerably lower, and sourcing malt or malt barley from abroad entails a lot of price risk, which is shown, for instance, in the barley price hike in 2007–8 (see Figure 17.9).

In order to ensure quality and security of supply, and to save on import costs, various breweries have started to vertically coordinate with farmers, exactly as has been observed before in Eastern Europe, the former Soviet Union, and even Africa (FAO 2009; Swinnen and Van Herck, Chapter 14 in this volume; World Bank 2006). Vertical coordination implies that breweries set up contracts with local farmers which include input provision (on credit and/or at subsidized rates) and extension, in order to incentivize farmers to produce the desired barley varieties for quality malt production, as well as to raise productivity (GoI 2007).[14]

SABMiller initiated a contract farming programme in 2005 with over 7,000 farmers in 12 districts of Rajasthan to improve the quality and supply of barley. The project, known as 'Sanjhi Unnati' (progress through partnership), involves multiple partners: the brewer (SABMiller), a maltster (Cargill Malt Eurasia), an NGO (Morarka Foundation), and the Rajasthan government. The contracts include a buy-back commitment by SABMiller. Genier et al. (2008) report that only 62% of the farmers who had bought seeds through the programme effectively sold their barley harvest to SABMiller, indicating contract enforcement imperfections. In the short run (as long as low returns to investment do not discourage these support programmes), these imperfections are expected to benefit, rather than to harm, farmers, as they motivate the buyer to increase producer prices (Swinnen and Vandeplas 2009). Indeed, in spite of the extra costs incurred by the company for input provision and extension, SABMiller's contract prices are on average slightly higher than the prices on the traditional wholesale markets ('mandis'), which would be the farmers' most likely alternative marketing channel for selling barley (Genier et al. 2008).

In 2009, SABMiller initiated a similar project involving over 2,500 farmers in Haryana. Other breweries followed suit: in 2006, United Breweries signed a partnership with PepsiCo for contracting out barley production to 1,200 farmers (corresponding to roughly 4,050 hectares of land) in Rajasthan.[15] Currently, SABMiller and United Breweries are procuring around 20% and 10%, respectively, of their barley needs through contract farming. There are reports in the media that South Asia Breweries and Asia Pacific Breweries are in talks with PepsiCo to explore the possibility of sourcing their raw materials through contracts as well (Dogra 2008).

Future Development of the Indian Beer Market

Strong growth is still expected for some time to come in the Indian alcohol market. Increased globalization, international mobility, and high income growth in urban centres has led to the Westernization of Indian diets

[14] The Union Ministry of Food Processing Industries also launched a scheme in 1992–3 for the development of hop production in India under the pretext of saving on foreign exchange (MOFPI 2007b).
[15] PepsiCo India is one of the pioneers in contract farming in India, and is currently contracting out potato and citrus production for its own processing facilities. In a bid to benefit from PepsiCo's expertise, LT Overseas and United Breweries have outsourced management of their production contracts—mainly involving the provision of infrastructure and technical support services—for basmati rice and barley, respectively, to PepsiCo.

(e.g. Pingali 2007). Not only have Western foods such as pasta and cheese gained popularity, but the growing Indian middle class is also increasingly turning to beer and wine (Renuka 2002). Gradually, alcohol seems to have become a basis for social enjoyment, rather than an instrument for intoxication. Moreover, whereas, traditionally, specialized alcohol shops and bars serving alcohol have catered mainly for adult male consumers, social taboos on alcohol consumption by women are slowly fading away, especially in the major cities. In states like Maharashtra, where wines and beers are now also sold in supermarkets, women are increasingly gaining the confidence to buy alcohol (Euromonitor 2009). In other states, governments are also becoming increasingly liberal in allotting licences for alcohol shops, leading to an increased number and diversity of outlets. For example, in 2009, Barista, a major chain of coffee shops in India, announced that they would apply for a licence to sell beer and wine in their coffee lounges in Delhi—taking another step in the direction of promoting the acceptability of alcohol to the general public.

India's climate is a major asset in the development of the beer market, as beer is an ideal drink in hot weather. Statistical data suggest that beer consumption as well as production are peaking in the summer months (from April to June; see Figure 17.10) (United Breweries Limited 2004). Another promising feature of the Indian market is its very young consumer profile: half of India's

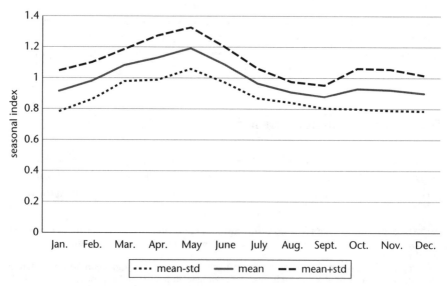

Figure 17.10. Seasonal variation in beer production, 1993–2009
Source: Authors' calculations, based on data from the Central Statistical Organization.

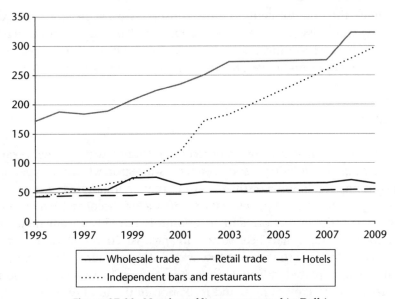

Figure 17.11. Number of licences granted in Delhi
Source: Government of NCT of Delhi (2010). Available at <http://excise.delhigovt.nic.in>.

population is below 25 (US Census Bureau 2009), and it is widely assumed that behavioural changes take place much more swiftly in young societies.

The changing attitude with respect to alcohol consumption is also evident in recent developments on the policy front. The latest Model Excise Policy, drafted by the Ministry of Food Processing Industries (MoFPI) in 2006, envisages a more liberal alcohol distribution system, especially for beverages with moderate alcohol content, such as beer, wine, and ready-to-drink mixes (RTDs) (Government of Haryana 2009).[16] This idea has already been adopted in the latest Excise Policies of several states, leading to a variety of measures such as the elimination of the limit on licences for beer, wine, and RTDs, the introduction of new types of licences (e.g. for wine bars or pub-microbreweries), and a duty structure based on the alcohol content. This trend is visible, for example, in the sharp increase of beer and IMFL retail licences in Delhi, as well as of licences allowing independent bar and restaurants to serve alcohol (see Figure 17.11).

Moreover, the eleventh five-year plan has provisions for the promotion of the wine industry with a view to opportunities for adding value to farm products such as grapes, for income and employment generation, as well as

---

[16] Along these lines, several state excise policies state that one of their policy objectives is 'to wean away people from hard liquor to low content alcohol such as wine and beer by making their availability relatively easier [...]' (Government of Chandigarh 2007; Government of Haryana 2009).

to honour the commitment to shift consumers away from hard liquors (Planning Commission 2008; MOFPI 2006). Similarly, the development of the beer industry holds great potential for linkages with, and increased profitability of, barley farms, as we explained in the previous section.

Conclusion

Given the ambivalent perception of alcohol in Indian society, high taxation levels, stringent regulations, and preferences for stronger drinks, per capita beer consumption in India is still low by international standards. Regulations, involving an amalgam of policy instruments such as licences, high taxes and import duties, FDI restrictions and price controls, have historically moderated the growth of the Indian beer sector. In the past 20 years, the sector has witnessed strong growth due to several waves of deregulation. Further deregulation may be expected, driven, among other factors, by WTO negotiations.

Moreover, high growth rates and relaxation of the rules on foreign direct investment in the last decade have attracted foreign investment in this area, and have led to a large differentiation in the market, with a greater emphasis on quality. This has translated into important shifts in backward linkages in the brewery sector: contract farming schemes are being set up by the major brewers and may significantly benefit local rural development.

In combination with quickly rising incomes and changing attitudes towards alcohol consumption in India, currently observed growth rates may continue in the years ahead, helping India eventually to secure a more prominent position on the global map as far as beer consumption is concerned.

References

AB InBev (Anheuser-Busch InBev) (2007). 'Press Release—Inbev Announces Zone Leadership Changes'. Media Reports, 16 May. Retrieved 2 February 2009 from <http://www.ab-inbev.com/go/media/global_press_releases/press_release.cfm?theID=7&theLang=EN>.

APB (Asia Pacific Breweries) (2008). 'India...It's Tiger Time: Asia Pacific Breweries' Indian Arm launches Tiger Beer in Mumbai', 16 April. Retrieved 3 February 2010 from <http://www.apb.com.sg/newsroom/news_080416.html>.

APBCL (Andhra Pradesh Beverages Corporation Ltd.) (2010). Website. Available at <http://www.apbcl.gov.in>.

Benegal, V., G. Gururaj, and P. Murthy (2003). 'WHO Collaborative Project on Unrecorded Consumption of Alcohol'. Project report by the National Institute of Mental Health and Neurosciences, Bangalore, India, and World Health Organization, Geneva. Available at <http://www.nimhans.kar.nic.in/deaddiction/Publications.html>.

Brown, J. M. (1972). *Gandhi's Rise to Power: Indian Politics 1915–1922*. Cambridge: Cambridge University Press.

Buckland, C. E. (1902). *Bengal under the Lieutenant-Governors: Being a Narrative of the Principal Events and Public Measures during their Periods of Office, from 1854 to 1898*, 2nd edn. Calcutta: Kedarnath Bose. Available at <http://www.archive.org/stream/benga-lunderlieut02buckiala/bengalunderlieut02buckiala_djvu.txt>.

Cassels, Nancy Gardener (2004). 'The East India Company's "Abkarry" and Pilgrim Taxes: Questions of Public Order and Morality or Revenue'. Paper presented at the 18th European Conference on Modern South Asian Studies, at Lund, Sweden, 6–9 July. Available at <http://www.sasnet.lu.se/EASASpapers/22NancyGardner.pdf>.

Central Board of Excise and Customs (2009). 'Beverages, Spirits and Vinegar'. Customs Policy for 2009–10, Chapter 22, Section IV. CBEC, Department of Revenue, Ministry of Finance, Government. Available at <http://www.cbec.gov.in/customs/cst-0910/chap-22.pdf>.

Goyal, S. K., K. S. C. Rao, N. Kumar, A. Nauriya, B. M. Gupta, K. M. Chenoy, K. V. K. Ranganathan, M. R. Murthy, and D. N. Sharma (1983). 'Functioning of Industrial Licensing System: Capacity and Production in Organised Industry'. *Economic and Political Weekly*, 18/18: 694–708.

Dogra, S. (2008). 'Barley Farming the Next Big Thing', 22 May. Retrieved 3 February 2010, from <http://www.business-standard.com/india/news/barley-farmingnext-big-thing/323702/>.

Euromonitor (2009). Beer—India, Country Sector Briefing. Euromonitor International.

European Council (2006). 'Report to the Trade Barriers Regulation Committee', July. Retrieved 3 February 2010 from Examination Report Concerning an Obstacle to Trade, within the Meaning of Council Regulation (EC) No. 3286/94, Consisting of Trade Practices Maintained by India Affecting Trade in Wines and Spirits. Available at <http://trade.ec.europa.eu/doclib/docs/2006/july/tradoc_129462.pdf>.

Evans, T. (1895). 'A Brief Sketch of our Indian Excise Administration'. LSE Selected Pamphlets. Available at <http://www.jstor.org/stable/pdfplus/60221761.pdf>.

FAO (2009). 'Barley—Malt—Beer. Agribusiness Handbook'. Rome, Italy: FAO. Available at <ftp://ftp.fao.org/docrep/fao/012/i1003e/i1003e00.pdf>.

Food Safety and Standards Authority of India (FSSAI) (2009). Draft Food Safety and Standards Rules and Regulations, 2009. Available at <http://www.fssai.gov.in/>.

Gandhi, M. K. (1954). 'On the Eve of Dandi March', in S. Narayan (ed.), *Satyagraha in South Africa*, vol. III. Ahmedabad, Gujarat, India: Navjivan Publishing House.

Genier, C., M. Stamp, and M. Pfitzer (2008). 'Corporate Social Responsibility in the Agri-Food Sector: Harnessing Innovation for Sustainable Development'. Draft report prepared for FAO, Rome, Italy. Available at <http://www.fsg-impact.org/ideas/pdf/CSR in the Agri-food Sector.pdf>.

Government of Chandigarh (2007). Excise Policy of UT, Chandigarh for the year 2007–8, 15 February. Retrieved 3 February 2010 from Department of Public Relations, Chandigarh Administration. Available at <http://admser.chd.nic.in/uploadfiles/press/pressnote/pr1084.pdf>.

Government of Haryana (2009). Excise Policy of the Government of Haryana 2009–10. Retrieved 3 February 2010 from <http://haryanatax.com/Excise/ExcisePolicy09-10.pdf>.

Government of India (GoI) (1980). *Fourth Report of the National Police Commission, Government of India*. Available at <http://bprd.gov.in/writereaddata/mainlinkFile/File848.pdf>.

GoI (2006). Department of Industrial Policy and Promotion. Retrieved 3 February 2010 from Ministry of Commerce and Industry, Government of India. <http://siadipp.nic.in/policy/changes/pn4_2006.pdf>.

—— (2007). Chapter 5: Policy on Fruits and Vegetable Processing Industries. Retrieved 3 February 2010, from Ministry of Food Processing Industries, Government of India. <http://www.mofpi.nic.in/ContentPage.aspx?CategoryId=845>.

Government of Karnataka (2007). Karnataka Grape Processing and Wine Policy, Retrieved 2 February 2010 from Proceedings of the Government of Karnataka. <http://www.karnatakaindustry.gov.in/documents/Karnataka%20Grape%20Processing%20and%20Wine%20Policy%20-%202007.pdf>.

Government of Maharashtra (2008). Maharashtra State Excise Department. Retrieved 2 February 2010, from Maharashtra Government. <http://stateexcise.maharashtra.gov.in/>.

Government of Mizoram (2007). The Mizoram Liquor Total Prohibition (Amendment) Act 2007 (Act No. 4 of 2007), 5 April. Retrieved 3 February 2010, from Acts passed by the Government of Mizoram. <http://mizoram.nic.in/printing/acts/2007/mltpamend2007.pdf>.

Government of NCT of Delhi (2010). Notification F.10(56)/96–97/IMFL/Ex. Office of the Commissioner of Excise, Government of NCT of Delhi, New Delhi.

Government of Punjab (2009). Excise Policy for the Year 2009–10. Retrieved 3 February 2010 from Punjab Government Excise and Taxation Department. <http://www.pextax.com/excise_policy.htm>.

Government of Tamil Nadu (2002). Topic No. 7: State Excise. Retrieved 3 February 2010 from Report of the 12th Finance Commission. <http://www.tn.gov.in/budget/12thfincomm/>.

Hansard (1888). Government of India (Frontier Policy): Resolution. *Official Report of Debates in the UK Parliament, Motions of the Commons Sitting of 13 March 1888*, 3/323: 1093–180. <http://hansard.millbanksystems.com/commons/1888/mar/13/government-of-india-frontier-policy>.

—— (1889). East India (Abkari Department). *Official Report of Debates in the UK Parliament, Motions of the Commons Sitting of 30 April 1889*, 2/335: 817–77. <http://hansard.millbanksystems.com/commons/1889/apr/30/east-india-abkari-department>.

Henson, S., and T. Reardon (2005). 'Private Agri-food Standards: Implications for Food Policy and the Agri-food System'. *Food Policy*, 30/3: 241–53.

Indiastat (2009). *India Statistics—Statistical Analysis, Data Information & Facts about India*. Available at <http://www.indiastat.com/>.

IMF (2009). World Economic Outlook Database, October 2009. Available at <http://www.imf.org/external/data.htm>.

Jacob, Sarah (2010). 'UB to Benefit from Andhra Pradesh's New Beer Policy', 8 July. Retrieved 27 October 2010 from *Economic Times*. <http://economictimes.indiatimes.

com/news/news-by-industry/cons-products/liquor/UB-to-benefit-from-Andhra-Pradeshs-new-beer-policy/articleshow/6140804.cms>.

Kurian, B. (2004). 'Inbev, S&N Vie for UB Stake—"Sale Process Not Connected to Bid for Shaw Wallace"', 8 December. Retrieved 3 February 2010 from The Hindu Business Line. Available at <http://www.thehindubusinessline.com/2004/12/08/stories/2004120802800200.htm>.

Lakshman, N., and A. Carter (2007), 23 April. 'The Great Indian Beer Rush'. *Business-Week*. New York: Bloomberg L.P. <http://www.businessweek.com/magazine/content/07_17/b4031068.htm>.

Mehta, P. S. (2006). *A Functional Competition Policy for India*. Consumer Unity & Trust Society, Centre for Competition, Investment and Economic Regulation. Jaipur, India: Academic Foundation.

MoFPI (Ministry of Food Processing Industries) (2007a). Retrieved 3 February 2010 from Government of India. <http://mofpi.nic.in/ContentPage.aspx?CategoryId=399>.

—— (2007b). Retrieved 3 February 2010 from Government of India. <http://www.mofpi.nic.in/ContentPage.aspx?CategoryId=425>.

—— (2006). Report of the Working Group on Food Processing Sector. Retrieved from Eleventh Five Year Plan. <http://mofpi.nic.in/images/File/Eleventh FYP.pdf>.

Pingali, P. (2007). 'Westernization of Asian Diets and the Transformation of Food Systems: Implications for Research and Policy'. *Food Policy*, 32/3: 281–98.

Planning Commission (1956). Second Five Year Plan. Government of India, Planning Commission, Yojana Bhnavan, New Delhi. Retrieved 3 February 2010. <http://planningcommission.nic.in/plans/planrel/fiveyr/welcome.html>.

—— (1961). Third Five Year Plan. Government of India, Planning Commission, Yojana Bhavan, New Delhi. Available at <http://planningcommission.nic.in/plans/planrel/fiveyr/welcome.html>.

—— (2008). 'Agriculture, Rural Development, Industry, Services, and Physical Infrastructure'. Retrieved 3 February 2010 from Volume III, Eleventh Five Year Plan 2007–12. <http://planningcommission.nic.in/plans/planrel/fiveyr/11th/11_v3/11th_vol3.pdf>.

Pryor, A. (2009). *Indian Pale Ale: An Icon of Empire*. Milton Keynes: The Open University, Walton Hall.

Rahman, L. (2003). 'Alcohol Prohibition and Addictive Consumption in India'. Paper presented at the Second Annual Postgraduate Conference, hosted by the Leverhulme Centre for Research on Globalisation and Economic Policy (GEP), University of Nottingham, 10 April. Available at <http://globalisationandeconomicpolicy.org/shared/shared_levevents/conferences/2003_PG_Rahman_paper.pdf>.

Reddy, D. N., and A. Patnaik (1993). 'Anti-arrack Agitation of Women in Andhra Pradesh'. *Economic and Political Weekly*, 28/21: 1059–66.

Renuka, M. (2002). 'Ready for the Fizz'. *India Today*, 22 April. <http://www.india-today.com/itoday/20020422/business.shtml>.

Rose, J. H., A. P. Newton, E. A. Benians, and H. Dodwell (1929). *The Cambridge History of the British Empire*. Cambridge: Cambridge University Press.

Saxena, S. (1999). 'Country Profile on Alcohol in India', in L. Riley and M. Marshall (eds.), *Alcohol and Public Health in Eight Developing Countries*. Geneva: WHO, 37–60.

Singh, N. K. (ed.) (2003). *Encyclopaedia of Bangladesh*, vol. 21: *Public Administration in Bangladesh*. Delhi, India: Anmol Publications Pvt. Ltd.

Supreme Court of India (1997). *Bihar Distillery and ANR v Union of India and Ors*, 29 January 1997. Retrieved 3 February 2010 from <http://www.indiankanoon.org/doc/883373/>.

Swinnen, J., and A. Vandeplas (2009). 'Rich Consumers and Poor Producers: Quality and Rent Distribution in Global Value Chains'. IFPRI Discussion Paper 932, Washington. Available at <http://www.ifpri.org/sites/default/files/publications/ifpridp00932.pdf>.

United Breweries Limited (2004). Letter of Offer to the Equity Shareholders of the Company. Available at <http://www.sebi.gov.in/dp/ublfinal.pdf>.

Unnikrishnan, C. (2008). 'UBL, SAB Miller Sue AP Govt on Beer Price'. *Wall Street Journal*, 15 November. Retrieved 3 February 2010 from Livemint. <http://www.livemint.com/2008/11/14234417/UBL-SAB-Miller-sue-AP-govt-on.html>.

US Census Bureau (2009). International Data Base (IDB). Available at <http://www.census.gov/ipc/www/idb/index.php>.

WHO (2004). *Global Status Report on Alcohol 2004*. Geneva: World Health Organization. Available at <http://www.who.int/substance_abuse/publications/global_status_report_2004_overview.pdf>.

World Bank (2006). 'Market Linkages in the Slovak Agri-Food Sector'. Environmentally and Socially Sustainable Development Unit, Europe and Central Asia Region, Working Paper 43. Washington: World Bank. Available at <http://siteresources.worldbank.org/INTSLOVAKIA/Resources/MarketLinkages.pdf>.

World Trade Organization (2010). 'India—Certain Taxes and Other Measures on Imported Wines and Spirits', January. Retrieved from Dispute Settlement: Dispute DS380. Available at <http://www.wto.org/english/tratop_e/dispu_e/cases_e/ds380_e.htm>.

Part V
Conclusion

18

Beeronomics: The Economics of Beer and Brewing

Johan F. M. Swinnen and Thijs Vandemoortele

The chapters in this book demonstrate that 'beeronomics' covers a vast set of economic issues: economic history, development, demand and supply, geography, trade, investment, technology, health and nutrition, quantity and quality, industrial organization, competition, science and innovation, taxation, regulation, political economy, and so on. This concluding chapter summarizes some of the key insights of this book, organized in five sections: a historical perspective on the product 'beer', consumption, industrial organization, trade and international expansion, and government regulation. In a final section, we discuss a set of unresolved issues and a future research agenda in the field of beeronomics.

Beer: What's in a Name?

Throughout history, different types of alcoholic beverages that were made from a whole range of ingredients have been labelled 'beer'. Both technological innovations and changes in consumer preferences have caused important changes in the type of 'beer' consumed. In ancient civilizations, beer was not filtered and people drank it directly from large jars through straws in order to avoid gross sediment (Hornsey 2003). Until the Middle Ages, the preservation and taste of beer were enhanced by adding a mixture of spices to the brewing process—so-called 'grut'. A major innovation was the use of hops in the brewing process. It allowed better preservation and also changed the taste. A few centuries later, several scientific discoveries changed the brewing, transport, and marketing of beer. These included the discovery of yeast, and the invention of glass bottles and cooling equipment. A major change occurred in the nineteenth century with the development of 'lager beers'. Until then, beer was brewed using a 'top-fermentation' process, in which yeast rose to the top of the fermenting brew. A new beer production process used a 'bottom-fermentation' process, in which yeast sinks to the bottom of the brewing vessel. 'Lager' beer was clearer than the ales that then existed. Since lager beer of a consistent and reliable quality could be produced throughout the year, it gained market share at the cost of traditional ales, and came to dominate the beer market globally. However, other types of beer remained popular in some European regions, such as Belgium, Ireland, England, and Bavaria (Poelmans and Swinnen, Chapter 1 in this volume).

During the first half of the twentieth century, several grain shortages and high grain prices caused US brewers to brew beer of lower alcohol content and to use cheaper substitutes for barley. The resulting lager beers were lighter in colour and were therefore called 'light lager' or 'American lager' beer. By the end of World War II, 'light lager' had gained a major share of the North American beer market and US consumers had become used to drinking it (Rabin and Forget 1998).

Later in the twentieth century, 'diet' or 'light' beers were developed in response to a growing demand for low calorie drinks. Light beer has been a great success in the US, but much less so in other countries. In 2005, it was the most popular beer category in the US (Tremblay and Tremblay 2005).

Since the 1980s, consumers in the US have shown a renewed interest in 'older' beer styles, such as porter, pale ales and brown cask ales, stout and bitters. This phenomenon is known as the 'microbrewery movement', since many of these beer styles were initially produced by new small-scale producers (Tremblay and Tremblay, Chapter 8 in this volume). Similar trends in consumer preferences can now be observed in many European countries, where there is renewed consumer interest in—and growing production of—a wide variety of non-lager beers (see the section on microbreweries).

Consumption

Global beer consumption is much higher than consumption of any other alcoholic drink, not only in terms of volume, but also in value terms, and the gap is growing. In 2007, the value of global beer consumption was around 112 billion euros, compared to 55 billion euros for wines and 94 billion euros for spirits and other alcoholic drinks. Not surprisingly, beer consumption varies considerably across countries and over time. Production and trade conditions for beers and its substitutes, as well as government regulation, have been important determinants of consumption patterns.

Traces of beer drinking have been found all over the world since several millennia BC.[1] In parts of North Africa and Europe, beer consumption gave way to wine during the Greek and Roman Empires when viticulture spread. During the Middle Ages and the Renaissance period, beer consumption grew, especially in northern, central, and western European regions. Beer consumption was at historically high levels in the fifteenth and sixteenth centuries because of income growth, urbanization, and increased health concerns with consumption of polluted water. Estimates put average beer consumption at between 200 to 400 litres per person per year for various towns in (what is now) Belgium, the Netherlands, and Germany (Unger 2001). These numbers are much higher than current beer consumption levels—which are around 80 to 100 litres per capita per year on average for these countries (Colen and Swinnen, Chapter 7 in this volume).

Beer consumption declined strongly from the seventeenth century with the arrival of new substitute products. Substitutes came through trade from newly colonized territories (e.g. tea, coffee) and from technological innovations in distilling (e.g. large-scale production of spirits such as gin, jenever, whisky, etc.) and in carbonating water (e.g. soda water and later soft drinks such as Coca-Cola) (see Unger, Chapter 2; Poelmans and Swinnen, Chapter 1, both in this volume).

With scientific breakthroughs allowing large-scale production of lager beer and the Industrial Revolution causing income growth, beer consumption increased significantly during the nineteenth and most of the twentieth centuries. Growth in beer consumption in the twentieth century was interrupted by the two world wars in Europe and by Prohibition in the US.

Over the past 25 years, consumption has shown markedly different evolutions among countries. Consumption per capita is still highest in Western and Central Europe, but has declined strongly over the past two decades in traditional beer-drinking nations in Europe and the US. For example, per capita consumption has declined by between 14% and 30% in Germany, Belgium, the US, and the UK since 1980. In contrast, there has been tremendous growth in per capita beer consumption in emerging countries such as China, Russia, Brazil, and India. A remarkable example of strong growth in beer consumption is the 'perfect storm' in the Russian beer market (Deconinck and Swinnen, Chapter 16 in this volume). Although Russia was traditionally a vodka-drinking country, per capita beer consumption increased more than fivefold between 1996 and 2007. A combination of rising incomes, an increase in the real price of vodka together with a decrease in the real price of beer, quality improvements by foreign investors, a ban on vodka commercials, and

---

[1] Archaeological findings show that Chinese villagers drank beer from 7000BC and that in North Africa traces of beer-brewing activities go back to the sixth millennium BC.

aggressive beer advertising led to the growing popularity of beer consumption, in particular among younger generations.

Similarly, per capita beer consumption in China has grown rapidly since 1980 thanks to increasing average household incomes, rural–urban migration, the constant real price of beer, and the increasing popularity of eating out (Bai et al., Chapter 15 in this volume). Since 2003, China has been the largest beer market (in volume), ahead of the US. However, Chinese per capita beer consumption is still three times lower than that of spirits, and considerably lower than per capita beer consumption in Western and Central Europe and the US. Hence, as in the other emerging countries, there remains huge potential for additional growth.

Various chapters in this volume show that the determinants of beer consumption and, in particular, the effect of income are complex. Freeman (Chapter 6) studies beer consumption in economic recessions. Psychological theories have suggested that, during recessions, beer consumption rises in response to the stress of an economic downturn, while economy theory predicts that consumption should fall as income falls. Freeman's research, based on US data, shows that beer consumption is a normal good (i.e. its consumption increases with income) and behaves pro-cyclically when one controls for (changes in) age distribution and different consumption habits per age group. Beer consumption increases when income increases, and decreases during recessions, i.e. with higher unemployment and lower incomes. Yet, although statistically significant, the economic significance of this pro-cyclical behaviour is weak at best.

These findings are consistent with many studies finding positive but low income elasticities, reviewed in Colen and Swinnen (Chapter 7). However, in their analysis, Colen and Swinnen show that both across and within countries, the relation between income and per capita beer consumption is not constant but displays an inverted-U shape. Hence, at low levels of income, income growth leads to more consumption of beer, while at higher levels of income, income growth reduces per capita beer consumption.

In addition, they find that, in 'traditional beer-drinking nations', trade openness reduces the share of beer in total alcohol consumption as the availability of wine increases. In fact, they document a convergence in alcohol consumption patterns between these different types of countries, i.e. countries that were traditionally mostly beer, wine, or spirits drinkers. Other factors such as climate, (state) religion, and the relative price of beer also determine beer consumption.

Finally, consumer preferences and incomes affect not only the total level of consumption, but also the nature of the beer. For example, preferences for low calorie beers have induced a strong growth in 'light beers', especially in the US. In recent years, increased consumer demand for more variation and specialty beers has induced strong growth of craft beers in the US and Europe (Tremblay and Tremblay, Chapter 8). In contrast, consumer preferences in China are substantially different from those in traditional Western beer-drinking countries. Chinese beer consumers typically prefer large quantities of undifferentiated, light beer with low-alcohol content and at low price—'cheaper than water' (Bai et al., Chapter 15). These preferences partially explain why foreign firms had and still have difficulties penetrating the Chinese beer market with their high-quality Western-style beers at premium rates.

Several chapters in this volume present evidence that consumer preferences for beers are not stable, but can be influenced by income (see above), by advertising (George , Chapter 12), by social networks, i.e. peers' consumption behaviour (McCluskey and Shreay, Chapter 9; Deconinck and Swinnen, Chapter 16), and by new experiences. New experiences may be induced by technological innovations (e.g. lager beers), government regulation (e.g. the British ban on wine imports—see Nye, Chapter 4), experiences of other cultures (McCluskey and Shreay, Chapter 9), or industry responses to shortages (e.g. American lager in the US in the mid-twentieth century—Tremblay and Tremblay 2005).

Industrial Organization

A crucial component of beeronomics is the industrial organization of the brewing industry. There are various aspects to this: the shift from households to monasteries to commercial companies as the dominant organizations of brewing; growing consolidation over time; the recent search for diversity and experience and the revival of small breweries; and vertical coordination in the brewing industry—both upstream and downstream. We will discuss each of these in this section.

From Households to Monasteries to Commercial Breweries

For millennia—from 7000 BC to the eighth century AD—beer brewing was mostly done in the household, like the preparation of food. Women played an important role as they were responsible for the domestic chores and thus also for preparing food and brewing beer. An important change came around AD 800 and in particular during the rule of Charlemagne. Under his rule, Christian monasteries spread over Europe and became 'centres of brewing'. Initially, most monasteries were located in Southern Europe where the climate allowed viticulture. The expansion of Charlemagne's empire to Northern Europe supported the spread of monasteries, which switched to brewing beer because of the cooler climate.

This lasted for several centuries until the twelfth and thirteenth centuries when income growth and the development of trade and urbanization induced an increase in demand for beer, which, in turn, induced the growth of commercial breweries. Two other factors played an important role as well. Technological innovation, in particular the role of hops in beer conservation, dramatically changed the process of brewing. In addition, government preferences and regulation were important. Until the arrival of hops, beer was flavoured and preserved with grut, a combination of herbs, which breweries had to buy from their local ruler, who used it to tax breweries indirectly. Because the advent of hops undermined this tax revenue, local rulers gradually switched to imposing direct beer taxes. However, since monasteries enjoyed exemptions on these direct beer taxes, local rulers favoured commercial breweries and the role of monasteries as centres of brewing started to decline.

From the fourteenth century, commercial breweries became dominant. During the Reformation in the early sixteenth century when the power of the Catholic Church diminished, the role of monasteries as brewing centres declined further. A final blow to monastery brewing was dealt by the French Revolution. During the revolution many European monasteries were destroyed and the monks chased away. Beer brewing was no longer a priority for the remaining monks, and commercial breweries took their place.

While commercial brewing has dominated the beer industry ever since, 'monastery beers' have made a remarkable recovery in recent years. Trappist beers, brewed by Cistercian monks, are a famous type of Belgian abbey beers. They regularly obtain top scores in international competitions and have seen significant commercial growth in recent years. In addition, large commercial breweries have started producing 'abbey beers' to profit from this new demand. Also some of the recently established microbreweries copy the monks' traditional brewing techniques and ingredients to brew their craft beers.

Consolidation

As soon as brewing shifted to commercial companies, economies of scale and, with it, the optimality of large versus small breweries became important issues. Since the sixteenth century, technological improvements and increasing fuel prices required brewers to make substantive investments in fixed capital, for example, the copper brewing kettle. The indivisibility of this unit in brewing induced breweries to increase production so as to reap potential economies of scale. Additionally high urban land prices, rising raw material costs, costly provision of clean water, and controlling the risk of fire induced a shift to larger breweries.

Ever since, the scale of breweries gradually increased. However, the dramatic consolidation of the beer industry and rapid scale increases occurred only in the twentieth century. World War I triggered important changes. During the war, many breweries in occupied territories (e.g. Belgium, France) and in Germany closed down due to a shortage of employees and inputs, and the removal of equipment by occupying forces. After the war, these breweries needed substantive investments to reopen. This induced smaller breweries to close down or to merge with larger brewers who could afford the required investments in re-equipment and modernization of the breweries. This process also allowed the large-scale introduction of the bottom-fermentation process, which increased scale economies and concentration further.

Since the end of World War II, the number of brewers has been sharply declining worldwide through massive consolidation and concentration in the beer-brewing industry. Part of this consolidation occurred through a shakeout of small local brewers, but a substantial share was accounted for through mergers and acquisitions by the largest players in the beer market. The consolidation and concentration process of the brewing industry in the 1950s and 1960s was driven by technological progress that enabled the automation of brewing and the acceleration of packaging. These innovations implied larger economies of scale, increased brewers' minimum efficient scale, and forced smaller brewers to quit, or to merge with or acquire other breweries (Adams, Chapter 13).

A very important factor in the dramatic consolidation in the European and US beer markets in the 1950–2000 period has been the changes in mass media, particularly the growth of commercial TV. In her fascinating research, Lisa George (Chapter 12) shows the dramatic impact of the spread of commercial TV on the spectacular shakeout of many regional and local brewers and the subsequent high concentration in the US beer industry. From its earliest days, commercial television has been heavily used by the beer industry to advertise. The spread of commercial television lowered the costs of transmitting information to consumers. The indivisibility of the television market induced breweries to consolidate in order to acquire larger geographic areas and lower advertisement costs per consumer, and to benefit from economies of scale. Small (local) breweries either quit or were overtaken by large (regional and national) brewing companies. Additionally, the large sunk investments in television advertising served as an entry barrier that protected national brewers from new competitors.

The commercial TV factor can explain why extreme consolidation occurred much earlier in the US than in Europe. Commercial television was introduced in the early post-war period and spread fast in the US, followed by strong consolidation in the beer industry in the 1960s and 1970s. In Europe, the spread of commercial television took place much later. Until the early 1990s, TV media was totally dominated by state TV channels which did not allow advertising. The spread of commercial TV with advertising only took off in the 1990s and 2000s—the period characterized by strong consolidation in breweries.

To date, the German beer sector is still less concentrated, not only than the US but also than other European countries. A combination of different factors explains this difference (Adams, Chapter 13). Due to both strict regulations on brewing ingredients (the German 'Reinheitsgebot'), which reduced beer's shelf life, and the government's promotion of reusable bottles, which are more costly to transport than cans, scale-augmenting packaging technologies were adopted to a lesser extent by German brewers than, say, brewers in the US, where the use of cans was supported by law. This prevented Germany's larger breweries benefiting from economies of scale and related transportation cost advantages. In addition, the German tied-house system (a contract between a retailer and a brewer which requires the retailer to sell only beer from that brewer) reduced the likelihood of a shakeout of small producers. In combination, these factors led to a lower concentration of breweries in Germany than in other countries.

Similarly, the Chinese brewery sector is at present relatively less concentrated, but for a different reason than for Germany. After China's economic reforms in the 1970s, breweries served as status symbols for China's counties and provided employment as well as tax revenues. For that reason, each county had one or more breweries, which were, as a consequence, small and inefficient. Therefore, until the 1990s, the Chinese brewery industry was marked by low concentration. However, even in the 1990s, when foreign investors tried (but failed—see below) to penetrate the Chinese beer market by capturing national Chinese brands, consolidation did not take off. Only in the last decade have branding and advertising expenditures grown, requiring larger sunk investments and providing benefits of scale. Consolidation, mainly through mergers and acquisitions, is now growing in China, but not yet to the same extent as in other beer-producing countries (Bai et al., Chapter 15).

Microbreweries

The growing domination of increasingly standardized lager and light beers contributed to an increasingly concentrated beer market, which, in turn, led to a countermovement—the 'microbrewery movement' (Tremblay and Tremblay, Chapter 8). The first microbreweries were established in the US at the end of the 1970s, but there was a real surge of microbreweries in the 1990s and 2000s. In Europe, where strong consolidation in the beer sector occurred (much) later, this phenomenon is more recent. Microbreweries are typically small-scale firms, offer a variety of different, high-quality beers, and adhere to old European brewing traditions (Tremblay and Tremblay, Chapter 8). They contrast with large-scale 'macrobreweries' that take advantage of scale economies and produce homogeneous, lager beers.

The importance of the microbrewery segment is illustrated by the fact that, in recent years, for the first time in centuries, the number of breweries has increased again in traditional beer markets, such as the US and Belgium. This increase is mainly driven by the upsurge of microbreweries (Tremblay and Tremblay, Chapter 8; Persyn et al., Chapter 5). Several factors have contributed to the success of microbreweries. Increasing consumer income has created a larger demand for variety, prestige, and local products—characteristics which craft beers offer. Consolidation led to a decrease in the number of varieties and breweries. Additionally, microbreweries face lower transportation costs and are more flexible at adapting to changing tastes and preferences.

Growth in the microbrewery segment is strong. From 1977 to 2009, the number of US craft brewers grew from two to over 1,700 brewers (Tremblay and Tremblay, Chapter 8). By the beginning of the twenty-first century, the microbrewery segment accounted for 5–7% of the total US beer market (Poelmans and Swinnen, Chapter 1). In Europe, too, growth has been strong in recent years. For example, in Belgium, abbey beers are the fastest-growing segment of the Belgian beer market (Persyn et al., Chapter 5).

Competition between the macro- and microbrewery segments is limited, since they offer beer of different styles and at different price levels. In fact, US microbreweries were initially 'contract breweries', i.e. they outsourced production to macrobreweries and benefited from those macrobreweries' overcapacity in production. Despite limited inter-segment competition, macrobreweries have reacted to the microbrewery countermovement by developing their own craft- and abbey-style brands in order to benefit from the brand image, and by participating in microbreweries. The latter benefit from this participation as it provides them with access to macrobreweries' distribution system.

Where the process of consolidation in the large macrobrewery segment during the second half of the twentieth century was supported by the spread of television, the growth of small-scale microbreweries has been promoted by different media, such as the internet (George, Chapter 12). The internet allows better targeting of individuals with particular tastes and lowers the cost of aggregating individuals based on preferences. Additionally, order-placing through the internet allows the traditional distribution channels that favour large brewers to be circumvented. Hence, where television created consolidation, the internet allows for lower minimum efficient scales and supports the activities of small microbreweries.

Vertical Coordination

An important economic and policy issue in the beer industry is the role of vertical coordination, both upstream and downstream. Breweries have tried to influence beer sales by vertically integrating with the trade and retail sale of beer.

DOWNSTREAM

On the downstream, retail side of the brewing sector, vertical coordination is common practice (Slade, Chapter 10). Examples are resale price maintenance (the brewer sets the minimum, maximum, or exact price a retailer can charge), exclusive dealing ('tied houses'—requires the retailer to sell only the brewer's beers), exclusive territories (the brewer assigns a geographic market to each retailer), quantity forcing (the retailer must purchase a minimum amount of beer), and tying products (selling a product to a retailer only if that retailer purchases another product as well). Brewers may have both efficiency and market power motives to impose such vertical restrictions on their retailers. On the one hand, these restraints may enhance efficiency by preventing retailers' free-riding on other dealers' services and by getting rid of double marginalization.[2] On the other hand, they may increase market power by facilitating collusion at some link in the supply chain, and by creating an exclusive distribution network that makes competitors' entry more difficult and costly.

One of these vertical practices, the 'tied-house' contract, is or was widespread in several countries. Under such contracts, a retailer or bar owner buys beer exclusively from one specific brewer, while that brewer provides the retailer or bar owner with inputs (equipment, credit, etc.) at below-market prices (Adams, Chapter 13). The system provides brewers with a guaranteed sales outlet, and allows retailers or bars to overcome financial constraints.

The impact of these vertical arrangements on concentration in the industry is complex. Adams (Chapter 13) argues that the tied-house system in Germany reduced the likelihood of a shakeout of small brewers due to short-term foreclosure effects. The system also serves as a vehicle for long-term brand image development as an alternative to television.

However, in the UK brewery sector, the tied-house system had the opposite impact on concentration because of limited entry in the retail market. During the eighteenth century, the British government limited the number of bars by requiring bar owners to obtain a licence from their local authority. Consequently, once all bars had become tied houses, changes in the distribution structure had to take place mainly through mergers and acquisitions at the level of the brewers. This interaction between the tied-house system and the licence-to-open regulation supported the creation of an oligopoly in the British brewing sector (Nye, Chapter 4).

Some governments have forbidden the use of the tied-house system. For example, in the US, most states prohibited tied-house contracts after the

---

[2] Double marginalization occurs when both brewer and retailer exercise market power and sell at a price above marginal cost—the final price is then higher than what would maximize joint profits (see Slade, Chapter 10).

repeal of Prohibition in 1933. The absence of tied houses in the US opened the door for an escalation of sunk (television) advertising costs, which led to a shakeout of small brewers and a highly concentrated US beer industry. Interestingly, governments in some European regions prohibited tied-house-type contracts and retail activities by brewers in the Middle Ages and the Renaissance period not because of competition concerns but to control tax evasion by the breweries (Unger 2004).

UPSTREAM
Upstream, brewing companies have at times set up vertically coordinated systems to organize the supply of essential inputs. For example, in the Middle Ages, brewers organized themselves and vertically coordinated with the shipping industries to ship clean water to their breweries (Unger, Chapter 2). In recent times, the absence of malt and other supplies of required quality and consistency induced foreign investors, after taking over local breweries, in Eastern Europe, India, and China, to set up supply chains to secure these inputs (Swinnen and Van Herck, Chapter 14; Arora et al., Chapter 17). Often, these foreign brewers first tried to deal with local shortages by importing inputs from their traditional suppliers abroad. However, logistical problems, import restrictions, and exchange rate fluctuations typically induced companies to establish contracting schemes with local companies and grain farmers. To secure the supply of high-quality barley and malt, brewers provided local farmers and malting companies with technical assistance, credit, and high-quality inputs, for example seeds.

Trade and International Expansion

Trade

Trade in beer is costly because it is a voluminous product, consisting mainly of water. That is why trade in beer has traditionally been limited to neighbouring regions. As a consequence, expansion of brewing companies occurs mostly through mergers, acquisitions, and brewing licences for in-country production of foreign beers rather than actual trade of beer.

Despite these constraints, trade in beer has grown substantially in volume and value in the past two decades. For example, US beer imports increased from around 0.5 billion litres in 1980 to 3.5 billion litres in 2007 (Tremblay and Tremblay, Chapter 8). Belgian beer exports more than quadrupled from less than 250 million litres in 1980 to more than 1 billion litres in 2007 (Persyn et al., Chapter 5). In this way, trade has grown as strongly as global production. (In other words, the share of trade in total production has stayed roughly constant.) As Colen and Swinnen (Chapter 7) show, increased trade openness is correlated with substantial changes in beer consumption globally and seems to contribute to converging patterns of alcohol consumption.

International Mergers and Investments

Until the early 1990s, consolidation was mostly in domestic markets, but this has since changed dramatically. Consolidation in the beer industry at the international level was marked by large takeovers. Currently, the global beer market is dominated by a few multinational players. Probably the best illustration of this process is the company AB InBev. In a mere 20 years, AB InBev has grown from two small Belgian breweries (Piedboeuf and Artois Breweries, producing respectively 70 and 350 million litres in 1971) to become the largest brewing holding in the world, owning breweries all over the world, producing 36.5 billion litres, about one-quarter of global beer consumption (Persyn et al., Chapter 5). Several factors seem to have played a role.

First, the decline in consumption in traditional 'beer-drinking nations' induced a search by their local brewing companies for expansion abroad. Second, the fall of the Berlin Wall in 1989 opened up a vast market consisting of traditional beer countries, with capital-constrained breweries which were offered for sale in the privatization process in Eastern Europe. The Eastern European beer market constituted an attractive investment opportunity for West European breweries because of its strong beer tradition, high beer consumption levels, relatively high incomes, and geographical and cultural proximity to Western Europe. Additionally, Eastern European brewers faced lower production costs but strong capital constraints, and their brewing facilities were in need of major upgrading. Because of import restrictions and limited demand for foreign beers, acquisitions rather than exporting or licensing turned out to be the optimal strategy to penetrate the Eastern European market (Arnold et al. 2000; Marinov and Marinova 2001). Between 1991 and 2005, a vast proportion of the Central and Eastern European breweries were bought by Western companies such as AB InBev, Heineken, SABMiller, and the Carlsberg Group. By 2009, the market leader in all countries in the region (except Slovenia and Belarus) was a foreign investor, and in almost all countries the combined market share of foreign investors exceeded 50% (Swinnen and Van Herck, Chapter 14).

This process of global consolidation through acquisitions and mergers spread from Eastern Europe to other parts of the world, in particular North and South America and Asia. The huge potential for growth in the Chinese and Indian beer markets has stimulated major investments, takeovers, and joint ventures by Western companies (Arora et al., Chapter 17; Bai et al., Chapter 15).

Several mergers have also occurred between European and American companies, starting with the takeover of Labatt, the premier Canadian-US brewer by Interbrew in 1995. Later Interbrew and AmBev, Brazil's largest brewer, merged into InBev, which in 2008 took over Anheuser-Busch to form the current AB InBev. During the same period, Miller merged with Coors and later SAB to form SABMiller; and Heineken acquired the Mexican brewer FEMSA. The result has been a dramatic consolidation at the global level: the world's four biggest brewing companies (AB InBev, SABMiller, Heineken, and Carlsberg Group) now account for over half of the global beer production. Another illustration of these dramatic changes is the fact that in 2010 the largest US-owned brewery was Boston Breweries—a company which a few years earlier was still considered a 'microbrewery' (Tremblay and Tremblay, Chapter 8).

Foreign Investment and Ownership

In summary, there appear to be several 'models' of global integration. The first model is that of traditional beer-consuming countries, where the decline in local consumption induced the main brewing companies to search for export markets for growth. Examples are Belgium, with AB InBev, and the Netherlands, with Heineken.

The second model is that of traditional beer-consuming countries, where the main breweries have been taken over by foreign companies. Examples are the US, Canada, and Eastern European countries. The reasons for this are not always the same. In Eastern Europe, for example, the liberalization and privatization process offered weakly capitalized companies in large beer markets—a unique opportunity for foreign companies. In other countries (e.g. the US), companies have been less export oriented because of continued growth on their domestic markets.

The third model is that of new (and large) growth markets, such as China, India, and Russia, which have attracted much interest from foreign brewers in the past 20 years. However, the foreign companies' success at investing in these three markets and the resulting market structure have differed significantly. In Russia, much as in Eastern Europe, with privatization the vast majority of brewing companies were taken over by foreign investors. The Russian market is now dominated by five large international brewers: Carlsberg Group, AB InBev, Heineken, Anadolu Efes, and to a lesser extent SABMiller (Deconinck and Swinnen, Chapter 16).

In India, foreign investors have been able to capture an important share of the market since the economic liberalization started and foreign investments were allowed, but the largest brewing company (Kingfisher) remains firmly in Indian hands.

In China, the opening of the beer market attracted much interest in the 1990s and significant foreign investments through joint ventures with Chinese companies. Typically, foreign investors put a strong emphasis on providing high-quality beer. However, this strong focus on quality and premium beers has been one reason why FDI failed in China at the beginning of the 1990s (Bai et al., Chapter 15). Besides management and marketing issues, the price strategy of demanding high-price premiums for high-quality beer was unsuccessful, since Chinese consumers prefer cheap, light beer in large quantities. In combination with the specific characteristics of the early foreign joint ventures (foreign investors' ownership share was limited to 49% of the joint venture; and labour management was restricted under strict labour regulations), this led to the failure of the initial foreign investments in Chinese beer companies. Local breweries, however, have learned from foreign technologies and have since grown rapidly. While foreign breweries have invested again in recent years, the Chinese beer market is dominated by Chinese breweries. The top ten largest Chinese and foreign firms in China produce respectively 46% and 19% of Chinese beer consumption.

Finally, Germany is, again, the exception to these models. Germany, a traditional beer market, has been characterized by limited external expansion by German brewers and by low FDI inflows. Since the sixteenth century, beer production in Germany has been subject to stringent purity regulations, although imports have been exempt since 1987 (van Tongeren, Chapter 3). Hence penetrating the German beer market with foreign brands that typically do not comply with these purity requirements is only possible through imports, not through FDI, and this only from 1987 onwards. Additionally, the factors that caused a lack of consolidation in the German market (see previous section) meant, on the one hand, that there were no large breweries looking for foreign expansion and, on the other, that the German breweries were less attractive to foreign investors.[3]

Government Regulation

Throughout history, governments have been heavily involved in the beer market. Since the early days of commercial brewing, governments have regulated the brewing industry for a variety of reasons and through a large set of different instruments. Important reasons for government regulation were (a) taxation; (b) protection of local brewers' interests; (c) market power concerns;

---

[3] One exception to this is Beck's, Germany's number one export beer, which was acquired by AB InBev (then Interbrew) in 2002.

and (d) health concerns. In this section, we discuss some government regulations and how they have shaped the beer and brewing sector.

Taxes and Government Revenues

As is demonstrated in the historical analyses in this book, taxes on beer have for centuries been a major source of tax revenue—sometimes staggeringly high—for some European governments. For example, around 50% of the UK government's revenues in the eighteenth century consisted of beer taxes and wine tariffs. From the fourteenth to the seventeenth centuries, taxes on beer made up a substantial share of towns' income in the Low Countries as well—frequently above 50% and in some cases even up to almost 90% (Unger 2004). Beer taxes thus had major implications for government activities. For example, Nye (Chapter 4) argues that excise taxes on beer provided the British government with large revenues to sustain its activities during international wars and expansion. The large beer taxes had other consequences as well.

First, there are instances where governments prevented the diffusion of an innovation because it endangered their tax base. For example, during the Middle Ages, before hops were used, beer was flavoured and preserved with grut, a combination of herbs. Breweries had to buy grut from the local ruler, who used it to tax breweries indirectly. Brewing was only allowed when a licence to use grut, the 'Grutrecht', had been obtained. The discovery of hops as a better preservative threatened this tax revenue and therefore hops were banned in many regions for a long time. For example, while the use of hops was already known in Germany around AD 800, its use was forbidden in Holland until the fourteenth century and in England until the fifteenth century. Once the Grutrecht no longer generated sufficient tax revenues, local rulers started imposing taxes directly on beer (Unger 2004; Poelmans and Swinnen, Chapter 1).

Second, governments have tried to increase taxes by regulating the structure of the beer industry. For example, the British government promoted increasing concentration in the beer sector for tax purposes. It implemented laws that limited entry into the brewing industry and restricted retail sales. Together with the threat of removing tariffs on French wine imports in case of tax evasion, the oligopolistic structure of the brewing industry facilitated the collection of high excise taxes on beer and allowed brewers to shift the tax burden onto consumers. Similarly, in the second half of the sixteenth century, town authorities in the Low Countries repealed output restrictions to allow consolidation to take place in the beer industry, which, in turn, made surveillance and tax collection easier for the authorities.

Third, beer taxes may have changed an entire nation's preferences for beer. For example, before the Anglo-French war of 1689–1714, Britain imported large quantities of cheap wine from France. During the war, trade between Britain and France was completely disrupted. In the absence of French wine as a cheap substitute, Britain's domestic beer industry flourished. After the Anglo-French war, the brewing industry successfully lobbied the British government to impose almost prohibitive tariffs on French wine. The fact that these tariffs were set by volume effectively excluded cheap French wine—beer's most competitive substitute. At the same time, the British government set high excise taxes on beer which generated massive government revenues: wine tariff revenues and beer excise taxes made up half of the British government's revenue. Compliance by the brewing industry was assured by the threat of lowering import tariffs on wine, and by the oligopolistic structure of the British beer sector which considerably facilitated tax collection and allowed brewers to shift the tax burden onto consumers. The taxes and tariffs had long-term consequences in terms of shaping British consumer preferences, since the British masses collectively turned to beer as their most important alcoholic beverage (Nye, Chapter 4).

Quality and Protectionism

Throughout history, governments have also aimed to regulate the 'quality' of beer and its contents. One example is the German Reinheitsgebot (purity law), originally a Bavarian beer law from 1516, which is one of the oldest food laws that still exists today, albeit with several adjustments (van Tongeren, Chapter 3). Similar regulations were introduced across Europe (Unger 2004). These laws laid down which ingredients were allowed to be used during the brewing process, and often stipulated beer prices. The laws' aim was said to be to protect consumers from harmful ingredients that were added to preserve beer, and to regulate prices. However, van Tongeren (Chapter 3) and Unger (Chapter 2) explain that a key purpose was also to protect local (or existing) breweries by creating entry barriers, and in some cases also to reduce prices of bread grains—which was politically important for rulers seeking to prevent social unrest.

The protectionist elements led to trade disputes. For example, the nationwide application of the Reinheitsgebot triggered several intra-German trade disputes. The regulation was also contested when the European Union started its economic integration process. The German government was forced to repeal the law in 1987 after the European Court of Justice ruled that the Reinheitsgebot imposed a non-tariff barrier to trade. Since then, imported beers need no longer adhere to the strict input requirements, although German brewers continue to use the same production methods, based on the original Reinheitsgebot. In line with local consumer preferences,

German brewers still refer to the old legislation as a guarantee of traditional quality.[4]

Competition Policy

There has been substantial concentration in the beer industry, as explained above. Larger concentration and consolidation can result from shakeouts of small brewers, or from mergers and acquisitions.

Increases in scale may have both efficiency effects and market power effects (Slade, Chapter 10). Through realizing economies of scope in production ('multi-product economies') and economies of scale by sharing facilities ('multi-plant economies'), merged breweries may increase their combined efficiency. However, the reduction in the number of brewers that goes with it may also increase the scope for collusion between the remaining brewers and the potential to extract rents from consumers, through raising prices. Slade (Chapter 10) reviews a number of case studies on the UK and concludes that several mergers that went ahead had little effect on prices, while proposed (but prohibited) mergers would have substantially raised prices and reduced consumer welfare. Accordingly, government intervention is warranted in some cases, but not always.

Governments have often tried to regulate mergers and acquisitions and influence concentration. In some cases, governments have tried to constrain consolidation; in other cases, they have stimulated it. For example, during the fifteenth and sixteenth centuries, output restrictions on beer production (e.g. restricted frequency of brewing, maximum size of each brew) limited the ability to reap the benefits of scale economies and protected smaller brewers. However, in the second half of the sixteenth century, town authorities in the Low Countries were more interested in improving their tax income than in protecting small brewers. The rising capacity of breweries and the subsequent reduction in the number of brewers translated into easier surveillance for taxation purposes, so governments repealed output restrictions and consolidation was able to take place in the beer industry (Unger, Chapter 2). As explained above, in the eighteenth century, the British government supported the oligopolistic nature of the brewing industry by restricting entry at the retail and wholesale level, on top of the technology innovations that were already inducing higher minimum efficient scales. The reason for this was that it led to higher profits—and thus a larger tax base—and lower tax enforcement costs.

---

[4] According to van Tongeren (Chapter 3), the law's repeal had limited consequences. As expected, it triggered a decrease in real consumer prices, which did not, however, lead to an increase in total beer consumption. In contrast, consumption per capita declined further in line with the general Western European trend. Imports increased only slightly due to strong brand loyalty on the part of German beer consumers and their preferences for local products, along with Germany's bottle-return system.

Governments' attitudes towards mergers and acquisitions have not been static even in recent times. For example, in the US, there was a considerable shift in attitudes regarding the potential competitive harm of mergers in past decades (Elzinga and Swisher, Chapter 11). Before the mid-1970s, the US Supreme Court adopted a zealous approach to anti-merger enforcement. Virtually all concentration was considered harmful to competition; small breweries needed to be protected; and trends towards concentration had to be stopped. Yet, from the mid-1970s onwards, there was a substantial shift towards more sophisticated economic analyses of proposed mergers. In line with these economic arguments, the US Supreme Court considered a combination of consumer welfare protection, potential entry, efficiency gains, and the failing firm defence when dealing with mergers that could potentially harm competition. This had major implications for the US brewery industry. Without this shift in attitudes towards mergers, the US brewery industry—with a four-firm producer-concentration ratio of 95%—would have been considerably less concentrated than it is now.

Governments are not only concerned with horizontal competition issues, but also with vertical restraints, such as the tied-house contract, imposed by brewing companies on the retail sector. For example, in 1989, the UK administration adopted measures that forced breweries to divest themselves of 14,000 tied houses. The aim was to lower retail prices and to increase consumer choice. However, because tied-house contracts also prevent double marginalization,[5] the divesture had the opposite effect. The scaling down of the tied-house system led to double marginalization and higher retail prices, and hence lower consumer welfare (Slade, Chapter 10).

Since 1999, the tie's maximum duration, before it comes up for renewal, is five years under EU legislation. Before, for example in Germany, these exclusive contracts could last for 20 years, but their duration has been gradually reduced. In most US states, the tied-house system was banned by law after the Prohibition ended in 1933 (Adams, Chapter 13).

Health and Nutrition Concerns

For many centuries, in particular in the Middle Ages, beer was considered a healthy alternative to polluted water and a nutritious complement to people's food. This nutritional perspective on beer has obviously changed. Consumers

---

[5] Double marginalization occurs when both brewers and retailers exercise market power and sell at prices above marginal costs—final prices are then higher than they need to be to maximize joint profits. The use of a two-part tariff, by which the brewer sets a price per unit purchased and a fixed fee that is independent of the amount purchased by the retailer, may overcome this double marginalization problem. Tied-house contracts introduce just such a two-part tariff, namely price per barrel of beer and e.g. the rental payment. For more information, see Slade (Chapter 10).

in rich countries are now concerned about too great a calorie intake from beer, leading to the growth of the low calorie beer market, which is particularly strong in the US. Similarly, with the arrival of no-alcohol substitutes such as tea, coffee, and sodas, and improvements in (drinking) water quality, health perspectives on beer consumption have focused mostly on the negative aspects of alcohol intake.

Public health concerns are an important driver of government regulations that restrict consumption of beer and alcohol in general. Social costs of excessive drinking and alcohol abuse include, amongst other things, prevention, support and treatment costs, alcohol-related crime, motor vehicle crashes, and excess morbidity and mortality which result in productivity losses (Sindelar 1998). These social costs are potentially large. Based on a substantive literature review, Rehm et al. (2009) conclude that an estimated 3.8% of all global deaths are attributable to alcohol; that countries spend more than 1% of their GDP on alcohol-attributable costs; and that the greatest contributor to total alcohol-attributable social costs is the cost of productivity loss (72.1%).

One of the best-known examples of regulations to restrict the use of alcohol is the Prohibition ruling that banned the production, sale, and transportation of alcohol for consumption in all of the US from 1920 until 1933. India, too, has experienced prohibition rulings in several of its states. India has always had an ambivalent attitude towards alcohol consumption. On the one hand, several Indian deities glorify alcohol intake, but, on the other hand, anti-alcohol movements are strong. These movements have their roots in both religious traditions and Gandhi's 'civil disobedience' campaign against the British as part of India's freedom struggle (Arora et al., Chapter 17). Therefore, the development of India's beer industry has been hampered by a multiplicity of regulations, such as taxes and price regulations, distribution licences, restrictions on production and FDI, and trade restrictions such as export fees and import tariffs. Also prohibition rulings—which are a state matter in India—have been or are being imposed in several states of India. However, a nationwide prohibition has never been implemented. An important factor is the contribution of alcohol taxes to government's tax revenues.

Alternatively, governments may impose taxes to (partially) recover the social costs. Governments may also limit or ban alcohol advertising, especially to prevent under-age alcohol use (Nelson 2005). Interestingly, governments sometimes distinguish between different types of alcohol, with potentially important implications for the beer market. For example, the Russian government excluded beer from its ban on alcohol advertisements from the late 1990s. Deconinck and Swinnen (Chapter 16) argue that this may have had a major effect on the dramatic growth of beer consumption (and the decline of vodka) in the past decade in Russia.

Concluding Comments

This final chapter summarizes a broad set of insights on the economics of beer and brewing, analysed in greater detail in the chapters of this book. From this review, it is clear that this book makes an important contribution to a better understanding of the economics of beer and brewing. However, it is also evident that there is much room for additional research. Many chapters raise as many questions as they answer.

The research agenda is too long to list; let us just give a few examples. First, Nye (Chapter 4) concludes that it is still an open question whether the dramatic rise in British beer taxes throughout the eighteenth century restrained growth during the critical early decades of the Industrial Revolution. Second, Tremblay and Tremblay (Chapter 8) argue that it is difficult to predict the future of microbreweries. Despite the impressive growth of the craft beer segment, craft brewers are faced with the challenge of maintaining their flexibility and small craft brewer image, while expanding in size. Third, McCluskey and Shreay (Chapter 9) conclude that there is much to study concerning the effect of culture and the dynamics of peer effects on beer consumption and preferences. Fourth, the analysis of George (Chapter 12) on the impact of television advertising on concentration in the beer industry raises questions as to what these results imply for current and new media innovations. Fifth, according to Bai et al. (Chapter 15), it is unclear whether Chinese domestic brewers will be able to retain their dominant position in the Chinese beer market. Since foreign brewers mainly supply high-quality beers, demand for foreign beers will rise as Chinese incomes are rising. It is unclear and open to future research how Chinese brewing companies will react, and how the Chinese beer market will evolve.

In summary, we could give many more examples, but this short list illustrates some of the many unresolved questions. Hence, we can conclude that this book demonstrates that beeronomics can be a serious scientific field, with thorough economic analysis on a set of important issues for our societies. It also shows that there is a rich future for researchers interested in beeronomics.

References

Arnold, S., J. Larimo, M. Miljan, R. Virvilaite, E. Frize, and N. Starshinova (2000). 'A Comparative Analysis of the Beer Market in Selected European Countries: Estonia, Finland, Lithuania, Russia and the UK', in P. Chadraba and R. Springer (eds.), *Proceedings of the 8th Annual Conference on Marketing Strategies in Central and Eastern Europe*. Vienna: Wirtschaftsuniversität, 7–25.

Hornsey, I. (2003). *A History of Beer and Brewing*. Cambridge: The Royal Society of Chemistry.

Marinov, M., and S. T. Marinova (2001). 'Foreign Direct Investments in the Emerging Markets of Central and Eastern Europe: Motives and Marketing Strategies'. *Advances in International Marketing*, 10: 21–52.

Nelson, J. P. (2005). 'Beer Advertising and Marketing Update: Structure, Conduct, and Social Costs'. *Review of Industrial Organization*, 26: 269–306.

Rabin, D., and C. Forget (eds.), (1998). *The Dictionary of Beer and Brewing*, 2nd edn. Chicago: Fitzroy Dearborn Publishers.

Rehm, J., C. Mathers, S. Popova, M. Thavorncharoensap, Y. Teerawattananon, and J. Patra (2009). 'Global Burden of Disease and Injury and Economic Cost Attributable to Alcohol Use and Alcohol-Use Disorders'. *The Lancet*, 373: 2223–33.

Sindelar, J. (1998). 'Social Costs of Alcohol'. *Journal of Drug Issues*, 28/3: 763–80.

Tremblay, V., and C. Tremblay (2005). *The U.S. Brewing Industry: Data and Economic Analysis*. Cambridge, MA: MIT Press.

Unger, R. W. (2001). *A History of Brewing in Holland, 900–1900: Economy, Technology and the State*. Leiden: Brill.

—— (2004). *Beer in the Middle Ages and the Renaissance*. Philadelphia: University of Pennsylvania Press.

Index

Note: page numbers in *italics* refer to Figures and Tables.

357